Mary Işın has lived in Turkey since 1973 and started researching Ottoman cuisine in 1983. She is the author of a Turkish cookery book, an encyclopedic dictionary of Ottoman cuisine and a transcription of an Ottoman cookery book as well as many articles on food history. She is also editor of *A King's Confectioner in the Orient* and an eighteenth-century Turkish dictionary of Persian culinary terms.

'Mary Işın has written an amazing work about every kind of Turkish confectionery, pastry, pudding, preserve and ice cream. The recipes are historic ones and the introduction and background text provide a fascinating insight into the Turkish past and the culture that created what is at the heart of one of the richest cuisines. I found it riveting.'
                                                                    – Claudia Roden

'The Turks have been famous for their sweet tooth since the days when so many confectioners worked at the Topkapi Palace that they had their own mosque. Sweets permeate Turkish life. Mary Işın has gathered a mountain of information on this rich subject – recipes from the Middle Ages to the present, science, history and folkways. It's a sweet read.'
                                                      – Charles Perry, food historian

'A fascinating and informative exploration of the role of sweetness in Turkish culture over the centuries.'
     – Laura Mason, food historian and author of *Sugar-plums and Sherbet*

'Mary Işın has penned a masterpiece in its field. This is a dizzying book that carries us into daily life, social life and the world of customs and traditions.'
                                        – Selim Ileri, writer and novelist, *Zama*

Sherbet & Spice

The Complete Story of Turkish Sweets and Desserts

MARY IŞIN

I.B. TAURIS

LONDON · NEW YORK

Published in 2013 by I.B.Tauris & Co Ltd
6 Salem Road, London W2 4BU
175 Fifth Avenue, New York NY 10010
www.ibtauris.com

Distributed in the United States and Canada Exclusively by Palgrave Macmillan
175 Fifth Avenue, New York NY 10010

ISBN: 978 1 84885 898 5

A full CIP record for this book is available from the British Library
A full CIP record is available from the Library of Congress

Library of Congress Catalog Card Number: available

Typeset by JCS Publishing Services Ltd, www.jcs-publishing.co.uk
Printed and bound by TJ International Ltd, Padstow, Cornwall

Contents

Illustrations

Colour Plates

I dedicate this book to my mother, Sheila Maureen Butler,
who for the past thirty years has searched for books
and other material to assist with my research, spent many hours in
her local library writing out extracts from rare books,
and been unfailing in her encouragement.

Acknowledgements

Many people generously shared their knowledge with me in the course of writing this book: Mustafa Afacan, Dr Leyla Ateş, Prof. Dr Nurhan Atasoy, Nalan Aydın, Dr Hülya Bilgi, Suna Birsel, Dr Paul Buell, Merete Çakmak, Abdurrahman Cerrahoğlu, Musa Dağdeviren, Dr Yücel Dağlı, İbrahim Denizci, Mustafa Denizci, Asuman Devres, Mehmet Doyran, İsmail Erdoğan, Dr Ayşe Erdoğdu, Nurtekin Erol, Sevim Gökyıldız, Suphi Görgen, Prof. Dr Feza Günergün, members of the Gurmeyizbiz group, Feyzi Halıcı, Nevin Halıcı, Filiz Hosukoğlu, Tijen İnaltong, Prof. Dr Acar Işın, Yavuz Işın, Prof. Dr Mustafa S. Kaçalin, Seyit Ali Kahraman, Selmin Kangal, Şevket Kılıç, M. Sabri Koz, Michael Krondl, Garo Kürkman, Prof. Dr Günay Kut, Turgut Kut, Ian Martin, Laura Mason, Dr Joyce Matthews, Atilla Özbek, Hanım Özdağ, Özden Özsabuncuoğlu, Ersu Pekin, Charles Perry, Keith Robinson, Maeve Robinson, Dr Aygun Şahin, Mert Sandalcı, Prof. Dr Nil Sarı, Ali Şekerci, Aylin Öney Tan, Berrin Torolsan, Ömür Tufan, Gezgen Tugay, Rahmi Tütüncüoğlu, Müjgân Üçer, Necati Asım Uslu, Celal Vecel, the Veren family, Prof. Dr İsmail Yakıt. I warmly thank them all and affectionately remember those who are no longer with us.

I also wish to thank the individuals and organizations that have let me use material from their collections to illustrate this book: Gökçen Adar, Vecihe Zaman Arseven, Cengiz Kahraman, Murat Kargılı, Mert Sandalcı, O.C. Tekinşen, K.K. Tekinşen, Sadberk Hanım Museum, Topkapı Palace Museum, Ankara Ethnographic Museum and the Turkish Naval Museum Archive; and last but not least the photographers: Cüneyt Akçıl, Yusuf Çağlar, Sinan Çakmak, Hadiye Cangökçe, Mustafa Dorsay, Hakan Ezilmez, Pınar Öztemel, Bahadır Taşkın and Erkan Veren.

Notes on the Pronunciation of Turkish Characters

All Turkish names and terms are spelt according to modern Turkish orthography, which is phonetic. The following letters differ in their values from those of English and should be pronounced as follows:

c as in *j*ar
ç as in *ch*air
ğ is silent, but extends the previous vowel
ı (undotted i) as in f*i*r
ö as in *oeu*vre
ş as in *sh*op
ü as in m*u*te

Glossary

batman a measurement of weight that is generally taken to be 6 kilograms, but varied widely from place to place and time to time.

börek layered pastries with savoury fillings made of *yufka* paste.

çiçek suyu distilled water of flowers, most commonly citrus fruit blossom, but many others were also used.

dirhem 3.207 grams.

dolma stuffed dishes, mainly vegetables, but also fruits, some fish and mussels.

helva the Turkish form of a word transcribed from the Arabic script as *halwa* or *halwah*. It is a general term covering many different sweetmeats (see Chs 15–18).

imaret public kitchen attached to a mosque that provided meals twice daily for employees of the mosque complex, students, travellers and the poor.

kadayıf the Turkish form of a word usually transcribed from the Arabic script as *qatâ'if*. Turkish cuisine has three types of *kadayıf* (see Ch. 24).

kantar English quintal, an ancient unit of weight and capacity used in the countries of the eastern Mediterranean that varied considerably from country to country. In Turkey the *kantar* was equivalent to 44 *okka* or 56.452 kilograms.

kıyye see *okka*.

kile a grain measure with widely differing values over time and place, and depending on the type of grain being measured. Calculated according to information in the late fifteenth-century endowment deed for Sultan Mehmed II's hospice, it was equivalent to 6.4 kilograms.

miskal 4.8 grams.

okka 1,283 grams. Also *occa* or *oka*.

pekmez molasses made by boiling fruit juice, usually grapes, to a thick syrup.

tahin sesame seed paste.

vukıyye see *okka*.

yufka thinly rolled circles of pastry.

zerdali apricots from an ungrafted tree grown from seed.

Preface

When I settled in Turkey in 1973 I was amazed by Turkish cuisine. My mother-in-law Nimet Işın and her brother Cevat Görgen, a merchant navy captain, were both keen cooks, and the whole family were keen eaters. I started compiling a recipe book and decided that the introduction should include something about the history of Turkish cuisine. Since I knew nothing about this I contacted Günay Kut, a professor noted for her work in this field. Among the books she recommended were two written in 1948 and 1952 by Professor Süheyl Ünver, a doctor and medical historian who pioneered research into Turkish food history. That was how it all began.

The more I read, the more fascinated I became with the lives of people in Turkey in past centuries as mirrored in their food and culinary traditions. Sweets and desserts are especially interesting in this respect because of the role they play on special occasions. Their diversity is extraordinary, ranging from syrup-soaked pastries to milk puddings. Some are familiar, some are shared by other eastern Mediterranean cuisines and others are unknown outside Turkey. Every single one is delicious. I have included over ninety authentic historical recipes that I hope adventurous cooks will be tempted to try.

Introduction

You have eaten of the world's sweet blessings, whereas I have only been
  able to afford bran and millet.
Yet both of us have gone to bed at night with our hunger satisfied.
                                        Yusuf Has Hacib (eleventh century)[1]

T URKEY'S HISTORICAL CUISINE HAS ROOTS in many cultures, including
      those of Persia, the Middle East, Central Asia, the Byzantine Empire
      and the lands ruled by the Ottoman Empire in Asia, Africa and Europe.
Threads of these many culinary legacies were woven into Ottoman cuisine,
which evolved into a distinctive food culture that came to dominate throughout
the Near East and the Balkans.

Turkish confectionery owes its oustanding diversity partly to these varied
roots – above all the legacies of two other imperial cuisines, the Safavids of
Persia (1501–1736) and Abbasids of the Arab world (750–1238) – and partly to
innovations during the Ottoman period (1299–1923). Anatolia, the Asia Minor
of the Romans and heartland of the Ottoman Empire, has been a melting pot
of peoples and cultures for thousands of years. With the advent of the first
farmers in the fertile lands of southeastern Turkey watered by the Tigris and
Euphrates, Neolithic culture flourished in Anatolia, giving rise to precocious
Neolithic settlements such as Çatalhöyük in southern central Turkey, where
the earliest buildings date to the seventh millennium BC. It is in this Neolithic
period that *aşure*, a pudding made of wheat berries, dried fruits and pulses, has
its origins, as part of ancient fertility rites associated with the grain harvest.
This venerable pudding, the oldest in the Turkish repertoire, is a cousin of the
English frumenty and other related dishes carried far and wide across the globe
with the spread of wheat cultivation. Another confection with roots in Anatolia
is *tatlı sucuk* (nuts threaded on a string and dipped in grape juice thickened
with starch), but this has never spread far beyond Turkey's boundaries, despite
being exported in large quantities to Arabia, Iran and India in past centuries.[2]

Cakes soaked in honey or sugar syrup that feature in medieval Arab cuisine may have evolved from Roman puddings consisting of bread or cakes soaked in honey recorded in the fourth or fifth centuries AD.[3] Similarly, puddings made from dried dates stuffed with nuts and soaked in honey are a shared feature of Roman, Arab and Ottoman Turkish cuisines.[4]

Among the many contributions of medieval Persian and Arab cuisines are the earliest sweets made of sugar – *nöbet şekeri* (sugar candy), *peynir şekeri* (Edinburgh rock, pennet), *koz helvası* (nougat), *badem şekeri* (sugared almonds), *keten helvası*, flour helva, *kadayıf*, *muhallebi* (milk pudding thickened with rice flour), *zerde* (saffron pudding) and fruit preserves. While some of these have changed hardly at all in a thousand years, others have undergone a considerable metamorphosis and/or diversification.

The numerous dishes combining meat with sugar or honey which were a hallmark of medieval Arab cuisine and had a powerful impact on both Turkish and European cuisines were gradually abandoned in the post-medieval period. Just a few relics of this tradition remain, such as Turkish *tavukgöğüsü* (milk pudding thickened with shredded chicken breast) and English mince pies, in which the meat they once contained is still represented by suet. Another parallel development in Turkish and European culinary evolution was a sharp drop in the use of spices and aromatics from the fifteenth century onwards.

Out of Central Asian foodways evolved *sütlaç* (rice pudding), *güllaç* and a range of savoury and sweet pastries made with the paper-thin pastry that was a staple of nomad Turcoman cuisine.

Untangling the complex threads of origin and influence is often impossible, since the Christian, Jewish and Muslim peoples of the Ottoman Empire lived side by side and exchanged foodways for over six centuries. Further complicating the situation is the fact that the region was a hub of trade, receiving a steady stream of expensive spices and exotic foodstuffs such as preserved ginger, mango and tamarind from India, coffee from Yemen and lotus berries from Egypt. Many previously unknown foodstuffs introduced from Asia, Africa and America became so acculturated that memories of their distant homelands faded away, as in the case of maize from America and okra from the Congo. Okra had been unknown in Near Eastern cuisines before the Ottoman period, but made a deep impact on Turkish cuisine.

Food played a central role in private and public life for the Ottomans, and sweet foods in particular were endowed with symbolic significance by people of every class and faith. No social event or public occasion, including birth, marriage, religious festivals and official ceremonies, was complete without the particular sweet foods associated with it. When a baby was born, sugar or syrup was smeared on its mouth so that it would be sweet spoken, and sweet dishes such as *mafiş* and *zülbiye* were brought as gifts to the mother by her friends; *zerde* was served at wedding and circumcision feasts; *lokma*, *un helvası* (flour helva) or *irmik helvası* (semolina helva) were served after funerals; sweets such as *akide* and sugared almonds were distributed at *mevlit*s (memorial ceremonies); *lokma* was distributed to school children at the ceremony marking a child's first day at school; *güllaç* and baklava were made during Ramazan (Ramadan); *aşure* was made on the tenth day of the month of Muharrem; *Nevruz macunu*, an electuary made of forty or more ingredients, was distributed at Nevruz, the ancient Persian new year; *akide* sweets were presented by the janissaries to the grand vizier and other state officials as a symbol of loyalty, while the palace reciprocated with trays of baklava for the janissaries; and *gaziler helvası* was made for the souls of dead soldiers after battles. Some of these customs survive in Turkey today, and local variations on this theme are endless.

Sweet foods were held in particularly high regard in Islamic culture, perhaps reflecting the role of the Persians and Arabs in the expansion and spread of sugar cane cultivation and sugar refining technology. The Turks carried the spiritual significance of sugar and sweets to new heights, naming the three-day festival following Ramazan the Şeker Bayram or Sugar Feast. Two apocryphal oral traditions of the Prophet Muhammed – 'The love of sweets springs from faith' and 'True believers are sweet' – were frequently quoted by Turkish writers in past centuries and decorated the walls of Turkish confectionery shops.[5]

The Ottoman upper classes, who could afford the finest and most expensive ingredients from far and wide and employ skilled cooks able to prepare gourmet dishes to match, created an *haute cuisine* marked by diversity and innovation. From the fourteenth century onwards the rose, quince and bitter orange preserves of former centuries were joined by scores of new varieties: green almond, cornelian cherry, aubergine, green walnut, peach, mulberry, watermelon, barberry, jujube, stonecrop, sour grape, sage gall, persimmon, wild apricot, quince blossom and judas tree flower, to mention but a few. Islamic medicine was a rich source of new confectionery items. Medicines such as electuaries (*lohuk*) and other pharmaceutical preparations made palatable by honey and sugar gradually became eaten purely as sweetmeats flavoured with fruit juice or spices such as cinnamon.[6] Eventually these were made by confectioners instead of pharmacists. A similar English example is pastels, which can be throat pastels sold in a chemist or fruit pastels. Turkish delight (*lokum*), the most celebrated of all Turkish sweets, dates back only to the eighteenth century, when it evolved as a modified version of two much older confections, *pelte* and *tatlı sucuk*. Other innovations include *kazandibi* (a type of caramelized milk pudding), *ekmek kadayıf* and ice cream thickened with salep.

In the kitchens of the palace and the wealthy elite new variations on old dishes were constantly being thought up by cooks eager to win the hearts of their gourmand employers through their stomachs. In this way many sweet dishes changed beyond recognition. One typical example of this process is *kadayıf*, which originated as a griddle cake in medieval Arab cuisine, but in early Ottoman times underwent a metamorphosis into pastry threads cooked on a griddle. This version became so popular that it spread throughout the Near East, overshadowing the original *kadayıf* pancake. Helva made with sesame paste was similarly unknown in pre-Ottoman times, yet is so ubiquitous in the region today that its absence can hardly be imagined. The Arab *ma'mûniyya*, a pudding made from chicken breast, rice and almond milk, which entered European cuisine under such names as *mammonia* and *mawmene*[7] was transformed in Turkish cuisine into deep-fried balls of rice flour helva sprinkled with sugar, nuts and rose water.[8]

Regional dishes were another source of diversity. Under the empire's centralized administrative system, provincial governors, judges and other state officials appointed to towns and cities around the empire introduced favourite dishes from the capital Istanbul to their circle of acquaintances in the provinces, while adding local specialities that they had enjoyed to their own culinary repertoires. Examples of local sweet dishes recorded in eighteenth- and nineteenth-century cookery books are *yengem duymasın helvası* made in the town of Zihne in Salonika, *peynir lokması* made in the island of Lesbos, the *ishakiyye helvası* of Bursa and the *sarmalı kadayıf* of Diyarbakır. Guests who enjoyed an unusual dish would ask their host for the recipe. When the *kadı* of İzmir ate dinner at the home of the customs officer Ahmed Ağa in 1764, he enjoyed a pudding called *nuriyye*, which Ahmed Ağa explained had been invented by one of his female servants and was known nowhere else. It was arranged that she go to the *kadı's* house and teach the recipe to one of his own female cooks, but as an additional precaution the judge wrote down the recipe:[9]

Nuriyye

Method: First prepare the dough, taking sufficient white flour for one batch, lemon juice and ten egg whites. Oil the hands with olive oil as you knead these ingredients together. If you have no lemons use verjuice (sour grape juice) instead. Then divide the dough into pieces and roll each into a very thin circle.[10] Fold each circle in four and fry in plenty of clarified butter, remove and drain well. Then place in a pan of boiling syrup. When the fried pastries have absorbed the syrup, arrange half of them neatly in a deep baking tray. Spread a layer of clotted cream on top and then arrange the remaining fried pastry over this. Place the tray over a slow charcoal fire and cook until the pastry expands and softens. Remove from the heat and sprinkle rose water and cinnamon over before serving.

In similar fashion the fame of dishes unique to palace cuisine spread beyond the palace walls into the city, and recipes for these found their way into cookery books. Examples include *saray etmeği* ('palace-style bread pudding'), *saray lokması* ('palace-style doughnuts') and *süzme saray aşuresi* ('palace-style *aşure*'). This was a two-way process, with dishes made in other households adopted into palace cuisine. One of the ways in which this occurred is illustrated by the case of the seventeenth-century scholar, poet and gourmet Nev'îzâde Efendi (1583–1635), who presented his own version of *pelte*, a pudding for which he was renowned, to the sultan and was rewarded with the title of Pelteci Efendi (Master Pelte Maker):[11]

> This *pâlûde* is an ancient confection, but the great scholar Nev'îzâde Efendi meticulously and painstakingly brought this dish to such a glorious state and renown that words hardly suffice to describe it. Indeed, despite his modesty he was obliged to present one or two celadon dishfuls each to the foremost doctors of canonical law and to the chief black eunuch in the imperial palace for his royal highness the sultan, perhaps in that illustrious presence. And when those great men were pleased with the gift, from respect he sent some again and again, and his title became Pelteci Efendi. By giving a new refinement and form to *rahatü'l-hulkum* [*pelte*], he introduced a way of preparing the dish superior to that of his predecessors. Truly he was a respected man of noble character, a most excellent person who would give not just *pâlûde* but his life for those he loved and his friends.

Another person who presented dishes to the palace was Mehmed Efendi, who was appointed *şeyhülislâm* (head of canonical scholars) in 1775. His culinary offerings are known to have been appreciated by Sultan Abdülhamid I (r. 1774–89).[12] Ottoman sultans occasionally attended gatherings known as *helva sohbeti* given by high-ranking state officials, and there tasted dishes prepared by their host's cooks. When Mahmud II (r. 1809–39) visited royal lodges or parks on the shores of the Bosphorus, grand houses in the vicinity would send dishes prepared in their own kitchens,[13] and one day in Ramazan he ate his evening meal at the house of Şeyhülislâm Dürrîzâde Abdullah Molla, after paying a surprise visit. Abdullah Molla was renowned for his excellent table and Mahmud praised both the food and the beautiful dishes in which it was served. However, seeing that the crystal bowl in which the stewed fruit was served at the end of the meal was of coarse quality in comparison to the others, he could not resist asking the reason:[14]

> Dürrîzâde welcomed the sultan. Since the time was late, everyone immediately sat down and ate the food, which was more delicious than they had expected. Sultan Mahmud sat opposite the master of the house and broke his fast. He was not only impressed by the wonderful flavour of the food, but also by the precious and beautiful dishes in which each course was served, all except the crystal bowl in which the *hoşaf* [stewed fruit] was served after the pilaf, and he asked why this was not as fine as the rest of the tableware. Dürrîzâde replied, 'I do not allow lumps of ice to be added to the *hoşaf*, because it would spoil the flavour. So as you see, I have the *hoşaf* served in a bowl fashioned from ice.'

The sultan had not realized that the bowl was made of ice, and when recounting the incident later admitted how ashamed he was to have criticized it. After dinner he made amends for this *faux pas* by telling his host, 'Your cook is excellent. If you wish let us exchange him with mine.'

Great value was placed on creative cookery, and the names of some celebrated cooks known to us from historical sources include Mehmed Usta, who had a repertoire of 1,500 dishes. The constant process of innovation, refinement and diversification in the kitchens of the elite class created a sophisticated cuisine fit for demanding gourmets. One such gourmet was Seyyid Hasan (1620–88), sheikh of the Sünbüliye mystic order, who recorded the menus of meals eaten with his large circle of friends and acquaintances in his diary kept between 1660 and 1664.[15] Other Ottoman men were interested not only in eating but also in cooking. As we have already seen, the poet Nev'îzâde Efendi invented an improved version of *pelte*, and the court historian Ahmed Câvid (d. 1803) used to make his own *börek* (layered savoury pastries) and fruit preserves.[16] An infantry officer Mahmud Nedim, who was taught to cook as a child by his mother, wrote a cookery book for his army colleagues in 1898.[17]

Although the *haute cuisine* of Istanbul and major cities featured expensive and exotic ingredients such as musk, ambergris and mango preserve, it was still essentially rooted in the culinary traditions of ordinary people. Dishes such as bulgur, *börek* and helva were to be found on the tables of all classes, those of the upper classes distinguished principally by finer quality and more varied ingredients. While sesame paste helva for the well-off was prepared with egg whites and white honey, and flavoured with rose water, lemon juice or white mulberry juice, the commonplace version for *hoi polloi* substituted gypsophila root for egg whites and *pekmez* (grape syrup) for white honey, and contained no extra flavourings.[18]

The sweetmeat *keten helva*, which is known by a variety of regional names, is an interesting example of a dish shared by high and low alike. Introduced to Turkey from Iran or Khorasan in the Seljuk period, probably in the thirteenth century, this sweetmeat was made at home in cities, provincial towns and even some villages around Turkey until recently, despite demanding specialized skill to make.[19]

At grand Ottoman meals sweet courses were not served at the end but in the middle or between the savoury courses. In Europe the custom of reserving desserts for the end of the meal began in France in the eighteenth century and gradually spread to England and other parts of Europe.[20] As a result, Western visitors to Turkey in the nineteenth century were dismayed to find the sweet courses being served at intervals throughout the meal, as illustrated by the following description by a German army officer, Helmuth von Moltke, of a banquet given for foreign diplomats to celebrate the circumcision of Sultan Mahmud II's sons:[21]

The first dish was a roasted lamb stuffed with rice and raisins . . . Then came *halwa*, a sweet dish made with flour and honey, then again a roast, again a pudding, some hot, some cold, some sour, some sweet, each dish superb; but the manner in which they were combined was hard for a European stomach to comprehend and nor was there any wine. Ice cream was served in the middle of the repast.

When the English poet and painter Edward Lear travelled to Albania in 1848, he was invited to a magnificent dinner by Osman Pasha, governor of Skodra:[22]

As for the legion dinner, it is not to be described. I counted up thirty-seven dishes, served, as is the custom in Turkey, one by one in succession, and then I grew tired of reckoning (supposing that perhaps the feast was going on all day) though I think there were twelve or fourteen more. But nothing was so surprising as the strange jumble of irrelevant food offered: lamb, honey, fish, fruit; baked, boiled, stewed, fried; vegetable, animal; fresh, salt, pickled; solid; oil, pepper; fluid; sweet, sour; hot, cold – in strange variety, though the ingredients were often very good. Nor was there any order in the course according to European notions – the richest pastry came immediately after dressed fish and was succeeded by beef, honey, and cakes; pears and peaches; crabs, ham, boiled mutton, chocolate cakes, garlic, and fowl; cheese, rice, soup, strawberries, salmon-trout, and cauliflowers – it was the very chaos of a dinner! . . . On the whole, there was much to amuse, though I should not like to dine with Pashas often.

The custom of serving one or two sweet dishes among the savoury ones continued in traditional circles until the end of the Ottoman period, as menus for Ramazan meals at the Kâdirihâne dervish lodge in Istanbul reveal.[23] One of these included two desserts, *ekmek kadayıfı* and *elma tatlısı* (apples cooked in syrup), served amid savoury courses consisting of noodle soup, kebab, a dish of dried okra, *su böreği* (a layered pastry similar to lasagne), *ekmek kadayıfı*, *kefal paçası* (mullet in aspic), celeriac and pilaf.

This mixing of sweet and savoury courses is still encountered in parts of Turkey at celebratory meals.[24]

OTTOMAN CULINARY INFLUENCE ON EUROPE

From the early sixteenth century onwards there were many diverse Ottoman influences exerted on European cuisine. The watermelon travelled from Turkey via Hungary and became known as 'Turkish gourd' or 'Turkie Coocomber' in English and *turquin* in French, while the Turkish name *karpuz* (from the Persian *harbuz*) entered German twice, once as *arbuse* for watermelon and secondly as *kürbis* for the gourd family *Curcurbitae*. Similar linguistic traces of Ottoman culinary influence abound in Hungarian and Polish as well as the Balkan languages: in addition to fruits and vegetables, dishes like *dolma* (stuffed vegetables, from the Turkish verb *dolmak*, 'to be filled'), *tarhana* (dried soup mix made of flour or wheat berries with yogurt, from the Persian), salep (a drink made with dried orchid root, whose name entered English as 'saloop') and of course coffee, to mention but a few.

A number of puddings and candies were among these introductions into Europe, rice pudding being one of the earliest, introduced into Italy in the early sixteenth century. Close political and trade relations with Italy led to Turkish influences on the cuisine of Venice in particular. Rice pudding is first recorded in 1529, on the menu served at Ercole d'Este's wedding banquet, where it is described as 'Turkish-style rice' cooked with milk, sugar, butter and rose water.[25]

Later in the sixteenth century sherbet, a sweetened drink made with fruit juices, ground nuts or spices, entered Venetian cuisine and spread from there to the rest of Italy, and then on into France and other parts of Europe. In 1577 the Grand Duke of Tuscany, Francesco I de' Medici, wrote to Mafeo Veniero of Venice, asking for recipes for preparing 'Turkish *sorbette*'.[26] Fruit and almond sherbets also made their way to Sweden in the early eighteenth century, when King Charles XII of Sweden returned home with his retinue and his Turkish creditors, after five years of asylum in Turkey between 1709 and 1714.[27] When the new fashion for sherbet reached England in the seventeenth century, crunchy slabs of flavoured sugar called *sert şerbet* or *şerbetlik şeker*,[28] which were dissolved in water to make sherbet, were imported.[29] In the early nineteenth century, however, England's sherbet vendors turned to a cheap substitute made of sugar, bicarbonate of soda and citric acid; and when the fashion for 'Turkish sherbet' and 'Persian sherbet' passed, this fizzy powder survived as the basis of children's sherbet sweets that are still popular in England today.

In summer Turkish sherbet was cooled with snow and ice, and when this beverage was introduced to Italy, the techniques for storing snow and ice were carried with it. Although this was an ancient practice known to the Romans, it had since been forgotten, until reintroduced into Italy and France from Turkey in the sixteenth century.[30]

Hungary was another gateway by which Turkish foodways entered Europe. As well as the fruits and vegetables already briefly mentioned above, some confectionery items also took this route. *Koz helvası* (nougat),[31] which originated in the Arab world, was introduced from Turkey into central Europe via Hungary, where it was known as *törökmez* ('Turkish honey'), and from there to southern Germany and Austria, where the nougat on sticks sold at fairs is still called *Türkischer honig*.[32] Culinary interaction between Turkey and Austria was considerable, even though the two countries were as often at war as at peace. Names such as *Beç ekmeği* ('Austrian bread'), *Beç poğaçası* ('Austrian buns') and *Beç tavuğu* ('Austrian hen' – guinea fowl) illustrate the Austrian influence on Turkish cuisine, while among the Turkish foods that travelled in the opposite direction to Austria coffee was the most famous. As one writer on Austrian cuisine puts it, 'Coffee came to Austria with the Turkish army that besieged Vienna in 1683 and, although the Turks lost, the coffee won.'[33] Baklava also made its way to Austria, where it evolved into the famous *apfelstrudel*.[34]

The nineteenth century saw two more items of Turkish confectionery make an impact on Europe. Around the middle of the nineteenth century *çevirme*, a soft confection made with fruit juice or flavoured with spices and nuts, was introduced to France, where it acquired the new name of *fondant*.[35] *Lokum*, or Turkish delight, the flagship of Turkish confectionery, was an eighteenth-century invention, based on earlier starch-based confections. By the 1830s *lokum* was already delighting foreign visitors to Istanbul. Exports began around the middle of the century, and 'lumps of delight', as it was first called, were on sale in England in the early 1860s.[36]

Tracking down the history of sweetmeats, and establishing who influenced whom is not always easy, and sometimes impossible. An intriguing example is *demir tatlısı*, fritters made by dipping decorative iron moulds in batter and then into hot fat. The Turkish name 'iron pudding' refers to the openwork iron moulds made of beaten iron or sheet iron, fashioned into any design the blacksmith or his customer fancies. The earliest recipe is in Bartolomeo Scappi's Italian cookery book published in 1570,[37] and these fritters are found in many cuisines around the world under a variety of names: Iran (*nan-i panjara*, 'window bread'), Italy (*frutte di Sardegna* or *frittelle* in the sixteenth century), England (stock fritters or fritters of arms in the seventeenth century), Sweden (*struvor*), Norway (*rosetbakkelser*), Finland (*rosetti*), the United States (rosette fritters), Mexico (*buñuelos de viento*, 'wind fritters') and Indonesia (*kembang goyang*, 'swaying flowers'). A pastry requiring considerable skill on the part of both blacksmith and cook must have been around a very long time to travel so far and wide.

1. *Demir tatlısı* fritter moulds heating up in olive oil in the village of Keramet in western Turkey. The iron moulds are made by local blacksmiths (Photograph: Füsun Ertuğ).

EUROPEAN INFLUENCE ON TURKISH CONFECTIONERY

Up to the nineteenth century the tide of influence flowed largely from east to west. Since then, however, westernization has had a huge impact on Turkish confectionery, particularly in the cities. There are few recorded examples of western European influence on Turkish confectionery prior to the nineteenth century. We know that Greek and Frankish (European) confectioners kept shop in the district of Galata at the mouth of the Golden Horn in the seventeenth century.[38] Described as masters of the arts of confectionery and pharmacy, reflecting the close association between the two, these confectioners made trees and fruits of sugar that amazed those who saw them, and 'sweetmeats of many colours fragrant with musk and ambergris, fit for a sultan and unsurpassed in any land'. There were apparently sixty such shops in Galata, and others in the districts of Kasımpaşa, Eyüp and Hocapaşa. European confectioners were sometimes hired from Italy for special events. In 1675, for example, Venetian confectioners were employed in preparations for festivities held to celebrate the circumcision of Sultan Mehmed IV's sons Mustafa (later Mustafa II) and

2. *Demir tatlısı* fritters being made in the village of Keramet in western Turkey (Photograph: Füsun Ertuğ).

Ahmed (later Ahmed III) and the wedding of his daughter Hatice Sultan to the vizier Mustafa Pasha.[39]

In the first half of the nineteenth century, Western influence gathered momentum as French confectioners discovered the Istanbul market and opened shops in Beyoğlu, the hilltop district above Galata where diplomats, foreign merchants and other foreign residents congregated.[40] Customers at these fashionable establishments included not only foreigners but also members of the Ottoman upper classes and the royal palace. Wealthy Ottomans even imported French *bonbons* from Naples and Marseille for special occasions such as weddings.[41]

French puddings and pastries began to win favour, and recipes to appear in Turkish cookery books. One recipe for a French-inspired pudding called *zübde-i hünkârî* (royal cream) even includes maraschino liqueur, a startling innovation for an Islamic country:[42]

Zubdayi Khunkâri

Place 140–170 g of powdered sugar, three-quarters of a teacup of rose water, a little musk, two or three small glasses of maraschino, and 42 g of dissolved gelatine in a bowl and mix well. Then add half a litre of fresh cream, stir three or four times and pour into a mould. Leave to set on ice, then remove from the mould and serve.

Several such recipes containing alcohol are found in an Armenian cookery book dated 1876, written in Turkish in the Armenian alphabet. These reflect the fact that Ottoman Christian communities in Istanbul led the fashion for French cuisine, and were, moreover, not prohibited from drinking alcohol. One of these recipes is for *mabeyin pudingası*, a pudding flavoured with kirsch, Malaga rum and madeira.[43] Although *pudinga* is a corruption of the English word 'pudding', the word found its way into Turkish as a second-hand borrowing from French. However, a real English pudding is recorded at a banquet held by Sultan Abdülhamid II for the British ambassador Lord Dufferin in 1882, at which, in honour of the sultan's English guest, the menu included *ploompouding*.[44]

Turkish recipe books of this period begin to feature *pudinga*s, *pudnika*s, biscuits, creams, gateaux and tarts. Meanwhile new ingredients that arrived from Europe at this time, such as potatoes and rolled oats, make occasional appearances. In 1900 Mahmud Nedim recorded a recipe for potato fritters soaked in syrup,[45] and Mehmed Reşad's cookery book published in 1921 contains a recipe for porridge made with imported Quaker Oats.[46] Pearl barley was sometimes used in *aşure* instead of husked wheat grains,[47] and cornflour (maize starch) is occasionally specified in place of the traditional wheat starch, described as *kola*, from the French *colle*, or *kornfluvur* from the English, both of which words must have mystified Turkish readers.[49]

With the establishment of the Turkish Republic in 1923, Turkey turned its back on the Ottoman period. Modernization was everything, and modernization meant Europeanization. Traditional culture was now regarded as retrograde, and although Turkish people remained faithful to their cuisine in their own homes, cookery books set about converting their readers to the superior French way of cooking. A book on confectionery published in 1939 is an extreme example of this trend. Entitled *The Turkish Woman's Book of Confectionery*, it would have been more appropriately titled 'The French Woman's Book of Confectionery', because its pages are filled with crèmes, marmalades, gateaux, biscuits, pains d'Espagne, cakes, fondants, tartelettes, mille-feuilles, savarins, *pudings* and petits fours, overshadowing the sad handful of Turkish recipes grudgingly permitted to remain.[49] Nougat is here, but under its French name – the author not deigning to use the Turkish term *koz helvası*. He explains that he has written the book 'to meet the needs of modern Turkey today', and those needs were apparently French food. This was a time when only the fortunate few could afford modern gas or electric ovens in their kitchens, and in towns the time-honoured method of baking was to deliver your tray of baklava or *kurabiye* (a type of shortbread) to the local bakery. But the book's anonymous author regarded public bakers with disdain because 'they have no idea of the temperature required to bake a gateau.'

In 1966 a second 'revised' edition of this book was published. In actual fact it had not been revised, but completely rewritten by the celebrated cook and cookery writer Ekrem Muhittin Yeğen, who reinstated Turkish confectionery.[50] Most of the French recipes were discarded and replaced by classic Turkish puddings and sweet pastries. Just fifteen foreign recipes were allowed to remain.

Turkish confectionery has not survived those decades of discrimination completely unscathed. Customs like offering *çevirme* to visitors have virtually died out, while chocolate's stranglehold on the market has marginalized many traditional sweets. Cheesecake is the latest craze, and few people even recall the numerous Turkish puddings and sweet pastries made with fresh unsalted cheese, such as cheese-filled baklava, cheese *lokma* and cheese helva.[51] Wafers made the traditional way have been ousted by tasteless factory-made versions.

Now the surge of interest in traditional cuisine, both historical and provincial, over the last thirty years is fast making up for decades of neglect. On the confectionery front the *muhallebici* or 'pudding shop', a Turkish institution that was on the brink of extinction in the 1980s, has staged an unexpected comeback, and traditional sweets such as the boiled sweets known as *akide* are regaining popularity. Some traditional sweets forgotten in the cities have managed to survive in small provincial towns, such as lollipops in the form of hollow animal figures.[52]

The stories behind Turkey's huge variety of sweets and puddings are as fascinating as their flavours, and exploring them is a voyage of adventure. In the words of Mevlânâ Celâleddin Rûmî (1207–73), 'This sea of sugar knows no shore, no boundary.'[53]

1 Şeker   Sugar

If, seeing the beauty of the sugar cane, the heart pours out its blessings
Sweetness and flavour begin to shout aloud from the root of every
   tooth.

Mevlânâ Celâleddin Rûmî (1207–73)[1]

AS WELL AS SUGAR CANE and sugar beet, the main raw materials of
modern industrial sugar production, natural sugars are present in a
bewildering variety of plants, including even lichens and seaweed.[2]
Syrup can be obtained in commercially viable quantities from many cereals,
trees and fruits. In North America several varieties of maple tree provide
sufficient syrup to support an enormous industry, and long before the European
colonization of the New World, Native Americans were producing a type of
brown granulated sugar from boiled maple syrup, and hard sugar cakes made
by pouring the syrup into wooden moulds.[3]

Palm sugar or jaggery is another variety still produced extensively in India,
Malaysia, Java and other parts of Southeast Asia. In the nineteenth century raw
sugar obtained from palm species such as *Arenga pinnata*, *Borassus flabellifer*
and *Phoenix sylvestris* was often exported to England under the guise of cane
sugar, and only experts were able to distinguish them.[4]

In many parts of Turkey the sugary sap produced by pine trees in springtime
used to be a traditional snack, and was also eaten for its medicinal properties.
Peeling off the bark of pine trees to obtain the sap-impregnated membrane
known as *çam soymuğu* or *yalamuk* was so widespread that it was prohibited
under the Turkish Forestry Act of 1956.[5]

A 'peculiar sort of sweet carrot' in the province of Sivas in central Turkey
attracted the attention of the traveller Frederick Burnaby in 1876, and in an
entrepreneurial spirit he regaled his readers with plans for a sugar refinery:[6]

If an enterprising inhabitant were to start a manufactory of this article of consumption, he would speedily make an immense fortune. Beetroot and a peculiar sort of sweet carrot abound throughout the district. The first-mentioned vegetable can be bought for eight shillings a ton. It might be grown for very much less. Any amount of water-power could be brought from the neighbouring mountains to bear upon machinery. Coal is also to be found in the neighbourhood. This part of Anatolia is supplied with sugar from Constantinople. If it were manufactured on the spot, the profit would be very great, for the cost of carriage would be saved; in all probability it would utterly supplant the Constantinople sugar, and soon find a market throughout the whole of Asia Minor.

The founding of the Turkish sugar industry in the 1920s shows that this was no pipedream but a prophetic vision, although none of the twenty-five sugar refineries eventually established made use of Sivas's famous sweet carrot.[7] Today this carrot survives only in the memory of old people in the province. Yet it used to be eaten as fruit for dessert, and was so famous that it features in a local legend supposed to have taken place in the early fifteenth century during Timur's whirlwind conquest of Anatolia. The story goes that Timur's daughter was kidnapped, and although she was soon restored to her father, he was determined to take revenge. The girl had no idea where her kidnappers had taken her but gave her father a carrot as a symbol of the unknown place where she had been concealed. Getting the point immediately, Timur marched on Sivas and razed the city.[8]

In Turkey fruit molasses known as *pekmez*, made principally from the boiled and clarified juice of grapes, but also mulberries, pears, carobs and diverse other fruits, has always been an important sugar substitute in puddings, preserves and other confectionery. The history of *pekmez* can be traced back to Central Asia, where the eleventh-century Turkish scholar Mahmud of Kashgar recorded it in his dictionary of Turkic dialects, showing that it has been around for nearly a thousand years and probably far longer.[9]

Sugar syrup produced from cereals also has a venerable history. In the seventh century the Chinese knew how to manufacture syrup from millet, rice and barley starches,[10] and the fourteenth-century traveller Ibn Battuta speaks of a syrup called *naide* produced from wheat in Egypt.[11] Today syrup made from maize is increasingly used in the food industry, although the processing with enzymes to convert the natural syrup into a high-fructose substance has given it a bad name.

Whatever the source of the raw syrup, whether cereals or grape juice, the clarification process was much the same. After boiling the syrup so that the water content evaporated, an alkaline substance in the form of lime or wood ash, or marl in the case of *pekmez*, was added to remove the protein and other solid particles.[12] However, the next stage in the refining process, that of crystallization, was only possible for syrups with a high sucrose content, such as cane syrup. This was a crucial factor for commerce, since it was far more difficult and costly to transport syrup than dry sugar products such as granulated or loaf sugar.

Sugar cane has the highest sugar content of any other plant, and this superiority to rivals like jaggery meant that it played a leading role in the development of sugar refining technology. New Guinea is thought to be the original homeland of the sugar cane,[13] and from here it was introduced to India and China before the common era, to Iran in the fifth century, and from the seventh century onwards carried by the Arabs to Egypt and other parts of North Africa, Rhodes, Sicily, Spain and the Balearic Islands.[14] The ancient Greeks and Romans knew of sugar only as an exotic substance from India. Strabo (63/64 BC–c. AD 24) never tasted sugar and knew of it only from Nearchus (c. 360–300 BC), an officer in the army of Alexander the Great, who in India saw reeds that produced honey 'though there were no bees around'.[15] Pliny the Elder (AD 23–79), however, gives a detailed description that suggests Indian sugar was by then available in the West: 'It is a kind of honey that has collected in bamboo, white like gum, easily broken by the teeth, in pieces no larger than a hazel nut, and used only for medicine.'[16]

Sugar produced from cane syrup in India was called *sarkara*, the Sanskrit for gravel or pebble, from which the Persian *shakar*, Turkish *şeker*, Arabic *sukkar*, old Italian *zucchero* and eventually the English 'sugar' derive. Granulated and loaf sugar was being produced in India before 300 BC,[17] and the Chinese referred to hard sugar loaves made in India and Persia as 'stone honey'.

In the eighth century pure white 'stone honey' refined with milk had sufficient rarity value to be sent as gifts

3. Egyptian sugar cane (Mustafa Rasim, *Çiftçilik*, Istanbul AH 1302/1886, vol. 2, p. 172).

to the Chinese emperor from Bukhara and Khwarizm.[18] The raw product for the refined sugar produced in Central Asia probably came from Afghanistan, where there were 'many forests of sugar-cane' growing in the provinces of Lamghan and Ghandhara in the first half of the seventh century, according to the Chinese pilgrim and scholar Hiuen-Tsiang.[19] India and the southwest Persian province of Khuzistan were also famous for cane sugar production. After the Arab conquest of the latter region in 640, sugar refining technology was carried westwards to Egypt and other parts of the Mediterranean littoral. The consumption of 40,000 kilograms of sugar at the dazzling wedding feast for the daughter of the caliph of Baghdad in 807 illustrates the scale of the sugar refining industry at this period.[20]

The fame of Khuzistan sugar lasted for centuries. In a thirteenth-century Arabic cookery book, *Kitâb al-Wusla ila al-Habîb*, 'Khuzistan sugar fingers' are one of the ingredients in a dessert called *qawut*.[21] Samarkand was for centuries associated with sugar,[22] although whether sugar was ever actually produced there is unclear. However, both Khuzistan and Samarkand were eclipsed by Egypt in the poetic imagination. The thirteenth-century mystic poet and philosopher Mevlânâ was inspired by the sugar of Egypt to write:[23]

> My beloved has consumed so much sugar in the Egypt of love
> That my cry of appeal has left no sugar in the heart of the *ney* [reed flute].

Turkish scholar Mustafa Ali of Gallipoli (1541–1600) likened the sugar of Egypt to a sea flowing to Istanbul:[24]

> As if the sugar of Egypt were a sea
> Flowing ultimately to Istanbul.

This was no exaggeration in view of the way in which Egypt dominated the sugar trade until the mid-fifteenth century. The Chinese ruler Tai Tsung (627–50) had sent a delegation to India to learn the technique of sugar production, but this had produced nothing better than a sun-dried black molasses cake.[25] Several centuries on, the Chinese sugar industry looked to Egypt instead of India for the latest sugar refining technology. Egyptians visiting the court of the Mongol Khan in the thirteenth century travelled to the sugar-producing centre of Unken (today Yongchun) to pass on their knowledge:[26]

> ... you find a city called Unken, where there is an immense quantity of sugar made. From this city the Great Kaan gets all the sugar for the use of his Court, a quantity worth a great amount of money. And before this city came under

the Great Kaan these people knew not how to make fine sugar; they only used to boil and skim the juice, which when cold left a black paste. But after they came under the Great Kaan some men of Babylonia [Cairo] who happened to be at the Court proceeded to this city and taught the people to refine the sugar with the ashes of certain trees.

The advanced sugar refining technology of Egypt was also taken to India, where high-quality white sugar was being produced during the Moghul period, as attested by King James I's ambassador Thomas Roe. When Roe visited Mir Jamalüddin Husain, viceroy of Patan, in 1615, the viceroy presented him with 100 snow-white sugar loaves:[27]

> He gave me for a present, as is the manner when anyone is invited, five cases of sugar candy, dressed with musk, and one loaf of the finest sugar as white as snow about 50 pounds weight, desiring me to accept of one hundred such loaves against I went away: which, said he, you refuse of me thinking I am poor, but it costs me nothing, it is made in my government, and comes gratis. I offered to accept when I was going, but he pressed to take it now for fear he should be then unprovided. Thus calling himself my father, and I myself his son, we took leave of one another.

In later centuries, however, the Indian sugar industry went into decline, and local sugar was eventually superseded entirely by imports from China and Egypt. In India refined white sugar became known as *Chini* (Chinese) and sugar candy as *Misri* (Egyptian), while loaf sugar was known by the Arabic term *kand* (originally from the Sanskrit *khanda*, meaning 'broken', and source of the English word 'candy').[28] By the beginning of the nineteenth century even the fact that sugar had ever been produced in India had been largely forgotten, as this passage written by Thomas Williamson in 1810 reveals:[29]

> Although the sugar cane is supposed by many to be indigenous in India, yet it has only been within the last 50 years that it has been cultivated to any great extent . . . Strange to say, the only sugar-candy used until that time was received from China.

We can assume that the Turks were familiar with sugar from at least the eighth century, when it was sufficiently abundant in the cities of Central Asia to play a symbolic role in daily life. In Samarkand mothers fed their newborn babies with 'stone honey . . . desiring that it speak sweetly when grown up'.[30] This custom continued in Ottoman Turkish culture, as we learn from the late nineteenth-century writer Ali Rıza Bey (1842–1928), who relates that the midwife rubbed sugar on the mouth of a newly born baby to ensure that it was 'sweet tongued'.[31] The nineteenth-century Turkish painter Şeker Ahmed Pasha (1841–1906) was nicknamed Şeker because he was such a good conversationalist.[32]

Hiuen-Tsiang, whose journey between 629 and 645 took him through the land of the Göktürks stretching between Turfan and the Indus, was invited to a feast by the ruler Tong Yabgu in the city of Tokmak. While Tong Yabgu ate roast beef and mutton, his vegetarian guest was served a special menu of 'pure articles of food such as rice cakes, cream, sugar candy, honey sticks, raisins, etc.'[33] The 'honey sticks' must have been *fanid*, sticks of highly refined or pulled sugar that became known as 'pennet' in English.[34]

A couplet in the eleventh-century *Kutadgu Bilig* (Knowledge Befitting a Ruler) written in Uighur Turkic by the Karakhanid courtier Yusuf Has Hacib informs us that the upper echelons of society were eating sugar in abundance:[35]

> Whether satiated on sugar and helva or barley and millet,
> One is still hungry on awakening.

Another work from the same period, the *Divanü Lugâti't Türk* (Compendium of Turkic Dialects) by Mahmud of Kashgar, a scion of the Karakhanid dynasty ruling Central Asia and Transoxania, describes two Turkish desserts made with sugar. One of these was *usbari*, for which bread cooked in ashes was crumbled into butter and sprinkled with sugar. Another was a kind of rice pudding known as *uwa*, made of boiled rice mixed with sugar and chilled with ice, eaten as a *soğukluk* ('cool dish').[36]

The most detailed account of the different types of sugar exported to Europe from Egypt in the fourteenth century is by Francesco Balducci Pegolotti, an agent of the Florentine merchant firm of Bardi. He tells us that the finest triple-refined white sugar *zucchero mucherra* (from the Arabic *shakar-ı mukarrar*) was reserved for the use of the Mamluk sultan:[37]

> Loaf sugars are of several sorts . . . the *mucchera* is the best sugar there is; for it is more thoroughly boiled, and its paste is whiter, and more solid, than any other sugar . . . and of this *mucchera* kind but little comes to the west, because nearly the whole is kept for the mouth and for the use of the Soldan himself.

This may be the origin of the term 'royal sugar' (*sucre royal* in French and *Königszucker* in German).[38] Royal sugar was the finest refined white sugar, as white as snow and 'so transparent that a finger touching it, is seen through the thickest part of the loaf'.[39] As in earlier times, the best sugar continued to be a gift fit for kings, and the Mamluk sultan presented King Charles VII (1403–61, r. 1422–61) of France with 50 kilograms of sugar.[40] In 1461 another Mamluk sultan presented the Doge of Venice, Pasquale Malipiero, with gifts that included forty-two loaves of *zuccheri moccari* (triple-refined sugar) and five *scattole* of *zuccheri canditi* (sugar candy).[41]

Triple-refined sugar was moulded into conical loaves or rectangular sticks. The sticks were known in Turkish as *parmak şekeri* ('sugar fingers') or *kalem şekeri* ('sugar pens'). 'Sugar candy' was purified sugar crystals known as *sukkar-i kand* in Arabic and *nöbet şekeri* in Turkish. Pegolotti wrote of sugar candy, 'the bigger the pieces are, and the whiter, and the brighter, so much is it the better and finer.'[42] Another type of sugar mentioned in Persian texts was *sukkar-ı sulayman*, sugar refined just once and then solidified in cakes, which may have taken its name from the city of Sulaymanan in Khuzistan.[43] Common brown sugar, either in loaves or granulated, was known as *kızıl şeker* ('red sugar') in Turkish, *zucchero musciatto* in Italian and muscovado in English.[44] In the nineteenth century, however, we find brown sugar being described as 'Egyptian sugar' in Turkish, reflecting the decline in the quality of Egyptian sugar under pressure from European competition.[45]

Italian names for other sugar types being traded in the fourteenth century included *zucchero caffettino*, thought to take its name from the palm-leaf basket (Arabic *kaffa*) in which it was packed; *zucchero bambillonia*, meaning 'sugar of Cairo'; and *zucchero dommaschino*, meaning 'Damascus sugar'.[46] Damascus sugar was a high-quality white loaf sugar produced in Syria. When the German botanist Dr Leonhart Rauwolff visited the region in 1573, he observed that a large numbers of sugar loaves were produced at Tripoli:[47] 'Hereabout, and in other adjacent places, groweth a great quantity of sugar-canes, so that there is yearly sold a great many sugar-loaves that are made thereof.'

Loaves of lower-quality sugar quickly disintegrated into granulated sugar, as Pegolotti explained:[48]

> Powdered sugars are of many kinds, as of Cyprus, of Rhodes, of the Cranco of Monreale, and of Alexandria; and they are all made originally in entire loaves; but as they are not so thoroughly done, as the other sugars that keep their loaf shape . . . the loaves tumble to pieces, and return to powder, and so it is called powdered sugar.

Since sugar was rarely adequately refined, discerning Ottoman cooks clarified their sugar by adding egg whites to the boiling syrup and skimming until all trace of molasses had disappeared.[49] 'People of refined taste do it that way. If that is too much trouble then you might as well use boiled grape syrup instead,' remarked Mahmud Nedim in 1898.[50]

The problem with brown sugar, grape syrup and honey is that they have pleasant but forceful flavours of their own which interfere with the flavours of fruit preserves and sweet dishes. In elite cuisine this was an effect to be avoided at any cost, and Ottoman period recipes for sweet dishes emphasize the need to use the best grades of sugar. A manuscript baklava recipe dating from the sixteenth or seventeenth century specifies the use of granulated sugar candy, and if that is not available, then white Egyptian sugar.[51] Similarly an eighteenth-century *kadayıf* recipe instructs the cook to use Damascus sugar candy or *peynir şekeri* (white pulled sugar) and, as second best, European loaf sugar wrapped in blue paper.[52]

Loaf sugar, sugar candy and *peynir şekeri* required cutting into manageable lumps and then pounding to produce granulated sugar for cooking. Turkish author Refik Halid Karay (1888–1965) describes watching this chore in his childhood:[53]

> In those days sugar was sold in the form of conical loaves of different sizes. These were cut into pieces at home and stored. Watching soap being cut up with wire and sugar loaves being broken with a hammer was an amusement I never missed. I used to enjoy watching the young maids gathering particles of soap in their hair and sugar dust on their faces.

During the Ottoman period sugar was plentiful in the cities, but nevertheless more expensive than honey. In the mid-sixteenth century one *okka* (1,283 grams) of the finest white honey cost 10–12 *akçes*, while the same quantity of the finest sugar cost 18–20 *akçes*. According to Hans Dernschwam, only the wealthier classes could afford to eat sugar rather than honey.[54] A century later the price of Athens honey, which was regarded as the best of all, remained much the same, at 13 *akçes*, whereas the price of fine sugar soared to 40 *akçes*, three times its former level.[55] The seventeenth-century courtier Evliyâ Çelebi tells us that Defterdar Mehmed Pasha, gourmet and governor of Erzurum, refused to admit honey or brown sugar into his kitchen, allowing only Damascus loaf sugar to be used in his sweet dishes.[56] Only the privileged few could afford to be so fussy. Away from the major cities, where sugar prices were even higher than in Istanbul, even the wealthy classes used sugar sparingly, substituting grape syrup more often than not.[57]

In Europe the situation was little different, despite the steady expansion of colonial sugar plantations. As late as the second half of the eighteenth century,

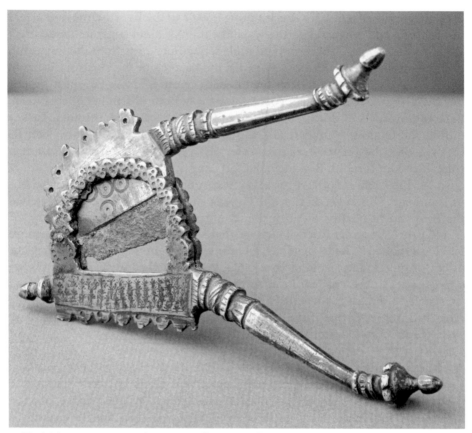

4. Turkish sugar cutters (Private collection; photograph: Mustafa Dorsay).

sugar was an expensive commodity in Europe, particularly in countries without sugar-producing colonies. In Germany, for example, 1 kilogram of sugar cost 5 gold marks, and guests were expected to dip a lump of sugar tied on the end of a string suspended from the ceiling into their cup of coffee to sweeten it.[58]

Until the eleventh century very few Europeans had even tasted sugar,[59] but as the Crusaders became acquaintanted with sugar in Syria and Palestine and carried parcels of it back home, sugar was increasingly sought after. For a long time Europeans were obliged to obtain their supplies from the Islamic countries, and began to seek ways of escaping this monopoly. Crusaders cultivated sugar cane plantations in lands conquered from the Arabs in Syria,[60] and after learning the techniques of sugar production set about establishing their own plantations and sugar mills nearer to home. In 1166 King Wilhelm II of Sicily presented a mill for crushing sugar cane to the Benedictine monastery in Monreale and sent an expert to teach the monks about sugar manufacture.[61] But it was the sugar plantations and mills set up in Cyprus from the thirteenth century onwards that were finally to tip the balance of the sugar industry in Europe's favour in the middle of the fifteenth century.[62] Now European rulers, like their Islamic counterparts, could enjoy the honour of sending gifts of sugar. Bertrandon de la Brocquière, a Frenchman who travelled through Turkey during the reign of Murad II (1421–51), reported that gifts sent by Jean III (r. 1432–58), the French Lusignan ruler of Cyprus, to the Turkish Karaman ruler Tâceddin İbrahim Bey, included forty sugar loaves.[63]

In 1471, 4 *kantars*[64] of 'Cyprus sugar' were purchased for the palace kitchens in Istanbul.[65] This suggests that the Cyprus sugar of commerce now matched the Egyptian in quality, a conclusion confirmed by the demand by James II (r. 1464–73), Crusader ruler of Cyprus, that all sugar produced in his kingdom be 'thrice-boiled'.[66] As Cyprus sugar became more abundant, European sugar prices dropped, and demand rose, with the result that sugar began to play a larger part in the cuisine. Prior to this sugar had been largely a medicinal substance, and faith in its efficacy was such that in 1492 Canon Pietro Casola remarked ironically that if the amount of sugar in Cyprus was anything to go by, Cypriots would live forever:[67]

> I can only speak of a great farm not far from Limasol, which belongs to a certain Don Federico Cornaro, a patrician of Venice, and is called Espicopia, where they make so much sugar, that, in my judgment, it should suffice for all the world. Indeed it is said to be the best which goes to Venice, and the quantity sold is always increasing. It seems to me that no one ought ever to die there.

The rest of Europe did not sit back and watch the French and Italian landowners in Cyprus make fortunes from their thriving sugar industry. Rising demand for sugar and the fat profits to be made spurred others to search for new places to grow sugar cane.

In 1521 the Turkish navigator Pîrî Reis described the city of Valencia as being 'surrounded entirely by sugar cane fields', although it is possible that these plantations were a legacy of Muslim rule in Spain, where sugar cultivation had been introduced in the ninth century, rather than a later endeavour to expand sugar production in Europe.[68] Portuguese entrepreneurs backed by Genoese financiers set about planting sugar cane in the Canary Islands and Madeira in the Atlantic. Hard on their footsteps came the first plantations in the New World, where sugar cane became one of the first cash crops.[69] As demand for sugar in the Old World soared, sugar manufacture was seen as the surest way to quick riches, not just for individuals but for entire countries; European powers scrambled for New World territories with cane-friendly climates like Surinam and the Caribbean islands.[70]

European sugar continued to be imported into Ottoman Turkey. Cyprus sugar was succeeded by 'Frankish sugar', purchased in 1489–90 for the hospital founded by Sultan Mehmed II. In the seventeenth century the rise of sugar production in Britain's New World colonies is reflected in the fact that 'English sugar' sold in Athens for 22 dollars per *kantar*.[71]

Egypt's once-legendary sugar industry was gradually sidelined by these developments. By the second half of the eighteenth century Egypt was producing sugar almost solely for home consumption, apart from small but steady sales to Turkey.[72] Despite increasing European competition, small loaves of fine *mükerrer* sugar from Egypt continued to be purchased for the Ottoman palace between the sixteenth and nineteenth centuries,[73] and Egyptian brown sugar remained popular among ordinary people because it was not only cheaper but thought to taste sweeter.[74]

Immense amounts of sugar were consumed at the Ottoman palace. The quantity steadily rose from 5 tons per annum in the late fifteenth century, to 35 tons per annum in the sixteenth century and 65 tons per annum in the mid-seventeenth century.[75] According to British ambassador Stanley Lane-Poole, 16,000 pounds sterling a year were spent on sugar during the reign of Sultan Abdülaziz (1861–76).[76] About half of that sugar was used by the confectioners for making syrups, pastes and preserves. Ottaviano Bon, Venetian representative at the Ottoman court in 1604–7, was astounded by both the amount of sugar and the fact that it was commonly presented as gifts:[77]

> And as for sugar, there is spent an unspeakable deal of it in the making of *Sherbets* and *Boclavas*, which not only the Seraglio useth, but are also ordinary presents, from one Bashaw to another, and from one friend to another; insomuch that it is a thing to be admired, that so great a quantity should so suddenly be consumed.

Huge expenditure on imported sugar became a cause for concern in the mid-seventeenth century. Evliyâ Çelebi describes a debate that supposedly took place between the Egypt merchants and the butchers during a guild procession in 1639. In fact the debate is veiled criticism of Ottoman economic policy. Retorting to the Egypt merchants, the butchers declare:[78]

> [The Egypt merchants] are a tribe of usurers and black marketeers. The Ottoman state has no need for their Egyptian rice . . . As for Egyptian sugar,

the honey of Rumelia, Athens, Wallachia and Moldavia, which is praised by God in the words 'rivers of honey' has seventy virtues. And if my lord the sultan did but wish it, hundreds of thousands of kantars of sugar could be produced in the provinces and sub-provinces of Alanya, Antaya, Silifke, Tarsus, Adana, Payas, Antakya, Aleppo, Damascus, Saida, Beirut and Syrian Tripoli. This would suffice to satiate the world, and we would have no need for your sugar.

This viewpoint might seem strange in view of the fact that Egypt was then part of the Ottoman Empire, but similar anxiety about securing sugar supplies was later to beset the European colonial powers, who threw themselves into the home production of beet sugar from the beginning of the nineteenth century. Sugar had become such a vital commodity that any prospect of a sugar shortage was dismaying. This was particularly true of Britain, which had come to lead the world in sugar consumption. The British diplomat William Eton, writing in the 1790s, proposed Egypt, Candia (Rhodes) and Sicily as alternative sources of sugar for England:[79]

Egypt produces a considerable quantity of sugar of a very good grain. Were that country under a better government, it might supply Europe with a great quantity. The sugar cane grows also very well in Candia and in Sicily, where, if the inhabitants were more industrious, or were there enterprising people of capital among them, this would become a product of much consequence. The same may be said of a great part of the coast of Barbary.

Eton's idea that Egypt's sugar industry was a good investment for British capitalists did not fall on deaf ears, and a few years later an Englishman established a sugar refinery in Egypt. James Webster visited this refinery in the 1820s, after it had become the property of the khedive:[80]

On our arrival at Eraramoun, we inspected the sugar maufactory belonging to the Pacha of Egypt, which was originally established by an Englishman, but is now conducted by an Italian. Quantities of sugar candy, which is in great demand among the Turks is manufactured, and also some rum, some of which we tasted and found to be excellent.

Evliyâ's vision of a domestic sugar industry was eventually fulfilled in the twentieth century, albeit based on sugar beet rather than sugar cane. Meanwhile, in the nineteenth century Turkey's sugar suppliers included the United States of America, Belgium, Russia and Denmark, as well as Egypt, showing that –

thanks to sugar beet – any country, with or without colonies, could now be the proud possessor of a sugar industry.[81] The high sugar content of sugar beet had been known for centuries, but the challenge of producing first syrup and then white sugar from beet only began to seem feasible when the spectre of sugar deprivation scared European countries into action.

The first person to produce beet sugar was a Prussian, Franz Carl Achard, prompted partly by a slave mutiny that took place in the Caribbean in 1791. Napoleon's blockade of British ships later created a sugar shortage in France, and this led to the first home-made French sugar loaf in 1808. Beet sugar offered a golden opportunity for Europe to break Britain's stranglehold on the sugar trade. In a bid to stem the beet sugar tide, British merchants offered Achard a bribe of 200,000 talers to abandon his research, but he refused.[82]

In Turkey the first attempt to found a Turkish sugar industry was in 1840, when Dimitri Efendi, a Greek merchant from Arnavutköy in Istanbul, approached the Ministry of Trade for permission to set up a sugar refinery. The ministry refused on the grounds that this would mean the loss of customs revenues on imported sugar – precisely the argument that had settled the squabble over precedence between the butchers and the Egypt merchants in favour of the latter two centuries earlier:[83] 'the treasury receives ten thousand pouches of gold in customs duty on the goods carried by the Egyptian galleons. Justice demands that we lead the procession, and that the butchers follow behind.'

Further attempts to found a local sugar industry were made by an Armenian, Davutoğlu Karabet, in 1867, a Frenchman, Michel Pasha, in 1879, Yusuf Bey in 1890 and Rauf Pasha a few years later. Sugar beet seeds were brought from Europe and samples of beet grown in Turkey were sent to Europe for analysis. But the challenge of growing a new crop on a sufficiently large scale, compounded by burdensome trade agreements with the European powers, prevented these initiatives getting anywhere. Not until 1926, three years after the proclamation of the Turkish Republic, was Turkey's first sugar refinery built. In 1955, after fourteen more refineries had been established, Turkey finally became self-sufficient in sugar.[84]

2 Nöbet Şekeri   Sugar Candy

No one to crush my sugar candy
No one to strain it through muslin.
What use is a palace or mansion
With no one to share it with me?

Turkish folk song[1]

ONCE UPON A TIME A confectioner's apprentice spoilt a batch of sugar syrup and was so afraid of his master's wrath that he dug a hole in the stable floor, tipped the syrup inside and covered it with manure. Days later, when the syrup was discovered, large, transparent sugar crystals had formed in it. Thinking that the attractive crystals would be popular with customers, the confectioner forgave his apprentice and set about devising a practical method of producing them.[2]

This method is as interesting as the appearance of these diamond-like sugar crystals threaded on strings. It requires a copper container slightly wider at the rim than at the base, and numerous small holes in the sides. Strings are threaded through the holes and stretched across the inside of the container. Then lime or clay is pasted to the outside to seal the holes, and boiled sugar syrup is poured into the container. This is then wrapped in sacking and left in a warm place. A week later huge crystals of pure sugar are found to have formed on the strings.

It seems plausible that this complex method began with an accidental discovery. What is more, burying the containers in manure so as to maintain a steady temperature over a long period was ancient practice, documented in Italy in the sixteenth century.[3] So the myth passed down through generations of Turkish confectioners has a core of truth.

Known in English as 'sugar candy' or sometimes 'rock sugar', these sugar crystals threaded on strings have a history that can be traced back more

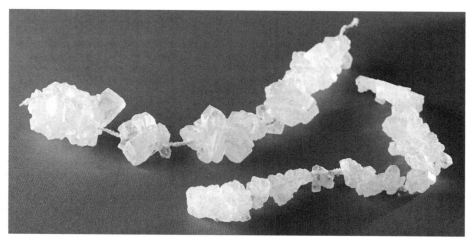

5. Strings of sugar candy crystals (Photograph: Mustafa Dorsay).

than 2,000 years. Megasthenes (c. 350–290 BC), who travelled to India at the beginning of the third century BC as an envoy of Seleucus I, one of Alexander the Great's former generals, records that 'stones are dug up of the colour of frankincense and sweeter than figs or honey.'[4] These were sugar candy crystals, presumably dug out of their warm bed of manure.

One of the earliest references to sugar candy in Arabic literature is in a treatise on bookbinding by Al-Mu'izz ibn Bâdîs (1007–61), who lists it among the substances used to make glue.[5] Sugar candy made from white sugar was one of the sugar types being exported to Europe in the fourteenth century, as recorded by Francesco Balducci Pegolotti (c. 1340), who wrote, 'the bigger the pieces are, and the whiter, and the brighter, so much is it the better and finer.'[6] By the sixteenth century sugar candy was being made in Genoa and Venice, according to the French pharmacist Michel de Nostredame (Nostradamus), who published an account of its manufacture in 1552. This very detailed working recipe in Nostredame's lively style is given in abridged form below:[7]

To Make a Very Fine Sugar Candy

Take nine pounds or so of nice white sugar-loaf or muscovado (for beautiful materials make for a beautiful work, and ugly ones for an ugly or nasty one) and dissolve or liquify it in a sufficient amount of water . . . As soon as it is boiled, take some specially-made unglazed earthenware pots and place in each of them a little stick of pine-wood, or a length of reed, in order that the sugar may candy throughout as a result of having something to form around. When the sticks have been properly fitted inside them all, pour the still-hot sugar into each pot, put its lid on (which should be of earth[enware?]) press it in thoroughly and seal it roughly with clay, for no other reason than to keep the heat inside for longer. Then immediately bury it under some dung – which should be warm – in some hidden or secluded place . . . Cover them up well and leave for nine whole days and nine whole nights.

At the end of nine days, take them out of the dung heap, open them and pour out the syrup which has not yet candied and you will see that out of nine pounds of sugar, five or six pounds will have candied – perhaps more, perhaps less . . . You should also understand that if the sugar were to stay under the dung longer than nine days and the dung were hot, the sugar would de-candify because the steam from the dung contains moist fumes that would penetrate inside to some extent, and there would be as much [sugar] de-candifying itself as candying . . . Then break the pot and remove the sugar, which will all have candied.

Anybody can make this, but it is disgraceful for a lot of idle chatterers to say that beautiful sugar candy can be made from an impure sugar. 'Quia ex non musico non fit Musicus' ['For you can't get good music out of a bad musician'].

This, then, is how to make sugar candy as it is made in Genoa and Venice.

The most interesting aspect of this method is that instead of the strings used at a later period, a wooden twig or reed is placed in each earthenware pot. This almost certainly reflects the age-old method used in the Islamic world, where palm branches were used instead of pine sticks.[8] A clue as to where and when crisscrossing strings replaced sticks is found in the Ottoman palace kitchen accounts for 1471, where an entry specifies 'string for the sultan's sugar'. Evidently the technique of using strings in copper vessels instead of twigs in pots had already been developed in the Islamic world when Nostredame was writing, but Italian confectioners had not yet learned of this new method.

In England sugar candy was known from at least 1390,[9] and gave its name to the mineral barite, called 'sugar candy stone' because of the deceptive resemblance of its crystals.[10]

In some Quarries, on the South-west Part of the Island [Portland opposite Weymouth], there is found a Sort of Stone, which they call (with good Reason) the *Sugar-candy-Stone*, of which there are two sorts, *viz.* one pale, like *white Sugar-candy*; and the other of an *Amber-colour*, like the *brown Sugar-candy*; and indeed, they much resemble *Sugar-candy* in the *Lump*, that any Person might be imposed upon by them, till his Tongue and Teeth convinced him, that they were nothing but an insipid Exudation of Juices, petrified, chrystallized, and candied up by Nature in this Manner.

Sugar candy continued to be made in England until the first quarter of the twentieth century, but it appears to have been forgotten in France by the end of the nineteenth century since the French artist Pretextat Lecomte, who watched its manufacture in Istanbul in 1902, described it as a 'Turkish speciality'.[11]

The Turkish name *nöbet şekeri* is a corruption of the Persian *nabât shakar*, which literally means 'plant sugar', to distinguish it from the ancient sweetener, honey. The corruption of *nabât* to *nöbet* was helped by the fact that *nöbet* means 'fit', 'attack' or 'paroxysm' and sugar candy was used as a remedy for coughs. In the fifteenth century the Turkish physician Ibn Şerif described sugar candy as 'the finest of all sugars',[12] and it was used not only in medicine, but in cookery – by those who could afford it – to make syrup for baklava and other puddings. Defterdar Mehmed Pasha, a seventeenth-century Ottoman government minister, insisted on Syrian sugar candy being used in all the sweets made in his kitchen, including baklava, helva, milk puddings and stewed fruit.[13] Sugar candy made in Syria and known as *Şam nebatı* (Damascus sugar candy), was the best of all, and is specified in an eighteenth-century Turkish recipe for *kadayıf*.[14]

In the seventeenth century such extravagant consumption of sugar candy was a privilege of the rich alone, since in 1640 it cost 100 aspers per *okka*, almost double the price of the finest loaf sugar, which sold at 60 aspers per *okka*.[15] Most ordinary people probably never tasted sugar candy except to cure a cough. So when the confectioners marching in a guild procession in 1639 tossed sugar candy to the watching crowds, it would truly have been an occasion to remember.[16]

Istanbul's confectioners were still making sugar candy until 2004, when lower-priced imports from Iran made it uneconomical.[17] Traditionally they had used rectangular copper containers measuring approximately 100 centimetres long, 50 centimetres wide and 50 centimetres high, with perforations for the cotton threads in the short sides. The syrup was boiled to 120°C and poured into the container, which was then covered with a lid, wrapped in sacks, and left for fifteen days. Later on the copper containers were replaced by much larger containers made of galvanized sheet iron and measuring about 2 metres in length, with three rods, two at either end and one in the middle, to which the strings were tied. Fifty kilograms of sugar produced twenty of sugar candy, and the caramel-coloured syrup left over from the process was used to make *akide* (boiled sweets) or baklava syrup. *Nöbet şekeri* is still sold in Turkish spice shops, not as a sweet, but as a traditional remedy for coughs and sore throats.

3 *Peynir Şekeri*   *Pulled Sugar*

Pulled sugar and boiled sweets
The epicure needs sugar.

Watchman's rhyme[1]

PASTEL-COLOURED LUMPS OR STICKS OF pulled sugar in a variety
of flavours known in Britain as 'Edinburgh rock' are claimed to be the
invention of the nineteenth-century Scottish confectioner Alexander
Ferguson,[2] and a Scottish cookery writer describes Edinburgh rock as 'one
of the triumphs of the Scottish confectioner's art'.[3] Meanwhile in the Turkish
city of Konya, lumps of pulled sugar are described as *Mevlânâ şekeri* after
the thirteenth-century mystic philosopher Mevlânâ Celâleddin Rûmî, who
spent most of his life in the city. Both are urban myths, the reality being that
pulled sugar is one of the oldest sweets in the world, predating both Alexander
Ferguson and Mevlânâ. It was invented at least 1,000 years ago by Persian, Arab
(or possibly Indian) confectioners,[4] and one of the earliest recipes is given by
the Anadalusian physician and scientist Abu al-Qasim Khalaf ibn al-Abbas
Al-Zahrawi (936–1013), known in the West as Albucasis, and acknowledged
by Michel de Nostredame in the preamble to his own very detailed recipe for
penites.[5] The Baghdad physician Ibn Jazla (d. 1100) describes the technique
for creating the finest variety, made in Harran (in the southeastern Turkish
province of Urfa) and therefore known as *fânîd Harrânî*.[6] Ibn Sayyâr al-Warrâq
mentions pulled honey in his tenth-century cookery book, but does not attempt
to describe the method, instead instructing his readers: 'Order some to be made
for you.'[7] The term he uses is *nâtifü 'asel 'ala al-mismâr* (boiled honey pulled on
a nail), because once the boiled syrup was the correct consistency it was formed
into a rope, hooked over a nail (*mismâr*) and pulled until white in colour.

Pulled sugar was introduced into Spain by the Arabs, and had reached England by 1500. The Persian names *fânîd*, *pânîd* and *pânîdh* travelled via Arabic

into European languages, taking the form *alfenique* in Spanish, *alfenim* in Portuguese, *penite* or *succre panis* in French, and phanid, penid or pennet in English.[8]

In fifteenth-century Turkish medical texts, pulled sugar is referred to either by its Arabic name *fânîd* or Turkish *peynir şekeri*, meaning 'cheese sugar', probably because of its opaque white colour. The Turkish name was already in use in the 1420s, recorded by the physician Ibn Şerif, who explains that 'fânîd is what in Turkish is called peynir şekeri.'[9] Perhaps this term had been newly coined, since a few decades earlier another physician Celalüddin Hızır (d. 1417) defines *fânîd* by a different Turkish term, *parmak şeker* ('finger sugar', i.e. a sugar stick).[10] Other sources use the name *şeker-i kalem* ('pen sugar').[11]

Pulled sugar is made from boiled sugar syrup or honey that has cooled sufficiently to handle. It is stretched in the hands,[12] on a marble surface, or on a nail or hook in the wall. As it is stretched minute sugar crystals form in the paste, causing its colour to change from amber to a glossy satiny white. If not carefully sealed from the air, the pulled sugar quickly grains, becoming opaque and acquiring the familiar chalky texture. Pulled honey sticks were known in Turkish as *arşın helvası*, first recorded in Turkish sources in the first half of the seventeenth century as a sweetmeat that made children's mouths water.[13] In the eighteenth century the same sweet, known by the name *kamış helvası* (reed helva), was sold by Arab street sellers in Istanbul.[14] Friedrich Unger, royal confectioner to Otto I of Greece, who spent the summer of 1835 researching confectionery in Istanbul, gives the following recipe for *arşın helvası*.[15]

Arschin Halwassi

Boil the honey for sufficiently long that it hardens on a wet stick which you dip into it and then pass through cold water. Then pour it onto a buttered marble slab and pull it according to the pulled sugar method.

Arschin-halwa is in fact nothing else but *Peinir scheker* (pulled sugar), which will be described later. The difference is only that the Turks use honey rather than sugar and that this delicacy is called *Arschin-halwa*.

Ottoman pulled sugar was made in diverse shapes, colours and flavours, including rose, orange and cinnamon, as we learn from Unger's account:[16]

Peinir Schekeri (Pulled Sugar)

This confection . . . is consumed in great quantities in the Orient and represents the main item among the sweet goods of each *schekerdschian* (sugar baker). This pulled sugar the Turk produces with great dexterity and during the preparation lends to them all imaginable varieties of colours and shapes.

The writer of this work found often at the side of the shop of the *schekerdschian* a large marble slab, and up on the wall a great hook. In order for the sugar not to harden too soon he uses a pan of charcoal embers.

There is no difference between the method of preparation used here and the European. The Turk boils a quantity of sugar to cracking point, adds some lemon juice, so that it does not grain too quickly and is more malleable, colours it or leaves it white, pours it on the slab, pulls the sugar over the hook until it is finished, and then gives it different shapes. He prepares Peinir Schekeri of a white colour with vanilla pods, of a red colour with rose oil, yellow with orange oil, and with cinnamon oil etc.

Later on in the century pulled sugar flavoured with bergamot became so popular that *peynir şekeri* is defined in a Turkish–English dictionary dated 1890 as 'a softish white sweetmeat flavored with bergamot'.[17] And by 1926 the name *bergamot şekeri* (bergamot sweets) had gained currency for fruit-

6. Pulling a rope of sugar on a nail in the wall. This Turkish political cartoon dated April 1910 shows a figure in a fez (probably grand vizier İbrahim Hakkı Pasha) as a confectioner. The shadow puppet character Karagöz is telling him that his sweets have no flavour (*Karagöz* 187 (27 April 1910), p. 1).

flavoured pulled sugar.[18] The rope of hot pulled sugar was cut with scissors in alternate directions to form four-cornered lumps as broad as the thumb. These were flavoured by adding fruit syrup, such as lemon, orange, bitter orange or bergamot, to the boiled sugar, or alternatively applying rose, violet, cherry, mint and other oils to the hands while pulling the sugar paste. There may be some connection here with the honey-coloured sweets known as *bergamote*, which have traditionally been made in the French city of Nancy since 1850.[19]

Red and white pulled sugar sticks were served at a banquet consisting of scores of sweetmeats of every description given to celebrate the circumcision of Sultan Süleyman the Magnificent's sons Bâyezid and Cihângîr in 1539.[20] Their popularity continued through to late Ottoman times, when red-and-white striped pulled sugar rings and sticks were still favourites with children and sold by itinerant sweet sellers (see Plate 2). One Ottoman writer of the period mentions pulled sugar sweets being offered in silver dishes to guests at weddings.[21] Opium eaters, who craved sugar, carried boxes of pulled sugar around with them.[22]

In the late nineteenth century an English traveller who saw white-and-red striped sugar sticks in a Turkish confectionery shop in Eyüp and was apparently unaware of the Edinburgh variety, instead compared it to traditional English rock as sold in Norfolk villages:[23]

> I turned for consolation to the sweetmeat shop before mentioned – a genuine Eastern sweetmeat shop . . . and yet every one of those sweetmeats have I seen in Norfolk villages – Turkey rock, white and striped with red, and cocoanut paste, and hardbake – nay, even toffee, beloved of our youth!

H.V. Morton, writing several decades later, compares Turkish rock to that of Margate in Kent.[24]

> I was interested to see in Istanbul, in company with the usual sweets as are encountered all over the Arabic-speaking world, authentic bull's-eyes and sticks of Margate Rock. I never remember having seen these old-fashioned sweets anywhere else except in England, where their popularity has of late years been so well eclipsed by chocolate that you have to look for them now in village post offices. My first thought was that English manufacturers, finding a declining market for rock and bull's-eyes at home, had created a new one in Turkey.

It is not just the English who recall the sweets of their childhood with nostalgia. One Turkish writer says with a sigh:[25] 'What has become of those sweets and confectioners of the past! Our Turkish delight and boiled sweets are not what they were. If only by some miracle our old confectioners could be brought alive.'

Although pulled sugar had arrived in England via the Arab world many centuries earlier, Turkish-style pulled sugar sticks in different flavours and colours were evidently introduced into English confectionery at some point in the mid-nineteenth century, as shown by the English confectioner Henry Weatherley's recipe for 'Turkey Sugars':[26]

Turkey Sugars, Lemon, Peppermint and Rose

Take seven pounds of loaf sugar lowered, and boil to the crack, when half cold put in the usual quantity of flavor of either sort, and commence to pull on a large hook, fixed against the wall, till it begins to get stiff and shines, when you can form it into either straight or twisted sticks; to color the rose, keep some cochineal paste or carmine ready, and put it in the sugar on the slab.

The earliest Turkish recipe for pulled sugar is a translation from the Arabic by the fifteenth-century physician Şirvânî: from Bağdâdî's thirteenth-century cookery book *Kitâb al-Tabîkh*.[27] Şirvânî makes only one minor alteration, specifying that a tinned pan should be used:

Helvâ-yı Yâbise (Dry Helva)

The method for this is to take as much white sugar as desired, dissolve it with a little water in a tinned pan, skim off the scum, boil it until it thickens, then pour it onto a marble slab. When it has cooled slightly fold it and then placing on a large nail fixed into the wall, pull and rub with the hand until the sugar goes entirely white. Then again place on the marble and add some pounded pistachio nuts. Knead, spread out and fold until it cools, then cut as you wish and eat it. Some people colour this helva with saffron, and some mix in blanched almonds and roasted husked sesame seeds and fresh poppy seeds.

Pulled sweets owe their survival in modern Turkey not to children – who were the main consumers in the past, but have now been seduced by chocolate bars – but in part at least to the tradition of distributing small paper cones filled with mixed pulled and boiled sweets at ceremonies known as *mevlit*s, held to commemorate births, deaths and various religious feast days.

4 *Kudret Helvası*   *Manna*

We sent down manna and quails upon you.

Quran, 2:57.

FOR THOUSANDS OF YEARS PEOPLE believed that manna was a miraculous gift from God that rained down from the sky. The Old Testament account of God sending down manna and quails to feed the hungry Israelites is also found in the Quran and in the writings of Mevlânâ.[1] The Israelites soon became bored with manna, and began to 'remember the fish, which we did eat in Egypt freely; the cucumbers, and the melons, and the leeks, and the onions, and the garlick: But now our soul is dried away: there is nothing at all, beside this manna, before our eyes.'[2]

The manna spurned by the disgruntled Israelites is just one of many different varieties found on plants and trees around the world, particularly in mountainous, steppe and desert regions. It is produced by insects of diverse species that suck the sap from leaves or branches, absorb the nutrients they need and expel the carbohydrates in the form of sugar syrup.[3] Israeli entomologist Dr Bodenheimer (1897–1959) believed that the biblical manna was produced by two scale insects (*Trabutina mannipara* and *Najacoccus serpentinus*) living on the tamarisk species *Tamarix mannifera*, which grows in the Sinai Desert.[4] The manna produced by the insects dries in the heat and falls to the ground as granules. The theory that the biblical manna was an insect product has not gained wide currency, even though supported by the fact that the Arabic word *man* means 'plant lice' as well as the honeydew they excrete.[5]

It has also been proposed that the manna of the Israelites was a kind of lichen, *Lecanora esculenta* (cup moss), which grows in barren mountainous areas and used to be gathered for food in Kirghistan, Persia and Turkey.[6] When swept down by wind or rain in large quantities it was thought by local people to have rained from heaven. Known as *kudret buğdayı* in Turkish, this lichen was used as food in times of famine. Hâfız Veli Çimen of Karahalli in western Turkey recalls that when locusts stripped his family's wheat fields bare during the War of Independence (1919–23) he was sent to the mountains to gather lichen, which his mother mixed with barley meal to make bread.[7] The name *kudret buğdayı* could be translated as 'wheat of divine power', just as *kudret helvası* means 'sweetmeat of divine power'. However, Turkish theologian Prof. Dr İsmail Yakıt suggests that the name be interpreted as 'naturally occurring', since the natural world is the creation of God.[8]

Discounting the lichen, which is neither sweet nor an insect product and so not strictly a manna at all, two varieties of manna are found in Turkey in quantities significant enough to have a culinary impact. One of these is honeydew produced by the scale insect *Marchalina hellenica*, which is the source of the pine honey produced in southwest Turkey and Greece.[9] Known as *balsıra*, the honeydew is deposited on the branches of some pine species, mainly *Pinus brutia*, by the immature insects. During the hot summer months the quantity of the saccharine liquid increases and attracts bees, which collect this syrup instead of nectar from flowers. During the *balsıra* season Turkish beekeepers from far afield transport their hives to the pine forests of the region.

Surprisingly, Bodenheimer, who worked in Turkey for several years during the 1940s and studied traditional Turkish beekeeping, does not mention *balsıra* or pine honey. Even today the fact that pine honey is made from a variety of manna is very little known outside beekeeping, forestry and entomological circles.

The only Ottoman period account of *balsıra* I have encountered is in the seventeenth-century travel account by Evliyâ Çelebi, who came across it in the forests of Sivrihisar (today Seferihisar):[10]

The people have another product, a syrup called *balısıra* found on the pine trees in all the mountains here. A white substance appears on all the pine branches and a kind of little worm appears and eats into the branches. Then these worms excrete a white syrup onto the bark and twigs and this adheres to them. Then in the season the people climb into the pines and gather the honey into boxes, and the remaining honey is left on the trees and the bees of the province come to those pine-clad mountains and carry it away to their nests in their hives and make great combs of honey that are famous in the four corners of the world as Sığla or Sivrihisar honey, which has a fragrance like musk and raw ambergris.

And in these mountains the pastures and vineyards ring with the buzzing of bees' wings. And the bees gather the worm honey that is like ready-made helva and make honeycombs in their hives that weigh twenty or thirty *okka*s apiece, and from this is made strained honey as white as muslin that is sent as gifts to magnates and gentry.

The honey made by the worms in the trees is not comb honey, but an encrustation like thick syrup.

The other type of manna found in Turkey is oak manna, produced by aphids that breed in oak forests, particularly in the eastern provinces.[11] The manna is known by various local names: the Persian *gezengevî* or the cognate *gezo, men* from the Arabic *man*, and the Turkish words *kudret helvası* and *yağcı pelidi*.[12] The Persian *gezengevî* and *gezengübin* mean tamarisk honey, while *gez-meni* means tamarisk manna. Persian *gez* is also the name for *Astragalus adscendens*, another manna host-plant of western Asia, so *gezengübin* can refer to Astragalus manna or be used as a generic term for oak manna produced in western Iran, northern Iraq and eastern Turkey. It was also called *man-es-simma* (manna from the skies) in Persian and Arabic pharmacopoeas, and 'Diarbekir manna' or 'Kurdish manna' in historical English sources.[13]

The inconspicuous appearance of the tiny aphids on the oak leaves, the unpredictability of the manna's appearance, and the pleasing image of manna raining from heaven has meant that local people tend to perpetuate the myth even in the teeth of evidence to the contrary. There is sometimes little or no oak manna for several years running, followed by a glut year, probably depending on unknown factors relating to the life cycle of the insect and weather conditions.[14]

Mannas were valued in the Islamic world for their medicinal properties, and Evliyâ Çelebi refers to the laxative properties of the oak manna of Diyarbakır and Malatya:[15] 'By the command of God manna called gezengevi rains from the skies onto the leaves of oak trees in the mountains. It is a tasty laxative sweetmeat.'

If the honeydew on the oak leaves was collected before sunrise it could be shaken onto a cloth, and this formed the finest white variety.[16] However, some of the gatherers did not go to this trouble but merely pounded the leaves and manna together.[17] After the sun rose it melted to form a layer of transparent syrup on the leaves. In places where oak manna was abundant enough to form a commercial commodity it was gathered in skin bags. The manna dried into crystallized lumps which were so hard that when Bodenheimer first obtained a sample of Turkish oak manna from Elazığ he thought it was a stone:[18]

It is sold in large lumps of hard consistency, stone-like, and always mixed with small fragments of oak leaves. When I obtained the first specimen in

Turkey, I was certain that it was a stone covered superficially with a small amount of hardened honeydew mixed with the fragments of oak leaves. We learned much later only that the entire 'stone' was manna.

In the province of Bitlis the leafy branches are gathered in the mountains and carried back to the villages where they are rinsed in cauldrons of water and the sugary solution strained before boiling to produce a delicious dark syrup.[19]

In the first half of the twentieth century an estimated 30,000 kilograms of oak manna were sold annually in Iraq, two-thirds of it imported from Iran. The raw manna was purified by confectioners and mixed with egg white and almonds or other nuts to make nougat.[20] Local people in the manna-producing areas, on the other hand, boiled and strained the manna and then ate it for breakfast, diluted it with water to make a sherbet drink, or mixed it with flour and nuts to make cakes.[21]

One of the earliest accounts of oak manna is by the Roman historian Quintus Curtius Rufus, in his biography of Alexander the Great written c. AD 50. He writes that near the Caspian Sea there were many trees resembling oaks, whose leaves were covered with honey and which the inhabitants gathered before sunrise, lest the moisture should be dried up by the heat of the sun.[22]

The earliest mention of oak manna in Ottoman times is by the Dutchman Dr Leonhart Rauwolff, who travelled through the southeastern provinces of the Ottoman Empire in 1573. He noticed the manna among merchandise at Mosul bound for Baghdad:[23]

Among the rest I saw . . . another sort of manna as big as a double fist, which is very common here and is brought from Armenia, as they told me. It is of a brown colour, a great deal bigger and firmer, and not so sweet as that of Calabria, yet very good and pleasant to eat. Within it are several red grains, so small that one taketh no notice of them when one eats it. It looseneth the body very well, but not so much as ours, wherefore the inhabitants eat great pieces thereof in the morning, as the country-men on the mountains of Algave eat cheese.

The brown colour he mentions suggests that the manna must have been melted down, since Bodenheimer notes that the raw manna is white, becoming reddish after melting.[24] The 'red grains' were probably the aphids.

In Istanbul during the nineteenth century oak manna was sold in the Ramazan markets set up in mosque courtyards during the month of fasting, when sweetmeats of all kinds were purchased in readiness for the Şeker Bayram (Sugar Feast) at the end of Ramazan.[25]

Manna aroused a great deal of interest among European scientists during the nineteenth century, when French chemist Berthelot and German chemists such as Fluckiger obtained samples and carried out analyses.[26] In 1862 a sample of Turkish oak manna described as 'Diarbekir manna' was shown at the International Industrial Exhibition held in London.[27]

Other types of mannas mentioned in historical Turkish sources include *gezengübin* produced on species of *Astragalus* by *Cyamophila astragalicola* (an insect species of the *Psyllidae* family), which in Iran was used to produce nougat, just as oak manna was in Iraq;[28] *terengübin* produced by an unknown insect species on the camel thorn *Alhagi* and for centuries an important source of sugar in Central Asia, from where it was exported to China under the name of 'thorn honey';[29] *tıgala*, a manna produced by certain weevils of the *Larinus* species on *Echinops* which, despite being a product of Iran, was at one time known as 'Turkish manna' in Western literature because Europeans encountered it in Turkey;[30] *sükker-i üşer* produced on *Calotropis*; and *şir-hişt* produced on *Cotoneaster nummularia* or *Atraphaxis spinosa*. However, all of these mannas were confined to medicinal use.

By the second half of the nineteenth century Italian ash manna was rapidly superseding traditional Turkish and western Asian mannas for medicinal purposes in Turkey. Ash manna is thought to have been discovered by the Arabs during the period they ruled Sicily (827–1070), and they named a mountain on the island Jabal-i Mann, meaning 'Manna Mountain' (corrupted to Gibelman or Gibelmanna by local Sicilians).[31] Sicilian manna is the product of a large sap-sucking cicada (*Cicada orni*), whose names in German (*Mannazirpe*) and Swedish (*mannastreiten*) mean 'manna cicada'.[32] Although Sicilian manna is not the biblical variety, in 1927 the Italian government passed a statutory instrument declaring that the name 'manna' was 'reserved for the product obtained from the flowering ash or manna ash (*F. ornus* or *F. excelsior*)'.[33] Another urban myth had been born.

5 Confectioners and Confectionery Shops

> He who comes from a garden brings roses as a gift
> He who comes from a sweet shop brings sweets.
> Mevlânâ Celâleddin Rûmî (1207–73)[1]

IN 1244 A MAN CARRYING a tray of sweetmeats on his head came into the hall where Mevlânâ Celâleddin Rûmî (1207–73) was teaching law in Konya and handed him a piece of the sweetmeat. The sweet seller was Shems of Tabriz, and he became Mevlânâ's spiritual guide, transforming him from scholar into mystic philosopher and poet. When Mevlânâ returned to Konya years later,[2]

> he had become demented and would speak only in Persian rhymed couplets which no one could understand. His disciples used to follow him and write down that poetry as it issued from him, and they collected it into a book called the *Mathnawi*.

This anecdote reflects the spiritual significance accorded to sugar in Islamic culture, and its powerful metaphorical role in Mevlânâ's writings.

From Mevlânâ we learn that in thirteenth-century Konya, during the Seljuk period, there were both shops and street vendors selling confectionery. One of a series of Ottoman miniature paintings depicting a guild procession in 1582 shows a confectioner's shop being pulled along on a float. On the counter stands a pair of scales, and above this three shelves of conical sugar loaves and jars of sweets. The arched aperture behind the shopkeeper, who is sitting crosslegged, represents the entrance to the workshop behind. There is a parrot in a cage at the lower right corner (see Plate 1).

Guild processions were the advertising films of their day, played by live actors on floats decorated with the raw or finished products of the trade to which they belonged. The enigmatic parrot must be an image closely associated with the confectioners. References to parrots in mystic poetry by Mevlânâ, Kaygusuz Abdal (d. 1444), Ahmed Pasha (d. 1497) and others suggest an answer to the mystery, since the idea that parrots love sugar and on this account are 'sweet tongued' is a common conceit. The following example is from Mevlânâ's *Mesnevi:*[3]

> You are not a parrot that they should give you sugar,
> And listen to your sweet words.

So the parrot in the confectioner's shop symbolized the desire for sugar and the way in which eating sugar bestows the gift of eloquence. On a deeper level parrots also symbolized the attainment of spiritual awareness.

Other miniatures of this period depict confectioners' furnaces. Stoves of this type made of brick remained unchanged for centuries in Europe as well as in Turkey, providing the controlled heat required for sugar boiling and other confectionery techniques. Sixteenth-century Ottoman confectionery furnaces had an arched opening at floor level for laying the fire and cleaning out the ashes. Cooking was done by setting the tray or pan onto the circular well above the fire grate. Furnaces much like these were used by confectioners everywhere for centuries, and they were still in use in England in the late nineteenth century. In his *Confectioner's Handbook*, published in 1881, the English confectioner E. Skuse gives a diagram of a confectioner's furnace with a detailed description of how to construct one, including the cost of materials, and offers to build one for his customers in London at no charge, providing they pay his railway fare.[4] Even as late as 1928 'the old-fashioned brick furnace' had evidently still not outlived its usefulness, despite the advent of both electric and gas stoves, since it is described again in the twelfth edition of the same book.[5]

As well as confectionery furnaces, rectangular hearths with low stone walls on three sides were used for cooking over charcoal. Rows of such open-fronted hearths can still be seen in the *helvahane* (confectionery kitchen) at Topkapı Palace in Istanbul. These are described as 'low charcoal cookers surrounded by walls' by the Bavarian royal confectioner Friedrich Unger, who visited the palace in 1835.[6] Unger also describes 'walled-in pans set at a slant for the preparation of halwa' and 'a big walled-in flat pan for roasting the sesame, nougat etc.' Confectioners' shops were also equipped with ovens built into the wall, as illustrated in two early twentieth-century pictures, and described by Charles White in 1846.[7] When town confectioners were cooking large quantities of fruit preserves or syrup, they sometimes did this in the street outside their shops.[8]

The front part of the shop where customers were served had shelves for glass jars of sweets. Here sat the proprietor, where he could simultaneously keep an eye on his staff at work in the back room.[9] A painting of a Turkish confectioner's shop by the Maltese artist Amadeo Preziosi dating from 1857 shows a broad marble counter on which are a dish of sweetmeats beneath a bell jar and a pair of scales, shelves with various jars on the right and strings of *tatlı sucuk* suspended from the ceiling (see Plate 3).[10] In the back shop the figure of a confectioner at work can just be seen in the firelight. The wooden shop shutters, painted with flowers inside each panel, are lifted up to form an awning over the counter. Resting on a shelf behind the confectioner is what looks like a framed mirror, but is more likely to be one of the religious mottos beloved of Ottoman confectioners since at least the seventeenth century: 'The love of sweets springs from faith,' or 'The true believer is like helva.'[11] Charles White (1846) records that many confectioners' shops in Istanbul were adorned with framed and glazed inscriptions of this kind.[12]

When the French poet and novelist Théophile Gautier visited a confectioner's shop in Istanbul in 1852, he was struck first of all by the painted shutters. He and his companion entered the shop and sat on stools as they sampled the various sweets and drank cups of coffee while watching the confectioners at work:[13]

My friend made me enter one of the confectioners' shops to initiate me into the delights of Turkish gormandism, far more refined than people think it in Paris. The shop deserves a separate description. The shutters, drawn up like fans, like the ports of a ship, formed a sort of carved awning quadrilled and painted yellow and blue, above great glass vases filled with red and white sweets, stalactites of *rahat lakhoum* – a sort of transparent paste made with the best of flour and sugar and then coloured in various ways – pots of preserves of roses, and bowls of pistachios.

We entered the shop, which, though three people would have found it difficult to move about in it, is one of the largest in Constantinople. The master, a stout, dark-complexioned Turk, with a black beard and a good-humouredly fierce expression, served us, with an amiably terrible air, rose and white rahat lakhoum and all sorts of exotic sweets highly perfumed and very exquisite, although somewhat too honeyed for a Parisian palate. A cup of excellent mocha relieved by its salutary bitterness the cloying sweets, of which I had partaken too lavishly through love for local colour. At the back of the shop young boys, with print aprons around their waists, were moving upon the bright fire the copper basins in which the almonds and pistachios were being rolled in sugar, or were dusting sugar upon rolls of *rahat lakhoum*, making no mystery of their preparations.

Although there appears to be no room for customers in pictures of Turkish confectioners' shops such as the painting by Preziosi, we know that some confectioners provided stools or divans where customers sat to sample sweets and take refreshments. The famous French cook Alexis Soyer, who was sent to Istanbul by the British government during the Crimean War to improve the diet of soldiers in the British hospital run by Florence Nightingale, was taken to such a confectioner's in Üsküdar by the *kazasker* (chief justice) of Anatolia one evening in the month of Ramazan:[14]

Our progress came to an end at a confectioner's shop, the largest and principal one in Scutari. Here sherbets, coffee and chibouques [pipes], iced lemonade,

7. A confectioner at work. He is stirring a pan of jam while a tray of some kind of pastry dessert is baking in the oven behind him. A quince, a pear and an apricot are lying in front of him. In the foreground is a jar labelled *vişne tatlısı* (cherry preserve), another rectangular tray containing some kind of sweetmeat, perhaps Turkish delight, cut into squares, and a colander containing apricots (Cover illustration of *Tatlıcıbaşı*, a book of confectionery recipes by Hadiye Fahriye, published in Istanbul in 1926).

sweets, and all kinds of fruit in season, were handed to us, as we sat upon the divans in open view to the public, a great crowd having been attracted to the spot. Numbers entered and saluted the Pacha, and retired.

While some foreigners compared Ottoman confectionery shops unfavourably to fashionable establishments in Paris and London, Sir Adolphus Slade, who served in the Ottoman navy during the reign of Sultan Abdülmecid, was enthusiastic:[15]

The counters are covered with slabs of marble, always beautifully clean, particularly so where preparations of creams, wheys, etc. are sold, of which the Osmanleys make great consumption. The confectioners' shops are admirable in point of elegance, and the excellence of the article: everybody has heard praised Turkish sweetmeats; I may add that one is in danger of having a tooth-ache during his stay at Constantinople.

Around the same period John Auldjo described a 'large and handsome' confectioner's near the Fish Market, where he tasted a large number of sweets at one sitting:[16]

The day was wound up with the important business of tasting the different varieties of confectionery to be found in a large, handsome shop near the Balouk bazar. All were luscious, and many, particularly the preserved rose leaves, were even delicate. We partook of some thirty or forty different sorts; in which flowers, scents, fruits, and gums were mixed with sugar, until of the consistence of damson cheese.

Although Auldjo, like many other travellers, claimed that the Turks ate sweetmeats in large quantities, in fact his own capacity probably astonished Turkish onlookers, for whom accepting more than one sweet at a time was not regarded as good manners.

Charles White gives a detailed account of the various containers and equipment found in confectioners' shops on Alaca Hamam Street in the district of Eminönü. His description of the gilt paper, coloured gauze, ribbons, coloured paper and tinsel ornaments used to decorate their wares shows that confectioners went to a good deal of trouble to tempt customers:[17]

Higher up in Aladsha Hammam Street are the shops of several shekerjee (confectioners), whose trade is among the most conspicuous and profitable in the city. The different sweetmeats are symmetrically arranged, in vases, packets, or flat baskets, ornamented with gilt paper, and covered with coloured gauze, fastened with ribbons. Sticks of red and white candy, and small glass cups, filled with candied cherry, mulberry and plum pulp [*çevirme*], for sherbets, are suspended from the ceiling, interspersed with coloured paper and tinsel ornaments. All practical business is performed in a back shop. Here are ovens for baking, and stoves for preparing various preserves; copper pans for mixing the pulp, and large, flat copper heaters, on which the fluid is poured, candied, dried, and then cut up in diamond-shaped cakes for use.

Once the sweetmeats had been selected they were packed in colourful baskets and boxes,[18] or in the case of small purchases, in folded paper cones or the customer's pocket handkerchief, as we learn from Julia Pardoe:[19]

> . . . no Turk, however high his rank, returns home for the night, when the avocations of the day are over, empty-handed: it signifies not how trifling may be the value of his burthen – a cluster of grapes, a paper of sweetmeats . . . The father of the eldest son, Usuf Effendi, had brought home Ramazan cakes; but Soliman Effendi deposited on the tandour a *boksha*, or handkerchief of clear muslin wrought with gold threads, and containing sweetmeats.

Julia Pardoe's expectations of Istanbul's confectionery shops had been unrealistically raised by the hyperbole of an acquaintance who told her that 'the stalls of the sweetmeat-venders resembled fairy-palaces'. So when she eventually saw them for herself in 1836, she remarked, 'I can only say, that with every disposition to do ample justice to all I saw, my own ideas of enchantment are much nearer at Grange's or Farrance's.'[20]

The Ottoman upper classes were equally enamoured of the European-style elegance that Julia Pardoe found wanting in Istanbul, and in the early 1840s a Frenchwoman, Madame Meunier, opened a fashionable confectionery shop in Beyoğlu, the district of Istanbul where the diplomatic and Levantine communities congregated. Gérard de Nerval visited her shop in 1843 and wrote:[21]

> . . . although Turkish women make excellent fruit preserves, the Parisians remain unsurpassed where the manufacture of sweetmeats, bonbons and splendid packaging for these are concerned. As we were returning from the Sweet Waters we passed down the Grand Rue de Péra, which is similar to our Rue des Lombards. To watch the crowds and take some refreshment, we stopped at the principal confectioner's shop, run by Madame Meunier. The shop was full of eminent personages, wealthy Turks who had come to make

their purchases in person, because it is not wise in this country to entrust
simple servants with the task of buying bonbons. Madame Meunier had won
the trust of the *effendi*s (men of distinction), who knew that she would sell
them only the best.

European sweetmeats in porcelain dishes were among gifts presented to
the fourteen-year-old Münire Sultan, daughter of Sultan Abdülmecid, at
her engagement to İbrahim İlhami Pasha in 1858.[22] These may have been
purchased from Madame Meunier's or from another French confectioner's
shop, Vallaury's, on the same street.

There had been foreign confectioners in Istanbul before the nineteenth
century, notably the 'Galata confectioners', consisting of Greeks from Chios
and 'Franks' (probably Italians), who specialized in medicinal preparations
and figurative decorations made of sugar paste. In the seventeenth century
they kept sixty or seventy shops in the districts of Kasımpaşa, Eyüp, Suriçi and
the Jewish quarter of Hocapaşa.[23] They formed a separate guild of about 500
members who, like the other specialized confectioners' guilds – including the
helva makers, *akide* makers, *lokma* makers, *pâlûde* makers and *bâdemli köfter*
makers – were under the authority of the *hünkâr helvacıbaşısı* (royal chief
helva maker) and the *şehir şekercibaşısı* (chief confectioner of Istanbul). The
city confectioners evidently retained close ties with the palace until the end
of the nineteenth century, since the guild steward in the 1870s was a palace
confectioner called Şekerci İbrahim Efendi, who had been educated at the
palace school.[24] The sweet makers' guild had rooms on Asmaaltı Caddesi in
Eminönü, and the members paid an annual membership fee of one gold piece.

Each of the old craft guilds had its *pir*, 'patron saint' or founder, often
semi-mythical figures who were purported to have invented the article in
question. The *pir* of confectioners is variously identified as Hüseyin bin Nusayr
or Abdullah bin Mesut. Helvacı Ömer was *pir* of four separate branches of
confectionery trade: the helva makers, *kurabiye* makers, *güllaç* makers and
şerbet makers, leaving the *kadayıf* makers to his son Reşid.[25]

The guilds supervised the apprenticeship system and organized the ceremonies at which journeymen were raised to the rank of master craftsmen. In
1933, an elderly confectioner named Mehmet Ağa described the ceremonies of
the past, which were held in meadows outside the city in springtime. Ceremonial girding of the *peştemal*, an ankle-length silk apron, marked the craftsman's
new status as master:[26]

Without permission from the guild no one could open a shop. This
permission was granted at a ceremony held every spring at Kâğıthane. There

was feasting and the *peştemal* girding ceremony took place. The *peştemal*s were made of silk and woven in Bursa. Although the confectioners invited many other guilds to these celebrations, they never invited the tanners. The *peştemal* girding ceremony was conducted as follows: After the meal everyone rose and prayer rugs were laid out before the masters. A *hoca* prayed, and then the guild steward and the *yiğitbaşı* [a high-ranking guild official] of the confectioners sat beside the *hoca*. The *yiğitbaşı* was responsible for organizing the event and acted as mentor to the journeymen.

Mehmet Ağa had come to Istanbul from his native city of Çankırı in 1870 at the age of fourteen and become apprenticed to Osman Ağa, a fellow countryman from Çankırı. At that time there were seventy confectioner's shops in the city altogether and the neighbourhood of Bahçekapı at the southern mouth of the Golden Horn was the centre of the confectionery industry. Mehmet Ağa said that, even though his own shop was not among the most famous, up to the outbreak of the Balkan War (1912) he had sometimes employed as many as eighteen journeymen.[27]

The most famous Turkish confectioner of all time was Hacı Bekir, who was born in Kastamonu around 1760 and as a young boy was apprenticed to a confectioner in Istanbul. In 1777 he opened his own shop in Bahçekapı. Hacı Bekir is believed to have been appointed as chief palace confectioner during the reign of Mahmud II (1809–39), and to have perfected the art of making Turkish delight.[28]

Upon Hacı Bekir's death in 1856 his shop passed to his son Hacı Ahmed,[29] who was succeeded in turn by his son Ali Muhiddin.[30] But since the shop continued to be known as Hacı Bekir he achieved a kind of immortality. The journalist Burhan Felek, who was born in 1889, claimed in his memoirs to have seen Hacı Bekir, whereas in fact, the man he remembered seeing as a child must have been Hacı Bekir's grandson Ali Muhiddin.[31] Preziosi's famous painting of a Turkish confectioner is dated 1857 and may depict the elderly Hacı Bekir shortly before his death. Hacı Bekir undoubtedly deserved immortality. He was not only the first person to export Turkish delight, but he and his descendants always welcomed curious tourists into the back shop to watch boiled sweets and Turkish delight being made.

As an institution Hacı Bekir went from triumph to triumph, winning medals at a series of world fairs, including Vienna in 1873, Cologne in 1888 and Brussels in 1897. Sweets from Hacı Bekir continued to be purchased for the palace, and Ali Muhiddin Hacıbekir was appointed chief confectioner to Sultan Abdülhamid II in 1906 and to the khedive of Egypt in 1911.[32] Despite his celebrity status, Ali Muhiddin continued to permit foreign visitors to watch

8. A nineteenth-century postcard showing a confectionery shop with jars of sweets on the shelves at the back and along the counter (Courtesy of Mert Sandalcı).

his journeymen at work. One of these visitors was the Englishwoman Dorina Lockhart Neave, who lived in Istanbul from 1881 to 1907. Although she confuses the techniques of pulled sugar and Turkish delight, her vivid account of this visit brings to life an establishment that can have changed little since the time of Hacı Bekir himself:[33]

> It was too late for any further sight-seeing, so we hurried back to the Bridge, paying on our return journey a visit, absolutely essential after seeing Stamboul, to Hadji Bekir's Turkish Delight factory. This is situated most conveniently near the Bridge head, and consists of one small room where, under the opening of a large chimney piece, huge copper pans were kept filled with sugar syrup. Young boys stirred these incessantly for two hours at a time, over a large wood fire, until the mixture thickened, when various flavours were added, such as mastic, rose or vanilla. I was much amused to note that Hadji Bekir, the owner, who welcomed us into his shop, never attempted to sell us his Turkish Delight. With great ceremony he offered us plaited straw-covered stools to sit on, and cups of coffee were supplied with generous helpings of *rahat loukoum* (Turkish Delight) and boiled sweets in many colours. We were then invited to watch the process of making Turkish Delight, which thrilled me, as we were just in time to see a man take out of the coppers a great coil of the thick syrup that had been cooking. With a dexterous twist of the wrist he

threw the sticky substance, as thick as a coil of rope, into the air and caught it on a huge hook. With lightning speed it was spun through the cook's hands and thrown up again repeatedly onto the hook. Each time this process was resorted to the substance became thicker, and it shone with satin-like sheen. Finally, when the substance acquired the right consistency, the confectioner cut it up into squares, rolled these in the finest sugar procurable, and, when they were ready for consumption, handed them round to us to taste. From a shelf above his head he reached for a wooden drum-shaped box, and waited for orders for the quantity of Turkish Delight that was required. Until that moment we had in no way been given the slightest hint that we were expected to buy any of the goods for sale in the shop. We had been treated as honoured guests, with the usual beautiful manners of the courtly Turk, which always filled me with admiration; it was with the greatest diffidence that we asked what our account came to, and were surprised and relieved to find that we had been charged only for the boxes of Turkish Delight that we had been allowed to buy.

Another famous Istanbul confectioner of the period was Cemil Bey (1861–1913), who was also a composer, *ud* player and *hafiz*.[34] Istanbul was the main centre of the confectionery trade, but not the only one. Some provincial cities, such as Konya, Aydın and Uşak, were also renowned for their confectionery,[35] and the writer Halid Ziya Uşaklıgil (1867–1945) came from a long line of helva makers in Uşak.[36]

6 Sugar Sculpture

There came a hundred sugar lions
Nearly replicas of those in the wild.

Mustafa Ali of Gallipoli (1582)[1]

The confectioner fashioned
Sugar trees of many kinds.

Watchman's rhyme[2]

JUGGLERS, ACROBATS, FIRE-EATERS, STRONG MEN, sword-swallowers, tightrope walkers, illusionists, performing animals, automatons, firework displays, enactments of sieges and battles, and escapologists were among the entertainments at Ottoman period festivities celebrating royal weddings and circumcisions.[3] Other spectacles on these occasions were sculpted sugar models of gardens, castles and animals produced by the confectioners, which – after being paraded through the streets and main show ground where the sultan and other privileged spectators were seated on balconies – were broken up and eaten by the crowds or distributed among the royal family and high-ranking officials.[4]

Miniature illustrations of sculpted sugar gardens made for celebrations in 1582 and 1720 show colourful and intricately worked pavilions, pools containing fountains or rowing boats, fruit trees, cypress trees and flower beds (see Plate 5). Decorative artificial trees known as *nahıl*, representing the tree of life and symbolizing plenty and long life, were also carried in wedding and circumcision processions, and some of these were likewise made of sugar. Those made for royal celebrations were gorgeous affairs with decorations made of gold, silver, wax and coloured paper attached to the wooden trunk and branches.[5] At the wedding celebrations of Hatice Sultan, the eldest daughter of Mehmed IV, eight of the fifty *nahıl*s were made of sugar.[6]

*Nahıl*s were also carried in peace celebrations, perhaps symbolizing the hope that peace would be long-lasting. When the Treaty of Erdebil was signed between Ottoman Turkey and Iran in 1612, Shah Abbas I sent sugar *nahıl*s as well as thousands of packloads of food for the two armies attending the illuminated night-time celebrations. These festivities were so spectacular that when Evliyâ Çelebi visited Erdebil about thirty years later local people were still talking about them.[7]

At the festivities lasting fifty-two days for the circumcision of Murad III's sons in 1582, sculpted sugar figures of animals were carried on trays in procession through the streets. As well as the 100 lions mentioned in the quotation from the account of these celebrations by Mustafa Ali of Gallipoli at the beginning of this chapter, there were 100 lion cubs, 100 tigers and tiger cubs, 100 large elephants and 100 elephant calves, horses, camels, buzzards, vultures, falcons, partridges, peacocks, cockerels, ducks and geese.[8] Such were their numbers and variety that:

> The ground was transformed into a new world
> With wild animals and birds all of sugar.

There were also backgammon and chess sets made of sugar.[9] In a pair of miniatures illustrating the sugar sculptures we see a lion, leopard, camel, elephant, giraffe, horse, two mythological creatures with the body of a bird of prey and a woman's head wearing a crown, two storks, two geese, a tray of fish and two trays of unidentifiable spotted objects – perhaps the leopard cubs mentioned by Mustafa Ali? One of these miniatures is reproduced in the plate section (see Plate 4).

From another eyewitness, this time Reinhold Lubenau of Konigsberg, we learn that the sugar models also included giraffes, monkeys, mermaids, fish, watermelons, grapes, peaches, pomegranates, oranges, lemons, apricots, jugs, ewers, candlesticks, pools with fountains and castles.[10] Lubenau reports with regret that most of these sugar sculptures were spoilt by a sudden rainstorm just as they were being carried into the Hippodrome. More than 9 tons of sugar, and large quantities of cinnamon, cloves, aniseed and bitter oranges were used to make these sugar models, which were sculpted by Jewish craftsmen and painted by artists.[11]

Small sugar models of animals and fruits, such as elphants, horses, partridges, vultures, apples and quinces made by Istanbul's confectioners as novelties were sold in the street in the early sixteenth century, as reported by the writer Lâtifî in 1525.[12]

Sugar models continued to be made until the nineteenth century. At the royal wedding celebrations in 1836 for Mihrimah Sultan, daughter of Mahmud II, and Ferik Mehmed Said Pasha, the confectioners paraded with life-size models of a horse and rider, and carried roses and laurel wreaths made of sugar.[13] In 1874 the Italian writer Edmondo de Amicis described sugar figures served at the end of a traditional Ottoman meal in an Istanbul restaurant: 'a huge dish of sweetmeats, among which were conspicuous a steamboat, a fierce-looking lion, and a sugar house with grated windows'.[14] Since there is no evidence that sugar models were ever used to decorate the table at Turkish meals, however grand, it may be that the restauranteur had been inspired by the long-standing European fashion for sugar table decorations.

When Siyavuş Pasha, *beylerbeyi* of Rumelia, married the sister of Murad III in 1575, coloured sugar models of towns, forts and figures of various animals, including elephants and leopards, were carried in the bridal procession.[15] The German Lutheran minister Stephan Gerlach, who witnessed this event, reported that the total cost of these and other wedding preparations was 100,000 ducats. Sugar sculptures were not reserved for royalty, as this description by Gerlach of a bridal procession for an unidentified but clearly wealthy couple shows:[16]

> Those who followed carried perhaps fifty statues made of sugar. At the front were six or seven figures of elephants each ridden by a negro, then came two lions, three horses, four strange sea creatures, a peacock, stork, falcon and other diverse birds, cups, jugs, candlesticks and innumerable other objects, all made of sugar and colourfully painted, so that one might have thought that they were made of wood or some other material . . . After the wedding the bride distributes these sugar works to her friends, giving one a lion, one an elephant, and thereby gratifying them all.

The earliest account of sugar sculptures made for Ottoman celebrations dates from 1457, when sugar mosques, castles, pavilions and meadows bedecked with myriad flowers and fragrant herbs were displayed at the circumcision celebrations for Mehmed the Conqueror's sons Bâyezid and Mustafa.[17] The 'meadows' must be the forerunner of the sugar gardens that became such a feature of later festivities. The Ottomans loved flowers and gardens, and their custom of presenting cut flowers as gifts and decorating their turbans with flowers astonished sixteenth-century European travellers.[18] The sugar gardens made for the festivities held in 1675 to celebrate the circumcision of Mehmed IV's eldest son Mustafa included violet gardens.[19] On the eleventh day of celebrations sugar sculptures were carried in procession through the streets and afterwards, together with 1,000 trays of sweets, were set on the ground for the crowds to eat.[20] The circumcision was followed by the wedding of Hatice

Sultan, the sultan's eldest daughter. According to the poet Nâbî, the three sugar gardens made for her wedding contained sugar nightingales and other birds, lions, roe deer, fish and camels.[21] In his account of the celebrations, Nâbî describes these gardens in the following two couplets:[22]

> Three gardens filled with ornaments
> Boughs, leaves and fruit all of sugar.

> In each one or two fountains
> With water flowing at whim.

Larger sculpted figures of animals were carried on trays for the circumcision procession, as described by Dr Covel:[23]

> Then followed, in two files on each side of the way, 120 sugar-workes, borne on frames by two slaves a piece, sedan wise, made from 2½ foot to a yard and a half high, some more or less as the fancy required. They were Ostridges, Peacocks, swans, Pelicans etc., Lyons, Beares, greyhoundes, dear [deer], horses, Elephants, Rams, Buffaloes etc. (it is unlawfull to make figures of men); they were done brutishly and bunglingly.

Another Englishman, Thomas Coke, watched the same celebrations and tells us that Hatice Sultan's husband-to-be Musahip Mustafa Pasha sent his bride '30 mules laden with sugar-plums and sweet-meats; figures of several sorts of birds and beasts, of sugar, so ill-favouredly represented, that they could not be said to break the law against making images.'[24] Coke and Covel's disparaging remarks about the figures seem rather unjust when we look at miniature paintings of sugar sculptures made a century earlier in 1582 and half a century later in 1720. Although it is certainly possible that the miniature painters improved upon reality, the fact that Gerlach and Lubenau were not disappointed by the figures they saw a century earlier suggests that the figures were far from being 'ill-favoured'.

Miniature paintings (for an example, see Plate 5) show eight sugar gardens made by the palace confectioners in 1720, during the period known as the Tulip Era, for the circumcision festivities for Ahmed III's four sons, Süleyman, Mehmed, Mustafa and Bâyezid. Four of the gardens have pools, each containing a boat, ship or fountain, surrounded by small pavilions, fruit trees, cypress trees and flowers. The other four have a large pavilion in the centre surrounded by trees, flowers, birds in cages and paths. From contemporary accounts we know that the tulips, roses, jonquils and other flowers were made from coloured sugar, the pathways pebbled with sugared almonds of various colours, the flower beds edged with bricks made of *mermerî helva*, the soil made of brown granulated sugar, and the pools were filled with sherbet.[25] Each of the gardens was carried by sixteen or more brawny young men from the naval docks.

At the wedding of Mustafa III's daughter Şah Sultan to Mehmed Emin Pasha in January 1768 four sugar gardens were made, of which one was presented to the sultan, one to the princes, one to the princesses and one to the *valide sultan* (mother of the sultan).[26]

The fact that cane sugar hardens on cooling was exploited to produce sugar figures as early as the third century AD in Tongking, China. Little cakes of sugar made by sun-drying cane juice were sometimes given the form of human figures or animals such as tigers, lions and elephants.[27] This idea may have originated in China or, like sugar processing technology, in India, and moved westwards to appear in a thirteenth-century Arabic cookery book written in Spain:[28]

Cast Figures of Sugar

Throw on the sugar a like amount of water or rose water and cook until its consistency is good. Empty it into the mould and make of it whatever shape is in the mould, the places of the 'eyebrow' and the 'eye' and what resembles the dish you want, because it comes out of the mould in the best way. Then decorate it with gilding and whatever you want of it. If you want to make a tree or a figure of a castle, cut it piece by piece. Then decorate it section by section and stick it together with mastic until you complete the figure you want, if God wills.[29]

Sugar sculpture became all the rage throughout western Europe, and an English recipe entitled 'To make ymages in suger' appeared in *Curye on Inglysch*, written in the late fourteenth century.[30] In Europe these figures were used principally to decorate dining tables, and in sixteenth-century Italy it became fashionable to make even the plates and cups from sugar paste. After the meal these could be broken up and eaten, affording the guests additional entertainment.[31] European confectioners added gum arabic or tragacanth, egg white and sometimes starch to the sugar paste used for decorations to reduce its fragility and increase its malleability. Although we have no contemporary Turkish recipes, the intricate designs of the model sugar gardens depicted in Ottoman miniature paintings suggest that some such substances must have been added to enable the sugar paste to be carved. We know that tragacanth was used by Turkish confectioners, because nineteenth-century cookbooks have recipes for moulded sweets made with sugar and tragacanth and flavoured with musk. Jews escaping the Spanish Inquisition may have introduced Italian techniques of sugar sculpture to Turkey.[32] Italian sugar sculpture developed into a highly sophisticated art at this period, with banqueting table decorations designed by well-known artists.[33] There is evidence that the skills of Italian confectioners were sought in the seventeenth century, since for the combined royal wedding and circumcision celebrations of 1675 an unspecified number of Italian confectioners were hired from Venice in addition to 200 local confectioners.[34] The confectioners of Galata,[35] famous for their skill at modelling sugar trees and fruits, may well have mediated in bringing Italian confectionery fashions to Istanbul. These 500 confectioners included both Greeks from Chios and Europeans, and their display of sculptures made an impressive display in a guild procession held in 1639:[36]

> They carried cypresses and apple, pear, apricot, cherry and peach trees made of sugar, whose fruits were also made entirely of sugar. It was a marvellous sight, so that watchers might have thought them to be trees bearing sacred fruit.

Marzipan was another good modelling material. During the period of Arab rule in Spain marzipan had been shaped into flowers and fruits,[37] and Ottoman confectioners too shaped marzipan into fruits such as lemons, plums and apricots, which they brushed with diluted tragacanth and then glazed with sugar syrup.[38]

Hollow moulded figures made of boiled sugar on sticks were a popular children's sweet. These lollipops were most often in the shape of cockerels, hence their Turkish name *horoz şekeri* ('cockerel sweets'), but also came in innumerable other forms, such as giraffes, lions, rabbits, birds, donkeys, mermaids, horsemen, pistols and baskets. However, cockerels were always the favourite, especially those with sugar whistles attached (see Plate 6). These lollipops are immortalized in a poem by the twentieth-century Turkish poet Cahit Sıtkı Tarancı, who identifies them with childhood:[39]

Childhood
I counted out my coins to Affan Dede
He sold me my childhood
Now I have neither age nor name;
I don't know who I am.
No one should ask me a question;
I know nothing about what goes on.

This spring day, this garden;
Water plashing in the pool.
My kite high above the clouds,
My marbles shiny and bright
My splendidly spinning hoop;
I wish my cockerel lollipop would never end!

These lollipops are made in two-part moulds by pouring the boiled sugar into the closed mould, then pouring the excess back into the pan, leaving a thin coating that cools and sets in a matter of minutes. The sugar animal figures sold in the streets of Istanbul in the early sixteenth century may have been made by the same method, since filling moulds with boiled sugar and letting it solidify would have been both time-consuming and resulted in an expensive product.

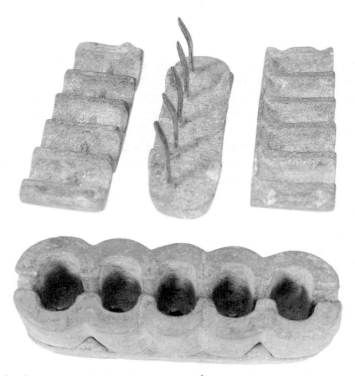

9. Mould for five sugar whistles (Courtesy of İbrahim Denizci; photograph: Cüneyt Akçıl).

Hollow figures are a fragile but affordable sweet, containing no more sugar than could be licked and crunched by a child at a single sitting. Similar sweets were known elsewhere in Europe, and the first record of hollow moulded sweets is in early seventeenth-century England, when Sir Hugh Plat described making hollow lemons, oranges and pears by pouring boiled sugar into plaster moulds and then swinging and turning them in the air:[40]

> Vse your Sugar in this manner: Boile refined or rather double refined sugar and Rose-water to his full height, viz. till by powring some out of a spoone, it will run at the last as fine as a haire, then taking off the cappe of your moulde, poure the same therein, filling vp the mould aboue the hole, & presently clap on the cappe, and presse it downe vpon the Sugar: then swing it vp and downe in your hand turning it round, and bringing the neather part sometimes to bee the vpper part in the turning, and *e conuerso*.

In the nineteenth century two English recipes describe the more practical method of filling the mould and then pouring off the excess. One is Henry Weatherley's description, published in 1865:[41]

Boiled Sugars in Moulds

There are many kinds of boiled loaf sugars, lowered and colored as for drops, and cast into iron moulds of all shapes, and before the whole mass sets pour it out, which leaves that only which clings to the shapes; as they are well oiled previously, they easily come out when the mould is parted.

Another English confectioner, Skuse, gives a more detailed account in his book written around 1881:[42]

Boiled-Sugar Figures

Iron moulds are made by confectioners' machinists for casting boiled sugars in, they may be had to turn out all kinds of figures, such as dogs, cats, elephants, etc. etc. They are very popular amongst the children, and sell well in certain districts, and show a handsome profit. The moulds are generally made in two parts, they must be well oiled, the sugar boiled as for drops, fill the mould full, and just before the whole mass sets pour as much of the sugar out as will run; this will leave only a thin coating which clings to the sides of the shapes, and will easily come out when the mould is parted, then you have the figure complete but hollow.

Despite their popularity these lollipops disappeared without trace in England, swept away by mechanized sweet production. In Turkey they were widely made until the 1990s by confectioners who produced them at home and sold them in the streets. Today only three of these *horoz şekeri* makers are still in business, in Bergama, Bursa and Mudanya. Until the 1950s the same confectioners also made sugar whistles known as *düdük şekeri*, consisting of a single or sometimes a double pipe, one playing a high and the other a low note, and another similar children's sweet called *çıngırak şekeri*, a hollow sugar sweet with a little bell inside.[43] Both hollow lollipops and whistles were always sold by itinerant street sellers, particularly at funfairs held on religious holidays.

7 *Akide*   *Drops*

Sweetmeat trays filled with red *akide*
Turned every corner of Istanbul into a Coral Bazaar.
Sâbit (d. 1712)[1]

A KIDE ARE BOILED SUGAR SWEETS flavoured with fruit juice or spices. This word, which originally meant thickened grape or sugar syrup, also meant faith or loyalty. The former meaning originated in the Syrian Arabic dialect, in which the word *akîda* meant to knot or to thicken.[2] So in fifteenth- and some sixteenth-century Turkish texts *akide* does not mean boiled sweets but grape syrup.[3]

The law code of Bâyezid II (r. 1481–1512) drawn up in the city of Manisa in the late fifteenth century specifies that the price of *akide* should be adjusted according to the price of grapes, so evidently *akide* here refers to boiled grape syrup, which was widely used as a sweetener in place of sugar.[4] From the beginning of the sixteenth century the corrupted form *ağda* gradually gained currency as the common term for syrup.[5]

The *ağda* sellers of seventeenth-century Istanbul had a bad reputation for charming their way into the affections of their women customers by singing seductive songs as they carried their barrels of grape syrup through the streets:[6]

> Let's strain syrup
> Let's swim like the moon
> Let's eat the *ağda*
> Sweet so sweet
> Let's go to the vineyard
> Let's enjoy ourselves
> O what *ağda*
> My beloved in the vineyard
> Her grapes in the vineyard.

Meanwhile *akide* acquired its new meaning of boiled sugar sweets, which were themselves new in the sixteenth century. *Akide*'s alternative meaning of loyalty was now picked up, and these sweets were used to convey a symbolic message by the soldiers of the Janissary Corps. When they received their three-monthly salaries they presented the grand vizier, other dignitaries and their own officers with gifts of *akide* sweets as a symbol of their loyalty to sultan and state.[7]

In time strict rules grew up concerning the quantities of *akide* presented to each official at the *ulûfe* ceremony: 500 drams to the grand vizier, 200 drams each to the commander of the Janissary Corps, and the two other highest-ranking janissary officers, and between 50 and 5 drams to various other janissary officers.[8]

As a similar reminder of faith and loyalty, *akide* sweets were distributed every Tuesday morning to the officials of the Council of State, which convened four days a week in the domed council chamber known as the Kubbealtı at Topkapı Palace:[9] 200 drams to the grand vizier, 150 drams each to the ministers and high judges, 100 drams each to the principal janissary officers, and 15–30 drams each to the clerks and officials of the Council of State, depending on their rank.

Mustafa Ali of Gallipoli's metaphorical use of the term *akide* – 'Every word he spoke was like an *akide* sweet' – in 1587 shows that these sweets were by now familiar to the reading public, and that their symbolic meaning could extend to anything pleasant and delightful.[10] With so much symbolism and so many flavours to choose from, it is not surprising that *akide* became the sweet of choice at circumcision celebrations, weddings, the Şeker Bayram (a three-day festival marking the end of Ramazan) and a host of other religious and social festivities. As the custom spread from the palace to the public at large, demand rose to such an extent that the guild confectioners could no longer produce *akide* in sufficient quantities. The result was a rash of bootleg confectioners and soaring sugar prices. In 1582 the government responded with a ban on unauthorized confectioners:[11]

Command to the Chief Judge of Istanbul,
The Chief Judge of the aforementioned city, Mevlânâ Zekeriya, has sent a letter to my royal court relating that the leading members of the guild of confectioners in the aforementioned city have applied to the court and reported that bootleggers have multiplied and are purchasing the sugar that arrives in the city to make *akide*, and that in consequence sugar prices have risen excessively from 20 or 30 *akçe*s per *vakıyye* to 45 or 50 *akçe*s per *vakıyye*, and requesting that hereafter bootleggers be banned. Therefore I command

that they be prohibited as in the past, and may care be taken that nothing is done contrary to my royal command.

Akide sweets were an essential part of circumcision banquets for the royal princes, the first recorded occasion being the circumcision of Sultan Süleyman the Magnificent's sons Bâyezid and Cihângîr in 1539. When the twelve-year-old Mustafa (the future Mustafa II) and two-year-old Ahmed (the future Ahmed III), the sons of Mehmed IV, were circumcised in 1675, 200 chestfuls of *akide* were carried in the procession.[12] At the circumcision of the four sons of Ahmed III in 1720, when 5,000 boys from poor families were also circumcised, the gifts presented by the guild of paper makers included four dishes of *akide*.[13]

Akide sweets were also presented to guests at ceremonies known as *mevlit*s held to commemorate the birth of the Prophet, and the births and deaths of ordinary people. In her memoirs Ayşe Osmanoğlu (1887–1960), daughter of Abdülhamid II, describes a *mevlit* ceremony held at the palace:[14]

During the Mevlid large silver trays of *akide* sweets, each carried by two cellarers, were brought and first offered to my father, and then by turns to everyone in the room. Each person took one sweet. The gentlemen-in-waiting brought the trays to the Harem side, and everyone took one from these heaps of diverse sweets. When the Mevlid was over my father would stand up. When he stood up everyone else did, and repeating their thanks left the room. He would say a few words to some of them. Decorated baskets and boxes of sweets would be distributed to all the guests. These were purchased from Hacı Bekir Efendi.

The palace always purchased its *akide* sweets from the most renowned confectioners in the town. The *şehir şekercibaşısı* ('chief town sweet maker') was equal in status to the *hünkâr helvacıbaşısı* ('chief royal helva maker'), who was in charge of the confectionery kitchens at the palace, and both these grandees marched side by side in guild professions.[15] The *akide* makers formed a company apart from the other confectioners, had their own shops – no fewer than seventy of them in Istanbul in the mid-seventeenth century – and even revered a different patron saint. While the patron saint of the confectioners and helva makers was Hüseyin bin Nusayr, that of the *akide* makers was Hazret-i Enes.[16] Evliyâ Çelebi tells us the names of Istanbul's famous *akide* makers in 1640: Fenâyî in Ayasofya Bazaar, Mevlevî Ahmed Çelebi in Unkapanı, Dede Beğ in Kasımpaşa and Sun'î Çelebi in Üsküdar.[17] Boiled sweets made by these masters would apparently last five years without losing their colour and sheen, and their glowing transparency was likened to Yemeni agate.

The oldest recorded varieties of *akide* are *elmasî* and apple, served at the royal circumcision banquet of sweets in 1539.[18] *Elmasî* means diamond-like, which speaks for itself as to their appearance although leaving us in the dark as to the flavour. The *kurs-ı limon* (lemon balls) served at the same banquet may also have been a type of *akide*. In later centuries the most popular of all was musk-flavoured, and the intoxicating fragrance of musk and ambergris from the *akide* sweets distributed to the crowd during the 1639 guild procession perfumed the air.[19] A register of fixed prices dating from the same period lists just two types of *akide*, plain (perhaps the *elmasî*) and musk-flavoured.[20] Lines from an eighteenth-century watchman's poem emphasize the superiority of the latter over any other:[21]

> None can compare to
> *Akide* flavoured with musk.

In the late nineteenth century musk *akide* was among the sweets served to guests on the Şeker Bayram. Abdülaziz Bey describes how this three-day festival was celebrated by a well-off Ottoman family:[22]

> That day the mistress of the house sent decorated baskets of many-coloured sweets to the midwife, her friends, her children's teachers, and former servants who had married, as an expression of her regard. Then guests would begin to arrive to offer bayram greetings to the master of the house. If these guests included ministers or state officials, they would be welcomed by the steward himself, who would take the guest's arm and accompany him to the room where the master of the house was waiting. Each guest would be offered small pieces of mastic-flavoured *rahat-ı hulkum* (Turkish delight), marzipan and musk-flavoured *akide* sweets on decorated silver trays by the chief cellarer and his underlings, and take one piece of their choice. Then the guests would wipe their mouth with a damp muslin cloth and return it to the plate.

Boiled sugar syrup was also used to make nut brittle, which, like nougat, was known as *koz helvası*. The syrup was poured into a tray in a thin layer and nuts pressed into the surface.[23] The hazelnut and pistachio helva served at the circumcision of Mehmed IV's sons in 1675 may have been similar.[24] Sweetmeats of this kind consisting of plain boiled sugar syrup mixed with sesame seeds or almonds are called *nâtıf* in fourteenth-century Arabic cookery books.[25] Similar sesame seed sweetmeats are still made at home in country districts in Turkey today, and factory-made versions wrapped in celophane are sold in Turkish shops and supermarkets. The thirteenth-century mystic Mevlânâ makes frequent mention of these sweets:[26]

> Be silent, walnut and almond helva have been placed before us;
> The almond helva will pray, and the other will say amen.

In the early nineteenth century *akide* sweets came in three shapes, none of them like the cut pieces familiar today. Instead they were either balls or circles, sometimes with a dip in the centre.[27] A rose-flavoured variety stamped in the centre with the word '*Maşallah*' ('May God protect') was known as *mühürlü akide* ('stamped *akide*').[28]

In the late Ottoman period, *akide* were flavoured with a wide variety of fruits, flowers and spices,[29] including cinnamon, clove, rose, violet, mint, lemon, orange, strawberry, hazelnut and almond.[30] Sometimes they were dyed red, either with cochineal or alkanet.[31] Bright attractive colours have always been an important aspect of the art of confectionary. In many cases the natural colour of the flavourings, such as fruit juices, citrus peel, and the petals of flowers such as sweet-scent pelargonium or roses would have been sufficient.[32] Chemical dyes became available in Istanbul in the first part of the twentieth century, and Hadiye Fahriye, author of a book on confectionery published in 1926, warns her readers against using harmful dyes in *akide*.[33]

The familiar shape of *akide* today, produced by cutting pieces off a rope of hot sugar with scissors, giving the rope a half turn at each cut, began in the mid-nineteenth century, and according to Reşat Ekrem Koçu was a shape invented by Hacı Bekir.[34] This was a period of innovations in flavour as well, with flavours such as tea, coffee, chocolate and cream appearing, some influenced by European bonbons.

One surprising use of *akide* was to decorate stuffed mackerel and other fish dishes. *Akide* sweets in a variety of colours were crushed and then sprinkled on the fish, the glinting colours giving the illusion that it was still alive. This was not only beautiful to look at but also delicious.[35]

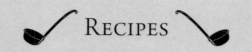

RECIPES

ŞEKERLI MÜŞKIFE HELVASI   (Şirvânî, c. 1430)[36]
SUGAR HELVA WITH POUNDED NUTS

Place three hundred *dirhem*s of sugar in a pan, and boil it over a medium heat to the consistency of *akide*. Take four hundred *dirhem*s of previously scalded, dried, pounded and sieved almonds and mix them into the sugar syrup. Pour this into a tray and spread it out using the fists. Then cut it in thin pieces with a knife and store it like *pişmâniye helvası*[37] to eat when desired.

GUWARLACK AKIDE   (Friedrich Unger, 1838)[38]
AKIDE BALLS

Boil a quantity of sugar to cracking point, colour red with cochineal just before removing it from the heat, or leave it white, and pour the caramel [Unger's term] on the marble slab. Cut it in pieces and roll into balls and you have the *guwarlack akide*.

BAHARLI AKIDE   (Hadiye Fahriye, 1926)[39]
SPICED AKIDE

Akide sweets are often flavoured with cinnamon and cloves. These are prepared and cut like other *akide* sweets, except that they are cut in pieces somewhat larger than plain *akide*, and instead of rolling into balls are customarily left as they are. Just before the *akide* is removed from the heat, for every one *kıyye* [1,283 g] of sugar stir in one *dirhem* of cinnamon or clove oil. Then pour the sugar onto a marble slab. If the flavouring is insufficient, then you should oil the marble slab with cinnamon or clove oil instead of almond oil, and before cutting into pieces rub a very little oil onto the surface. That will be sufficient.

BADEM HELVASI (Mihran Arabacıyan, 1876)[40]
ALMOND HELVA

Scald 120 *dirhem*s of sweet almonds, remove their peel, wash in cold water, dry with a cloth, and cut each almond widthwise into six pieces. Dry them in a clean frying pan or oven. Place 70 *dirhem*s of granulated sugar into a frying pan over red hot embers, toss in the hot almonds and stir. Spread part of the mixture on the base of a helva mould . . . and spread layer by layer until the mould is full. But you must do this quickly or it will set and be impossible to spread.

8 Ağız Miski   *Musk Lozenges*

> She gave me a kiss to serve as a musk lozenge.
> Nedîm (d. 1730)[1]

MUSK LOZENGES WERE EATEN TO sweeten the breath, hence their association with kisses and lips in Ottoman court poetry. The early seventeenth-century poet Ganîzâde Nâdirî (d. 1627) was one of many who mentions them:

> When at dawn a drop of dew fell upon the rosebud
> I thought it was a musk lozenge in the rosebud lips of my beloved.

In 1640 12.4 grams of these perfumed lozenges cost one *akçe*.[2] They were gifts fit for princes. At the circumcision festivities for the sons of Ahmed III in 1720 six plates of musk lozenges were among the gifts presented by the guild of paper makers.[3]

What were these so desirable musk lozenges that inspired Ottoman court poets?

The following recipe from an early nineteenth-century Turkish recipe manuscript shows that they were simple enough to make at home – so long as you could afford the musk:[4]

Recipe for the Sweets Known as *Ağız Miski*
Take a hundred *dirhem*s of sugar, fifteen *dirhem*s of starch, five *dirhem*s of gum tragacanth, and two grains of musk. Mix all these with rose water into a paste, then cut it into pieces as desired, dry them and then eat them.

Gum tragacanth is a substance obtained from milk vetch stalks. Although 380 species of milk vetch (*Astragalus*) grow in Turkey, only five are a commercial source of gum tragacanth,[5] which is a traditional Turkish export. In 1865 Weatherley advised confectioners to 'avoid buying cheap East India or common gums, they will not make good lozenges, Turkey gums have greater strength and tenacity, and the paste is easier to work and much smoother.'[6]

Musk lozenges are an example of the numerous sweets that began life as medications. Gum tragacanth mixed with rose water and pulled sugar was an old cough cure,[7] and this gum is still used in the pharmaceutical industry today. Lozenges lived a similar dual life as confection and cough cure in Europe, and musk lozenges are one of the oldest gum and sugar paste sweets in both East and West, probably due to a common origin in Islamic medicine. In Britain confectioners continued to produce musk lozenges into the 1920s, albeit replacing true musk with artificial musk essence.[8]

The association of musk lozenges with kissing was shared by the British, who sometimes called them 'kissing comfits'. In Shakespeare's *The Merry Wives of Windsor*, Falstaff declares:[9] 'Let the sky rain potatoes; let it thunder to the tune of "Green Sleeves", hail kissing-comfits and snow eringoes.'

Robert May's seventeenth-century recipe for musk lozenges gives this name alongside the less romantic 'muskedines' and 'rising comfits':[10]

To Make Muskedines Called Rising Comfits or Kissing Comfits
Take half a pound of refined sugar, being beaten and searsed, put into it two grains of musk, a grain of civet, two grains of ambergriese, and a thimble full of white orris powder, beat all these with gum-dragon steeped in rose-water; then roul it as thin as you can, and cut it into little lozenges with your iging-iron, and stow them in some warm oven or stove, then box them and keep them all the year.

Sugar paste to which gum tragacanth has been added is both edible and malleable. It can be shaped like potter's clay and hardens when dry. This was the perfect material for sculpted decorations and fancy sweets, and confectioners made good use of it. In 1836 Julia Pardoe observed 'gums, mixed with sugar, perfumes, and the juices of fruits, moulded into a hundred pretty shapes' in Istanbul's confectionery shops.[11]

A recipe for another type of moulded spiced lozenge made with gum tragacanth is given in a Turkish manuscript dated 1828:[12]

Moulded Sweets

Take sufficient gum tragacanth and soak it in water overnight. The next day take one or two *kıyye*s of sieved sugar and adding the gum slowly knead it to a paste. Mix some blanched and ground almonds, and some ground cinnamon and cloves to make a filling. Spread a thin sheet of the sugar paste into the mould, then sprinkle the filling over, cover with another sheet of the paste and press with the mould.

A similar Ottoman Turkish recipe for *kitreli şekerleme* (tragacanth sweets) is given by Friedrich Unger, in his book about oriental confectionery published in 1838:[13]

Khydrely Schkerleme

Roll out tragacanth to the thickness of a knife's back, spread a finger thick layer of almond paste (*badam kuftessi*) over, and spread tragacanth on top of it, and cut, or prick out, or roll with a pastry wheel into any shapes, dry and candy them.

9 *Misk*

Musk

Every part of the world was filled with the scent of musk and ambergris.
Yusuf Has Hacib (1070)[1]

USK MIGHT NO LONGER BE an ingredient of Turkish confectionery, but its memory lives on in the Turkish phrase *misk gibi* ('like musk') to describe any fruits or dishes with a delicious fragrance. Nearly a thousand years ago the same simile was being used by the Turks of Central Asia, as evidenced by the phrase *yıpar burdı* ('it smelt like musk') cited by Mahmud of Kashgar in his Turkish–Arabic dictionary.[2]

Whether musk had any culinary uses in Central Asia at that time, or was used only as a perfume, is unknown. Verses 25 and 26 of Surah 83 of the Quran mention a pure wine 'sealed with musk', suggesting that in Arabia musk may have been added to drinks in the early Islamic period.

In Ottoman Turkey musk was used above all in sherbet drinks. At the circumcision celebrations held in 1582 for Şehzade Mehmed, the son of Murad III, enormous amounts of musk were used to flavour the sherbet, and Mustafa Ali of Gallipoli specifies the exact quantities in his verse account of this event:[3]

> And sixty three pods of Tatar musk
> Were lost in the celebration sherbet.

Mustafa Ali's reference to 'Tatar musk' in this couplet refers to the fact that musk came from lands ruled by the Mongols and Central Asian Turks, for whom 'Tatar' was a blanket term.[4] Musk is a secretion of the musk deer, various species of which inhabit the Himalaya and forested mountainous regions of Siberia, Mongolia and China. During the mating season the male musk deer excretes this strong-smelling substance, which is produced by a gland enclosed by hairy skin, the musk 'pod' or 'cod' as it was known in English.[5] The musk pod was known in Ottoman Turkish as *misk göbeği* and in Central Asian Turkic as *kün yıparlığ*.

Musk was one of the most valuable commodities in all Asia, and must have been a mainstay of the economies in regions inhabited by musk deer, such as Tibet, where Marco Polo watched the animals being hunted in the thirteenth century:[6]

> I should tell you also that in this country there are many of the animals that produce musk, which are called in the Tartar language *Gudderi*. Those rascals have great numbers of large and fine dogs, which are of great service in catching the musk-beasts, and so they procure great abundance of musk.

Marco Polo again encountered musk deer hunters in northern China, in the region of Tangut, and this time gives a detailed description of the deer and its pod:[7]

> In this country too is found the best musk in the world; and I will tell you how 'tis produced. There exists in that region a kind of wild animal like a gazelle. It has feet and tail like the gazelle's, and stag's hair of a very coarse

10. Musk deer (James Wylde (ed.), *The Illustrated Natural History*, London, 1881, p. 232)

kind, but no horns. It has four tusks, two below, and two above, about three inches long, and slender in form, one pair growing upwards, and the other downwards. It is a very pretty creature. The musk is found in this way. When the creature has been taken, they find at the navel between the flesh and the skin something like an impostume full of blood, which they cut out and remove with all the skin attached to it. And the blood inside this impostume is the musk that produces that powerful perfume.

Musk deer have been hunted almost to extinction for their precious glands. Although they are now protected under international treaties, this has failed to stamp out illegal hunting. Since musk is worth four times its weight in gold,[8] it is no longer affordable for culinary use, but remains sought after in traditional Chinese medicine and by the perfume industry. China has endeavoured to meet demand by setting up musk deer farms, where the glands are removed without killing the animals.[9]

During the Ottoman period musk from both Nepal and Tibet was imported, but the latter was the most highly esteemed according to Seyyid Mehmed İzzet, writing in 1878.[10] In 1615 when the British ambassador Thomas Roe passed through Nepal on his way to the court of Jihangir, he was entertained by Mir Jamalüddin Husain, viceroy of Patan and former Moghul ambassador, who presented him with gifts that included 'five cases of sugar candy, dressed with musk'.[11]

Musk was a luxury ingredient affordable only by the wealthy, yet, not-withstanding the high price, consumption in Ottoman Turkey rose to such a degree that in 1610 there was insufficient musk to meet the sultan's needs, and merchants were prohibited from selling musk on the open market until the *miskçibaşı* ('chief musk procurer', an official responsible for supplying the palace with spices) had replenished palace stocks.[12]

The smell of musk endured in the empty pod, and this served cooks in good stead in emergencies. A recipe for Turkish delight in an early nineteenth-century cookery manuscript explains that instead of musk grains the empty musk pod can be used to scent the sugar.[13] The story that musk was mixed into the mortar of the Byzantine church of Haghia Sophia and the claim that its scent still lingers today might be apocryphal, but musk's clinging pungence is no myth.[14] Musk poachers in Nepal conceal the musk pods in bottles of ghee to prevent the smell from being detected.[15] As the Turkish saying goes, 'Musk gives its hiding place away.'

Musk's high value is emphasized by another traditional Turkish saying: 'To buy boiled sweets for the price of their musk'. Musk was so precious that at the Ottoman palace it was stored under the watchful eye of the chief cellarer, along with the sultan's gold, silver and bejewelled tableware.[16] The high price paid for musk is recorded in the palace kitchen accounts for September 1469, showing that a sheep was worth less than 2 grams of musk.

Musk was an ingredient of many sweets and puddings, including *aşure*, *pelte*, *güllaç*, helva, *akide*, *lokum* and *lohuk*. Baron de Tott, a Frenchman who lived in Turkey during the second half of the eighteenth century, complained about the excessive use of musk in sherbet:[17] 'This Sherbet, so much talked of in Europe, and so little known, is made of conserved fruits dissolved in water, but with so much musk as almost to destroy the taste of the liquor.'

Musk was appreciated as much as a mark of wealth and power as for its fragrance. An eleventh-century Turkish proverb recorded by Mahmud of Kashgar illustrates how musk was identified with riches: 'Even after the pod is empty of musk, the scent remains' was used of a man who had lost his fortune but still managed to avoid living in poverty.[18]

10 *Badem Şekeri*

Sugared Almonds

European sugar almonds
From time to time are tasted
Everyone enjoys them, sir
Who would refuse a comfit?

Comfits with allspice
Then there is orange peel
Coffee beans are delightful
Coriander comfits innumerable.

Watchman's rhyme[1]

NUTS AND SEEDS COATED IN sugar have been popular in the Middle East and Europe since at least the thirteenth century. Pistachio nuts, roasted chickpeas, coriander seeds, coffee beans and orange peel are just some of the many varieties, but above all it is almonds that exemplify this class of sweets. In the thirteenth century Mevlânâ refers several times to sugared almonds:[2]

He who shows respect receives respect
He who brings sugar eats sugared almonds.

In the seventeenth century sugared almonds were not only made by local confectioners but also by foreign confectioners who kept shop in the district of Galata.[3] Whether the 'European sugared almonds' mentioned in the watchman's rhyme were made by them or were imported is uncertain. In the late eighteenth century the European variety was slightly cheaper than the 'palace-style' sugared almonds made by local confectioners, but the latter were preferred for serving to guests at social gatherings because they were glossier.[4]

The Bavarian confectioner Friedrich Unger, on the other hand, expresses a poor opinion of Turkish-made comfits, so perhaps their quality had declined by the time Unger tasted them in the 1830s:[5]

> *Dragée*
> Under this name you find cinnamon, cloves, almonds, pistachios and sesame seeds coated with different colours in large quantities, but prepared such that one has never seen a worse *dragée;* yet the Orientals have no small opinion of their panwork;[6] and only with the greatest flattery on my part could I discover the secrets.

Comfits were one of the most popular 'nibbles' (*nukl* or *nokul*) served on social occasions. At the splendid circumcision festivities held for Mehmed II's sons Bâyezid and Mustafa in 1457, guests were served with sherbet followed by almond, pistachio, coriander, pine nut, cinnamon and clove comfits.[7] Seventeeth-century sources record cinnamon, clove, aniseed, coriander, almond, pine nut, pistachio nut, hazelnut, chickpea, ginger, fennel seed, bitter orange peel and coffee bean comfits,[8] while in the eighteenth century the most common types were made with hulled chickpeas, pistachios and almonds.[9]

Coating the comfits in sugar of different colours is first recorded in the fifteenth century, when the sugar syrup was dyed yellow with saffron,[10] and later writers refer to comfits in a variety of colours.[11]

Eating comfits with sherbet or wine was a custom that lasted for centuries and was widespread across both the Islamic world and Europe, reflecting the high degree of interaction between the Islamic and Christian worlds in the late medieval and early modern periods. Comfits were among the sweetmeats served on silver dishes at Timur's court,[12] and when Baron de Tott visited the Greek prince of Moldavia on his way to take up his new post as the French ambassador to the Crimean Khanate in 1767 he was served with sherbet, fruit conserves and comfits.[13] In 1519, when King Henry VIII received ambassadors from the French king Francis I, comfits were served with the wine on silver and gilt dishes.[14]

Sugared almonds of various colours were used as pebbles in the sugar models of gardens carried in the procession celebrating the circumcision of the sons of Ahmed III in 1720.[15] This was a convenient resemblance but also appropriate symbolism, since comfits were not just luxury foods but associated with good fortune and abundance; hence their role in various celebratory events. At the wedding of Mehmed IV's daughter in 1675 the gifts included thirty mule-loads of comfits and other sweetmeats.[16]

Ali Rıza Bey records that in the late Ottoman period it was customary at the ceremony held six days after the birth of a child to fill the potty kept beneath the cradle with sugared almonds and give these to the midwife.[17] In her memoirs the nineteenth-century Ottoman composer Leylâ Saz explains that coffee bean comfits were among the gifts given by bridegrooms of limited means to his bride and mother-in-law.[18]

At Greek weddings sugared almonds were showered over the bride and groom on their return home from the church,[19] and offered on trays to the wedding guests.[20] In Italy, too, *confetti* (comfits) were strewn over the bride, and throwing them was part of the fun of carnival celebrations.[21] The same custom was widespread at Turkish weddings, where 'coins, sugar-plums, millet, rice, and the like [were] strewn over a bride or cast to the public to be scrabbled for,'[22] and the tradition continues in many parts of Turkey.[23] This custom can be traced back to medieval Central Asia, where grains and coins were scattered over brides of the Karakhanid period (840–1212).[24]

Comfits were an alternative to the cereal grains that featured in many ancient rituals relating to fertility and abundance. In both eastern and western cultures tossing grain over the bride expressed the wish that she be blessed with children and prosperity. Baron de Tott records that the Crimean Tatars threw millet over the bride, and that this represented her portion:[25]

A Dish, of about a foot in Diameter, was placed on the Head of the Bride; over this a veil was thrown, which covered the Face and descended to the Shoulders; Millet then was poured upon the Dish, which, falling and spreading all round her, formed a Cone, with a Base corresponding to the height of the Bride. Nor was her Portion complete till the Millet touched the Dish, while the Veil gave her the power of respiration. This Custom was not favourable to small People, and, at present, they estimate how many measure of Millet a Daughter is worth. The Turks and Armenians, who make their Calculations in money, still preserve the Dish and the Veil, and throw Coin upon the Bride, which they call spilling the Millet. Have not the Crown and the Comfits the same Origin?

Comfits are among the hardest sweets to make, requiring professional skill and equipment to ensure successful results.[26] Before the advent of modern machinery, a little melted sugar was poured into a pan suspended on a chain, then the roasted seeds or nuts were tossed in and rolled in the syrup by swinging

11. French confectioners making sugared almonds in pans attached to the ceiling by chains. The same method was used in Turkey (*L'Encyclopédie de Diderot et d'Alembert*, 1763–72).

the pan. Then more syrup was added and the process repeated until sufficient layers of sugar had built up.

The first and only Turkish recipe for sugared almonds was written by Şirvânî in the fifteenth century:[27]

Sugared Almonds

Beat two egg whites in a pan and then add a *vukıyye* of sugar and [place over heat and] skim until it is the correct consistency. Then blanch a *vukıyye* of almonds and roast them in bran until all the moisture has evaporated and the bran colours. Then place a little of the sugar syrup into a pan with the almonds and hang up the pan [by a chain], hold it by the hand and swing it, then lift it down. Add more syrup, hang up the pan again and stir it rapidly until it coats the almonds. Go on adding the sugar as many times as you wish, whether more or less. If saffron is added to the sugar syrup it will colour it yellow. And if a little starch is added to the almonds they will be white and also it will make the sugar go further.

This time-honoured method was used in both the orient and the occident for centuries.[28] It was described by Théophile Gautier, who visited a confectioner's shop in Istanbul in 1852:[29] 'At the back of the shop young boys, with print aprons around their waists, were moving upon the bright fire the copper basins in which the almonds and pistachios were being rolled in sugar.'

Sugared almonds are not about to go out of fashion, despite the assault of the new-fangled chocolate-filled variety. As Cem Sultan, the son of Mehmed the Conqueror, wrote in the fifteenth century:[30]

Who can claim supremacy over sugared almonds?

11 Şerbetlik Şeker
Sherbet Sugar

As I burned with raging thirst
They handed me a glassful of sherbet.

Süleyman Çelebi (d. 1522)[1]

LARGE RED SQUARES OF GRAINED sugar flavoured with cloves are the last survivors of a large family of instant sherbet tablets once made by Turkish confectioners. This is used to make *lohusa şerbeti*, hot spiced sherbet traditionally made after the birth of a child to give the new mother energy and improve her supply of milk. Before the arrival of fizzy drinks, sherbet was the main beverage in a largely teetotal society. It was made in a myriad of flavours, using fruit juices, flowers, spices, seeds and nuts. Since fruits and flowers were in season for only a limited time and preparing fresh sherbet was time consuming, confectioners prepared convenient instant mixes that kept indefinitely and only needed diluting to prepare the sherbet of your choice. These took three forms: syrups (*şurup*), pastes (*çevirme*) and tablets (*sert şerbet, şerbetlik şeker* or *şerbet şekeri*).

Syrups remain fairly common today. Black mulberry and other syrups are still made at home in some rural areas, although the last surviving commercial brand has been squeezed off most supermarket shelves by fizzy drinks. Pastes (*çevirme*) are today a rarity produced by a handful of old-fashioned confectioners in a very limited range of flavours – mainly bergamot and mastic – and by the late Ottoman period were being eaten as a sweetmeat rather than diluted to make sherbet.[2]

Unlike syrups and *çevirme*, which were frequently made at home, sherbet tablets were the exclusive province of the professional confectioner. Boiled sugar syrup was flavoured with fruit juices, essential oils such as rose or cinnamon, or decoctions of spices, herbs and ground nuts, then stirred and worked against the side of the pan until the sugar grained. The mixture was poured onto a marble slab in a thick layer and when set was cut in diamond shapes, or for Ramazan in rounds with decoratively cut edges.[3]

Another version of sherbet sugar was *külşâhî şerbet*, prepared by pouring the same mixture into an earthenware mould in the shape of a truncated cone.[4] A hole in the base of the mould served for pressing the sherbet sugar out when it had set, and was covered by a piece of paper. Lumps were broken off this sherbet loaf and diluted or eaten as a sweetmeat.

In the 1830s the German royal confectioner Friedrich Unger recorded the following varieties of sherbet sugar made by Istanbul's confectioners: orange, cinnamon, rose, lemon, vanilla, salep (orchid root), pistachio, bitter almond, violet, jasmine, opium, barberry, strawberry, sour cherry, pomegranate, sour grape, apricot, peach, plum, date, pineapple and chocolate.[5] Sometimes additional flavourings were used, such as ambergris, which was added to pistachio sherbet for example, or colourings such as cochineal or spinach water. The favourite sherbet flavours in Ramazan were rose, orange and lemon. Salep sherbet was only sold in winter.[6]

The variety called *Nevruzî şerbet* or 'New Year sherbet' was made for the ancient Persian festival of Nevruz (literally 'new day'), corresponding to 22 March, which was the first day of the new year in the ancient pre-Islamic calendar. This was made with sugar, musk, ambergris and gold leaf, cut into small squares and decorated with further gold leaf laid on top.[7]

Sherbet sugar started out in life as a medical preparation and gradually transferred allegiance to confectionery. Its ancestor was a digestive mixture called *cevâriş* or *cüvâriş*, whose sugar content and method of preparation were much the same, except that when made as a medicine *cevâriş* was usually crushed to powder.[8] Made with pleasant-tasting ingredients and shaped in tablets, it made a delicious sweetmeat. A recipe for *cevâriş-i misk* in a work by the Turkish physician Celâlüddin Hızır (d. 1417) differs only from sherbet sugar in the number of active ingredients: mastic, musk, cloves, cinnamon, sandalwood and rose water. These were cooked with sugar syrup, then poured into a tray oiled with almond oil, and when set cut into pieces and stored in a box.[9] In fact these palatable ingredients lead us to suspect that Celâlüddin's patients ate this *cevâriş* as much for enjoyment as its health benefits. Similar medical preparations introduced from Islamic into European medicine were known as 'conserve', the earliest mention in the *Oxford English Dictionary* dating from 1502.[10] In Europe too these doubled as sweetmeats.

We know that *cevâriş* was consumed as a sweetmeat from at least the early sixteenth century, because it featured at a banquet held to celebrate the circumcision of Süleyman the Magnificent's sons Bâyezid and Cihângîr in 1539. Among the fifty-three types of sweetmeats served on this occasion were six varieties of *cevâriş*: pistachio, cherry, almond, lemon, coconut and gold leaf.[11]

Red sherbet tablets numbered among the gifts of sweetmeats and syrups sent by the groom to the home of his bride on their wedding morning.[12] As we have already seen, the clove-flavoured variety associated with childbirth was also red, a colour symbolizing good fortune and happiness.[13] In the late Ottoman period this sherbet was not only served to the new mother and her guests, but also sent as gifts to notify friends and relatives of the happy event:[14]

> Diamond-shaped sherbet tablets were purchased from confectioners' shops, boiled up and placed in jugs. The jugs were wrapped in red gauze. If the child was a boy the lid of the jug was left unwrapped, and if a girl, it was wrapped. The jugs were then sent to relatives, clerics and friends as a way of announcing the event. Tips were given to the servants who delivered the jugs ... [Visitors] brought gifts of gold for the baby, and sweet pastries such as *kurabiye*. Visitors were served first with coffee then hot *lohusa şerbeti*. It was customary after drinking the sherbet to offer up a prayer that God might make the mother's milk plentiful.

Sherbet sugar also featured at other social and religious celebrations. An inscription carved on the wall of the Helvahane Mosque at Topkapı Palace is the text of an endowment made by Mihrivefâ Hâtun, a housekeeper in the royal harem, in 1817. She left a legacy of 2,000 piastres for serving sherbet, rose jam, coffee and mixed sweets in paper cones at *mevlit* ceremonies to be held annually in memory of her friend Durnab Hatun and for her own redemption.[15] At these ceremonies a poem about the birth of the Prophet by the fifteenth-century Turkish poet Süleyman Çelebi was recited.[16]

One of the earliest accounts of Turkish sherbet is by the French botanist Pierre Belon, who journeyed to Turkey, Egypt, the Holy Land and Persia between 1546 and 1551:[17]

> Some are made of figs, others of plums, and of pears and peaches, others again of apricots and of grapes, yet others of honey . . . the sherbet-maker mixes snow or ice with them, to cool them: for otherwise there would be no pleasure in drinking them.

The fashion for Turkish sherbet in Europe began in Venice around this time, and from there spread to the rest of Italy. In 1577 Francesco I de' Medici, Grand Duke of Tuscany (r. 1574–87), wrote to Mafeo Veniero in Venice, asking him to send him the recipe for Turkish sherbets and other Turkish beverages.[18]

In the seventeenth century we begin to find references to sherbet sugar in English sources. Francis Bacon was one of the first to write about this novelty in 1627:[19]

> They have in Turkey and the East certain confections, which they call servets, which are like to candied conserves, and are made of sugar and lemons, or sugar and citrons, or sugar and violets, and some other flowers; and some mixture of amber [ambergris] for the more delicate persons: and those they dissolve in water, and thereof make their drink, because they are forbidden wine by their law.

An early first-hand account of sherbet sugar is by Henry Blount, an Englishman who visited Turkey in 1634:[20]

> They esteeme *Sherbets* made with Sugar, the juyce of Lemmons, Peaches, Apricockes, Violets, or other Flowers, Fruits, and Plumbes as each countrey affoords; these are dryed together, into a consistence reasonable hard, and portable for their use in Warre, or else-where, mingling about a spoonefull with a quart of water.

When sherbet drinking became fashionable in England in the mid-seventeenth century, sherbet sugar began to be imported. In December 1662 a coffeehouse called Murat the Great in Exchange Alley in London advertised its 'sherbets made in Turkie of lemons, roses, and violets perfumed' in the weekly *Kingdom's Intelligencer* newspaper.[21] In 1682–3 boxes of sherbet were among goods imported through the City of London;[22] France was importing sherbet paste by 1723.[23] In 1797 *Encyclopaedia Britannica* described sherbet and the 'perfumed cakes' used to make it:[24]

> Sherbet, or Sherbit, a compound drink, first brought into England from Turkey and Persia, consisting of water, lemon-juice, and sugar, in which are dissolved perfumed cakes made of excellent Damascus fruit, containing an infusion of some drops of rose water. another kind of it is made of violets, honey, juice of raisins, etc.

The English confectioner Jarrin of Bond Street devoted a whole section of his book, *The Italian Confectioner*, to 'conserve tablets', which are identical to Turkish sherbet sugar, except that they are made with the pulp of fruits and flowers rather than the strained juice.[25] His pistachio tablets are even coloured with spinach water in the same way as those made by Turkish confectioners. However, these tablets were not dissolved in water to make sherbet, but had acquired a uniquely European function – as 'an ornament to asiettes montées for the dessert'.[26]

By the middle of the nineteenth century a cheap substitute for sherbet sugar made from loaf sugar, carbonate of soda, cream of tartar and essence of lemon was being used in England to prepare a sherbet drink sold in the streets of London.[27] This was the forerunner of the carbonated drinks that still dominate the global soft drinks market. A recipe for this imitation sherbet, described as 'Persian Sherbet', is given by the English confectioner Henry Weatherley:[28]

Persian Sherbet

Mix fourteen pounds of fine powder sugar with five and a half pounds tartaric acid, and five pounds of carbonated soda; before the soda is added, work into it one ounce of essence of lemon; a little orange essence adds to the fragrance and flavor; there is a cheaper article made but the above is not to be surpassed.

These fizzy sherbet powders are still popular ingredients of traditional English sweets like sherbet dabs and sherbet fountains. A strange metamorphosis indeed.

RECIPE

Sert Scherbet with Orange Water   (Friedrich Unger, 1838)[29]

Boil any amount of sugar to a feather (the finer the sugar the more beautifully white the scherbet becomes); now work the feathered sugar with a wooden spatula until it forms a flour on the walls of the pan, always mixing it in with the [rest of the] sugar, and thus the sugar becomes thick.

Meanwhile add some orange water, just so much that the scherbet only becomes firm, but remains smooth and keeps a pleasant taste.

If too much orange water were added the scherbet would stay soft and rather resemble *lohuk*[30] than *sert scherbet* without being one or the other.

When the sugar has been worked for a while and has started to thicken, then pour it in the thickness of three knife-backs on a marble slab, let it stand for a few moments and then cut into diamond shapes with a knife. Let it get quite cold, break it, and the *sert scherbet* is ready.

12 Macun

Soft Toffee

The physician of spring offered felicitations for Nevruz
With red roses instead of crimson *ma'cun*.

Seyyid Vehbî (d. 1736)[1]

MACUN IS A GOOEY TOFFEE in garish colours traditionally sold by street sellers in many parts of Turkey. Today they can still occasionally be seen plying their wares to children in busy parks, squares and waterfront promenades. The colourful *macun* is sold in circular tin trays divided into triangular compartments. Once the customer has made their choice from the flavours on offer, the *macuncu* scoops up some of each in turn, using a screwdriver-like implement called a *macuncu mablağı* or *macunkeş* and coils it around a small stick, the contrasting colours creating a striped effect.

In the past the flavours commonly consisted of mastic, bergamot, cinnamon, rose, mint, plum and lemon.[2] The trays were made either of copper or wood,[3] and when the vendor stopped on a street corner, he set the tray on a tripod that he carried around with him. Vendors in provincial towns and villages often dispensed with trays, instead carrying the *macun* in a curved container divided into several compartments that they strapped around their waist with a leather belt.[4] They would sell to the crowds in wedding processions, at the spring festival of Hıdrellez, on public holidays and on market days.[5]

In Istanbul some *macun* sellers competed for custom by playing music. These were usually former members of military bands who played marches, folk songs or polkas on the clarinet or bugle.[6] Others entertained their younger customers with trays like roulette wheels, with a spinning pointer mounted in the centre. The child spun the pointer and was served the flavour of the draw. This is described by Mary Adelaide Walker, an English portrait painter who lived and worked in Istanbul for thirty years in the second half of the nineteenth century:[7]

Another collection of sweet temptations much carried about is of the 'stick-jaw' description. The black, brown, red, white, and yellow substances are disposed on a flat metal dish, divided into compartments radiating from the centre, where there is a stick which the appreciative twirl round, and the dealer, with an iron skewer that serves for all, scoops out a halfpenny or a farthing lick from the sweet at which the point may stop.

Macun originated as a class of pharmaceutical preparation in classical antiquity. *Mesir macunu*, a type traditionally made in the western Turkish city of Manisa from dozens of different spices, takes its name from Mithridates, the Pontic ruler who died in 63 BC. Mithridates lived in fear of being poisoned by his sons, and was obsessed with finding an antidote. By experimenting with animals that were fed an antidote and then bitten by poisonous snakes and insects, he eventually developed an antidote called mithridaticum, and took regular low doses to develop his immunity to poison. Consequently, when he was defeated by Pompey after a long resistance against Roman conquest, Mithridates was obliged to commit suicide by his sword, since poison had no effect. Pompey is said to have carried off the documents and books in Mithridates' library to Rome, where Italian physicians began to make mithridaticum. When Hâfize Sultan, the mother of Sultan Süleyman the Magnificent, founded a hospital in Manisa, she reputedly had the formula for mithridaticum brought from Venice to use in her hospital, but as a cure-all rather than an antidote.[8]

Islamic physicians made hundreds of kinds of *macun*, most of them designed to strengthen the body and soothe the spirit. The active ingredients were mixed with three times the amount of honey, which made the medicine more palatable and acted as a preservative.[9] The sweet flavour meant that some *macun*s doubled as sweetmeats.

The most famous *macun* with such a dual function in the Ottoman

12. Turkish *macun* seller in an early twentieth-century photograph (Photograph: Max Fruchtermann).

period was *Nevruz macunu* or *nevruziyye*. Nevruz was the ancient new year, celebrated by Turks and Persians on 22 March.[10] The eleventh-century Islamic scholar Birûnî investigated the history of Nevruz and relates various beliefs and legends concerning its origin and history: God was said to have created the sun and the vegetable world on Nevruz; the Prophet Muhammed was said to have been presented with helva on a silver tray on Nevruz and distributed it to his followers, declaring that this was 'the day that God gave life to this sleeping world'; and the mythological ruler of ancient Persia Jamshid was said to have discovered the sugar cane on Nevruz and commanded the first sugar to be made.[11] Birûnî explains that he found these stories in the works of old authors, so evidently the connection between Nevruz and sweetness went back a long way.

13. Cartoon depicting a *macun* tray with a spinning pointer like a roulette wheel. One of the children has spun the pointer to select the flavour. The shadow puppet theatre character Karagöz, who is in the role of *macun* seller, holds a number of sticks in his hand, onto which the gooey *macun* will be coiled (*Karagöz*, 784 (31 July 1915), p. 4).

According to Armin Vámbéry, nineteenth-century turcologist and British spy, Nevruz was celebrated 'from the eastern borders of the Ottoman Empire to China' and was more important in those countries than religious holidays.[12] This was not so in Ottoman Turkey, but nevertheless Nevruz did not pass unnoticed. Manisa's *mesir macunu* was distributed to the populace at Nevruz, a custom that is alive and well today. Thousands of people gather in Manisa while the governor, mayor and local members of parliament toss 3 tons of *mesir macunu* wrapped in small coloured celophane packages from Sultan Mosque onto the crowds below.

The sixteenth-century writer Mustafa Ali of Gallipoli refers to *nevruziyye* as *mesrititus* (a corruption of mithridaticum), and warns that women servants should only be allowed to eat this *macun* on the day of Nevruz,[13] presumably because it was regarded as an aphrodisiac. It was also widely believed to protect those who ate it from being bitten by poisonous creatures such as snakes and scorpions.[14] This belief, dating back to Mithridates and his search for an antidote, is further confirmation that *nevruziyye* and *mesir macunu* are one and the same thing, both having their origin in the antidotes called *tiryak*, from the Greek *theriake*, origin of the English word 'treacle'.

According to ancient Persian tradition seven foods whose name began with the Persian letter *sin* were associated with *nevruziyye*. Sources disagree about whether these were ingredients or eaten with it. According to one source these were *sumak* (sumac), *sebze* (vegetable), *sünbül* (hyacinth), *semek* (fish), *sirke* (vinegar), *sîr* (garlic) and *senced* (oleaster).[15] The eighteenth-century Ottoman poet Seyyid Vehbî provides a slightly different list: *sumak* (sumac), *sirke* (vinegar), *salata* (salad), *süci* (wine), *semek* (fish), *sîb* (apple) and *sefercel* (quince).[16] Ayşe Osmanoğlu, the daughter of Sultan Abdülhamid II, recalls that at the palace *nevruziyye* was eaten after tasting seven foods whose names begin with the letter 's': *susam* (sesame), *süt* (milk), *simit* (bread ring), *su* (water), *salep* (orchid root), *safran* (saffron) and *sarımsak* (garlic).[17]

The night when *Nevruz macunu* was made at the palace was called Ot Gecesi (Herb Night). While the *macun* was cooking under the supervision of the royal physician, illusionists, magicians and musicians would entertain the confectioners until dawn.[18] The finished *macun* would then be packed into lidded crystal or porcelain jars and presented as gifts to the sultan, his mother, wives, sons and daughters, viziers and other grandees. The jars were wrapped in gauze, tied with ribbon and delivered with illuminated greeting cards attached.[19] Until the beginning of the First World War it was common for pharmacists and physicians to prepare *Nevruz macunu* in elegant jars as gifts for their patients at Nevruz.[20]

Ayşe Osmanoğlu records that the Persian embassy used to send *macun* and other Nevruz gifts to her father, Abdülhamid II:[21]

> At Nevruz the Persian Embassy would send macun and diverse Persian sweets in precious porcelain vessels and decorative boxes placed on trays wrapped in fabric as a gift for my father. The Nevruz sweets were decorated with small Persian gold coins bearing the portrait of the Shah of Persia arranged to spell my father's name. My father would give these to us or send them to anyone he wished to favour.

Although some sources assert that *nevruziyye* was made of forty-one different ingredients, this is contradicted by Ottoman-period recipes, which call for sometimes more and sometimes fewer ingredients. These include ambergris, musk, rose water, cloves, cochineal, almond oil, cinnamon, sandalwood, cardamom, nutmeg, coconut, ginger, coriander, angelica, sugar . . . the list goes on and on. The *macun* was always red in colour and always topped with gold leaf.[22] Evliyâ Çelebi describes it as 'spring helva with gold leaf', so we know that this tradition goes back at least to the seventeenth century.[23] Confectioners sold their *nevruziyye* in gilded paper cones or glass jars, and sometimes set up temporary stalls in mosque courtyards during Nevruz.[24] As well as *macun* they also made two sweetmeats called *nevruzî şerbet* containing musk, ambergris and gold leaf, one soft and one the hard crystallized type described in the previous chapter.

Other types of *macun* were eaten as desserts at meals. Seyyid Hasan (1620–88), a sheikh of the Sünbüliyye mystic order, records *macun* flavoured with mint and sweet flag (*Acorus calamus*) respectively served at meals he ate with his friends and fellow dervishes.[25]

13 Çevirme   *Fondant*

That which the Arabians call Lohocks, and the Greeks Eclegma, the Latins call Linctus, and in plain English signifies nothing else but a thing to be licked up.

Nicholas Culpeper, 1653[1]

I F YOU ADD THE JUICE or essential oil of any fruit, flower or spice to boiled sugar syrup and then stir it in just one direction for an hour, you will have made the viscous sweetmeat called *lohuk* or *çevirme*. The former term comes from the Arabic *lâ'ûk* and the latter is the Turkish name meaning 'turning' in reference to the stirring required. In the year 2000 these sweetmeats were on the brink of extinction and could only be found at the confectioner's Hacı Bekir, which has continued to make bergamot- and mastic-flavoured *çevirme* for a dwindling number of customers. Then suddenly various brands of mastic-flavoured *çevirme* began to reappear, some locally made and others imported from Greece.[2] The Greeks seem to have played a part in this miraculous recovery, because the Turkish producers were at a loss as to what to call this 'new' confection, and plumped either for 'mastic jam' or 'mastic *macun*', neither of which is correct. In Greece this confection had never fallen out of favour, and was known as *glyko koutaliou* ('spoon sweets'), because of the tradition of serving them to guests with a spoon, a custom that has virtually died out in Turkey.

In Ottoman times serving *çevirme* was part of the ceremony of receiving guests. This sweetmeat was offered before coffee, which is why recipes are found under the heading 'Confections Served Before Coffee' in some cookery books.[3] Bowls of *çevirme* were placed on a tray, together with spoons and glasses of water, and each guest in turn took a spoonful of *çevirme*, drank some water, and then placed the spoon into their glass.

Many travellers have left accounts of Ottoman hospitality rituals, but not many of them were high enough in rank to experience the full-blown version.

One such traveller was Lord Charlemont, a rich young Irish aristocrat, who after leasing a captured French warship sailed from Malta to Istanbul in June 1749. In Istanbul he was received by the minister of interior Nailî Efendi, who took a liking to this charming and courteous young man and treated him to the full panoply of preserves, coffee, sherbet, rose water, pipe and incense:[4]

I lost no time, but was immediately conducted by Pisani [Charlemont's interpreter] to the apartment of the Reis Efendi, one of the principal officers of state, who unites in his person the higher offices of Secretary of State, and Chancellor of the Empire. I found him sitting upon his sofa, and, having been presented, was received with the most cordial, easy, and unaffected politeness. Having first enquired into my name and rank he desired me to sit down by him. He told me that he was happy in the opportunity of seeing me, and much obliged to Pisani for procuring him that pleasure. He then asked me several questions concerning my travels, as: where I had been, whither I intended to proceed, how I had amused myself, whether I liked the abode of Constantinople, etc. He called for coffee, and his servants presented me with a silver vessel, filled with a sort of perfumed marmalade with a large gold or gilt spoon. Of this marmalade, by the direction of Pisani, I put into my mouth a spoonful, which served instead of sugar to the coffee, which was then brought in.

Having drunk it, I was going to rise, and to take my leave, but the Reis Efendi desired me to sit still, telling me that he would treat me according to my condition. The servants then served me with iced sherbet, a liquor much used by the Turks and commonly made with liquorice, orange juice, and water, of which when I had tasted, one of them flung out of a silver bottle with a long and very narrow neck rose water upon my hands and habit, with which, having finished to sprinkle me, another servant presented me with a silver urn having its cover pierced full of holes and shaped something like those incense pots which are used in Catholic churches. This, it seems, was full of burning perfumes, but as I did not well know what to make of it, I unluckily laid my hand on its cover, and burned my fingers, at which ridiculous accident the Reis Efendi laughed heartily, and with great good humour told me that he was pleased to see me begin to accommodate myself to their customs, to which he hoped I should not be long a stranger.

Pisani then showed me the method of perfuming myself, by holding the urn between my two hands and putting it into my bosom under my gown or pellice. This manner of presenting with sherbet and perfumes is considered by the Turks as the highest compliment they can pay to a guest of distinction whom they desire to honour.

Both this 'marmalade' and the 'conserves' described by travellers like Baron de Tott and Julia Pardoe were *çevirme*. Tott describes it as 'conserve of roses, flowers of orange, and lemon-pulp' and Pardoe as 'conserves, generally strongly impregnated with perfume, such as rose, bergamotte, and citron'.[5]

The origin of *çevirme* was a medical electuary called *lohuk*. Made with a high proportion of sugar or honey, it quickly found a new identity as a sweetmeat. Below is an example of an early fifteenth-century medicinal *lohuk* recipe:[6]

14. Set of spoons and forks and silver filigree basket for serving *çevirme* and fruit preserves to guests.

Lu'ük-ı Züfa

Beneficial for asthma and chronic coughing and rids the body of green phlegmatic humours in the lungs. Cook 20 *dirhem*s each of blue iris root and hyssop in three *rıtıl*s of water until reduced to one *rıtıl*, then add a *rıtıl* of sugar and cook to the correct consistency.

A few years later, another physician gives a recipe for a sweetmeat he calls *helvâ lâ-dakîk lehâ* ('helva without flour'), but which is actually the earliest recipe for *çevirme*, as the emphasis on constant stirring shows. Thanks to this recipe we can date the development of *lohuk* as a sweetmeat rather than a medicine to the first half of the fifteenth century:[7]

Helvâ lâ-dakîk lehâ

The art of making this is to dissolve 450 *dirhem*s of white sugar in 38 *dirhem*s of rose water in a tinned pan over a gentle heat, skim and then continue stirring and boiling until it begins to thicken. Add sufficient pounded and crushed sweet almonds, and stir until cooked. When done, pour into a bowl and sprinkle 75 *dirhem*s of white powdered sugar over. Eat when set.

Lohuk as a medicine was introduced from the Islamic world into Europe, but there its potential as a sweetmeat went unrecognized. In 1653 the English physician, pharmacist and astrologist Nicholas Culpeper devoted a whole chapter of his *Complete Herbal* to *lohock*, with recipes for coltsfoot, poppy, raisin, pine nut, purslain, fox lung, squill and colewort *lohock*, prefaced by the following general description:[8]

Of Lohocks

That which the Arabians call Lohocks, and the Greeks Eclegma, the Latins call Linctus, and in plain English signifies nothing else but a thing to be licked up. They are in body thicker than a syrup, and not so thick as an electuary.

The manner of taking them is, often to take a little with a liquorice stick, and let it go down at leisure.

They are easily thus made; Make a decoction of pectoral herbs, and the treatise will furnish you with enough, and when you have strained it, with twice its weight of honey or sugar, boil it to a lohock; if you are molested with much phlegm, honey is better than sugar; and if you add a little vinegar to it, you will do well.

Culpeper's *lohocks* are generally made with pulled sugar, sugar candy or granulated sugar, and the reader is instructed to stir it 'stoutly', 'swiftly' or 'diligently' with a wooden pestle, which is what causes graining and, as the stirring proceeds, lends the mixture a smooth soft texture. Almost identical instructions are given in Turkish recipes for *lohuk* or *çevirme* as a sweetmeat.[9]

Çevirme was poured into glasses or china bowls and sealed with paper,[10] ready to be offered to guests. Sets of special spoons were made for this purpose, some in the form of spatulas with slender cylindrical handles.[11]

The journalist Burhan Felek (1889–1982) describes how *lohuk* was presented to guests when he was a child:[12]

When visitors were received good families offered them a sweetmeat, which in Ottoman times we called *lohuk* but which confectioners called çevirme. This was a kind of white paste flavoured with mastic or bergamot. It was served on silver trays.

As many glasses as there were people in the room, including the hostess, would be filled with water, and the same number of spoons plus one extra placed in a special goblet. A bowl filled with *lohuk* would be placed in the centre of the tray and offered to the guests one by one, beginning with the oldest and most respected. Guests familiar with this custom would dip their spoon into the *lohuk*, pull out a spoonful, place it in their mouth and then lick vigorously. Then they would pick up a glass, drink sufficient water, and place the spoon into the glass. Soon afterwards coffee would be brought in.

Turkish novelist Selim İleri recalls his mother making cornelian cherry *çevirme* when he was a child in the 1950s:[13]

I loved cornelian cherry çevirme. It was made just like jam, except that the cornelian cherry juice was strained through muslin, then poured into the pan, and stirred constantly in one direction until really thick, using a wooden spoon. When it was thick enough, lemon juice was poured in. Then it was given one last stir. 'Are the *tatlı* bowls ready?' she would ask, and the çevirme was poured into the bowls. They had to be '*tatlı* bowls' . . . Now in that expression '*tatlı* bowls' I seem to hear the voice of a way of life. Traditions that have faded away are speaking.[14]

Stirring *çevirme* was exhausting on the arms and required skill, so it was often purchased ready-made from confectioners, who prepared it in huge semicircular tinned copper pans and stirred it with a correspondingly huge wooden paddle. As they stirred, sugar crystals formed, causing the syrup to thicken and turn white; then as the stirring continued, the crystals were broken down to a uniform size, resulting in a smooth, viscous texture. German confectioner Friedrich Unger, who visited Istanbul in 1835, describes this texture as 'soft and similar to a pomade', and explains that confectioners set their pans of *çevirme* over cold water or ice while stirring.[15]

None of the recipes specifies how long the *çevirme* should be stirred, but the Turkish recipes warn that any pause or change of direction in the stirring will be disastrous:[16]

> Once you have begun stirring, you must continue without pause. Because if you get tired and leave off or sometimes turn your paddle in the other direction all your trouble will be wasted. It is necessary to have a helper to take turns when you become tired.

Similar advice is given by Mehmed Reşad in 1921: 'Stir it constantly in one direction with a paddle made of boxwood and a cubit in length. Since it is impossible for one person to do this by themselves, two people must take turns.'[17]

When a friend and I tried Celâl Pasha's recipe our arms ached after just twenty minutes. The syrup quickly thickened and became too stiff to stir. The result was gritty instead of smooth. The sugar had needed a lot more arm-breaking stirring to convert it into *çevirme*: an impossible task for novices.

Çevirme was made in every imaginable flavour. The French traveller Poullet, writing in 1668, records lemon, essence of violets, roses, jasmine or other fragrances, and explains that it was stored in china pots.[18] Friedrich Unger provides the longest list of flavours, including orange (made with orange juice, orange peel, orange-flower water or orange oil), cinnamon, rose (made with rose water, rose oil or fresh rose petals), rose water and opium, lemon, vanilla, salep, green tea, bitter almond, pine nut, pistachio, chocolate, violet (made with fresh petals or pounded violet root), jasmine, mignonette, opium, barberry, strawberry, pineapple, sour cherry, sour pomegranate, sour grape, apricot, peach, plum, banana and date.[19] The famous musk-flavoured *devâ-i misk* made in Edirne was another variety. Charles White adds mulberry to the list of flavours and tells us that in the 1840s confectioners sold their *çevirme* – which he describes as 'candied cherry, mulberry and plum pulp, for sherbets' – in small glass cups that they hung from their shop ceilings.[20] Late nineteenth-century cookery books cite several more flavours: raspberry, ambergris, jonquil, bergamot, whole sour cherry, stonecrop, bitter orange, citron, lily, mimosa, clematis, mastic, mandarin orange, and a combination of rose water and musk.[21]

Abdülaziz Bey relates that gifts sent to the bride by the groom on the wedding morning included crystal bottles of syrups and *çevirme*, either plain or flavoured with bergamot or mastic in lidded bowls.[22]

From the 1920s *çevirme*, alias *lohuk*, alias *lohuk şerbeti*, alias *tatlı*, began to disappear from Turkish life, together with the customs in which it played a part. But around the same time it returned in a new western guise as fondant, which – apart from the stirring in one direction – is made by the same method and with the same ingredients. Fondant emerged in France a few decades after Friedrich Unger's detailed recipes for *çevirme* were published in German. In the course of his investigations of Istanbul's confectionery in 1835 Unger took a liking to this soft sweetmeat and described it in detail in his book, remarking that his readers would find it easy to make:[23]

> I will only quote the favourites that I tasted in Constantinople and whose precise recipes I collected, and the reader will find that when he understands some of the preparations, he will be able to make all kinds of *lohuk-scherbet* with the greatest of ease.

Nowhere does Unger compare *çevirme* to fondant, or point to a similarity to any French confection. Instead he compares it to pomade. Had fondant existed at this period in Europe, a confectioner of Unger's standing, with the professional experience to warrant appointment to a royal court, could hardly have been unaware of the fact. We can conclude that fondant was as yet unknown in Europe in the 1830s and 1840s. The earliest reference to fondant in French sources seems to be *pâte de fondant*, translated as 'fondant paste' in the English edition, in Jules Gouffé's cookery book dated 1867:[24]

> Boil some sugar to the ball, and bring it back to the blow by adding some fruit juice or any of the flavourings described in the preceding recipes. When the sugar is cold, work it with a wooden spatula until it forms a smooth thick paste.

In Gouffé's next book, *Le Livre de patisserie*, published in 1873, he gives a recipe for *glace de fondant* (fondant icing), which includes lemon juice, as specified by Unger and Turkish sources.[25] By 1877 fondant had found its way into *Encyclopaedia Britannica*.[26] In 1881 the English confectioner Skuse published recipes for cream fondants, in which lemon juice is replaced by cream of tartar as a graining inhibitor.[27]

This soft sweetmeat was a revolutionary departure for European confectionery, as Skuse explains: 'At a time when practically all sweetmeats were hard, these soft creamy confections, melting in the mouth, whence their name, attractive in form, flavour and colour, soon became as popular here as in the country of their origin.'[28] This country of origin was France and *fondant* meant melting or melted in French, previously applied to juicy fruit or the flux used in enamelling.

The sudden appearance of a new sweetmeat just a few decades after the publication of Unger's book with its almost identical recipes for *çevirme* is unlikely to be a coincidence, especially since one of his declared objectives was to seek out new articles of oriental confectionery that might be well received in Europe.[29] As a royal confectioner, anything new which Unger offered his royal employer and members of the court had a good chance of spreading rapidly along the European grapevine. It took a professional confectioner to understand the techniques involved just by watching, and even so Unger overlooked the fact that the confectioners stirred in a single direction, which gives Turkish *çevirme* its viscous texture and is where it diverges from European fondant. Consequently fondant made by European confectioners sometimes became 'white and stiff in appearance like an irregular lump of white curd' and then had to be reheated in order to pour into moulds.[30] Later on, European confectioners began to add glucose to ensure the desired smooth texture. So fondant in Europe developed a life of its own, first as moulded sweets and sugar mice with string tails, and later as a filling for chocolates.[31]

RECIPES

LOHUK SCHERBET WITH ORANGE WATER   (Friedrich Unger, 1838)[32]

Boil approximately ¾ *occa* of sugar to a feathered syrup. As soon as you take it from the fire, add ¼–½ liquor glass of lemon juice. This is required for every *lohuk scherbet*.

Stand the pan in the water until it has cooled down a bit, and work the syrup until it starts to thicken, then pour in sufficient orange water that the *scherbet* when poured does not become firm, but soft and similar to a pomade.

The Turks themselves quite often prepare fairly large quantities in the street in front of their shops, in great tinned pans. They work and stir the syrup with a great spatula with such dexterity that it is evident they often prepare it. They also quite often place the pan on ice rather than in cold water so that the sugar cools more quickly and the scherbet becomes more delicate and fine.

As already mentioned, they make it somewhat softer in winter than in summer because the softer *lohuk scherbet* ferments more easily in the great summer heat.

CREAM FONDANTS   (E. Skuse, 1881)[33]

B oil 7lbs. of sugar with three pint of water and 2lbs. of glucose with three pints of water, to the degree of feather 243 by thermometer, pour it on the slab, then with a pallet knife rub the syrup against the plate until it all becomes white and stiff in appearance like an irregular lump of white curd; take this off the plate and put again in the pan, and melt it over a slow fire, stirring it all the time; when it melted sufficiently thin to pass through the runner fill up your moulds.

ÇEVIRME   (Dr Celâl Pasha, 1891)[34]

A fter bringing one *kıyye* of sugar to the boil with half a *kıyye* of water, skim and continue to boil. And occasionally, that is every four or five minutes, put a drop of the sugar into cold water. If it dissolves immediately the consistency is not yet right, but on the contrary if it does not dissolve but instead sinks to the bottom of the glass and forms a lump like a chickpea, then it is ready.

Then remove the pan from the fire and set it aside until the sugar begins to crystallize, and when it seems that it will crystallize entirely, then take a boxwood pestle a cubit in length and the thickness of an ordinary pestle, and beginning in the centre of the pan start to stir rapidly, always in one direction. When it goes white and acquires an sheen like clotted cream then it is ready. Once you have begun stirring, you must continue without pause. Because if you get tired and leave off or sometimes turn your paddle in the other direction all your trouble will be wasted. It is necessary to have a helper there to take turns when you become tired.

This is the basic method for all varieties of *çevirme*. Because when you begin to stir the sugar you add two, four or five drops of essences such as mint, cinnamon, cloves and bergamot, depending on their strength and so make *çevirme* in each of these different flavours. Only vanilla or mastic should be added while the sugar is boiling.

LOHUK ŞEKERI   (Mehmed Reşad, 1921)[35]

After boiling two *okka*s of sugar in one cup of water until it dissolves, add the juice of four lemons. Then remove the pan from the heat, and when it begins to cool stir it constantly in one direction with a paddle made of boxwood and a cubit in length. Since it is impossible for one person to do this by themselves, two people must take turns. When the sugar has become as white as snow it is ready.

While stirring the *lohuk* sugar add essence of lemon, a very little pounded mastic or similar flavourings as desired.

CORNELIAN CHERRY ÇEVIRME   (Hadiye Fahriye, 1926)[36]

Take a *kıyye* of cornelian cherries, press to a pulp and strain the juice. Add sufficient sugar to this juice and boil to a thick syrup. Then add a lentil-sized piece of alum and stir clockwise until the texture is like that of *macun*. Then place in bowls and put away until needed.

14 Reçel   *Preserves*

With His sugar in His rose garden I was transformed into *gülbeşeker*.
Mevlânâ Celâleddin Rûmî (1207–73)[1]

THE PRESERVATION OF FRUIT IN honey or grape juice molasses can be
traced back to the Roman period, when whole uncooked quinces, figs,
apples, plums, pears and cherries were submerged in honey or a mixture
of honey and *defrutum*.[2] Quince paste – ancestor of both British marmalade
and the largely forgotten *ayva murabbâsı* of Turkish cuisine – made in Portugal
and Spain was the earliest type of jam to be made with cooked fruit, and was
being exported to Rome in the second century AD.[3] The Islamic physician and
philosopher Ibn Sinâ (980–1037), known to Europeans as Avicenna, advised
travellers to carry fruit preserves to eat on sea voyages.[4] The exquisite flavour
of rose jam, known as *gülbeşeker*, inspired the mystic philosopher Mevlânâ to
instil it with sacred symbolism:[5]

O rose, that escapes from the rose garden and mingles with sugar,
What caused you to leave the rose garden?
O rose, you are sweeter than sugar itself, and more worthy of sugar . . .
Now you have become *gülbeşeker*, food of the heart, light of the spirit
By *gülbeşeker* I mean our existence by the grace of God;
Our being is like iron and the grace of God a magnet.

The superior flavour of *gülbeşeker* lay, as its name ('rose and sugar') proclaims,
in the fact that it was made of sugar rather than honey or molasses, so the
delicate fragrance of the rose petals was not overwhelmed. The use of sugar
revolutionized preserves, and led to a sharp increase in the number of varieties.
A fourteenth-century Turkish medical book gives recipes for *gülbeşeker*,
green almond and ginger jams, and also mentions walnut and gourd jams.[6]

Fifteenth-century Ottoman sources add preserves made of citrus peel (citron, bitter orange and lemon) and Indian gooseberry[7] to the list, and one document tells us that gourd jam made with honey, cinnamon and cloves was served to guests at the Fâtih mosque complex in Istanbul.[8] In the sixteenth century there was an explosion of jam varieties in Turkey, and each century added to the number. Many of these are still familiar today, such as cornelian cherry, aubergine, green walnut, peach, mulberry, watermelon, citron and pear, but others have fallen into oblivion, such as green almond, melon, ginger, barberry, pineapple, medlar, jujube, stonecrop, sour grape, sage gall, salep, persimmon and ungrafted apricot (*zerdali*), as well as most of the flower jams, such as violet, jonquil, quince blossom, mallow flower, judas tree flower, borage flower and jasmine.

Apart from rose, citrus and other cultivated plants, gathering sufficient blossom to make jam is virtually impossible nowadays. Even a century ago the tradition of making flower petal jams was beginning to die out, as Ali Rıza Bey lamented in 1922:[9]

> Until recent times there were many enthusiasts who loved gardening and trees. They grew sufficient vegetables, roses, and delicious fruits for the needs of the household and grafted the bushes and trees themselves. Households made jams, syrups and preserves in every season. Those enthusiasts have disappeared.
>
> In the past violets, tulips, hyacinths and jonquils were grown in the gardens of Eyüp and Bahariye,[10] and purchased by confectioners to make preserves and syrups.

The Turkish term for fruit either whole or in pieces preserved in syrup is *reçel*, deriving from the Persian *riçâr*, which originally meant electuary, pickles and various preserved or fermented condiments, especially those made with milk or yogurt.[11] In Iraq the term came to refer to jams made of the juice of fruit such as apples, quinces and raisins cooked with grape molasses.[12] The Arabic term *murabbâ* and Persian *perverde* were at first used in Turkish for any type of fruit preserve, later acquiring a more specific meaning in Turkish as a jam made of fruit juice or sometimes fruit pulp. In the latter sense the term *murabbâ* has now been superseded by *marmelât*, from the French term *marmelade*.[13]

An early Turkish preserve recipe, recorded by Şirvânî, physician to Sultan Murad II (1421–51), is made of slices of citrus peel preserved in sugar and then left in the sun, resulting in a kind of candied peel. The process is complex and involves more than two months of preparation:[14]

Murabbâ of Citron

Cut the citron, clean the peel [i.e. remove the flesh and membranes] and cut into slices. Soak in salt water for seven days, changing the water every two days. Then soak for one day and one night in lime water,[15] and a further seven days in fresh water, changing the water every day, until all the salt has been extracted. Then soak in sugar syrup for ten days. As the peel absorbs the syrup add more, until the slices are sweet. Remove from the syrup. Prepare a clarified sugar syrup and boil the slices in this until the syrup thickens. Then soak for thirty to forty days in rose water syrup. Remove, arrange on trays, cover with clean muslin and leave in the sun to dry. When it has crystallized place in wooden jars and eat when desired. Bitter orange and lemon peel may be treated in the same fashion.

Removing the bitterness from the peel is clearly a priority here; soaking for several days is still the rule for most Turkish citrus preserves.

At the circumcision celebrations for Sultan Mehmed II's sons Bâyezid and Mustafa held in the city of Edirne in 1456, guests were served with trayfuls of sweetmeats and in addition given boxes of crystallized fruit to take home.[16] Later on, however, candied fruit fell out of favour, until it reappeared as a European introduction in the early nineteenth century,[17] when – according to Charles White – it was produced in large quantities by 'Italian and Swiss settlers' in the Galata district of Istanbul.[18]

Crystallized fruits were part of the trousseau of Mihrimâh Sultan, daughter of Sultan Mahmud II (r. 1808–39) when she married Admiral of the Fleet Mehmed Said Pasha in 1836. On the seventh day of the eight-day wedding festivities her splendid trousseau, packed on forty mules and twenty carriages, and carried on 160 trays, passed in procession through the streets, watched by hundreds of thousands of people.[19]

Although we have nineteenth-century recipes for rose jam, how the *gülbeşeker* eaten by Mevlânâ in the thirteenth century was made seemed doomed to remain a secret forever. Fortunately, preserves of this kind introduced from the Muslim world were popular in Europe at this period and a poem written around 1265–70 by a contemporary of Mevlânâ's, the Dutch poet Jacob van Maerlant, contains a recipe for *gülbeşeker*:[20]

Rose Sugar

Rose sugar (*suker rosaet*) is made in the following way: rose petals that have been rubbed fine with sugar are put in a glass jar and left in the sun for 30 days; the contents must be stirred daily; the jar must be well sealed and it will remain good for three years.

A nineteenth-century recipe for sun-cooked rose jam, called *gülbeşeker şemsiyesi* ('sunshine rose sugar'), fills in a few missing details:[21]

Gülbeşeker Şemsiyesi

Method: Take half a *kıyye* of rose petals and cut away the white parts with scissors. Place in a vessel with a *kıyye* of sugar and knead until blended, then, using the hands, place in lidded bowls glazed on the inside. After this arrange the bowls on a copper tray and when the sun is hot take off the lids and place the tray in full sunshine. In the evening replace the lids. Put the tray in the sun the following day and so continue for about a month until the surface crystallizes and goes white, when it is delicious. Prepare violets in the same way.

The idea of eating *gülbeşeker* for its therapeutic benefits as well as enjoying it as a sweetmeat lingered into the late Ottoman period. One spoonful taken in the evening aided the digestion and cured constipation.[22] Bitter orange preserve relieved indigestion brought about by over-eating on the Feast of Sacrifice.[23] The enduring link between fruit preserves and medicine is illustrated by the fact that a Turkish medical doctor wrote a book of recipes for fruit syrups, jams and conserves in 1891.[24]

In Europe the first confectioners were pharmacists or alchemists,[25] and one of the earliest books devoted to fruit preserve and sweetmeat recipes is a tract published by the French pharmacist, physician and astrologer Nostredame in 1552.[26] The preserves include lemon peel, bitter orange peel, walnut, sour cherry, quince, pine nut and green almonds. When his bitter orange peel recipe is compared to that written by the Ottoman physician Şirvânî a century before, there are some striking resemblances: in both the peel is soaked in salt water for about a week, and then in syrup for about a month.[27]

The confectionery kitchen at the Ottoman palace was at the same time a pharmacy, and the lists of purchases in the accounts registers include almost as many pharmaceutical substances as cookery ingredients. There was a similar link between medicines and confectionery in Europe. In Germany the guilds of pharmacists retained a monopoly on the production of sweetmeats into the first half of the seventeenth century, and in return for these rights produced sweetmeats for the royal courts.[28]

In sixteenth-century Turkey preserves diversifed to such an extent that no fewer than eighteen varieties were served at a banquet of sweetmeats during the circumcision celebrations for Süleyman the Magnificent's sons in 1539: citron whole and in pieces, *mürekkep*,[29] bitter orange, *ufak limon* ('small lemon'),[30] gourd, watermelon, quince, apple, cornelian cherry, aubergine, green walnut, pear, *gökçe*,[31] peach, sour cherry, cherry and carrot.[32] Before long, preserves became part of the rituals of hospitality and high dining in the upper circles of society. Talks between the Swedish ambassador Nicholas Rolamb and Melek Ahmed Pasha held in Silister in 1656 were followed by a banquet that concluded with fruit preserves.[33]

In the eighteenth and nineteenth centuries a distinction was made between two types of preserves: one called *tatlı*, which had a thicker consistency and a long shelf-life,[34] and the other called *reçel*, which had a thinner syrup and only kept for a few days. *Reçel* is identical to the European compôtes of the period, which were sweeter than today's stewed fruit. Because *reçel* was boiled for a shorter time and contained a lower proportion of sugar, and therefore did not require the addition of lemon juice to prevent crystallization, the flavour of the fruit was pure and unmasked. This type of preserve was poured into bowls to be eaten almost immediately, while *tatlı* was kept in glass or ceramic jars.[35] Nevertheless, since jams had to be made when the fruit was in season, it was common to prepare thick preserves and dilute them when *reçel* was called for. The preference for preserves with a thin syrup was a custom exploited by confectioners, as Hadiye Fahriye explains:[36]

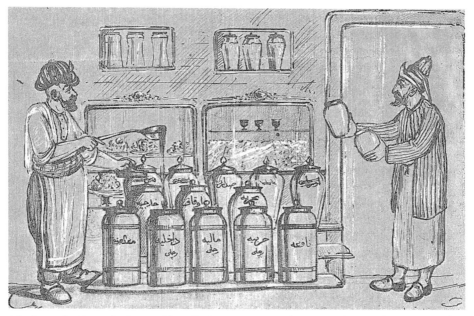

15. A confectioner's shop selling fruit preserves in huge jars during Ramazan. The customer has brought his own jars to be filled (*Karagöz*, 119 (16 September 1909), p. 1).

By adding a little water [to thick jams and syrups] and bringing them to the boil they can easily be given the desired consistency. This is the method confectioners always use, because they are obliged to keep the jams and syrups that they prepare in their various seasons until the holy month of Ramazan. So a few days before Ramazan they take a cauldronful of thick sour cherry or strawberry jam, and by diluting it sufficiently obtain two or even three cauldronfuls of jam to sell.

Jams were an essential part of the *iftar* meal at nightfall during Ramazan. The fast was broken with a spread of olives, dates, cheeses and various jams in tiny dishes, accompanied by sesame-strewn bread rings. Then after an interval the main meal followed.

Preserves of various kinds became part and parcel of Ottoman hospitality rituals from the seventeenth century onwards. Guests were offered a spoonful of whole fruit preserve, quince jelly, *gülbeşeker* or *çevirme* (fondant, as described in the previous chapter) before drinking coffee, which was served without sugar. These preserves were all thick enough to be spooned up without dripping, made with three measures of sugar to every one measure of fruit and some lemon juice to prevent crystallization.[37] A cookery book dated 1844 gives four recipes for 'sweetmeats [*tatlı*] served before coffee': two for quince jelly, one for *gülbeşeker* and one for Turkish delight.[38]

The *tatlı* was served to guests in silver or porcelain sets consisting of a goblet for spoons known as *kaşıklık*, spoons with long handles, lidded bowls for the sweetmeats, water glasses and a tray on which all this paraphernalia was placed. These sets were vehicles for ostentatious display, and one European traveller describes a set with a silver *kaşıklık* in the form of a boat used in the home of a Greek family:[39]

As soon as we were comfortably established round the tandour, a servant brought in a tray on which were arranged a large cut glass vase, filled with a delicate preserve slightly impregnated with *attar de rose*, a range of crystal goblets of water, and a silver boat, whose oars were gilt tea-spoons. One of these the lady of the house immersed in the preserve, and offered to me; after which she replaced the spoon in the boat, and I then accepted a draught of water presented by the same hospitable hand; the whole ceremony was next gone through with my father.

Sweetmeats were also placed beside the bed of a guest, in case they felt hungry in the night. The earliest account of this custom is by Baron de Tott in the late eighteenth century, when he visited the country home of his Greek interpretor:[40]

A small octagonal Tower, inlaid with ebony and mother-of-pearl that stood by the side of the Bed, and served for a Table; upon it was placed a large silver Candlestick, which held a yellow wax candle two inches thick, and three feet high, whose wick, nearly as big as one's finger, produced a very disagreeable smoke. Three China-salvers, filled with conserve of roses, flowers of orange, and lemon-pulp, with a little golden spatula, the handle of tortoise-shell, to serve for a spoon, and a crystal vessel full of water, surrounded this obscure Luminary.

The 'spatula' Tott describes was a *gülbeşeker* spoon[41] traditionally used for eating *tatlı*. These spatula-like spoons were still used by some Istanbul families in the mid-twentieth century.[42]

A tray of sweetmeats at the bedside is also described by Julia Pardoe in 1836:[43]

In each [bedroom] a tray is conspicuously set out with conserves, generally strongly impregnated with perfume, such as rose, bergamotte, and citron; and covered goblets of richly-cut crystal, filled with water. The custom appears singular to an European, but it is by no means unpleasant; and I had not been long in the country ere I found the visit of the servant, who knelt down at my bed-side, and handed the tray to me on my awaking, a very agreeable one.

The custom of offering preserves to guests has long since been forgotten in Istanbul, but lives on among some families in Antalya, and until recent years in İzmir.[44] One of the most detailed accounts of this ceremony is by Lady Fanny Blunt, wife of a British consul who lived in Turkey for nearly twenty years in the mid-nineteenth century:[45]

It is the custom throughout Turkey to offer as refreshment the *tatlou*, a rich kind of preserve made from fruits or flowers such as roses, lilies, violets and orange blossom. It is brought in soon after the entrance of a visitor. The service used for the purpose may be of the most costly or of the simplest description. That used in Turkish harems is always of some precious metal and comprises a salver, two preserve basins, a double spoon basket and a number of goblets and spoons. The edge of the salver, like that used for coffee, is surrounded by a gold embroidered cloth; the slave who offers it does so on bended knee. In addition to the *tatlou*, in Turkish konaks [large houses] sherbet, immediately followed by coffee, is offered to visitors when about to leave or when the hostess is desirous of being relieved of their company.

The guest who was offered preserves picked up a spoon from the goblet, took a spoonful of whichever variety he/she preferred, and afterwards placed the spoon in the second compartment of the 'double spoon basket', or a second goblet provided for used spoons or, in homes with neither of these objects, in their own glass after drinking the water.

This custom seems to have its advent in the second half of the seventeenth century, because earlier accounts of Ottoman hospitality rituals mention only coffee, sherbet and perfume. One of the earliest accounts of being offered jam is Henry Maundrell, who visited the pasha of Tripoli in Lebanon in 1697:[46]

> When you have talked over your business, or the compliments, or whatever other concern brought you thither, he makes a sign to have things served in for the entertainment; which is generally a little sweetmeat, a dish of sherbet, and another of coffee.

Aaron Hill, who in 1699 visited his relative, Lord Paget, then British ambassador at Constantinople, provides interesting details about the etiquette of offering refreshments to visitors:[47]

> When they are entered, they advance to that elevated part of the Floor call'd the *Soffrai* [misspelling for *sofa*], and place themselves cross-leg'd opposite to each other, on cushions richly cover'd, with their hands upon their Laps, like our Women. Now begins discourse, which is hardly enter'd, when several Pages, richly dress'd, bring a silk or muslin Handkerchief finely embroider'd; and spread it on the Stranger's Lap; then comes another with a Salver, containing several sorts of sweetmeats in little Spoons, like those we use for tea, some of these he eats, and is immediately attended by a third with a Dish of Coffee, that drank, the handkerchief is taken away, and they withdraw; but the Visitor has hardly renew'd his Discourse, when they return again with another handkerchief, which being spread as before, one sprinkles sweet water in his Face from a Silver Bottle, and another smoaking his Beard and the inside of his Vest with burnt perfume from a golden incense pan, they withdraw again; these two ceremonies are usually perform'd at the Page's discretion as to the time between them; but there remains a third, which they must wait their Master's call for, and that is, the bringing in a large Dish of sherbit of an excellent flavour, which as soon as the Stranger has drank he takes leave and goes away; for its their Custom never to call for that Liquor, till they grow weary of their Visitor's Company.

Foreign travellers were sometimes not aware that they were expected to take a single spoonful of the sweetmeat served to them, or found the custom parsimonious. English cavalry officer Frederick Burnaby's first experience of the custom was in 1876 at the residence of the Armenian bishop in İzmit:[48]

> Refreshments were now brought in on a silver tray, and several kinds of jam handed round in little silver dishes. The guest taking a spoonful of jam is expected to swallow it, he then drinks a glass of water. This is an economical refreshment, a very little jam goes a long way in the entertainment.

Burnaby's disparaging attitude reflects the low status of fruit preserves in the European sweetmeat hierarchy. If bonbons, chocolates or candied fruits had been offered instead, he would no doubt have considered it bad manners to take more than one, never mind empty the dish, as a guest did at the home of Mrs Schneider, wife of an American Protestant missionary living in Bursa in the first half of the nineteenth century:[49]

16. A palace page carrying a small pot of *çevirme* or fruit preserves ('Page Portant Les Confitures', in *Tableau Général de l'Empire Othoman*, 2 vols, Paris, 1789, Plate 59).

In America when a person makes the social call on his friend, if the lady of the house were to offer him a single tea-spoonful of sweet-meats (which would only tantalize his appetite without satisfying it) it would be a gross insult. Here it is one of the highest expressions of politeness. I well remember that about ten years since, immediately after our arrival in Broosa, an English traveller called on us. He was a stranger to Eastern etiquette. Our servant brought in a waiter containing a vase of jelly, a tea-spoon and a tumbler of water. The jelly was presented to the gentleman. He took the vase in hand and began to eat. He happening to relish it continued eating it, saying occasionally 'you have some very nice jelly, Mrs Schneider,' to the no small amusement of present company.

The Baron de Tott's servant committed a similar breach of etiquette in the palace of the Prince of Moldavia in 1767:[50]

The same ceremony was repeated in the Anti-chamber, in favour of my Lackey, who was far from practising my oeconomy on this occasion: his appetite, less delicate, refused nothing: he ate all they gave him, of ginger, comfits, and conserves, and swallowed, at a single draft, all the Sherbet.

Although fine fruit preserves are as delicious as any other confectionery, they have sadly lost some of the prestige they once enjoyed in Turkey. As in Western countries they now rate little higher than peanut butter or chocolate spread, to be ignominiously plastered on bread instead of savoured for their own sake. This is not to say that *reçel* was not eaten with bread at breakfast in the Ottoman period. It was – as a late eighteenth-century Ramazan verse tells us:[51]

> Let me have for breakfast
> A hundred thousand omelettes
> And dip my bread in
> Forty-eight thousand *okka*s of jam.

Menekşe hamîrisi, a kind of violet petal jam made in the same way as *gülbeşeker*, was a delicacy reserved for the breakfast tables of the upper classes. This was eaten with a little lemon juice and accompanied by whey cheese.[52] German army officer Helmuth von Moltke, who served in the Ottoman army during the reign of Mahmud II, recorded that it was customary to eat some rose jam with a glass of water before breakfast, and recommends the practice to his readers.[53]

Fruit preserves were once valued as wedding gifts in palace circles, illustrating the esteem in which they used to be held. Baronne Durand de Fontmagne, who lived in Istanbul for a year and a half in 1856–8 following the Crimean War, was shown the gifts about to be sent to the Ottoman princess Refia Sultan before her marriage to Ethem Pasha.[54] She noted that these included various preserves in 'not less than five hundred pots of very fine Dresden china'. This was a tradition that went back a long way. When Hatice Sultan, the daughter of Mehmed IV (r. 1648–87), married Musahib Mustafa Pasha two centuries earlier, the groom's gifts to the bride included '30 mules laden with sugar-plums and sweet-meats'.[55]

Some preserves made in distant provinces of the empire were transported to Istanbul, such as citron preserve from Egypt,[56] quince jelly from Amasya, orange flower, lemon peel, citron peel and rose jams from Chios, *gülbeşeker* from Edirne and a variety of different kinds from Adana.[57] Those with a thick consistency were packed in woodchip boxes and sold in a covered bazaar that once stood near the waterfront in Istanbul.[58]

Preserves made of tropical fruits and roots were imported into the Ottoman Empire from as far as India.[59] When the rebel khan of Bitlis, a city on the western shore of Lake Van, was defeated by an Ottoman army in 1658, his treasury was found to contain not only precious fabrics, jewellery, jewelled tableware and illustrated manuscripts, but hundreds of jars, small and large, made of jasper and İznik chinaware containing expensive preserves made from Khorasan plums, Bukhara plums, emblic myrobalan (*Phyllanthus emblica*), chebulic myrobalan (*Terminalia chebula*), nutmeg, ginger and coconut. The entire treasury was sold at auction, but when the time came to sell the preserves the jars were found to be empty – out of curiosity so many people had sampled these unusual preserves that nothing was left.[60]

The royal confectioners made preserves from fruit and flowers grown in the palace gardens and royal estates. A register kept by the palace confectioners between the early seventeenth and early eighteenth centuries records twenty-five different varieties, including quince blossom, date, jujube, watermelon, melon, violet, medlar, aubergine, pear, peach and green almond.[61] In some cases these were made with sugar alone, and sometime with a combination of sugar and honey in a ratio of three or four to one. They were stored in silver and china jars. Large quantities of fragrant varieties of roses were grown in the palace gardens for making rose water, *gülbeşeker* and rose syrup. Preserves were made in a special kitchen known as the *reçelhane*, which opened off the main confectionery kitchen.

After Mahmud II abandoned Topkapı Palace as his imperial residence in the nineteenth century, influential foreign guests were granted permission to visit the palace, and when the conducted tour was over they were offered refreshments that included rose or violet preserves.[62] Hundreds of kilograms of violets for making these preserves and sherbets for the sultan were sold to the palace by outside suppliers.[63]

Preserves were often made with grape molasses, and still are in country districts of Turkey today. Pumpkin preserve made with *pekmez* is particularly popular. However, preserves of this kind have never been held in the same esteem as those made with sugar, because the grape molasses lends its own dominant flavour and also spoils the colour of the fruit. For Ottoman gourmets the appearance of preserves was just as important as flavour and fragrance, and indeed sometimes more so. Jujube preserve was a favourite of novelist Refik Halid Karay (1888–1965), who describes its appearance enthusiastically yet remains silent on the subject of its flavour:[64] 'I preferred jujube jam with its greenish flesh visible through its greenish peel and whitish stone whose presence could be sensed.'

The emphasis on appearance evidently went back many centuries, as we see from the following account by the German physician Dr Leonhart Rauwolff during his travels in southeast Turkey and Syria in 1573:[65]

17. Pair of Kütahya ware jars inscribed 'Jujube Preserve' and 'Apricot Preserve' respectively, early twentieth century (Courtesy of Sadberk Hanım Museum; photograph: Selamet Taşkın).

They have many sorts of preserves, very well done with sugar and hony, very artificially (chiefly those they carry about to sell upon plates very well garnish'd) made up and set out with several colours and shapes very beautiful to behold.

Various other methods were used to give preserves a decorative appearance, such as rolling slices of citrus peel into tight spirals, a method still common today,[66] using whole fruits like wild pears and green male figs or adding nuts. In Istanbul a small wedge of orange peel or a pine nut was sometimes inserted into the base of each fig[67] or blanched almonds were added to apricot, melon and pumpkin preserves.[68]

Jam making was one of the most important domestic tasks in Ottoman housesholds, as related by the Frenchman Pretextat Lecomte, who lived in Istanbul during the reign of Abdülhamid II (1876–1909):[69]

Preserve making in Turkey is an art; the mistress of every house takes pride in preparing it herself. When this significant operation takes place in a house, all other concerns are banished, all other interests are sacrificed, the world does not appear to gravitate around its natural poles, but to revolve, in these serious moments, around the pot or the concoction of the precious sweetmeat.

According to the writer Sermet Muhtar Alus, for a woman to purchase her jam from a confectioner's was almost a stain on her reputation as an honest woman:[70]

Well-brought-up ladies made their own jam, or at least supervised its making, and then stored it away for Ramazan, while idle and frivolous ones wasted time until Ramazan suddenly struck, and then bought it from Hacı Bekir in Bahçekapısı, Rifat in Meydancık, Udî Cemil in Şehzadebaşı or Şekercigüzeli in Fatih.

Another danger awaited those idle ladies who bought jam from shops: European marmalades were made of glucose instead of sugar and adulterated with carrot, beet and pumpkin – and were expensive, to boot, according to one Turkish cookery writer.[71]

Soaking in lye to remove bitterness or improve texture is a widely used technique in Turkish jam making. As we have seen above, Şirvânî's citrus peel jam involved soaking the peel in lye, and sage galls were similarly treated to remove the bitterness,[72] while in the case of soft fruits such as strawberries and apricots the lye prevented the fruit becoming mushy. Lye has the most striking effect on the texture of melon, watermelon and pumpkin preserves, which acquire a crunchy shell around a melting interior.

Unusual preserves such as green pistachio shell, French lavender and *Lagenaria* gourd with pistachio nuts illustrate the extraordinary diversity of regional Turkish preserves.

RECIPES

GREEN ALMOND PRESERVE   (Friedrich Unger, 1835)

This preserve was made for the sultan in the seventeenth century using 6 kıyyes of honey to 35 kıyyes of sugar.[73] The recipe below is based on that recorded by Friedrich Unger during his visit to Istanbul in 1835.[74] The green almonds must be gathered in late March or early April while they are tender.

1.5 kg unripe almonds
650 g honey
3.35 kg sugar
2 litres water

Boil the tender green almonds in plenty of water until they soften (2–3 hours) then drain. Mix the sugar, honey and water and bring to the boil, simmer for 10 minutes. Toss in the almonds, bring to the boil, remove from the heat and set aside for 24 hours. The following day drain the syrup into a second pan and bring to the boil. Return the almonds, bring back to the boil and again set aside for 24 hours. Repeat this for six days altogether. Do not let the syrup become too thick or darken in colour. If necessary dilute with a little water before bringing to the boil.

1. Confectioner's 'shop' being pulled along on a float in a guild procession in 1582. Conical sugar loaves fill the top two shelves and there are glass jars of sweets on the lowest shelf. Below the shelves are a pair of scales and a parrot in a cage. In Turkish and Persian poetry parrots were often associated with sugar owing to their ability to talk sweetly (*Sûrnâme-i Hümâyûn*, TSM H1344, a detail from fol. 161v; photograph: Bahadır Taşkın; courtesy of Topkapı Palace Museum).

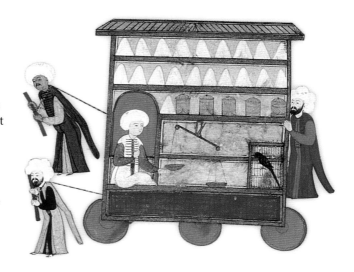

2. Colour lithograph by the Italian painter Jean Brindesi of a confectionery vendor selling sweets to a small girl. The sweets on his tray include pulled sugar rings piled on upright sticks and lollipops in the form of birds (*Souvenirs de Constantinople*, c. 1860; courtesy of Sadberk Hanım Museum).

3. Istanbul confectioner's shop. Colour lithograph after a painting by the Maltese artist Amadeo Preziosi. The five cylindrical sweetmeats hanging from ceiling behind the confectioner are *sucuk*, strings of nuts coated with grape juice thickened with starch (*Stamboul Recollections of Eastern Life*, 1858).

4. Animal figures made of sugar being paraded through the streets during the circumcision celebrations for Sultan Murad III's sons in 1582. The animals represented here include a giraffe, horse, stork, swan and elephant, with leopard cubs and fish made of sugar heaped on trays. A second miniature (24r) not reproduced here shows a sugar lion, leopard and camel. Sultan Murad III is watching the scene from a balcony at the upper left (*Sûrnâme-i Hümâyûn*, TSM H1344, fol. 25v; photograph: Bahadır Taşkın; courtesy of Topkapı Palace Museum).

5. Two sugar gardens made for the circumcision festivities for Ahmed III's sons in 1720. The gardens contain a castle and pavilion respectively, diverse fruit trees, and cypress trees with grape vines twined around them (*Sûrnâme-i Vehbi*, TSM A3593, fol. 161r; photograph: Hadiye Cangökçe; courtesy of Topkapı Palace Museum).

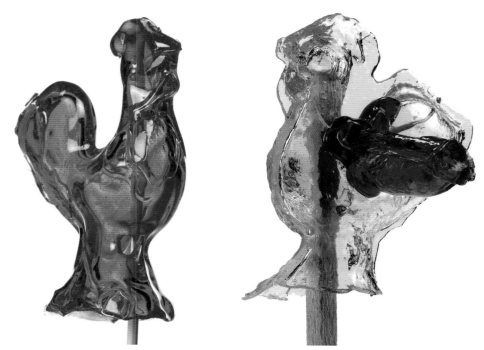

6. Hollow lollipops in the form of cockerels, made by two of Turkey's last *horoz şekeri* makers. A red sugar whistle is attached to the one on the right (Photograph: Hakan Ezilmez – YKKS and Mary Işın).

7. Hollow lollipop in the form of a cavalry soldier made by İbrahim Denizci (Photograph: Cüneyt Akçıl; courtesy of İbrahim Denizci), and the mould (Photograph: Hakan Ezilmez – YKKS).

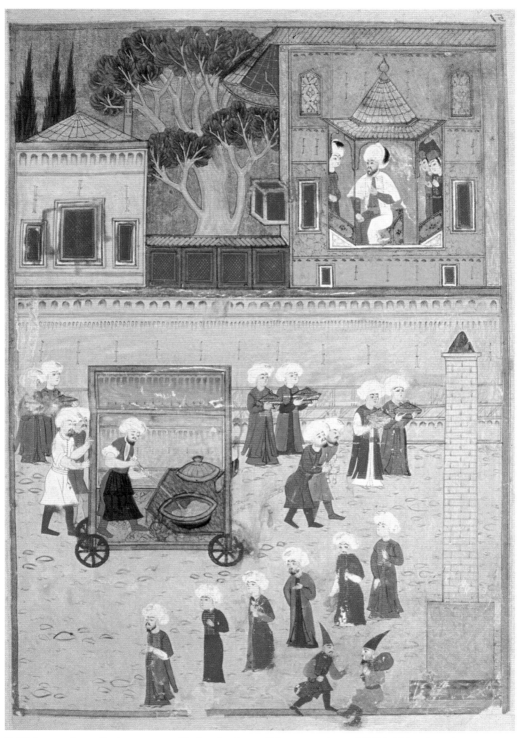

8. Helva maker stirring a pan of helva in the guild procession of 1582 (*Sûrnâme-i Hümâyûn*, TSM H1344, fol. 51v; courtesy of Topkapı Palace Museum).

9. Confectioners frying *memuniye* balls on a confectioners' furnace (*Sûrnâme-i Hümâyûn*, TSM H1344, detail from fol. 311v; photograph: Bahadır Taşkın; courtesy of Topkapı Palace Museum).

10. An Albanian seller of *susam helva*, a kind of sesame toffee made with honey. The figure holds a hammer to break up the hard toffee. The picture's caption is 'Halwa mileo!' ('honey helva'), the street cry of these sellers (Friedrich Unger, *Conditorei des Orients*, 1838, Bayerische Staatbibliothek, Oecon, 1777, facing p. 30; courtesy of Bayerische Staatbibliothek).

11. *Pelte* makers in the 1582 guild procession in Istanbul (*Sûrnâme-i Hümâyûn*, TSM H1344, fol. 300v; photograph: Bahadır Taşkın; courtesy of Topkapı Palace Museum).

12. A dish of *pelte* decorated with almonds can be seen on the upper table in this miniature depicting a banquet at the festivities for the circumcision of the sons of Sultan Ahmed III in 1720 (*Sûrnâme-i Vehbi*, TSM A3593, fol. 85r; photograph: Hadiye Cangökçe; courtesy of Topkapı Palace Museum).

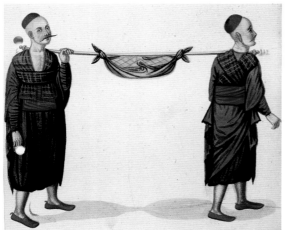

13. Two janissary soldiers carrying a tray of baklava made in the palace kitchens on the fifteenth of Ramazan (Painting from an album in Ankara Ethnographic Museum; photograph: Hadiye Cangökçe; courtesy of Ankara Ethnographic Museum).

14. Dishes of pilaf topped with *zerde* and behind them whole spit-roasted sheep on platters set on tripods laid out for the janissary soldiers, who are standing in rows on the left. This feast was part of the celebrations for the circumcision of Sultan Ahmed III's sons in 1720 (*Surname-i Vehbi*, TSMK A3544, fol.150v; courtesy of Topkapı Palace Museum).

SOUR GRAPE PRESERVE   (Mehmed Kâmil, 1844)[75]

This recipe dates from 1844. Sour grape preserve is mentioned in a fifteenth-century medical book.[76]

Take one *kıyye* of sugar and clarify in the customary manner. Skim off the froth and bring to the boil. When it begins to reach the correct consistency add a hundred sour grapes that have been sliced in half with a sharp pen-knife and the pips removed with a toothpick. When the syrup comes to the boil again and thickens sufficiently, remove from the heat and pour into lidded bowls. then immediately place these in cold water, so that it cools rapidly and its beautiful colour does not spoil. Then eat it with a *gülbeşeker* spoon. The same can be prepared with unripe seedless grapes.

WATERMELON PEEL PRESERVE

This preserve is made from the layer of white crisp flesh beneath the outer green rind. It was prepared by palace confectioners for the sultan from the sixteenth century onwards. An eighteenth-century palace document gives the ingredients as 60 kıyyes of sugar and 20 kıyyes of honey for 150 watermelons.[77] The following recipe is adapted from two modern recipes.[78]

1 large watermelon (only the white outer layer of flesh)
1 kg sugar
1 lemon
2 heaped tablespoonfuls of quicklime[79]

Using a long steel or wooden spoon, stir the quicklime into 7 cups of water in a steel container (avoid aluminium) and wait for 2 or 3 hours until the lime has sunk to the bottom and the water is clear (a very slight film may remain on the surface). Without agitating the pan, carefully pour off the clear water into another pan.

Cut the watermelon into pieces, peel off the green outer rind and remove the red flesh. Cut the white flesh into small cubes and place in the pan of lime water. Soak for an hour, then drain the watermelon and rinse well about eight times. Place the sugar into a pan, add a cup of water and bring to the boil. Toss in the well-drained watermelon and boil until the syrup thickens. Finally add the juice of one lemon, boil for a further 10 minutes and remove from the heat.

AUBERGINE PRESERVE   (Cevat Kolak, 1960s)

This is one of the preserves made for the sultan from the sixteenth century onwards. In the eighteenth century palace confectioners used 2,000 aubergines, 44 kıyyes of sugar and 30 kıyyes of honey.[80] It remains a popular preserve in some of Turkey's regional cuisines, but in cities it is almost impossible to obtain the baby aubergines required. The following is adapted from a modern recipe dating from the 1960s.[81]

    1 kg very small aubergines (finger-length)
    1 kg sugar
    1 lemon
    1 flat tablespoon vanilla sugar
    1 kg quicklime

Stir the quicklime into 4 litres of water in a steel container (using a long steel or wooden spoon) and set aside for at least an hour until the lime has sunk to the bottom and the water is clear. Without agitating the pan, carefully pour away the clear water and add 4 litres of fresh water. Repeat this four times. Save the last pan of clear water to soak the aubergines.

Peel the aubergines and pare away the stalks until all that remains is a conical cap. Toss into a pan of water. When all the aubergines have been peeled set the pan on the heat and bring to the boil. Cook until just tender. Be careful that they do not overcook. To test for the correct degree pierce one of the aubergines with a fine skewer and lift it up. If the aubergine falls off the skewer it is sufficiently cooked. Place the aubergines into the pan of clear lime water and leave for 30 minutes. Then wash them in plenty of water eight times, squeeze each one to remove the excess water and set aside.

Place the sugar into a pan, stir in a cup of water and bring to the boil. Add the lemon juice, bring back to the boil and then toss in the aubergines. Boil for about an hour until the aubergines have absorbed the syrup. Sprinkle the vanilla sugar over the top, place a lid on the pan and leave to cool. When the aubergines are cold, carefully place them in a jar and pour the remaining syrup over.

15 Helva:
Home-made Varieties

Silence, tonight the sultan has entered the kitchen
With a bright face and cheerful demeanour he is cooking
This is a sight never before seen
Our sweet beloved is cooking helva for us.
                                    Mevlânâ Celâleddin Rûmî (1207–73)[1]

THE TURKISH WORD *HELVA* COMES from the Arabic *halwa*, meaning any sweet confection, so its varieties cover a huge range of flour and sugar confectionery that could not possibly fit into a single chapter, and *keten helva* requires a separate chapter of its own. The remainder have therefore been divided into helvas whose ingredients include flour or semolina that are usually made at home for immediate consumption, and those that are commercially produced by professional confectioners.

The broad definition of helva also leads to a problem of interpretation when the word appears in texts without any clues as to the type which is meant. An example is found in the diary of the French linguist Antoine Galland, when he described the entertainment put on by the helva makers in the procession accompanying the Ottoman army led by Sultan Mehmed IV out of Edirne on its way to wage war against Poland on 4 May 1672:[2]

The fruit sellers and the confectioners advanced in much the same order. Two men at the head of the others each carried a large basin on his head containing baskets of diverse sorts of fruit; but what was most amusing was a man who preceded the corps of confectioners who wore a chemise that descended to his heels and was covered all over with *alva* [sic.], that is to say

sweetmeat, from top to bottom, and grabbed handfuls from his buttocks that
he ate and flung at the crowd. His beard, which was very long, was so covered
that it could not be seen and his bonnet was made of sweetmeat.

What sort of helva could this be? It was sticky enough to stick to the clown's
clothes and beard and soft enough to grab in handfuls, so perhaps it was some
kind of toffee or nougat.

There are other curious puzzles relating to helva, such as the *bayram helva*
whose ingredients are listed in a notebook kept by the palace confectioners
in the seventeenth and eighteenth centuries. As usual the method is not
described, evidently because the confectioners did not need reminding –
unfortunately for us. The ingredients fit none of the other Ottoman-period
helvas: sugar, clarified butter, eggs, honey, almonds, tamarind, black pepper,
sesame oil and an unknown ingredient called *sad* that might possibly be a
misspelling of *süd* (milk).[3] Then there is the tantalizing reference to helva
made with *boza* (a thick beer made of millet or rice) for Sultan Mehmed II in
1471,[4] and to *dellâliye helvası*, whose ingredients are entirely unknown, which
was made for religious festivals in the reign of Sultan Selim II (r. 1566–74).[5]
In the case of *kabak helvası* (marrow helva) made with marrow, honey and
almonds recorded in the eighteenth century we are more fortunate because
this confection is still a famous speciality of the province of Burdur.[6] It is made
by adding grated marrow to boiled sugar syrup, stirring constantly until the
texture becomes jelly-like, then spreading on a plate and decorating with
blanched almonds.

Setting these riddles aside let's turn to the topic of home-made helvas,
beginning with *un helvası* (flour helva), the most ancient variety, known as
afrûşe in Persian and *habîs* in Arabic. Other Turkish names were *hanegî helva*
or *helva-i hâne* (both meaning 'home-made helva') or *ter helva* ('fresh helva'). A
variation with a crumbly rather than a pasty texture known as *gaziler helvası* is
first mentioned in a poem by the mystic poet Kaygusuz Abdal (d. 1444).[7]

By the late nineteenth century the name *gaziler helvası* ('warriors' helva'),
was already puzzling civilians. When the journalist Mehmed Tevfik (1843–93)
asked a scholar if he knew the origin of the name, he received the jocular reply
that the helva was so difficult to digest that anyone who survived eating it was
a true warrior.[8] In fact *gaziler helvası* was made after battles in the memory
of comrades killed in action, as we learn from Evliyâ Çelebi's account of a
seventeeenth-century sea battle between a Turkish ship and enemy galleons
near the island of Sönbeki (Syme or Nisos Simi) off the Mediterranean port of
Marmaris.[9] When the battle was over the survivors cooked *gaziler helvası* and
recited prayers for the souls of the departed.

Gaziler helvası was still a feature of Ottoman army life at the end of the nineteenth century, when the infantry lieutenant Mahmud Nedim included a recipe in his cookery book written for fellow soldiers. He begins by describing how to make this helva in ordinary quantities at home, then explains how to make it for a company of soldiers. He bases the quantities not on the number of people it is being made for but on the quantity of clarified butter available:[10]

Gaziler Helvası (Warriors' Helva)

Now let us come to helva in army cauldrons:

The number of people should never be considered. If you have more than 15 *kıyyes* of clarified butter then this should be divided between two cauldrons. If you have just 15 *kıyyes* then prepare the helva in one cauldron. If this method is followed exactly the result will be excellent. Put the clarified butter into the cauldron and set it over the fire. When it begins to scorch toss a spoonful of water into the cauldron and when the sizzling stops remove from the heat. Let it cool slightly. Then two soldiers should rub the flour between their fingers as they pour it into the cauldron, while another stirs it with a large wooden beater. When it is the consistency of thick yogurt set the cauldron back on the heat. The heat should be low. Be careful not to let the bottom scorch. As before, when the right stage is reached pour some of the boiling syrup from the other cauldron and stir, and then five minutes later pour in some more. In short, if this method is followed the helva will be delicious. But the syrup must be hot or the fat will be exuded [from the roux], and to avoid that care alone is sufficient.

Gaziler helvası was a favourite pudding at winter gatherings known as *helva sohbeti* (literally 'helva conversation').[11] Nuts could be added, but this was not common, according to Mahmud Nedim. Sometimes a few almonds were added merely for the purpose of testing whether the roux was ready by their colour. Below is the oldest of all *gaziler helvası* recipes, from a manuscript dating from the sixteenth or seventeenth century:[12]

Helvâ-i Gaziler

Take 400 [*dirhems*] of honey, 200 of butter, and as much flour as necessary. After the butter has boiled, slowly add the flour until it becomes like batter. Then add a blanched almond and cook until the almond reddens. If no almond is added then the way to tell whether it is cooked sufficiently is that it emits a fragrance and also by bubbles that appear if you take some up in a spoon. Then tip the rapidly boiling sugar or honey syrup into the pan at one go, and when it is blended well, remove from the heat. After it has cooled rub between the hands so that it crumbles. It will be a lovely white colour.

Another version of this was known as *mülûkî gaziler helvası*, *mülûkî* meaning 'fit for kings'. And so it was: double the regular amount of sugar or honey was used, a huge quantity of almonds was added, and after cooking in the pan this helva was pressed into a deep baking tray and baked:[13]

Mülûkî Gaziler Helvası
½ *kıyye* of butter
1 *kıyye* flour
300 *dirhem*s milk (just under a litre)
1 *kıyye* honey
2 *kıyye*s almonds

First cook *gaziler helvası* by the usual method. However, the sugar or honey should be twice the ordinary quantity. Then add an abundance of almonds. If you prepare 3 *kıyye*s of helva then use 3 *kıyye*s of blanched almonds, which should be roasted in a pan for a while and then crushed to small pieces in a mortar before adding to the helva. Mix well and then place in a deep baking tray, pressing it firmly down. Cut into diamond shapes or any shape you please, and then bake in the oven as for *revani*[14] until the surface browns. Remove and arrange on a dish and it is ready to eat.

Other varieties of home-made helva were prepared with starch, semolina or rice flour instead of flour. The simplest form of starch helva was known as *asûde helvası*, and a variety with a crumbly texture as *reşidiyye helvası*. In 1539 'reşidiyye with almonds and saffron' was served to guests at the circumcision banquet for the sons of Süleyman the Magnificent and for this special occasion the helva was made with the following ingredients for 'one dishful' (sufficient for at least ten people seated around the same table): 2.5 *vukıyye*s of starch, 1 *vukıyye* of butter, 1.5 *vukıyye*s of honey or sugar, 100 *dirhem*s of almonds and 2 *dirhem*s of saffron.[15] No almonds or saffron are mentioned in eighteenth- and nineteenth-century recipes for *reşidiye helvası*, but some call instead for rose water, ground cinnamon and cloves to be sprinkled on top before serving.[16] Like *mülûkî gaziler helvası*, *reşidiyye helvası* could also be baked in the oven until the surface turned 'like agate'.

A variety of starch helva made with honey was known in Istanbul as *leb-i dilber* ('lover's lips' or 'lips of the beloved'), presumably shaped to suit the name. This helva is among foods served at a banquet celebrating the Ottoman conquest of Rhodes in 1522.[17] A story ascribes its invention to the Macedonian town of Zikhni (today in Greece), where it was known by the curious name *yengem duymasın helvası* ('don't-let-my-aunt-know helva') or *ninem duymasın helvası* ('don't-let-my-granny-know helva'):[18]

> A bad-tempered old woman in Zikhni had a married son and a daughter. When her daughter and daughter-in-law asked to make helva the old woman refused and they decided to steal the key to the larder. They secretly took butter, honey, starch and a pan. Because they were very young and inexperienced and ignorant of the art of making helva, they asked God for aid and cooked it. The helva was admired by everyone, and years later it is famous and still talked of.

Memuniye was a festive type of helva served at palace banquets and on religious holidays. It was made from rice flour, clarified butter, milk, sugar or honey, and in some cases shredded chicken breast, then rolled into small balls and fried (see Plate 9). According to Şirvânî's recipes dating from around 1430, the helva balls were sprinkled with powdered sugar, sliced almonds, and rose water flavoured with musk.[19] *Memuniye* was made with chicken breast for Sultan Mehmed II (1451–81),[20] but without the meat for a palace banquet in the early sixteenth century.[21]

Memuniye derived from an Arab dish named *ma'mûniyya* after the Abbasid caliph Ma'mun.[22] In its original

18. Palace confectioner carrying a dish of hot helva with the steam pouring out of the holes in the lid ('Un Halvadji', Comte de Choiseul-Gouffier, *Voyage pittoresque de la Grèce*, Paris, 1782).

form this was never fried, and was in fact identical to the Turkish pudding *tavukgöğüsü* (rice flour pudding made with chicken breast) that is still popular today.[23] The *ma'mûniyya* of Arabic cuisine made its way into western European cuisines at an early stage, under such names as *mammonia* and *mawmenny*.[24] In Turkey this pudding took on a dual persona, the original version becoming known as *tavukgöğüsü*, while *memuniye* became fried helva balls.[25] This would explain why Meninski defined *memuniye* as *panis saccharites* (sweet bun) or *marzapane* (perhaps in reference to the version of *memuniye* containing almonds for which Şirvânî gives a recipe) in his dictionary dated 1780.[26] A later Turkish–English dictionary follows Meninski's definition: 'A kind of shortbread, marchpane'.[27]

Purchases of '*memuniye* spoons' or '*memuniye* moulds' in the fifteenth and sixteenth centuries show us that the balls of helva were shaped using a special implement, probably something like a modern ice-cream scoop.[28] Fifteen of these were purchased for a banquet given to the Austrian ambassador in 1573.

Helva-yı hâkânî ('princely helva') was 'the sultan of all helvas';[29] in other words it did not get its name because it was eaten by rulers, but as a ruler in its own right. This helva was made with equal quantities of flour, starch and rice flour cooked with butter, to which boiled honey or sugar and boiling milk were added. Pieces of the helva were then shaped like dates and sometimes mixed with clotted cream.[30]

Sabunî helva, which had a consistency somewhat like Turkish delight, was made of starch, honey, butter or sesame oil and almonds. This was sometimes made by professional confectioners. A red-tinted version made in Istanbul in the nineteenth century was called *et helvası*.[31] This is another helva with a long history that can be traced back to the Abbasid period.[32]

The city of Bursa was famous for *ishakiye helvası*, made with ground rice. Ground almonds and sometimes milk were added, and when the helva was cooked it was moulded using coffee cups.[33] The author of an eighteenth-century cookery manual writes that when he was living in Bursa in 1730, he and Arapzâde Abdürrahman Efendi were invited to the home of a local dervish and there ate *ishakiye helvası* whose flavour was unsurpassed.[34] He asked his host for the recipe and recorded it in his manual. Below is Türâbî Efendi's English recipe published in London in 1864.[35]

İshâkiyye

Put on the fire a stewpan with a pound of fresh butter: when melted, add gradually a pound and a half of rice-flour, with three-quarters of a pound of almonds, skinned and well pounded, and keep stirring until it becomes a gold colour; then immediately add a pint of boiling milk, with two pints of boiling syrup, which you have previously prepared of loaf sugar and water . . . instantly put the cover over, and let it remain for five minutes; then stir it well with a fork, dish it up in moulds the size of a small teacup, letting it bear the impression of the mould, and serve with some white sugar sifted over.

As we have already seen in the case of *gaziler helvası*, helva had spiritual significance in Turkish culture, above all as a funeral food. Flour or semolina helva is still made for funerals and memorial services, hence such regional vernacular names as 'soul helva' or 'pick and spade helva'.[36]

Helva could also be a festive food, served on occasions such as guild ceremonies for journeymen graduating to the rank of master[37] and at meals held to reconcile friends on bad terms, as described by the historian Ahmed Câvid around 1800:[38] 'When friends are estranged their friends arrange a reconciliation meal. They cook helva and invite them both to dinner, and persuade them to patch up their quarrel.'

In Istanbul it was customary to eat *un helvası* on the last evening of Ramazan to mark the beginning of the three-day *bayram*. Abdülaziz Bey tells us that in grand houses the cooks would prepare *un helvası* decorated with gold leaf and serve it on a tray with burning tapers around the edge.[39]

Semolina helva made with milk was a staple of Ottoman-era picnics in woods and meadows along the Golden Horn and the Bosphorus. Picnickers also cooked spit-roasted lambs, dug pit ovens to bake lamb or cook kebabs in sealed earthenware jars, and ate the meat accompanied by vineleaf dolma.[40]

Home-made helvas are always at their most delicious when eaten fresh and warm. Semolina helva, wisps of steam still rising from the golden mound, is served in Ankara's tripe restaurants in the early hours of the morning. In the Ottoman period earthenware or copper helva dishes had domed lids pierced with holes to let the steam out while keeping the heat in, so the helva did not become damp. The palace cook shown in the engraving (Fig. 18) is holding a helva dish, with the steam wafting out of the holes in the lid.

RECIPES

HELVÂ-YI TER (Şirvânî, c. 1430)[41]

Take one *nüki* (641.5 grams) of honey, one *nüki* of butter. Place the clarified butter in a pan, let it melt and then stir in sufficient flour that has been passed through a fine sieve. Cook the roux on a gentle fire until it is no longer raw. Place the honey to melt on a hot fire and add 1 *dirhem* of saffron that has been soaked in a spoonful of water, and when the honey boils add the roux and stir until it is well blended, then remove from the fire and place on trays, bring it and let them eat.

HELVÂ-YI HÂKÂNÎ (Anonymous, eighteenth century)[42]

The name *hâkânî* means that this helva is the sultan of all helvas. When well cooked it is a delicate and pleasing helva. There are three or four kinds. The most famous of all is this: Take 200 *dirhem*s of pure white flour, 200 *dirhem*s of wheat starch and 200 *dirhem*s of rice flour. Clarify 1 *vukıyye* of butter, then place on a slow fire and add the different flours, stirring unceasingly with a wooden spoon. When the roux is cooked, add 3 *vukıyye*s of honey or clarified sugar syrup and 2 *vukıyye*s of milk, all of which should be boiling. Cover the pan tightly and let it stand for a quarter of an hour, then uncover, stir place on plates and let it be eaten.

DILBER DUDAĞI (Anonymous, 1828)[43]

Taking as your measure a container of 1 *kıyye*, take two measures of honey and one of water and two fingers less than a measure of clarified butter. Place these in a pan. Then take a flat and loose measure of wheat starch and one of water, blend the starch well in the water, then stir it into the honey. Cook it, stirring with a wooden spoon. Eventually the fat will sweat. Then pour off the fat once or twice. When the helva does not stick to the palate and has a gum-like consistency it is cooked. Then spread the helva in a baking tray and send it to the bakery. Bake until the surface is golden like agate. Mix some ground blanched almonds with granulated sugar, spread this on top, and sprinkle flower water and rose water over. Serve.

16 *Helva:* Commercial Varieties

TAHIN HELVASI

FOREMOST AMONG THE PRINCIPAL VARIETIES of helva made by commercial confectioners is *tahin helvası* or *tahine*,[1] made with ground sesame seeds. This is the commonest type in Turkey and the Middle East; today it is often mass produced in large factories, although small confectionery firms still exist in the provinces.

A vivid description of confectioners making *tahin helvası* in late nineteenth-century Istanbul is given by Pretextat Lecomte:[2]

> The manufacturing process for Turkish *halva* is rather curious. It makes use of a large basin approximately one metre and forty centimetres in diameter; this basin is fitted into a low wall which forms the furnace; close to the ground is contrived a cavity where one puts the wood which is used for cooking.
>
> Let us see the workmen at work. Above the basin hangs a large beater at least two metres long suspended by chains from the ceiling. Three men are there, waiting. The basin is filled with sugar, together with a certain quantity of water, the fire is lit, and soon the sugar starts to dissolve. Suddenly, one of the men seizes the large beater and begins to turn it about in the basin, regularly and rhythmically. As the beater alternately strikes the opposite sides of the basin it produces a sound which appears to mesmerize the craftsman and allows him to regulate his blows.
>
> Nothing is so fascinating as the image projected onto the area of bare wall which is animated by this great figure silhouetted in the reflection of the fire, following an enormous arc as it swings vigorously from right to left. Rap, rap; while in the background two men wait behind in silence. All at once one of them

moves forward, stands behind the other as he works, follows the movements of his body for a few seconds, then abruptly seizes the beater with two hands; rap, rap. Work continues in this way, the workmen taking turns at the task; which continues for three hours without respite, the beats continuing monotonously at a steady rate. A moment's cessation, an irregularity or a change of movement can compromise the desired result irremediably. The ingredients are water and sugar, of little complexity in effect, but the handling admits of no negligence. When the sugar is sufficiently concentrated and beaten, oil of sesame is added, *tahin* in Turkish; and finally when thoroughly mixed, and the preparation is ready, it is poured into an untinned, smaller copper basin, with a diameter of approximately forty-five centimetres; a little oil of sesame is added and the paste allowed to cool sufficiently until a workman can work it by hand without burning. This last task takes half an hour, after which the paste is left to cool; then it is removed from the mould. The resulting semispherical mass of *halva* is sold for four and a half to five piastres the ocque (approximately 1 fr. the kilo). This *halva* is despatched to all the interior, in round boxes containing one hundred drammes to half an ocque (a hundred and twenty grams or two hundred and forty grams approximately).

The only part of the process that has escaped the eye of Pretextat Lecomte is the addition of a decoction of 'helva root'. Perhaps the confectioners chose to deceive him as to the nature of the 'water' added to the sugar, which must have been a decoction of helva root. Helva root is obtained from five species of *Gypsophila*, out of around fifty native to Turkey, and has been an important item of trade and export for centuries, although the amount has been decreasing in recent decades because of diminishing populations of the wild plants.[3]

19. The dried roots of *Gypsophila* used to make *tahin helvası* (sesame helva), *koz helvası* (nougat) and *nâtif*. They are boiled in water and the decoction then beaten to form a white froth which is used as a substitute for egg white (Photograph: Mustafa Dorsay).

British archaeologist Charles Fellows saw camels loaded with helva root near the town of Elmalı in southwestern Turkey in 1840:[4] 'I observe camels loaded with roots, resembling very fine horse-radish (the *Silene*): this is found plentifully here, and used in making a sweetmeat; but it is principally obtained as a substitute for soap, and used in the raw state.' The root contains saponin, which causes the decoction to foam when beaten, hence the confusion with soapwort (*Saponaria officinalis*), which also contains saponin but is not used for helva making.[5]

The method of making *tahin helvası* is much the same today as described by Pretextat Lecomte, except that the laborious stirring of the helva root decoction and sugar is now done by machine, and the helva is prepared in rectangular instead of hemispherical blocks or the thin slabs described below by Olivier.

Going back further in time to the early nineteenth century we have another expert witness, the Bavarian confectioner Friedrich Unger, who tells us that helva root was a substitute for egg white in low-priced helva made by confectioners in Istanbul in 1835.[6] The helva root was boiled in water, drained, and fresh water added. Then the roots were removed and the decoction boiled until it became glutinous. Unger explains that this water was then mixed with 'bad honey or beckmesi (*pekmez*)'[7] until reaching the correct consistency, and finally mixed with *tahin*.

Fine helva, on the other hand was made with large quantities of egg whites, white honey and white sugar:[8]

Fine Halwa

Take 7 *occa*s of white honey and approximately 2 *occa*s of caster sugar, place this mixture on the fire and skim it thoroughly to remove all impurities.

Put this in a pan walled-in at a slant, make a gentle fire underneath, so that you can endure holding your hand on the pan, and start to stir with circular movements with a big spatula (approximately 5 feet long and furnished with a round disc at the base). As soon as the honey starts to thicken, beat the whipped whites of 100 eggs into the mixture, and then stir with the abovementioned spatula until the honey is thick . . .

Brush a warm pan with *dahin*, weigh 3 *occa*s of *agda* [boiled sugar syrup], pour it in, and with your hand work approximately 2 *occa*s of *dahin* into the aforementioned *agda* while it is still hot. In this way the *dahin-halwa* is ready.

As soon as these two basic ingredients are combined, it is laid on marble slabs or on boards to be sold.

As this recipe reveals, *tahin helvası* is essentially nougat mixed with *tahin* (sesame seed paste), which radically alters the texture from brittle to crumbly.

Charles White, who visited Istanbul in 1844, reported that the finest type of *tahin helvası* was flavoured with rose water, lemon juice or white mulberry juice;[9] these were probably types made by confectioners at the palace and in wealthy households. *Tahin helvası* made with *pekmez* used to be widely made in Turkey, and is still made today in some places, such as the town of Ermenek in Karaman.[10]

French naturalist and agricultural expert Guillaume Antoine Olivier was another traveller who watched *tahin helvası* being made during his journey around the Ottoman Empire in the 1790s:[11]

> Troas affords few vines, though the rising grounds and hills are very fit for that culture; but the inhabitants are not there accustomed to make wine. The grapes are employed in making a confection, called *petmés* [*pekmez*] in Turkish, of which the Orientals make a very great consumption during the whole year: they put it into ragouts; they employ it, in lieu of sugar and honey, in most of their choice dishes; in short they make of it, with sesamum reduced to paste, a sort of *nogat*, or almond-like cake, which would not be despised in Europe. I saw a great deal of it at Constantinople, at the Dardanelles, and in most of the towns of Turkey. The process consists in mixing those two substances in boilers exposed to a moderate fire, and in stirring it about without interruption, with a large wooden spatula, till the mixture be sufficiently thickened. It is poured on large slabs of marble or sheets of copper, and by its cooling, are obtained cakes which are made an inch and a half in thickness. This nogat is sold retail, at five or six sous a pound.

Tahin helvası was a staple food almost everywhere in Turkey. A slice eaten with bread made an easily prepared, nourishing and high-calorie meal for manual labourers and travellers,[12] and was indispensable for Orthodox and Gregorian Christians, who were not allowed to eat meat and dairy products during Lent and other fasts of between one and six weeks' duration, nor on Wednesdays and Fridays on a regular basis: totalling more than half the year in all. Pretextat Lecomte remarked:[13]

> There are certain times of the year at which the *halva* becomes, so to speak, the only food of the Christian and Armenian population. Two pennies' worth of halva and two pennies' worth of bread and you have a Lenten breakfast that is simple and inexpensive.

When Charles MacFarlane and his companion arrived in the Aegean town of Turgutlu late one evening in 1828, 'all the *kibabjis*[14] in the bazaars had already disposed of their savoury edibles to the hungry children of the prophet, and had not a morsel left for two equally hungry Ghiaours. He could get nothing but some *khalva*, a detestable Turkish sweetmeat.'[15]

Koz Helvası (Nougat)

Koz helvası is the ancestor of *tahin helvası*. Both were made with honey or sugar syrup and either egg whites or helva root. The Turkish name *koz helvası* literally means 'walnut helva', but is also used as a generic term for nougat containing any kind of nut, or even no nuts at all. If made with a soft rather than brittle texture it was known as *sakız helvası* (mastic helva). On account of its white colour a still more ancient name was *ak helva* (white helva), a term which is found, for example, in a Turkish medical book written by the physician Ibn Şerif around 1425.[16] The earliest recipes for nougat are found in a tenth-century Arabic cookbook, where a syrup of boiled honey and egg whites is mixed with almonds, pistachios, hazelnuts, walnuts, coconut, pine nuts, sesame seeds or hemp seeds.[17] This nougat was called *nâtif*, a term which was also used for a variety of nut brittle sweets made without egg white.[18] Later on, sugar and fruit molasses appear as alternatives to honey as in, for example, a *nâtif* recipe in the fifteenth-century Arabic cookery book *Kitabü't-Tibâha*.[19]

Plain nougat, *ak helva*, was served at palace banquets,[20] and features on a list of retail prices for the year 1640.[21] The pistachio helva and almond helva served at a palace banquet in 1539[22] could have been nut brittle or nougat.

In 1553 the German traveller Hans Dernschwam, who accompanied an Austrian embassy to Turkey, watched confectioners in Istanbul prepare nougat:[23]

> Among other things there is a kind of white confection, which is called *halwa* made of almonds, honey and egg white. They cook it in a big pan over a glowing fire, it is tough like a glue, they stir with a stick of wood, it becomes so hard afterwards that they must cut it into pieces with a strong knife. This is regarded as a delicious confection and marcipan. When one gets hold of it, one cannot have enough of it.

From this description it appears that Dernschwam was unacquainted with nougat before tasting it Istanbul, so we can tentatively date the spread of nougat into Central Europe to the late sixteenth century. Nougat found its way from

Turkey to Austria, probably via Hungary, since, as mentioned earlier, in both countries nougat is today still known as 'Turkish honey' – *törökmez* in Hungary and *Türkischer Honig* in Austria, where it is sold in the form of a fairground treat on a stick.[24]

In France the belief that nougat was invented in Marseille in the sixteenth century suggests that it was actually introduced from Turkey,[25] since Marseille was the main port of entry for Turkish exports into western Europe (Turkish delight later arrived in France via Marseille in the nineteenth century).[26]

In Istanbul nougat and nut brittle of various kinds – the most popular in the nineteenth century being *susam helvası* (boiled honey or sugar mixed with sesame seeds) – was sold in the streets on rectangular or circular trays. The seller was also equipped with a small pair of scales and a hammer to break the brittle helva into pieces:[27]

> Sellers of *susam halwa*, who in addition quite often offer other finer *halwa* types for sale, are usually Albanian boys from 12 to 14 years of age. On their heads they carry a long rectangular board, three sides of which have raised edges. On this board there is a piece of the coveted *halwa*, usually looking very disgusting, often a small pair of scales and a dirty chopper.
>
> Their dress is usually as unclean as possible, and their horrible cry: 'Hălwā Mĭlĕŏ Hălwā, Hălwā Mĭlĕŏ' sounds the whole day long. They are also commonly found in Greece. They obtain their wares from the shops of the *halwadschian* [confectioners].

Pretextat Lecomte also describes the helva vendors:[28]

> Now we come to *halva*, which is a nougat of the country. There are two kinds of *halva*: that which is manufactured and sold by the Albanians, composed of worked sugar, mixed then with nuts; another kind is made with sugar simply boiled and very concentrated, that has not been beaten; this sugar is poured onto a marble with roasted pistachios and hazelnuts, and allowed to crystallize.

Another type of nougat was *müdeccel helvası* prepared in thin crisp sheets and sold in the district of Galata in Istanbul in the eighteenth century.[29] Known as *kavred* in Persian, it is mentioned by the Persian poet Bushaq of Shiraz in the fifteenth century. A version of this, called *yaprak helvası* (leaf helva), is still made in the town of Safranbolu in northern Turkey. Around twenty of the nougat sheets are sandwiched together with ground walnuts and cut into rectangular pieces.

20. One of the wafer moulds used at Topkapı Palace in Istanbul. On one face is a seal of Solomon motif, with hatching on the other (Courtesy of Topkapı Palace Museum, TSM 25/3058; photograph: Hadiye Cangökçe).

21. A cast-iron wafer mould with a ship motif on one face and a bird on the other. The mould weighs 7 kilograms and is 79 centimetres long (Photograph: Hakan Ezilmez – YKKS).

KÂĞIT HELVASI

Literally meaning 'paper helva', *kâğıt helvası*, consists of wafers 20 centimetres in diameter sandwiched together with soft nougat. In the past the nougat was mixed with roasted almonds or pistachio nuts.

Wafers of this kind, made by pouring batter onto a circular iron mould incised with designs on both faces, can be traced back to the twelfth century, and claims have been made that a wafer iron dating from much earlier was discovered at Carthage in the early twentieth century.[30] Wafer moulds continued to be made by blacksmiths in Turkey until the 1930s, and traditional wafers were still being made with these moulds over open fires until about thirty years ago.[31]

The earliest recipe for the soft nougat used to sandwich the wafers together dates from the eighteenth century, and is titled *mülûki sakız helvası*, meaning 'soft nougat fit for a king':[32]

22. The shadow puppet character Karagöz is selling shares in the Turkish Maritime Lines company. When Hacıvat asks him why the shares are in the form of *kâğıt helvası* wafers, Karagöz replies that at least you can eat wafers. Presumably in 1910 the shares had slumped in value (*Karagöz*, 191 (11 May 1910), p. 1).

Mülûki Sakız Helvası

Take 100 *dirhem*s of sugar, 10 *dirhem*s of helva root, 25 *dirhem*s of flour and 15 *dirhem*s of clarified butter. Cook the flour with the clarified butter as if preparing helva and set aside. Then boil the helva root in 50–60 *dirhem*s of water and, straining off the liquid, boil it with sugar until it is the consistency of pulled sugar. Then pour onto a marble slab or tray and when nearly cool gradually work in the roasted flour little by little, then pull it on a hook until it turns sufficiently white. Mix with sufficient blanched pistachio nuts. Obtain a sufficient quantity of the white wafers used for *sakız helvası*, spread the helva between them in the same way, or alternatively cut it into small morsels. In short, do as you wish and eat them. This is *sakız helvası* fit for a king.

Another later recipe for *sakız helvası* calls for cutting the wafer sandwich into small squares or slices.[33]

Sadly, today *kâğıt helvası* is mass produced using the almost tasteless wafers used for cheap ice-cream cones.

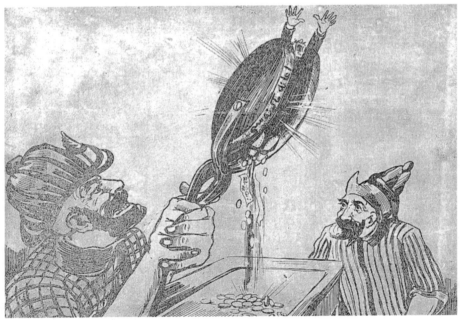

23. Cartoon published in the satirical newspaper *Karagöz* in 1913 showing a rich man being squeezed in a wafer mould to force him to make charity contributions. The Balkan Wars had just ended and many people were suffering from hunger (*Karagöz*, 547 (20 August 1913), p. 1).

BULAMA

Egg whites or helva root were also beaten with *pekmez* to make a confection called *bulama, çalma pekmez* or *telbis*.[34] Like *tahin helvası, bulama* required long and constant beating. *Bulama* so closely resembles honey, that in the past it was used as an adulterant.[35]

A nineteenth-century recipe describes the process of making *bulama* as follows:[36]

> . . . when the boiled molasses has cooled to the point where the hand can bear the heat, two or three people must beat it for about two hours until it is transformed into a white foam. Then ground *kurs*,[37] musk in the pod, cinnamon and cloves are added and stirred in. Fill into small jars.

During his journey on foot across Turkey in 1912 the British traveller W.J. Childs came across a woman making *bulama* near the city of Amasya:[38]

> In this land are curious processes of manufacture: of preparing food, of cultivation, and the like, which leave you wondering by what series of accidents they were discovered. One of these strange processes I saw now. An even, beating sound came from beside the road; I knew what it was, but had never yet seen the operation that caused it. Not many European men, even in Turkey, see a Turkish woman making *pekmez*; but this was the sight I saw on peering cautiously through the willows. *Pekmez* is grape juice, boiled, and then prepared by beating, which changes it from a thin watery food to a thick partially-crystallized substance like clouded honey, but of a colour nearly as dark as treacle. These methods are fairly obvious; the curious part is that the beating must be done with the open hand, and nothing else. You cannot make *pekmez* by beating with wood, or bone, or metal, so you are told. And further, once the beating has begun it must go on to the end without ceasing, or the *pekmez* will be spoiled – there must be no cessation of blows at all. After the grape-harvest, therefore, Turkish towns and villages resound with the making of *pekmez*. You hear beating all day and beating all night. For the process is a long one – so long that the women and girls take turns at the work, and beat until their hands are blistered and painful. It is said that sometimes the labour lasts a day and night. What I saw now behind the bushes was a woman kneeling on the ground before a shallow, open bowl nearly two feet across. With arms bare and open hands she was steadily slapping the contents, and by her half-closed eyes and look of resignation I supposed she had not only been at the work some time, but that the obstinate stuff was still far from being *pekmez*.

In the eighteenth century tiny boxes of *bulama* sold in grocery shops were a favourite with children,[39] and *bulama* is still sold today in circular chipwood boxes. When visiting the southeastern Turkish city of Gaziantep in the 1570s, physician and botanist Dr Leonhart Rauwolff saw two types of *pekmez* and reported that the thick variety was the most sought after and exported in 'little barrels':[40]

> The Turks not being allowed to drink wine by their law . . . boyl the juice of the grapes up to the consistence of honey which they call *pachmatz*, chiefly these that live at Andeb [Gaziantep], a town between Bir and Nisib. They have two sorts of this rob [syrup], one very thick, and the other somewhat thinner, the former is the best, wherefore they put it up into little barrels to send into other countries, the latter they use themselves, mix it sometimes with water, and give it to drink (instead of a julep) to their servants, sometimes they put it into little cups, to dip their bread in it, as if it were honey and so eat it.

Köpük Helvası

In many parts of Turkey a white foamy sweetmeat made of sugar syrup (or in the past grape juice syrup) whipped with a decoction of helva root is made. Known as *köpük helvası* ('foam helva') this is the basis for *koz helvası* and *tahin helvası*, and so sometimes called 'raw helva'.[41] In Arab countries and Central Asia, however, this foam is known as *nâtif*, which was the term for nougat and nut brittle used in Arabic cookery books written between the tenth and fourteenth centuries.[42] All these early recipes include egg white, and none makes mention of helva root.

Claudia Roden tells us that in Syria this sweet foam is eaten as a sweet,[43] and the same custom is widespread in Central Asia, where it is known as *nishala* or *rishala* by the Uighurs, *nishalda* by the Kirgiz, Kazaks and Uzbeks, and as *nishalla* by the Tajiks.[44] In Tajikistan and Uzbekistan it is made with either helva root or egg whites.

In Turkey's southeastern cities of Mersin, Antakya and Kilis *köpük helvası* is used as a topping for semolina shortcakes stuffed with nuts known as *kerebiç*, which are eaten on festive occasions.

17 Keten Helva (Pişmâniye)

Here comes the Persian confectioner
Bringing his *keten helva*
Making everybody happy
From their pockets luring money.

Mint water mint candy
It is you I really fancy
Red and white together
In strands my *keten helva*.

Music-hall song (c. 1900)[1]

KETEN HELVA IS THE MOST fascinating of all Turkish sweets, in terms of the complex method of creating it, its unusual texture and interesting history. Appropriately, no other Turkish sweet has been known by so many different names: *pişmâniye, peşmek, peşmânî, tel helvası, telteli, çekme helvası, depme helvası, saray helvası, külük helvası* and *met helvası. Pişmâniye, peşmek* and *peşmânî* remind us of its Persian origins, all deriving from the Persian word *pashm* meaning wool, in reference to the texture of fine strands. This texture also inspired the Turkish name *keten helva* ('linen helva'), the Greek name *molia tis grias* ('old woman's hair')[2] and the Chinese name 'dragon's beard'. How this sweetmeat found its way to China is as yet unexplained, perhaps it was via the Silk Road during the period of Mongol rule.[3]

Keten helva is often likened to candy floss, but although both have a texture of fine strands, the resemblance ends there. Ingredients, flavour and method are all quite different, as we shall see.

Keten helva is made in three stages: first flour and melted butter are stirred over heat for nearly an hour. Then sugar syrup is boiled to crack, pulled until it turns white and satiny, and shaped into a ring about 20 centimetres in diameter. Now comes the stage that requires the greatest skill. The pulled sugar ring is generously sprinkled with roasted flour and placed in the centre of a large circular tray. Three, four or more people sit around the tray, place both hands on the ring and squeeze it, simultaneously moving it in an anticlockwise direction. This requires a flawless rhythmic movement so that the ring does not become thinner in some parts and eventually break, ruining all the work. The ring gradually expands and when it is nearly as large as the tray, it is folded over in a figure of eight and the process repeated. More flour is sprinkled on at intervals and gradually the flour and pulled sugar blend together. Each time the ring is folded, the number of strands doubles. The ring should be folded at least ten times, making 1,024 strands (1, 2, 4, 8, 16, 32, 64, 128, 256, 512, 1024).[4] In the province of Adapazarı home-made *keten helva* is folded fifteen to sixteen times (making a total of 32,768 or 65,536 strands).[5] In nineteenth-century Bayburt, however, it was customary to fold it forty times, which raises the strand count to an astonishing 1.1 trillion (1,099,511,627,776 to be precise), and gives a very fine thistledown texture.[6] The finer the strands, the better the keeping qualities.

Very few of the recipes for *keten helva* make any attempt to describe the folding process in meaningful detail, because, as one cookery writer put it in 1925, 'experience has shown that it is impossible to make it from written instructions, without watching this helva being made and being together with those making it.'[7] When the helva was ready it was divided or cut into portions. The finer variety would be pressed into a shallow dish and then cut into lozenges. Sometimes it was spread in two layers, with a layer of finely ground nuts mixed with allspice in the centre.[8] Today in İzmit and Gaziantep it is formed into small beehive shapes.[9]

The earliest recipe for *keten helva* dates from the first half of the fifteenth century. This Turkish recipe uses clarified tail fat from the fat-tailed sheep and honey instead of butter and sugar, and glosses over the complexities of blending the pulled honey with the roasted flour:[10]

24. *Keten helva* made commercially in Mudurnu. This variety is folded over forty times, and the result is as fine as thistledown (Photograph: Sinan Çakmak).

Pişmânî Helva

The method is to place some clarified strained tail fat in a pan, bring it to the boil and then to take some fine white wheat flour that has been sieved through a silk sieve and let one person add sufficient quantity of this to the fat while constantly stirring with a helva maker's beater, and keep on stirring until the roasted flour is cooked to exactly the right degree. Then place the roasted flour in a large tray, wash the pan in hot water to remove the scum and grease. Put some honey in the pan over a gentle fire and stir constantly with a helva maker's beater until it turns to *akide* [syrup boiled to crack]. Remove from the heat, pour into a tray and let it cool down a little until you can touch it with your hand without burning. Pull the *akide* until it turns white, and heat up the tray slightly. Shape the *akide* into rings and blend it with the roasted flour until it forms strands like fine hair. Then spread it out in the tray, pressing with your fist and cut it with a knife, place it in a container and store until you wish to eat it.

Keten helva was served at Ottoman palace banquets in the early sixteenth century, such as that given in 1522 to celebrate the conquest of Rhodes, and the magnificent circumcision celebrations for the sons of Süleyman the Magnificent in 1539.[11] We know that in the 1580s *keten helva* was being made by a specialist class of confectioners, since in the guild procession of 1582, the *peşmine helva* makers (*cemâ'at-i halvâ-yi peşmîne kârân*) marched as a separate group, following the *pelte* makers.[12]

Pretextat Lecomte watched *keten helva* being made in Istanbul at the end of the nineteenth century. His account has some inaccuracies, but this is not surprising in view of his unfamiliarity with the complex method:[13]

There is yet another kind of *halva* called *Ketan halva*, which is as to say, threads of flax; in vulgar speech it is called 'old woman's hair'.[14]

This *halva* presents, in its tenuity and its whiteness, of a shining lustre, the appearance of those silver-plated wires that waft in the wind during campaigns and which are so poetically called *les fils de la Vierge* ['threads of the Virgin', i.e. tinsel].

Ketan halva demands a very long and complicated preparation lasting six to seven hours. When the sugar has melted and reached a certain degree of concentration, it is placed in a *tepsi* or large round tray. Around this tray is put pure white flour which has been lightly roasted in hot melted butter. The concentrated sugar is turned around the tray, at a certain distance from the edges; one then imparts a turning movement to it, the purpose of which is to make it gradually take up a certain quantity of butter and flour; this operation continues until the mixture of butter and flour has been completely absorbed. During this process of manipulation, a certain heat is maintained under the tray to prevent it cooling; finally the paste is worked lengthily, pulling and pulling again, bringing it back again, drawing again until the sugar is separated into fine filaments having the appearance of white silk. In addition to the Turks, the Persians also excel in the manufacture of this confection.

Just how difficult it is to make *keten helva* is shown by the fact that in earlier centuries it was one of the dishes used to test a cook's skill.[15] Yet despite its complexity *keten helva* was not the preserve of professionals but was widely made at home for helva parties held on winter evenings. Until a few decades ago this custom was widespread in provincial towns and cities; now *keten helva* making is rapidly becoming a lost art, remembered only by a few elderly people.

One of the places where *keten helva* is still made at home is the village of Şıhlar, in the Toros Mountains. According to local people, the village was founded in the thirteenth century by a religious scholar called Pirce Alaaddin from Khorasan, who brought the art of making *keten helva* with him to Turkey.

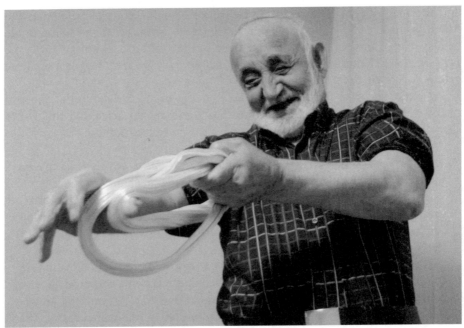

25. Mehmet Veren pulling the rope of sugar in preparation for making *keten helva*. The Veren family of Kastamonu is one of the few Turkish families that still make *keten helva* at home (Photograph: Erhan Veren).

26. Fatma Tokuş and Ayşe Yıldırım of Şıhlar village turning and stretching the rope of honey in the roasted flour (Photograph: Mary Işın).

This story fits what is known about the migration of Turkic people from Khorasan and Bukhara at this period, and places this sweetmeat's origin either in Persia or in an area under Persian influence, as the name *pişmâniye* indicates. In Şıhlar honey is used instead of sugar, which is an interesting survival of early practice, reflecting a time when sugar was an expensive luxury for city dwellers and a rarity in rural and remoter provincial areas of the country. *Keten helva* is traditionally made with grape molasses in the Turkish city of Burdur, giving it a distinctive and delicious fragrance.[16]

In past televisionless days, making a sweet requiring so much skill was a chance for the experts to show off and entertain the other guests, as they watched the ring of sugar transformed into a mass of fine white silky threads. Rhymes, folksongs, jokes, conversation and music were all part of the fun on long winter evenings. Musahipzâde Celâl describes *keten helva* being made at helva parties in the Ottoman period:[17]

The main type of helva made at these parties was *keten helva*. A brightly tinned copper tray large enough to seat eight or ten people around it was brought out and a huge ring of boiled [and pulled] sugar as thick as two wrists was placed on it. Sieved flour [roasted with butter] was heaped in the centre. The experts at making the helva rolled up their sleeves and washed their hands and arms with soap and hot water. They took their places around the tray and recited the prayer to Pir Selmanı Pâk.[18] Then they began to turn the [ring of] hot boiled sugar from right to left, frequently dipping their hands into the flour in the centre. The guests watched as they played music and sang. The boiled sugar was folded over and over again to the accompaniment of folk songs and jokes until it turned into strands of *keten helva*, which was then distributed in handfuls to the guests. Minstrels played as they recited epic legends and songs. Games such as the cup and *tura* were played, and riddles and stories were told.

The following verses are from a twentieth-century poem about making *keten helva* at a helva party in Afyonkarahisar:[19]

> *Let's Pull Helva*
> Tonight we have gathered here in joy
> Come brothers let's pull helva.
> Press the sugar gently, don't break it
> Come friends let's pull helva.
>
> Our helva is sweet and in strands
> Our conversation will be delightful, friends
> Yearning for it on a winter's day in Afyon
> Come friends let's pull helva.

After a long career as a sweet associated with celebrations and parties given by people from all walks of life, from the humblest cottage to the Ottoman palace, *keten helva* is today mass produced by confectionery firms. The process has been partially mechanized, although turning and folding the pulled sugar in the roasted flour still has to be carried out by hand. Fine *keten helva* would keep for weeks if stored in airtight wooden or tin boxes, and could be taken on long journeys.[20] However, any contact with the air or extremes of temperature reduce its shelf life and this has prevented modern factory-made *keten helva* from being exported in significant quantities.

18 *Helva Sohbeti*

Helva Parties

For one or two days let us not mention the tulip
May pleasures be sweet with a helva party
Nedîm (d. 1730)[1]

O N LONG WINTER NIGHTS FRIENDS would hold a gathering called *helva sohbeti* ('helva conversation'), a custom that was widespread at every level of society, from palace circles to provincial towns and villages. Although the custom has long since died out in Istanbul, it lingers on in some other places. Similar winter gatherings of friends, each taking turn to be host, were a Central Asian tradition known as *sugdıç* in the eleventh century.[2]

Another related tradition was communal meals held by associations of artisans and tradesmen known as *ahî*.[3] In 1332 Ibn Battuta was a guest of the local *ahî* association in the town of Ladik, where he was 'served a great banquet with sweetmeats and quantities of fruit'.[4] As at the *helva sohbeti*, sweetmeats were a prominent feature on these occasions, at which each participant either contributed a dish or paid their share of the expenses. In nineteenth-century Istanbul the dishes each person should contribute were sometimes decided by drawing lots.[5] These gatherings, whether among friends or groups of craftsmen, were known as *ârifâne*, *erfâne*, *harfâne* or *irfâne*, names that all derive from the Arabic *harîfâne* ('in the manner of an artisan').[6] In the summer each guild held similar annual gatherings. Tents and food were carried to meadows and parks on the city outskirts, and here the guild members camped for two or three days. The apprentices played games and sports, and the highlight of the event was the ceremony at which journeymen were promoted to master's rank. The last such guild ceremony in Istanbul was held by the horseshoe nail makers in 1898. Hacıbeyzâde Ahmed Muhtâr was a chance witness of this event, and described it years later in the introduction to his cookery book:[7]

> I must confess that in all my life I never came across so enjoyable a gathering and do not expect ever to do so again. The amicability between the members of the guild, who ranged from young men of eighteen or twenty to old men of ninety, the respect of the younger for the elder and the kindliness of the elder towards the younger were impressed on my mind. And I never tired of watching them play traditional Turkish outdoor games like *geçme*, *benzetme*, *atlama*, *esir alma*, *meydan boğçası* and *kırma telli*.[8]

Helva parties were similar in many ways to these *ârifâne* gatherings, except that they were held in winter, and varieties of helva were the main refreshment. The term *helva sohbeti* is first encountered in the seventeenth century; earlier sources describe them as *gece sohbeti* ('evening party') or plain *sohbet* (party). In the Crimea in the seventeenth century they were known as *oda sohbeti* ('room party').[9]

The cosy and intimate atmosphere of a warm room, protecting the friends gathered there from the cold snowy winter night outside, was conducive to relaxed and cheerful chatter. Helva parties frequently featured in poems about winter called *şitaiyye*, as in the following couplet by the eighteenth-century poet Seyyid Vehbî (d. 1736):[10]

> If one winter night party were sold at auction
> I would pay a thousand summer days to purchase it.

Conversation was central to these parties, and the sixteenth-century writer Mustafa Ali expressed the wish that 'every gathering should be flavoured with salt, and every conversation sweetened with sugar.'[11] Eating helva at social gatherings was not just a gastronomic pleasure but a symbol of this sweet conversation.

Other entertainments at helva parties were reciting poetry, singing folk songs and hymns, telling stories and jokes, and playing party games.[12] Of the latter the favourite for centuries was the ring game, which is mentioned in poems by the fifteenth- to sixteenth-century poet Tirsî (d. 1512):[13]

> Play the ring game with your rival at the party tonight
> Stamp the mark on his forehead and cheek all right
>
> . . .

We heard you led the games at last evening's party
One two three black smudges on your face plain to see.

The 'mark' and the 'black smudges' refer to the forfeit of rubbing soot on the face of the loser.[14] In the version of the game played in Edirne the players chanted the following rhyme when the forfeit was inflicted:[15]

Red smudge black smudge
They call me face smudge
You are now a laughing stock
Hey hey ya lelli ya lelli
Poor wretch you're out of luck.

The game is a variation on the triple cup game, using ten coffee cups or coffee cup holders turned upside down, with a ring under one of them. Each team tries to guess where the ring is hidden. Although the game is basically very simple, poker-style strategies to deceive the opposing team, rhymes recited at various points in the game, levelling slurs against one's opponents, a system of winning points, comic forfeits and jokes requiring quick-witted responses made the game both fun and challenging.[16] Forfeits were usually of the ridiculous sort, such as dressing in a fur robe and imitating a dancing bear.[17]

A game unique to Edirne helva parties was the wheat game, which began with the repetition of simple words, but as the game speeded up, each person who made a slip of the tongue was given a nickname, which then had to be memorized by everyone else. To make it more complicated every nickname had its own rhyme:

Keşkek[18] simmering in the pot
The name Donkey Head is my lot.

Not all the rhymes used in these games were polite, and one anonymous eighteenth-century writer complained about 'people who go to winter parties and play vulgar games'.[19]

In court circles professional entertainers were a feature of opulent helva parties: musicians, mimics, story tellers, comedians, poets, singers and dancers.[20] Not everyone appreciated these ostentatious affairs, disliking their stiff and formal atmosphere.[21]

The simplest form of helva party held among friends did not include a meal.[22] The guests arrived after dinner, were served tea or coffee during the evening and finally ate *keten helva* before going home. At grander helva parties the helva was served at a late hour along with fruit, savoury pastries, stuffed turkey and a whole range of puddings.[23] Pickles were often included on the menu because their acidity counterbalanced the sweetness and high butter content of the helva.[24]

Pickles served at helva parties are the subject of the following couplet by Eşref Pasha (1820–94):[25]

> Were it not for your sour face, bitter words and cold behaviour
> Would they ever admit you to the helva party O sufi?

Cabbage pickle was best-loved,[26] and Sultan Selim III (r. 1789–1807) wrote the following tongue-in-cheek eulogy of the cabbage – without which, he declares, no helva party was complete:[27]

> With the arrival of winter the cabbage doth emerge
> Unafraid of cold, a noble vegetable the cabbage.
>
> In shape and size like the mace of King Keykavus,
> Its leaves like giant rose petals nourish us.
>
> Unlike okra threaded on a thousand threads,[28] the cabbage
> May be compared to a lion riding in a carriage.
>
> With joy and pleasure it is a perfect marriage
> No helva party is complete without a cabbage.
>
> İlhamî[29] sings its worth and many praises
> My dear cabbage, dear cabbage, dear cabbage.

Helva was equally indispensable, the favourite variety on these occasions being *keten helva*, whose interesting and complex method of preparation was part of the entertainment. According to Musahipzâde Celâl, the guests played music, sang and cracked jokes while they watched.[30] One of those curious similarities between seemingly unconnected food cultures is between helva parties and taffy-pulling parties, which were traditional in Wales, Canada and the United States.[31]

Helva parties were hosted by turn, and those gathered chose the person who was to hold the next party and informed them of the decision by placing a ball of helva in front of them. This custom went back at least to the sixteenth century, when it is mentioned in an ode to winter by the poet Cinânî (d. 1595):[32]

> At New Year they play with a ball and polo stick
> Just like a helva ball held in a bent finger.

When times were peaceful, soldiers also held helva parties. In the seventeenth century Evliyâ Çelebi tells us that the officers on guard duty at Baghdad Castle invited the city magnates to helva parties on the battlements,[33] at which the guests were entertained with music and singing. Sentries at Van Castle also whiled away the nights with helva parties, illuminating the moats with torches as a precaution against sudden attack. Songs and hymns were sung, and the regimental band would play.[34]

In Istanbul helva parties lost favour as a result of the new fashion for European-style entertainments,[35] but in provincial Turkey the custom survived until relatively recently. If only we could sometimes switch off the television set and spend a winter evening making helva together and playing parlour games.

19 Sucuk and Köfter

SUCUK AND KÖFTER ARE SWEETMEATS made of grape molasses thickened with wheat starch. Grape juice boiled down to a sweet syrup has been made since ancient times. Known as *defrutum* by the Romans, the Turkish name for this syrup is *pekmez*, and it has played an important part in Turkish cuisine for at least one and a half thousand years. Sixth-century Chinese sources record that the Uighur Turkic peoples of Central Asia exported *pekmez* to China, along with dried grapes, wine and fresh table grapes of the famous Mare's Nipple variety.[1] *Pekmez* was an important sweetener long before sugar became widely available, and, being cheaper than honey, it was used by ordinary people in sweet dishes. One of the earliest of such dishes to be recorded is a mixture of roasted meal and *pekmez* described in the eleventh-century Turkish–Arabic dictionary by Mahmud of Kashgar.[2]

Pekmez is still an ingredient of numerous Turkish sweets and puddings today. One of these is *sucuk*, ('sausage'), which consists of strings threaded with walnuts or pistachios dipped into *pekmez* thickened with starch. After several dippings these form knobbly sausages 20–30 centimetres long. In the past *sucuk* was also made with almonds, hazelnuts and raisins.

The earliest account of this sweetmeat is by the French traveller Bertrandon de la Brocquière in 1432, when he visited Afyonkarahisar in Turkey on his way home from the Holy Land:[3]

> They cook also a nice dish with green walnuts. Their manner is to peel them, cut them in two, and put them on a string; then they are besprinkled with boiled wine, which attaches itself to them, and forms a jelly like paste all around them. It is a very agreeable food, especially when a person is hungry.

In the mid-seventeenth century there were forty shops in Istanbul making almond and walnut *sucuk* (also known as *köfter*):[4]

These *köfter* makers thread walnuts and almonds on strings a span in length. They prepare a thick *palude* [grape juice thickened with starch] and dip the strings of walnuts and almonds into this, producing delicious *köfter* resembling those of Antep, which weigh a hundred *dirhem*s each . . . The *köfter* of Antep and Manisa, and that of Eğriboz [Euboea] and Istanbul is delicate and renowned everywhere.

Sucuk made in Antep, the city known today as Gaziantep, is as famous today as it was in the seventeenth century, when it was exported on camels to Arabia, Persia and India.[5] Other places famous for this confection at this period were Aydıncık,[6] Gelibolu (Gallipoli) and Malatya.[7] Wherever grapes were grown, *sucuk* was made, and still is today. Although commonly made with grape juice, it can also be made with mulberry juice, as it is in Gümüşhane in northeast Turkey, and one Ottoman source mentions a version made with plum juice.

Robert Walsh, an English chaplain who lived in Turkey in the early nineteenth century, describes *sucuk* as 'a long roll like a black-pudding, formed of walnuts, enclosed in a tenacious glue, made of the inspissated [i.e. thickened] juice of various fruits'.[8]

In 1355 when Ibn Battuta visited Baalbek he noted a sweetmeat made of thickened molasses, almonds and pistachio nuts called *al mulabban* or *jald al faras*. The latter term means 'stallion's penis', suggesting that this sweetmeat was similar to *sucuk* in shape as well as its ingredients, so this is possibly the earliest reference to these sweet 'sausages':[9]

> There is, too, a kind of *Dibs* (molasses) called after Ba'albakk, which is a syrup made from raisins, and they add thereto a powder [starch] which makes it harden. Afterwards they break the pot in which it is made, and it remains all of one piece. From it is made a sweetmeat called Al Halwah, by putting in pistachios and almonds. This sweetmeat is named also Al Mulabban. They call it also Jald al Faras (*Penis equi*).

A simpler version of this sweetmeat, also known as *köfter*, *kesme* or *pelte*, was prepared by pouring the starch-thickened grape juice into trays, which when set was cut into squares or lozenges. Today this type is still made in some parts of Turkey, notably Kayseri and Diyarbakır. Below is a recipe dated 1828 from a manuscipt scroll discovered in Larissa by the bibliophile Ali Emirî in 1917:[10]

Recipe for *Pelte*

The ingredients and consistency of *pelte* are exactly the same as for *sucuk*. However, when the consistency is reached the mixture is poured into high-rimmed trays to the depth of one and a half fingers and left in the sun to dry for two days. Then it is cut into rectangular pieces and placed on boards to dry in the sun for about fifteen days. Then it is washed and laid on sheets in the sun until the dampness has disappeared and stored in baskets. Once the cold weather of December comes and the sweetmeats have crystallized they can be opened.

A crystallized surface was the secret of good *köfter*. In Kayseri today *köfter* is cut into lozenges, dried on rush mats, then packed into an earthenware jar and left for a month until sugar crystals form a white crust on the surface.[11] The flavour is marvellous. In her book on the food culture of İncesu, a town in Kayseri province, Aysel Özen describes a now almost forgotten local custom known as *saya gezme*, when young men dressed up and went from door to door demanding *tarhana* and *köfter*:

On 9 January, the day known as *zemheri* that marks the beginning of the severest period of winter, it was traditional for seven or eight teenage boys to put on beards and moustaches made of wool, dress in loose ragged clothes, and tall colourful conical hats. Shaking tambourines with jingles and banging on tin sheets, they would knock noisily on each door they came to. As soon as the door was opened they would play and dance. Then one of them would climb on a chair and proclaim, 'He said *het*, he said *hüt*! He told me to lie next to *tarhana* and *köfter*'. Then he threw himself flat on the ground. The mistress of the house gave them gifts of food like flour, bulgur, *tarhana* and *köfter*. Sometimes the boys recited verses such as: If you give may you enjoy plenty / If you don't may a rat fall into your bulgur jar.

Köfter is the ancestor and rural relative of Turkish delight, differing principally in being made with grape juice instead of sugar. A recipe for *köfter* made with quinces, apples or citrons in a nineteenth-century recipe manuscript compares it to Turkish delight.[12] High pectin levels in these fruits means that no starch is required for the boiled syrup to set to a gelatinous consistency.

Sucuk attracted the atttention of other travellers besides Brocquière. In the early nineteenth century, Edward Daniel Clarke saw sailors eating *sucuk* at İğneada on the southwestern Black Sea coast:[13]

In those coffeehouses may be seen groups of Turkish mariners, each party squatted in a circle round a pan of lighted charcoal; and, either smoking, sipping coffee, chewing opium, or eating a sort of sweetmeat, in shape like a sausage, made of walnuts or almonds, strung upon a piece of twine, and dipped in the concocted syrup of new wine, boiled until it has acquired the consistence of a stiff jelly and bends in the hand like a piece of Indian rubber.

A few years later the Reverend Robert Walsh wrote that *sucuk* made in Çorlu was sent to Istanbul in large quantities:[14]

Their only manufacture is a confection in great request among the Turks; it consists of walnuts enclosed in a sweet gelatinous substance, made from the inspissated juice of grapes: it is formed into long cylindrical rolls, like black puddings, and so transported to Constantinople, where it is eaten in great quantities. We saw some cartloads of this confection leaving the town.

In the 1830s Julia Pardoe likened *sucuk* to 'huge sausages' perforated with twine and hung from the framework of confectioners' shops in Istanbul,[15] while Warrington Smyth, who was served *sucuk* among numerous other sweetmeats at the home of his Turkish acquaintance Mahmud Bey in Vrania (today Vranje in Serbia), described it as 'a glue-looking chain called *soojook*, made by dipping a rosary of walnuts into grape-juice boiled to a thick jelly'.[16]

The Turkish writer Musahipzâde Celâl mentions *sucuk* as among the articles sold in Istanbul's dried fruit and nut shops:[17]

Until recently there were nearly a hundred shops selling only dried fruit and nuts in a covered market at the end of the Fruit Quay. All kinds of dried fruit and nuts from Anatolia, Syria and Rumelia were sold in this market. Fruit *murabbâ* [jellied preserves made with strained fruit juice] in wooden boxes, different types of *pestil*, walnut and almond *köfter*, walnut *sucuk*, and *nardenk* [boiled juice of sour pomegranates, plums, apples and cornelian cherries] were also sold here.

This market is no longer standing, but dried fruit and nut shops are still plentiful in Istanbul and other Turkish towns today. Every neighbourhood has at least one such shop, selling dried mulberries, roasted chickpeas, nuts and raisins of every description, pumpkin seeds, *sucuk*, *pestil* and much more. Today, supermarkets and shopping malls have bowed to tradition and include well-stocked dried fruit and nut stands.

The four recipes for *sucuk* and *köfter* below all date from the nineteenth century.

RECIPES

Sucuk   (Anonymous, 1828)[18]

Take blanched almonds or shelled walnuts and three or four days in advance thread these on flax strings. Fashion a hook from a stick for each string and attach the string to the hook. Then boil up a quantity of grape juice and when it is reduced to the consistency of watery *pekmez* measure it and taking the necessary amount of starch blend it with one measure of grape juice, then blend with the rest of the grape juice and stir constantly as it boils. When it is sufficiently thick dip a red-hot charcoal ember into the mixture. If the ember is not extinguished but emerges red-hot then the correct consistency has been reached. Dip each of the strings of walnuts and almonds into the mixture and hang them on taut lines. When this has been completed, start from the beginning, dipping each of the strings in for a second time and hanging them on the lines. In short, repeat the process three times and afterwards hang them in the sun. Then for fifteen days put them out in the sun every day from morning until evening to dry. Then wash them clean and lay them out on sheets, covering them with another sheet so that no flies settle on them. Leave them in the sun like this for one day and when they are dry take them indoors. Store them in a basket made of rushes or twigs. Open in December, when they will have become the finest sweet *sucuk*, and eat them.

Zuzuqui   (Friedrich Unger, 1838)[19]

For this is required: 1 *occa* of fresh grape juice, and 60 grams of starch. Make up the starch with some water, strain, and cook it until thick with the juice. Then thread nuts spaced slightly, hang them up and pour the cooked mixture over them, let it get cold and repeat until the nuts are well covered and it has the shape of a long sausage. Sprinkle some icing sugar or starch over and leave it to dry. Instead of walnuts, peeled almonds and raisins etc. are often used.

QUINCE *KÖFTER* (Anonymous, 1852)[20]

Peel and core a sufficient quantity of quinces and cook them in pure water until they are soft. Then using a large spoon crush them to a purée. Add clarified sugar syrup boiled to a thick consistency and place on the fire. Boil until thick, then pour into a tray to a thickness of one finger and leave in the sun for three to five days to dry. Cut into pieces like baklava and store in bowls. This is a delicious quince *köfter* that resembles *rahatü'l-hulkum* [Turkish delight]. If citrons, apples and other similar fruits are prepared in the same way they are also delicious.

ŞIRALI *SUCUK* (Ayşe Fahriye, 1882–3)[21]

Take once-boiled clarified[22] grape juice and blend two parts of starch and one part of semolina with a third part of the juice, and stir into the boiling juice. When it thickens dip strings of hazelnuts or almonds several times into the mixture until the desired thickness is reached and hang on hooks to dry.

20 *Pelte*

Your mouth is like sweet *pâlûde* sprinkled with rose water
Your lips like *helva* and your cheeks delicate *güllaç*.
Aynî (fl. late fifteenth century)[1]

*P*ELTE IS A PUDDING THAT began life in Persia and has inspired poets over the centuries. Turkish *pelte*, *pâlûde* or *pâlûze* and Arabic *fâlûdhaj* all derive from the Persian *pâlûda*, meaning refined.[2] Writing in the thirteenth century, Mevlânâ extols *pâlûze* as 'pure taste and flavour':[3]

You have such flavours, you are so sweet
That you have forsworn fat and honey
Fry in your own fat, sweeten with your own honey
For you are *pâlûze*, pure taste and flavour.

The earliest Arabic recipes date from the tenth century, and are presumably closest to the Persian original.[4] Basically these consist of honey and sesame oil, thickened with starch, and flavoured with saffron, camphor or musk. Almonds are an optional ingredient, mentioned only in the first recipe. Yet by the thirteenth century, when Mevlânâ was writing, *fâlûdhaj* had evolved into a kind of marzipan formed into 'melons, triangles and other shapes'.[5] In the fifteenth century it was also shaped into cucumbers and apples.[6]

The *pâlûze* praised so highly by Mevlânâ is likely to have been the marzipan-type of the contemporary Arabic recipe, especially in view of the words 'let almonds become *pâlûde*' in a poem by the Turkish mystic Kaygusuz Abdal (d. 1444).[7]

Another thirteenth-century Arabic cookery book gives a recipe for starch-thickened *fâlûdhaj*, but the author regards this as inferior, telling his readers that it is better with ground almonds. The starch-thickened version may be the 'tasteless, colourless *pâlûze* sold in the shops and markets' mentioned by Mevlânâ in his *Divân-ı Kebîr*.[8]

Nevertheless, in Ottoman cookery *pelte* was always made with starch, perhaps because this version was lighter and more digestible than that made with ground almonds. Both of the fifteenth-century Turkish recipes for *pelte* written by Şirvânî, royal physician to Sultan Murad II, are lighter than the earlier Arabic versions, containing neither oil nor ground almonds.[9] One of them is made from honey and starch and served sprinkled with sliced almonds and rose water syrup, while the other is similar but given a sour flavour by the addition of either sumac or cornelian cherry juice. In 1502 confectioners in the city of Bursa made *pelte* from grape juice, starch, sesame oil, almonds and saffron.[10]

Pelte was a favourite pudding at the Ottoman palace, occurring frequently in sixteenth-century kitchen registers,[11] and in menus for meals served to members of the Imperial Council.[12] In the seventeenth century *pelte* made by the eminent religious scholar, poet and gourmet Nev'îzâde Atâî (1583–1635) won such renown that he was asked to present some to the sultan:[13]

> This *pâlûde* is an ancient confection, but the great scholar Nev'îzâde Efendi meticulously and painstakingly brought this dish to such a glorious state and fame that words can hardly describe it. Indeed, despite his modesty he was obliged to present one or two celadon dishes each to the foremost doctors of canonical law and to the chief black eunuch in the imperial palace for his royal highness the sultan, perhaps in that illustrious presence. And when those great men were pleased with the gift, from respect he sent some again and again, and became known as Pelteci Efendi [Master Pelte Maker]. By giving a new refinement and form to *rahatü'l-hulkum* [*pelte*], he introduced a way of preparing the dish superior to that of his predecessors. Truly he was a respected man of noble character, a most excellent person who would give not just *pâlûde* but his life for those he loved and his friends.

Nev'îzâde's *pelte* was made by the following method:[14]

Fâlûzec

This is what they call *pelte*. Certainly it is a fine dish, and if made from Damascus rock sugar and starch made from *peksimet* wheat[15] will be exceedingly white. First take one *vukiye* of white sugar and 4–5 *vukiye*s of water and boil to a syrup. Blend 40 *dirhem*s of wheat starch with a little water and strain through a hair sieve. Add this to the syrup and stir unceasingly for three hours. After removing from the fire add a coffee-cupful of rose water, which will impart a delicious flavour, and pour it into dishes or individual bowls if preferred.

That an intellectual such as Nev'îzâde Efendi should have been interested in cooking is no surprise. Other Ottoman statesmen and scholars invented new versions of dishes: Şeyh Muhammed of Bursa was known for a new type of *hakânî helva*, and Master of Ceremonies Naim Efendi was known for a new *yahni* (stew).[16] Nev'îzâde's improved recipe for *pelte* has several distinctive features: it is made of expensive ingredients – the finest rock sugar instead of honey or grape syrup, and the finest wheat starch – and requires constant stirring for three hours. Long stirring was a feature of many Ottoman sweetmeats. Carried out over a low fire, this process brought about significant changes in both texture and flavour. This is one of the key aspects of preparing Turkish delight, whose basic ingredients are also sugar and starch, so in both method and ingredients Nev'îzâde's *pelte* bears a striking resemblance to Turkish delight. Even more striking is the fact that the term *rahatü'l-hulkum*, the original name of Turkish delight,[17] is here used for *pelte*. We can conclude that his version of *pelte* was the forerunner of Turkish delight, which is first recorded in the mid-eighteenth century.

The office of *pâlûdeci* or *pelte* maker at the Ottoman palace was instituted during the reign of Sultan Süleyman the Magnificent,[18] and the need for specialist cooks for this deceptively simple pudding shows that a high degree of skill was involved. *Pelte* was held in such high regard that it was served in special china '*pelte* bowls' (*üskûre-i pâlûze*) 7.5 centimetres in diameter.[19]

Various claims have been made for *pelte*'s health-giving qualities. Seventeenth-century *pelte* sellers asserted that it improved the eyesight.[20] Today it is popularly believed to relieve coughs and when made with cooking apples is a home remedy for diarrhoea. *Pelte* made with *pekmez* is a light and nourishing dish taken as a gift to women after childbirth.[21]

Pelte could be sweetened with sugar, honey or grape syrup. Describing the fragrant Athens honey that was so famous throughout the Ottoman period, Evliyâ Çelebi says that just one cup of this honey is enough to sweeten *pelte* made with forty cups of water.[22] As we have already seen, both of Şirvânî's fifteenth-century recipes were made with honey, one flavoured with rose water syrup and the other with dried sumac[23] or cornelian cherry juice. A variation that only the rich could afford was *pelte* flavoured with musk, mentioned by the eighteenth-century historian Ahmed Câvid.[24] Mehmed Kâmil's 1844 cookery book includes *pelte* made with black mulberry juice, and in his recipe for plain *pelte* he says that various fruit juices can be used instead of water.[25] Plain *pelte* could be sprinkled with cinnamon or allspice.[26] Examples of fruit *peltes* mentioned in Ayşe Fahriye's 1882 cookbook are sour cherry, apricot, black mulberry, strawberry, quince, sour pomegranate, redcurrant, cornelian cherry, orange, plum and sour apple.[27] The earliest reference to *pelte* made with fresh fruit juice is al-Warrâq's tenth-century Arabic recipe for *fâlûdhaj* made with melon juice.[28]

Türâbî Efendi's *palûde*, published in his *Turkish Cookery Book* in 1864, is flavoured with 'essence of rose or orange-flower', and then poured into a mould previously oiled with almond oil.[29] When firm it is turned out and served, ornamented if desired with 'some skinned pistachios or almonds'.

Pelte as a Drink

Pelte made with a pouring consistency was served hot as a winter drink. In past centuries Istanbul's *sıcak pelte* ('hot *pelte*') sellers did a roaring trade. In the mid-seventeenth century there were not only seven shops making hot *pelte* in the commercial heart of the city, but also around 800 street vendors. They kept their *pelte* hot by means of a box of hot embers beneath the copper vessels. When a vendor arrived at his pitch, he would set up his large wooden tray arrayed with cups made either of Chinese porcelain or local Kütahya-ware china, and advertise his wares with the cry: 'I have spiced *pâlûde*, boiling *pâlûde*, my dears.' This hot *pelte* was sprinkled with ginger, cinnamon and rose water.[30]

Hot *pelte* was sold in the street at breakfast time until the mid-nineteenth century.[31] It was very similar to the hot salep drink sprinkled with cinnamon that is still sold on Istanbul's ferryboats in wintertime. At the Ottoman palace a version of hot *pelte* called *pelteşîn* was made of starch, sugar, rose water or orange-flower water and lemon juice.[32] An eighteenth-century recipe claims that *pelteşîn* is good for the digestion and prevents 'vapour in the brain'.

Zirbaç

Zirbaç or *zırva* was a feast-day pudding containing dried fruits and thickened with starch. It evolved from an Arab meat stew called *zirbaj* or *zirbaja*, made with chicken or mutton, which can be traced back to the tenth century.[33] In Ottoman times various dried fruits were added, and from the late fifteenth century the meat was dispensed with, transforming *zirbaç* into a rich fruity pudding. During the reign of Sultan Mehmed II it was served at the *imaret* (public kitchen) of Eyüpsultan on religious feast days, and at the Fâtih Imaret on Friday evenings and daily during Ramazan.[34] *Zirbaç* also featured at the banquets held to celebrate the circumcision of the princes Bâyezid and Cihângîr in 1539.[35] More than 2 tons of *zirbaç* was prepared at the palace of grand vizier İbrahim Pasha during the year AH 963 (1555–6), using 615 kilograms of honey, 614 kilograms of red raisins, 187 kilograms of almonds, 169 kilograms of figs, 169 kilograms of prunes, 169 kilograms of dried *zerdali*,[36] 369 kilograms of wheat starch and 2 kilograms of saffron.[37]

The fifteenth-century foundation deed for the Eyüpsultan Imaret in Istanbul specifies that *zirbaç* be served together with *zerde* on religious festivals.[38] A recipe in an early fifteenth-century Turkish medical book gives the ingredients as mutton or chicken, vinegar, sugar or honey, cinnamon, chickpeas and almonds.[39] Another dated c. 1530 retains the mutton and chickpeas, but adds apricots, wild apricots, raisins, black *arslanî* prunes and wheat starch.[40] This represents an intermediate stage in the Ottomanization of *zirbaç*, which by the sixteenth century had been transformed from a meat stew to a dried fruit pudding.

The tradition of serving *zirbaç* at *imaret*s continued into the late nineteenth century, albeit in a much simpler and more economical version, consisting only of wheat starch, sugar, raisins and figs in equal quantities.[41]

The word *zirbaç* had been corrupted to *zirba* or *zirva* in Turkish by the early sixteenth century, and the colloquial form *zırva* acquired the metaphorical meaning of 'nonsense', which is still current today, although the pudding itself is forgotten.[42]

RECIPES

SUMAC PÂLÛZE   (Şirvânî, c. 1430)[43]

Take one *nuki* of honey and add 50 *dirhem*s of starch. Take the sumac, which has been left to soak in water, strain it through clean muslin, and add the water to the honey to make a syrup that is not excessively sour but pleasantly tart. Blend the starch with water and strain through muslin, add this to the syrup and place over a gentle fire to cook, stirring until it is ready. Remove from the fire and pour into bowls. Pour rose water syrup over, sprinkle with almonds and bring [to the table] to eat. It is also nice made with cornelian cherries.

PÂLÛZE OR PELTE   (Ayşe Fahriye, 1882–3)[44]

Take 30 *dirhem*s of fine starch and one kilogram[45] of sugar, add sufficient water to attain the desired degree of sweetness. Cook for two or three hours, stirring constantly, until the starchy flavour has gone, it has thickened and become almost transparent, then pour into a dish and allow to cool.

If desired the expressed juice or syrup of sour cherries, apricots, black mulberries, strawberries, quinces, sour pomegranates, currants, cornelian cherries, oranges, plums or sour apples may be added shortly before removing from the heat, then brought to the boil for the last time and taken off the fire so that their fragrance may not be lost.

21 Lokum   Turkish Delight

Dandin dandin danaylı
My little boy is palace born
His daddy has brought him
Lokum so sweet
Ninni to my baby ninni.

Lullaby[1]

ALTHOUGH *LOKUM* IS A LATECOMER in Turkish confectionery, dating only from the eighteenth century, it soon became one of the most famous sweetmeats in the world. *Lokum* started to earn its international reputation in the first half of the nineteenth century, when foreign travellers began to visit Turkey in unprecedented numbers, attracted by the idea of the 'exotic Orient' in the European imagination. Istanbul was the main destination, and here foreign tourists tasted *lokum* and bought boxfuls to take back home. As the fame of *lokum* grew, the confectioner Hacı Bekir began exporting it to Europe around the middle of the nineteenth century.[2]

Despite enjoying *lokum* so much, foreign visitors were unsure what it was made of. The American naval physician James de Kay says the following in his memoir of his stay in Turkey in the early 1830s:[3]

> . . . a delicious pasty-mass which melts away in the mouth, and leaves a fragrant flavour behind. It is, as we are informed, made by mixing honey with the inspissated juice of the fresh grape, and the Turks, who esteem it highly, call it *rahat locoom* or repose to the throat, a picturesque name to which it seems fairly entitled.

In 1844 another traveller, Charles White, otherwise a faithful observer, claimed that the ingredient that gave *lokum* its jelly-like consistency was semolina:[4]

All articles made by confectioners are classed under the head of *shekerlama* (sugared things). The most renowned of these is *rakhatlacoom* (giving rest to the throat). This is a gelatinous substance, consisting of the pulp of white grapes or mulberries, semolina flour, honey, sugar, rose-water, and kernels of apricots.[5] It is sold in long rolls or slices at 8 piastres the *oka*.

Contemporary recipes show that *lokum* was made in the same way as it is today, thickened not with semolina but with wheat starch. Perhaps confectioners, keen to protect their professional secrets, deliberately misled inquisitive foreigners.

Friedrich Unger, chief confectioner to King Otto I of Greece, was the first foreigner to record an accurate account of how *lokum* was made. Unger published his *lokum* recipes in 1838, after spending several months in Istanbul researching oriental confectionery.[6] In his book he gives four recipes for what he ironically calls the 'mysterious *Rahatol chulkum*', listing the ingredients as sugar, starch, water, lemon juice and rose oil.

Yet despite Unger's revelation of the truth about *lokum*, the sweetmeat continued to mystify Europeans for decades to come. Perhaps the fact that his book was written in German limited the spread of this information, which might have helped European confectioners to imitate this popular sweetmeat. Nonethless they tried, producing something very different from Turkish *lokum* that was on sale in England in the 1870s, as we hear from E.C.C. Baillie:[7]

We paid a visit to the place where they sell the Turkish sweetmeats, and tasted several of them. The 'Turkish Delight', which seemed to be considered the proper thing to buy for our children, is something like little square lumps of very sweet jelly, powdered over with some white composition. The sweetmeat known by that name in England is very different.

Three decades on, European confectioners were no closer to producing *lokum*, according to the French artist and writer Pretextat Lecomte, writing in 1901:[8]

Seeing the *locoum* of so beautiful a colour, warm and transparent, one might well assume its composition to consist of many elements and that it must be a difficult thing to make; we will demonstrate that this is by no means the case. These elements are simple and number but two; sugar and starch. As for handling, it must be very skilful and very meticulous, it is in this that all the secret lies, and it should not be thought that this is a minor matter, which is why never, in Europe, has anyone succeeded in imitating *locoum*.

Pretextat Lecomte watched *lokum* being made and his detailed description is unsurpassed by any other, past or present. The uninterrupted stirring for two hours is one of the main reasons why European confectioners failed to produce an acceptable imitation:

> The manufacturer of *locoum*s starts by dissolving starch in cold water; this starch is then placed in a great basin with a certain quantity of sugar, the basin is put on a gentle fire and for two hours approximately two men take turns in working the mixture with a large beater (a kind of spade made of wood). The sugar must be beaten in the same direction and without interruption, otherwise the paste will separate, and not become uniformly thick; and the timing of the beating movement must be constant, its regularity being the only cause of differences occurring in the quality of the paste. If the paste were irregularly beaten, the sugar would crystallize, which is where the art of handling lies. When the paste is ready, it is poured into small wooden moulds forty centimetres in length by twenty-five centimetres broad and four centimetres deep, the moulds previously powdered with fine sugar powder so as to prevent it sticking.
>
> When the paste has cooled, the manufacturer reverses the contents of the mould onto a marble slab, and with the aid of a knife of a distinctive form, a kind of broad crescent attached at the centre to a handle, cuts up the *locoum* into thin strips approximately three centimetres wide, then these thin strips are quickly cut in their turn into small cubes. The marble has been powdered, again to avoid sticking, and the cut pieces are powdered in their turn, for the same reason. Consequently the shopkeeper is so habituated to powdering, that while speaking to you, he powders no matter what, and so upon leaving his small shop you always find your overcoat to have been dusted with flour in the same way.
>
> The *locoum* is sold at 7 piastres to 12 piastres the *ocque* (1 fr. 40 to 2 francs). We have said that the *locoum* contains various elements: pistachios, almonds, mastic, etc. These elements are introduced only after the cooking is complete, when they are tossed into the basin and the paste is stirred, then poured into the moulds; in the case of mastic it is reduced to a very fine powder, flung into the paste at the last moment of cooking and beaten into it.

As Pretextat Lecomte says, skill is everything in preparing *lokum*. No amount of written explanation can take the place of experience. If European confectioners had succeeded in making *lokum*, doubtless it would not be called 'Turkish delight' today, but have acquired a different name, just as *çevirme* turned into 'fondant'.[9] Having failed to make the real thing, English confectioners demonstrated their perseverance by producing imitations such as 'Fry's Turkish delight', a chocolate-coated red jelly that was launched in 1914.[10] Even as late as 1928 some English recipes for Turkish delight specified gelatine as the thickening agent, and sulphuric acid was sometimes added.[11]

Lack of knowledge about the properties of starch was one of the main obstacles to imitating *lokum* in Europe. Although starch occurs occasionally in medieval recipes, its use virtually died out, and only reappeared in English cuisine in the late nineteenth century. In eighteenth-century Europe starch was used not in cookery but to sprinkle on wigs, and even when the fashion for wearing wigs had passed, the German name for starch remained *Haarpuder* (hair powder).[12] In England, meanwhile, starch was used to stiffen linen, which was the only use Mrs Beeton had for it, and in the *Oxford English Dictionary* no culinary uses are mentioned in any of the quotations under the entry for 'starch' from the fifteenth century until the start of the twentieth.

In 1553 the traveller Hans Dernschwam was at a loss for a German term for starch, describing it as 'strong flour'.[13] Starch was no more familiar three centuries later, when Sir James Redhouse was writing his Turkish–English dictionary, which was published in 1890. So unused were English-speaking readers to the idea of starch as a cooking ingredient that he felt obliged to inform them that starch was 'used for food' in his definition of the Turkish word *nişasta*.[14] Elsewhere the same dictionary avoids mentioning the word 'starch' at all, substituting the enigmatic term 'strained wheat'.[15]

In Turkey, the Middle East and Iran, on the other hand, starch had been an important culinary ingredient for at least a thousand years. Its properties were intimately known and a whole panoply of starch-based sweetmeats and puddings had evolved.

In Turkey starch making was one of the traditional food-processing tasks carried out in the home, along with making *pestil* (fruit leather), *pekmez* (fruit molasses), *sucuk* and *tarhana* (a soup mix of fermented dough with yogurt). Lady Fanny Blunt, who lived in Turkey for two decades in the middle of the nineteenth century, tells us that starch was among the winter provisions prepared by city women when spending the summer on their country estates:[16]

When the Bey intends paying a long visit to his estate and is accompanied by his family, the bedding and other households necessaries are brought from town. It is astonishing to see how little luggage a Turkish family travels with on such an occasion. Each person will have a boghcha, containing his or her wearing apparel; the articles for general use comprise a few candlesticks, petroleum lamps, perhaps two leyen and ibrik for ablutions which in the morning and at meal times make the round of the house; kitchen utensils and a few tumblers, plates etc. are all that is needed for the villeggiatura of a Turkish family . . . The harem bring friends to stay and the days are spent in roaming out bare foot in the most *negligés* costumes eating fruit and helping to make the winter provision, such as *Tarhana*, *Kouskous* (pastes for soup and pilaf), *Youfka* [thinly rolled flatbread baked on a griddle], *Petmaiz* (molasses made from grapes), *Rechel* (preserves made with molasses from fresh or dried fruits), and *Nichesteh* (starch made from wheat, much used for making sweets).

In the absence of a starch tradition, European cuisine used isinglass made from the swim bladders of sturgeon and other fish or gelatine made from animal bones or calfs' feet for jellying liquids. Blancmange, the dish we most associate with corn starch today, was made with isinglass once the traditional method of thickening it with minced chicken breast had been abandoned in the late seventeenth century, and isinglass continued to be used until the late nineteenth century.[17]

Of the numerous Turkish confections made with starch, *lokum*'s closest relatives are *sucuk* – strings of nuts coated with grape or mulberry molasses thickened with starch, *pelte* – a soft pudding made with honey or various fruit juices, and *kesme* or *köfter* – a sweetmeat made of grape molasses thickened with flour or starch.[18] *Kesme* was served at a palace banquet given in 1660[19] and is still made in many parts of Turkey, such as Diyarbakır, Kahramanmaraş and Kayseri. One of the main differences between *lokum* and its cousins *sucuk*, *pelte* and *kesme* is the substitution of sugar for grape molasses, so allowing the use of flavourings that would have been overwhelmed by the molasses. This opened the way for a whole new spectrum of flavours and fragrances, such as fruits, musk and rose water. The other important distinction lies in the hours of laborious stirring used in making *lokum*. So a sweetmeat fit for gourmets was born.

Although *lokum* did not yet exist in the seventeenth century, its name, *rahatü'l-hulkum*, already did. Meaning 'ease to the throat', this slogan used by *pelte* makers to attract customers was the seventeenth-century equivalent of the Fry's slogan 'Full of eastern promise'. The *pelte* makers made even wilder claims for their product: 'Brings ease to the throat and strength to the eyes. Refreshing and filling pelte.' By the late seventeenth century *rahatü'l-hulkum* had become a synonym for *pelte*, as illustrated by this line of poetry by Sâbit of Bosnia (1650–1712):[20] 'The slave to sweets would give his life for ease to the throat.'

'Ease to the throat' as a figure of speech describing sweet, soft and delicious foods can be traced back to the tenth century, when the Arab writer Badi' al-Zamán al-Hamadhani (969–1008) uses the phrase in one of his stories to describe a type of marzipan called *lawzinaj:*[21] 'And I said to the confectioner, "Weigh out for Abû Zaid two pounds of throat-easing *lauzinaj* for Abu Zaid, because it slips into the veins."'

In the nineteenth century the term *rahatü'l-hulkum* was corrupted in colloquial speech, first to *rahat-lokum*, then to *latilokum*, and finally to *lokum*. The contraction and mutation process was helped by the fact that the word *lokum* already existed as a term for small pastries, probably corrupted from the word *lokma*, meaning 'morsel'.[22]

The shortened form *rahat-lokum* was already widespread by the 1830s, as Kay's transcription '*rahat locoom*' goes to show. When the famous French chef Alexis Soyer was sent to Istanbul by the British government during the Crimean War to improve catering at the British military hospital in Scutari,[23] Soyer was invited to dinner on several occasions by Ottoman dignitaries. The most splendid of these occasions was an *al fresco* banquet given by Selim Pasha in 1855, and Soyer notes that '*rahat locoum*' was served at the end of the banquet.[24] The term *latilokum* is first recorded in the late Ottoman period.[25]

Turkish delight began to be exported via Marseille in the mid-nineteenth century, and the word *rahat-lokum* entered French in a form that Pretextat Lecomte calls 'the Marseillais barbarism *ratacomb*'.[26] Meanwhile the earliest English term, 'lumps of delight', was first recorded by Lady Londonderry in 1840.[27] The 'lumps' are the English translation of *lokum* in the sense of morsels. Lady Londonderry was one of those killjoy tourists who find fault with everything, so it is ironic that she should have made this small but significant contribution to the history of *lokum*, despite refusing to taste it:

> Presents are sent of baskets of confectionery, called 'lumps of delight', which I never had the courage to taste; neither could I, during my stay at Constantinople, summon resolution to try a Turkish bath, which, from the description I had of it, seems by no means inviting.

Türâbî Efendi wrote in 1864, that *rahatü'l-hulkum* 'is commonly known in England as the 'Lumps or morsels of delight'.[28] The first record of today's English term 'Turkish delight' is in the memoirs of an Englishwoman, E.C.C. Baillie, quoted earlier in this chapter.

Imported Turkish delight had been available in England since early 1861, when the magazine *Punch* published a cartoon captioned 'Latest Importation in Sweets, Rahat Lahkoum or Lumps of Delight'.[29] Who was manufacturing the 'very different' sweetmeat sold in England as Turkish delight is uncertain. Apparently there was a glut of imitations at this period. An advertising pamphlet dated 1878 for *lokum* exported to Britain by the Krikorian Brothers declares: 'As there are many imitations, we have considered it necessary to register our Trade Mark as under, without which, none is genuine.'[30]

Lokum became so famous in England in the 1860s that specialist shops opened. In Charles Dickens's novel *The Mystery of Edwin Drood*, left unfinished at his death in 1870, Edwin Drood and his fiancée Rosa Bud visit the 'Lumps-of-Delight shop' in Cloisterham, the fictional name Dickens used for Rochester:[31]

'Which way shall we take, Rosa?'
Rosa replies: 'I want to go to the Lumps-of-Delight shop.'
'To the—?'
'A Turkish sweetmeat, sir. My gracious me, don't you understand anything? Call yourself an Engineer, and not know *that*?'
'Why, how should I know, Rosa?'
'Because I am very fond of them. But O! I forgot what we are to pretend. No, you needn't know anything about them; never mind.'

So he is gloomily borne off to the Lumps-of-Delight shop, where Rosa makes her purchase, and after offering some to him (which he rather indignantly declines), begins to partake of it with great zest: previously taking off and rolling up a pair of little pink gloves, like rose-leaves, and occasionally putting her little pink fingers to her rosy lips, to cleanse them from the Dust of Delight that comes off the Lumps.

LATEST IMPORTATION IN SWEETS.
RAHAT LAHKOUM, OR LUMPS OF DELIGHT!

Turkey's reputation for good confectionery which inspired German confectioner Friedrich Unger in the 1830s was still alive and well in the late nineteenth century, reinforced by the success of Turkish delight. 'The Turk is a past master in the art of making sweets, sugar-plums, jams, preserved and candied fruits and syrups,' wrote Eugène Chesnel in 1888. 'Let us not forget the *rahat locoum* or Lumps of

27. Cartoon published in *Punch* magazine in 1861. The caption reads: 'Latest Importation in Sweets. Rahat Lakhoum, or Lumps of Delight.' Evidently the arrival of Turkish delight in England was a newsworthy event (*Punch*, 12 January 1861, p. 12).

Delight which have achieved fame in Europe.'[32] For foreign tourists Istanbul's confectionery shops had become as much a part of the itinerary as the Blue Mosque and Topkapı Palace.

The earliest *lokum* recipe in Turkish sources is in an undated manuscript cookery manual dating from the late eighteenth or early nineteenth century.[33] From this recipe we learn that musk was the most esteemed flavouring, followed by rose water. Musk was not only added to the paste itself, but also to the powdered sugar sprinkled over the finished product. The tray into which the paste was poured and the scissors used for cutting it into pieces were oiled with almond oil:

Recipe for the *Rahatü'l-hulkum* Sold in Shops
Take one *vukıyye* of sugar, 75 *dirhem*s of starch, five *vukıyye*s of pure water, and half a *dirhem* of musk. First clarify the sugar in the usual way and blend the starch with water before stirring it into the sugar. Boil gently, stirring without interruption until it is ready, which you can tell by the following means: When you lift up a spoonful of the mixture if it forms a point hanging from the spoon then it is still uncooked, but if the end gathers like a button and becomes solid like sugar then it is cooked. Then remove from the heat, pour into a tray rubbed with a little almond oil, and

28. An Englishwoman carrying a cylindrical box of Turkish delight, accompanied by a man carrying six more boxes. The caption reads: 'Buying Sweetmeats ("Turkish delight") in Constantinople' (Drawing by W.D. Almond dated 1890, printed in the *Illustrated London News*, 14 November 1891, p. 632).

smooth it out. After it has cooled rub some more almond oil onto a large pair of scissors and cut into pieces like *lokum*. Take a large white European sugar loaf wrapped in blue paper and pound the sugar to the correct fineness, pass it through a muslin sieve so that it becomes like flour, and add one or two grains of musk or the empty musk pod to impart its fragrance. Toss the *lokum* in this, remove and place in a bowl. Keep to eat when desired. Those who cannot afford such expense [of musk] should add one or two cups of strong rose water before cooking, that its fragrance be more delicious and delicate. Wishing health to those who eat it.

Another recipe is given in Mehmed Kâmil's cookery book *Melceü't-Tabbâhîn*, published in 1844. Here the *lokum* is flavoured with both musk and rose water:[34]

Rahatü'l-hulkum
Method: Take one *kıyye* of the finest sugar and prepare a syrup with three *kıyye*s of water in a tinned pan. After placing it on a medium heat immediately take 75 *dirhem*s of the finest pounded starch and slowly stir into the syrup. It must be stirred constantly so that it does not form lumps or stick to the bottom of the pan. When well cooked put a couple of drops of the mixture onto granulated sugar, and if it dampens the sugar and absorbs it then the consistency is not yet right, but if it gathers into a ball and the sugar is unaffected then it is ready. Then blend 25 *dirhem*s of rose water with a grain of musk and after adding to the mixture stir a few more times before removing from the heat. Oil a tray with almond oil and pour in the cooked mixture. When cool cut into pieces of the desired size and toss into a mixture consisting half of sieved starch and half of powdered sugar, and stir until they do not stick together. It will be delicious.

No recipes earlier than the manuscript recipe given above are found in Ottoman-period Turkish cookery books. However, as we have already seen in the previous chapter, *pelte* as made by the religious scholar and poet Nev'îzâde Atâî (1583–1635) is so similar to *lokum* in terms of both ingredients and method that it clearly marks the final stage in the evolution of starch-based puddings such as *pelte*, *sucuk* and *köfter* into Turkish delight. The comparison of *sabûnî helva* to *rahatü'l-hulkum* in a treatise on cookery that dates from around the third quarter of the eighteenth century suggests that *lokum* was already a familiar sweetmeat in the mid-eighteenth century.[35]

If our sources of information had been limited to Turkish recipe books, we might have concluded that musk and rose were the only flavours available until the middle of the nineteenth century. However, Friedrich Unger's four recipes for *lokum* collected during his visit to Istanbul in the summer of 1835 include *lokum* with almonds and another kind with pistachios and musk, as well as two flavoured with rose water. Unger explains that the pistachio and musk variety 'is the finest and best liked in the Serail'.[36]

Later Ottoman cookery books reveal how *lokum* flavourings multiplied. In Ayşe Fahriye's book published in 1882 there are four *lokum* recipes, one flavoured with a mixture of musk and rose water, a second with clotted cream, a third with almonds and a fourth with pistachios.[37] Twenty years later Hadiye Fahriye gives recipes for eight varieties of *lokum*: plain, mastic, clotted cream, almond, pine nut, pistachio nut, hazelnut and 'double cooked',[38] but notes that any flavour desired can be made by adding essences or syrups, and cites as examples rose, violet, lemon and bitter orange.[39] Musk and violet are no longer made today, but newfangled flavours such as banana and chocolate have taken their place.

Opium addicts were particularly fond of *lokum*, and children used to play an unkind practical joke on opium eaters by offering them cubed lung dipped in sugar. Deceived by the spongy texture, the opium eaters would accept the offering then curse at the children as they spat it out.[40] Opium addicts' fondness for *lokum* may have inspired the urban myth about *lokum* made with opium or cannabis, which has even found its way into a serious modern work on drug abuse.[41]

SABÛNÎ HELVA

The family of sweetmeats made with starch also includes the toffee-like confection called *sabûnî helva* or *sabuniye*, mentioned above. There are recipes for *sâbûniyya* in thirteenth- and fourteenth-century Arabic cookery books.[42] This sweetmeat entered the Ottoman repertoire and continued to be made until the nineteenth century, when Unger came across it under the curious name *et helvası* ('meat helva') and recorded the following recipe:[43]

> **Et Halwassi**
> 4 *occa*s of honey, ½ *occa* starch, ½ *occa* water, ½ *occa* dahin oil (sesame oil), ½ *occa* blanched roasted almonds. Mix the starch and water. If half an *occa* of water is not enough add a little more, and pour this mixture through a sieve into the honey. Place the mixture on a low heat, where it is constantly stirred while the water evaporates, as in the yet to be described *Rahatol chulkum*, for 2–3 hours.

22 Güllaç   *Starch Wafers*

You are refined candy on a sweet tongue
In your sweet words are *güllaç* made of honey and sugar.
Dâî (d. c. 1421)[1]

GÜLLAÇ ARE STARCH WAFERS BAKED on a circular griddle. They are so thin that they are semi-transparent and so fragile that they break at a touch. The ninth-century poet Ibn al-Rûmî compared them to the wings of grasshoppers and the early sixteenth-century Ottoman poet Lâmi'î Çelebi likened them to jasmine petals.[2] *Güllaç* is a Turkic word meaning 'flower food',[3] in reference to the wafers' petal-like appearance. In Persian *güllaç* is known as *gûlaj* or *gûlanj*.[4] At their first appearance in writing, however, the wafers were nameless. Ibn Sayyâr al-Warrâq describes them in his tenth-century Arabic cookbook, where they are used as wrappers for *lauzinaj* rolls filled with ground almonds, walnuts or pistachios mixed with sugar, musk, rose water, and sometimes ambergris and mastic.[5] While *Kitâb al-Tabîkh* always specifies starch wafers for wrapping *lauzinaj*, the thirteenth-century *Kitâb Wasf al-At'ima al-Mu'tâda* only mentions them as an alternative. Most thirteenth-century Arabic *lauzinaj* recipes call instead for very thin flatbreads of the sort 'used for *sanbusaj*', suggesting that *güllaç* wafers were no longer commonplace.[6] Although both these cookery books explain how to make the wafers, in practice it was probably a task left to professionals. The wafers require a special implement – a flat circular iron griddle, referred to as a 'plate' (*tabaq*) in *Kitâb al-Tabikh* and as a 'mirror' (*mir'ât*) in *Kitâb Wasf al-At'ima al-Mu'tâda* – and special skill. The fifteenth-century Turkish physician Muhammed bin Mahmûd Şirvânî says in his recipe that 'skilled masters know the right consistency' for the batter,[7] suggesting that professional *güllaç* wafer production was already a specialist branch of confectionery in Turkey. In the sixteenth century palace confectioners did not make their own *güllaç* wafers but purchased them,

29. Circular packets of *güllaç* tied with ribbons hanging around the neck of the shadow puppet character Karagöz, who is returning from doing his Ramazan shopping. The other provisions he carries include a basket full of jars of preserves, a cylindrical packet of macaroni, a large earthenware jar of clarified butter from Aleppo, garlic sausages and joints of cured *pastırma* (*Karagöz*, 225 (5 September 1910), p. 4).

presumably from confectioners who specialized in their production.[8] By 1640 we know that Istanbul had forty *güllaç* shops.[9]

While the starch wafers of Arab cuisine were made of starch and water alone, the Turkish variety always included egg whites.[10] The earliest Turkish recipes for *güllaç* date from the fifteenth century:[11]

Tava Güllaç

Take one *nuki* of good starch, add to five egg whites and knead with a little water to make dough. Leave to stand for the amount of time it takes to grill kebab then blend with water to make a soft consistency. If the batter is too thick the sheets will be thick. The sheets should be as thin as paper; skilled masters know the right consistency. Then dip the sheets into syrup, fold in two and lay in a china dish. Sprinkle pounded sugar and almonds over them, and syrup flavoured with musk and rose water. Finally sprinkle some more pounded sugar and almonds over and eat.

To prevent the wafers sticking, the griddle was greased with hard-boiled egg yolk. This fifteenth-century tip works perfectly, and is worth trying with all kinds of pancakes and crepes.

A variation was made with thin omelettes instead of wafers. An even more unusual *güllaç* recipe is given in a late fourteenth-century Chinese encyclopedia. Here the use of the name *güllaç*, which does not appear in Arabic cookery books, and the layered structure of the pudding, which bears no resemblance to the *lauzinaj* of Arab cuisine, is a reflection of the Turkic influence on Chinese cuisine during the period of Mongol rule in China. Since starch was not available to Chinese cooks, bean paste was substituted:[12]

Güllach

Mix evenly egg white, bean paste and cream [to make a dough]. Spread out [dough] and fry into thin pancakes. Use one layer of white powdered sugar, [ground] pine nuts and [ground] walnuts for each layer of pancake. Make three to four layers like this. Pour honey dissolved in ghee ['Muslim oil'] over the top. Eat.

In the sixteenth century *güllaç* was an indispensable pudding on such occasions as the banquet held to celebrate the conquest of Rhodes in 1522, and the circumcision banquet held for Sultan Süleyman the Magnificent's sons Bâyezid and Cihângîr in 1539, when *güllaç* was one of fifty-eight varieties of puddings and sweets.[13]

The German traveller Hans Dernschwam describes how *güllaç* was made in Istanbul in 1553:[14]

Thus, beat strong flour [wheat starch] with egg white. Pour a little of this or take a spoonful of it in a hot pan, it becomes a wafer. Those they make as many as they need. Over that they sprinkle finely chopped almonds or nuts mixed with sugar, to the thickness of a finger, to which rose water and musk have been added. Another is laid on top and it is ready. This is also thought to be a good, delicious food.

Dernschwam probably watched the wafers being made by professional *güllaç* makers, but since musk was an expensive luxury beyond the reach of ordinary people it seems unlikely that these artisans also prepared the pudding that he describes. Dernschwam may have eaten this luxury version of *güllaç* at an official banquet, since he was travelling with the entourage of the Austrian ambassador Ghiselin de Busbecq.

In the seventeenth century *güllaç* continued to be served on festive occasions. Evliyâ Çelebi describes how gigantic thousand-layer *güllaç baklavası* were cooked in Belgrade for weddings and circumcisions.[15] Recipes for *güllaç baklavası* are found in numerous nineteenth-century cookery books, such as the following example, dated 1844:[16]

Güllaç Baklavası

Method: Take as many *güllaç* as desired and lay them in a suitable tray one by one, sprinkling some rose water and milk between each one. When half have been laid spread *kaymak* (clotted cream) over and sprinkle some fine powdered sugar, then lay the other half in the same way. When this is complete, pour boiling sugar syrup over, cover the tray with a lid and set aside. Later remove the lid and eat when cool. If there is no *kaymak* to be had, sprinkle ground hazelnuts or pistachio nuts instead. Alternatively, soak the whole *güllaç* sheets in rose water and watery syrup, fold in two, fill with *kaymak* or pounded hazelnuts, fold up like a bundle and lay on a dish, then as usual pour hot sugar syrup over. This method is also renowned.

Türâbî Efendi's recipe for *güllaç baklavası* in his *Turkish Cookery Book* published in England in 1864 is of exceptional interest for food historians because of the detailed description of how to make *güllaç* wafers at the beginning of the recipe. This was for the benefit of his English readers, who could not obtain them ready-made:[17]

Ghyulaj Baklawassi

Put in a basin the whites of twenty eggs, and whip them up well, then add about a pound of wheat starch by degrees, stir it well, and mix it well with water, to form a very thin batter; then put over a charcoal fire a circular and slightly-domed sheet-iron, the under side in the centre of which you have previously cemented with ashes half an inch thick, to prevent it from getting fiercely hot. When moderately hot, pour a portion of the batter over the centre, with a convenient spoon, sufficient to form a round cake, the size of a large dinner-plate, or larger, and which will be done in less than a minute: it ought to be very white, and as thin as tissue-paper. When you have prepared fifty or sixty pieces in this manner, lay half of them in a suitable baking-tin, one over the other, sprinkling between each piece some rose-water and milk as you lay them; then lay some clotted cream over, a quarter of an inch thick, and shake some powdered sugar over; then cover it with the other half of the cakes, sprinkling rose-water and milk between each one as before; then put in a stewpan a pound of loaf sugar, with two pints of water, and set it to boil until it becomes a syrup; then take it off and pour it over the cakes, till covered, and let it remain covered until cold; then cut it up in diamonds, dish up and serve. Pounded almonds or pistachios may be used, if clotted cream is not handy.

These cakes are sold ready made in Constantinople, and they can be obtained through any Turkish merchant residing in this country. It is a delicate and most delicious dish when properly done.

None of the Arabic or Turkish recipes for *güllaç* wafers compares to this for detail. If the khedive of Egypt had not given a banquet for 'some of England's fairest ladies and greatest statesmen' on board his yacht *Faiz-Jehad* moored at Woolwich on the Thames on 16 July 1862,[18] the intricacies of making *güllaç* pancakes during the Ottoman period would have been irretrievably lost to us. The banquet made such an impression on the khedive's guests that Türâbî Efendi was persuaded by numerous friends to publish a book of Turkish recipes. Although the recipes are mostly translated from Mehmed Kâmil's cookery book, Türâbî Efendi has added many details about techniques and ingredients for his non-Turkish readers that make the book of far greater historical interest than the original. We learn that Mehmed Kâmil's 'as many *güllaç* as desired' is between fifty and sixty wafers, that the clotted cream should be a quarter of an inch thick, that the syrup should be prepared from a pound of sugar boiled with two pints of water, and that the finished *güllaç baklavası* should be cut into diamonds to serve. The only point he omits is how to grease the griddle, and here Şirvânî's tip about using hard-boiled egg is the most effective solution.

Today the method of making *güllaç* wafers has undergone some changes in terms of materials and technique. In past centuries, beaten egg white was added to the wheat starch batter, but today *güllaç* makers omit the egg whites and use a mixture of maize starch and wheat flour instead of the traditional wheat starch. A circular iron griddle with a straight handle is heated over a stove and then held over a basin full of *güllaç* batter while a ladleful of the batter is poured over the griddle. The excess pours back into the basin, while the wafer cooks almost instantaneously on the hot plate.[19]

Charles White, an Englishman who lived in Istanbul for three years in the early 1840s, describes 'Gulatch (the rose dish)' as 'a kind of cream, thickened with fine starch, and scented with rose water'.[20] This does not sound like *güllaç baklavası*, but another pudding called *güllaç pâlûdesi*. The anonymous author of an eighteenth-century Turkish cookery manual gives a recipe for this dish, which he explains was a speciality at the home of Paşmakçızâde Abdullah Efendi (1680–1732):[21]

Güllaç Pâlûdesi

Of all the ways of preparing *güllaç* this is the most delicious and light. It was a speciality at the home of the late Şeyhülislam Paşmakçızâde Hazretleri, who was the father-in-law of my late father, and consequently this was always cooked and eaten in our house. Method: First clarify sugar in the usual way and prepare a syrup. Leave the pan of syrup at the edge of the fire to keep hot. Meanwhile place a baking tray with a high edge or a frying pan on a trivet and lay a burning charcoal fire beneath. Pour a ladleful of the syrup into the tray and when it begins to boil lay a single *güllaç* onto it and press with a spoon. When it is soaked in the syrup begin to stir. When it is dissolved, place another *güllaç* into the tray and stir that in. As that dissolves add another until it is the consistency of *pelte* then pour in another ladleful of the aforementioned syrup and more *güllaç*, stirring as before. Continue until the tray is full. Then remove from the heat, stir in a coffee-cupful of rose water and set aside.

When it is cold decorate with blanched almonds or pistachio nuts and serve. If two grains of musk are blended with rose water and added, it will be deliciously fragrant. However, let the syrup be more watery than usual, because while cooking the water will evaporate and it will reach the desired consistency.

One late Ottoman cookery book has a recipe for *güllaç* rolls filled with clotted cream or pounded nuts –reminiscent of the *lauzinaj* of medieval Arab cuisine:[22]

Güllaç with Kaymak

Undo the ribbon holding the packet of *güllaç* wafers and lay them beside you. Pour a little dilute syrup and some rose water into a tray and turn each *güllac* wafer in the tray until it is soaked. Then fold in half and fold the right and left edges inwards as if making *dolma*. Place a rectangular piece of fresh or dried *kaymak* on the *güllaç*. Fold the right and left edges over and roll up as you do when making stuffed cabbage, then arrange neatly on a dish. Or you may roll it up a little longer than a *dolma* and shape it into a ring and heap these rings on a dish. Or you may lay the sheets in an oval dish as if making *börek* and spread *kaymak* between every four *güllaç*. Whichever of these three methods is preferred, when the dish is full pour warm clarified syrup over and sprinkle a little more rose water (or at least flower water) and it is ready to eat. If no *kaymak* is available, use pounded pistachios, hazelnuts, almonds or walnuts instead, which is also delicious.

Sometimes these *güllaç* rolls were dipped in beaten egg, fried in clarified butter and soaked in syrup, a variation that lives on in Sivas province.[23] Known as 'fried *güllaç*', the earliest recipe for this is dated 1844 and calls for a filling of either hazelnuts or *kaymak*, whereas the English recipe published by Türâbî Efendi in 1864 specifies either ground almonds or pistachios:[24]

Ghyulaj Kizartmassi

Prepare twenty or thirty cakes as No. 186 [see above], and moisten them by sprinkling rose-water over, then fold them in two separately, put on each one some pounded almonds or pistachios, then fold them in square or triangular shape, dip them in egg, and fry them a delicate colour on both

30. Street vendor with packets of *güllaç* in a basket on his back (*Karagöz*, 121 (20 September 1909), p. 4).

sides in hot fresh butter; drain them, and then throw them in boiling syrup, prepared as above. When sufficiently soaked, take them out with a spoon, and arrange them tastefully on a dish, and serve hot or cold.

As time went on, *güllaç* became so closely identified with Ramazan that a late eighteenth-century rhyme refers to it as exclusive to Ramazan,[25] and still today *güllaç* wafers are virtually unobtainable at any other time of year. Descriptions of Ramazan in the late Ottoman period invariably mention *güllaç*. Abdülaziz Bey describes packets of *güllaç* wafers tied with coloured ribbon sold in grocery shops,[26] and Leyla Saz relates how housewives served *güllaç* to their guests at the evening *iftar* meal.[27] Many other writers, such as Mehmed Tevfik (1843–93), emphasize that *güllaç* was an essential part of the *iftar* meal,[28] and packets of *güllaç* appear in cartoons relating to Ramazan.

The *güllaç* made today in Istanbul, whether in restaurants, pudding shops or at home, is always prepared with sweetened milk and ground walnuts. This version has indeed become so much the rule that in Ramazan 2003 one Turkish journalist condemned the use of hazelnuts and pistachios in *güllaç* as 'a crime and a sin'.[29]

23 *Baklava*

Baklava is a cure for ills
Baklava brings joy to the heart
I have eaten my fill of it
Baklava is exemplary.

Watchman's rhyme (c. 1800)[1]

Touch me remember me
At the harbour wait for me
I am a fine lady
On sugar feed me.

Traditional Turkish riddle (*answer: baklava*)[2]

S INCE THE FIFTEENTH CENTURY BAKLAVA has been no ordinary sweet
pastry, but has acquired a venerable status in Turkish cuisine that is
summed up by this anecdote recorded in the 1930s by British statesman
Sir Harry Luke:[3]

A Turkish Grand Vizier once gave a dinner in Constantinople to a certain
Ambassador. The dinner was ample and, by the time that the *plat doux* (it was
baqlawa) had arrived, the Ambassador could eat no more. 'Supposing,' asked
the Grand Vizier, who noticed that his guest had passed the dish, 'that you
were in a very crowded apartment and that your king wanted to enter, what
would you do?' 'I would press against the others,' said the Ambassador, 'and
make room for him somehow.' 'That is exactly what you must do,' retorted the
Grand Vizier, 'for the *baqlawa*, who is the king of sweets.'

Celebrations of all kinds, from weddings to religious feast days, called for
baklava. Whether made by cooks in wealthy households or by housewives in

ordinary homes, baklava was a symbol that extended far beyond the realm of culinary prowess. In his autobiography, the novelist Aziz Nesin (1915–95) recalled his mother's mortification at not being able to afford to bake a tray of baklava for the schoolmistress when, as a child of five in 1920, Aziz first recited a surah of the Quran from memory.[4] A gift of baklava would have been more meaningful than the *börek*, a layered savoury pastry, that she was obliged to give instead.

Presenting baklava as a gift was a long-established custom, especially in Ramazan. Abdülaziz Bey, writing around 1910, relates that well-off families sent trays of baklava to friends, neighbours, their children's schoolteachers, and to college students who were unable to return home for Ramazan.[5] When Easter came around, Christian neighbours reciprocated with gifts of eggs dyed red, Easter cakes and boiled wheat sprinkled with almonds, sugar and spices.

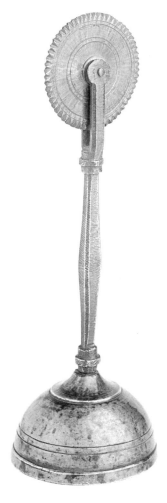

Novelist Hüseyin Rahmi Gürpınar (1864–1944) recalled that when, as a child of nine in 1873, he first fasted for one day during Ramazan, neighbours sent him a dish of baklava as a token of congratulation, unaware that he had secretly been eating meatballs, jam and stewed fruit in the kitchen. Hunger had got the better of his good intentions. His nurse caught him in the act and he compounded the transgression by offering her a bribe to keep silent: half the silver *mecidiye* his grandmother had promised him as a reward.[6]

No Ramazan was complete without baklava; it is a tradition that can be traced back to the fifteenth century, when baklava was made in the palace kitchens during Ramazan.[7] At the *imaret* founded by Sultan Bayezid II (1481–1512) in the city of Amasya, baklava made with saffron was served.[8]

31. Cast-brass pastry wheel used for cutting baklava into portions. The semicircular base was used as a pastry cutter for making the crescent-shaped filled pastries known as *fincan böreği* (Photograph: Mustafa Dorsay).

The earliest reference to baklava is in a poem by the mystic Kaygusuz Abdal, who lived in the first half of the fifteenth century:[9]

> Two hundred trays of baklava
> Some with almonds some with lentils.

Baklava filled with almonds is only to be expected, but lentils? The closest any other sources come to this is a nineteenth-century recipe for a baklava filling made with sweetened mashed beans. Perhaps lentils were the poor man's substitute for almonds, or it may be a joke – like the anchovy-filled baklava of Trabzon.[10]

Ottoman palace kitchen accounts for the year 1473, during the reign of Sultan Mehmed II (1451–81), record the quantities of *yufka* (tissue-thin pastry rolled out in circles) used to make baklava during Ramazan, but do not say what filling was used.[11] In 1503, however, walnuts were purchased specifically for the royal baklava.[12] The earliest recipes, discovered in a manuscript dating from the sixteenth or seventeenth century, call for an almond filling,[13] other ingredients being honey, sugar and clarified butter.[14]

Although Kaygusuz Abdal's poem is the earliest Turkish record of baklava, the thirteenth-century Arabic cookery book *Kitâb al-Wusla ila al-Habîb* contains a recipe for a sweet pastry very similar to baklava with the Turkish name *karnı yarık* ('split belly') given in addition to the Arabic name *kul wa-shkur* ('eat and give thanks'). The recipe uses the Turkish term *tutmaç* for the thinly rolled pastry: another indicator of its Turkish origin. The pastry can be shaped in two ways: either folded into broad strips then cut crossways and fried, or wrapped around the rolling pin and compressed to form a gathered hollow roll. The rolls are then formed into spirals, like the baklava known today as *sarığı burma* (coiled turban) or *bülbül yuvası* (nightingale's nest):[15]

> Another variety, called *kul wa-shkur* (eat and give thanks) and *garn yârûg* [*karnı yarık*, 'split belly']. Flour is mixed with clarified butter and kneaded with water, and it is rolled out with a rolling pin like *tutmâj*. Clarified butter is melted and the sheet of *tutmâj* is greased, and it is folded as wide as four fingers in bunches (or perhaps 'layers': *tâgât*). It is cut into strips (*shawâbîr*) and fried in sesame oil until brown. It is put in a plate and sprinkled with sugar, pungent rose water and pistachios. Another variety of it: it is kneaded as mentioned and rolled out as mentioned with clarified butter, and it is rolled around (*yutwâ 'ala*) the rolling pin and taken down from the rolling pin while it is standing up. And it is made into small round loaves and fried in sesame oil, and sugar and rose water are put on it.

If these complex baklava varieties were being made in the thirteenth century, we can safely assume that the simplest layered varieties date from even earlier.

Baklava has the closest ties to the pre-Anatolian Turkic cuisine of Central Asia of any of Turkey's sweet dishes. Tissue-thin pastry sheets are known to have had a long past in Turkish cuisine. The original meaning of the word *yufka* was thin or fragile, and so came to denote thin bread or pastry. In his Turkish–Arabic dictionary of 1074, Mahmud of Kashgar describes *yufka* folded and fried in butter, and another variety (*yalaci yuga*) so thin it crumbled at a touch.[16] Such folded and layered breads appear to have joined forces with the Arab culinary tradition of soaking pastries in syrup and so given rise to baklava.

The knotty question of the origin of the word *baklava* continues to vex linguists. The very similar word *oklava*, an old Turkish word meaning 'rolling pin', thought to derive from *ok* (arrow), is the basis for one theory proposed by the Turcologist Prof. Dr Mustafa S. Kaçalın, while Altaist Dr Paul Buell favours an etymology based on the Mongolian word *bakala-*, 'to wrap up in layers', combined with the Turkic verbal noun ending *-va*.[17]

This ancient tradition of folded and layered pastry leaves is reflected in *katlama* ('folded')[18] and *katmer* ('layered') – names for a large family of sweet and savoury pastries made all over Central Asia and Turkey today. The versatility of *yufka* sheets means that they appear in all kinds of guises, both savoury and sweet, in Turkic and Turkish cuisines. With the thickness varied as required, they can be wrapped, rolled, layered and sliced in seemingly endless variety, sliced into strips as noodles and boiled, fried or baked. Hardly a meal can be had in Turkey that does not include *yufka* in some form or other, and to varying degrees this is a feature of cuisines throughout the Middle East and the Balkans.

Rolling out *yufka* as thin as paper in a precise circle is an art, and in Turkish towns and cities most people rely on the local *yufkacı* (*yufka* maker) shop, where they are rolled freshly every day. Factory-rolled sheets in packets are available in supermarkets, but are so thick and inflexible compared to the hand-rolled variety that they are a desperate last resort. In the past, *yufka* rolling was not just a woman's skill, but something that almost every country-bred boy learned to master. Mahmud Nedim, an Ottoman army officer who wrote a cookery book for fellow officers who were either unmarried or whose families remained behind in their hometowns, tells his readers that if they do not know how to roll out *yufka* themselves they can ask one of the soldiers, 'most of whom know how to make *yufka*'.[19] Nor was cooking dishes from *yufka* entirely the preserve of women or professional cooks. Ahmed Câvid, historian to Selim III (r. 1789–1807), describes a *börek* (savoury layered pastry) that he used to make himself, layering twenty *yufka* with a filling of Mudurnu cheese, dill, parsley and eggs.[20]

Baklava's almost sacred status as a festive dish is due as much to the skill required to make it as to its luxury ingredients, requiring considerable quantities of honey or sugar, butter and nuts, which ordinary families could only afford on special occasions. *Yufka* making intrigued the French traveller Bertrandon de la Brocquière when he saw it for the first time in 1433.[21] During his journey across Turkey on his way home from the Holy Land, Brocquière watched nomad Turcoman women making *yufka* at their encampment near Antakya, the ancient Antioch:

> We halted among them; they placed before us one of the table-cloths before-mentioned, in which there remained fragments of bread, cheese, and grapes. They then brought us a dozen of thin cakes of bread, with a large jug of curdled milk, called by them *yogort*. The cakes are a foot broad, round, and thinner than wafers; they fold them up as grocers do their papers for spices, and eat them filled with the curdled milk . . . It was here I saw women make those thin cakes I spoke of. This is their manner of making them; they have a small round table, very smooth, on which they throw some flour, and mix it with water to a paste, softer than that for bread. This paste they divide into round pieces, which they flatten as much as possible, with a wooden roller of a smaller diameter than an egg, until they make them as thin as I have mentioned. During this operation they have a convex plate of iron placed on a tripod, and heated by a gentle fire underneath, on which they spread the cake and instantly turn it, so that they make two of their cakes sooner than a waferman can make one wafer.

The folded bread filled with yogurt served to Broquière by his Turcoman hosts is *dürüm*, the *türmek* of Central Asia recorded by Mahmud of Kashgar in his eleventh-century dictionary.[22] It is similar to the fast food that has recently become popular by the name 'bread wraps' in Britain and the United States.

Although medieval Arabic cookery books contain recipes for many sweet pastries, the only one for anything resembling baklava is the *karnı yarık* mentioned above. On the other hand, the Iranians knew baklava, which they called *lâberlâ*, *kûlânic* or *lûlânic*, all words again meaning 'layer upon layer'. This is among the myriad foods mentioned in the satirical poems of Bushaq of Shiraz (d. c. 1423–7), reflecting the extensive interaction between Turkish and Iranian cuisines from the eleventh century onwards.[23]

At the celebrations for the circumcision of Murad III's sons in 1582, 'trays of many-layered baklava' were prepared.[24] In the mid-seventeenth century Evliyâ

Çelebi claims with poetic hyperbole that baklava made for wedding feasts in Belgrade were the size of cartwheels and consisted of a thousand layers each![25] Evidently in elite circles the number of layers your baklava had was a source of pride. Ottoman period recipes diverge widely on this subject, ranging from eight to sixty layers.[26] In grand houses in the nineteenth century a minimum of a hundred layers was expected.[27] Of the three earliest recipes dating from the sixteenth or seventeenth century one is an eight-layered, one (titled royal baklava) is prepared with a type of puff pastry made by brushing melted kidney fat on the thinly rolled out sheets, which are folded up then rolled out again, and for the third the sheets are wrapped around the rolling pin, gathered into concertina rolls and arranged in a spiral in the baking tin as described in the thirteenth-century *karnı yarık* recipe.[28]

A technique for rolling out the sheets simultaneously is first recorded by Friedrich Unger, who observed it during his visit to Istanbul in 1835.[29] Each tiny ball of pastry is first rolled to a saucer-sized circle; these are heaped into a pile, and each dusted with plenty of wheat starch, and the whole pile is rolled out into a large circle. Batches of twenty sheets can be rolled out in this way.

32. Karagöz is making baklava by rolling out newspaper instead of pastry. He explains that sugar is unobtainable, now existing only in the newspapers (*Karagöz*, 1093 (17 August 1918), p. 4).

This method is still commonly used today by home cooks and professional pastry chefs.

Like the other arts, cookery was a barometer of wealth. While in the reign of Sultan Bâyezid II (1481–1512) the chief bakers at the palace, Sinan and Osman, were responsible for making baklava for Ramazan and religious festivals,[30] by the seventeenth century we find baklava makers (*baklavacı*) listed in a palace salary register as a separate class of pastrycook.[31] The high degree of specialization among cooks working at the palace or for wealthy dignitaries was one of the key factors in the development of Ottoman *haute cuisine*. Cooks spent their entire careers perfecting a particular type of dish for rich employers with sophisticated tastes, using the finest and most expensive ingredients.

The best baklava was so insubstantial that a coin dropped from a height of an *arşın* (65 centimetres) would pierce every one of its layers and strike the bottom of the baking tray.[32] This party trick had been around for a long time. In the seventeenth century baklava with clotted cream made in the home of Ferhad Pasha's descendants was described as 'without equal in the world, so delicate and crisp that a coin dropped onto it penetrates right through'.[33] The thousand-layer baklavas made in Belgrade were apparently so light that they too passed this test, despite their enormous size. Guild examinations required candidates for the rank of master cook to roll out the *yufka* for baklava so accurately that they precisely fitted the circular baking tray, as well as passing the coin-dropping test.[34]

The lightness of expertly made baklava has been most poetically expressed by James Stanislaus Bell, who described baklava that he ate in the town of Sinop on the southern Black Sea coast in 1839 as 'butterfly-things of pastry, which one might blow away, but for the honey their wings are clogged with'.[35]

Numerous types of baklava are made today but there were even more in the past. Ottoman cookery books record baklava filled with puréed beans, melon or unsalted cheese, which have been forgotten today.[36] Moreover, baklava was eaten hot, as we learn from recipes listed under the heading 'Hot Sweet Pastries' in one nineteenth-century cookery book.[37] However, the word 'forgotten' needs to be used with care, since dishes that have disappeared without trace in Istanbul have a tendency to turn up alive and well in Turkey's provincial cuisines. The pastry known as *katmer* in the southeastern city of Urfa is actually baklava with a filling of fresh unsalted cheese that is eaten hot, just as it was in Ottoman times. This is the *pièce de résistance* of special meals in Urfa, either made at home or ordered from pastry shops. At a time when cheesecake is all the rage in up-market cafés in Istanbul, it should not be hard to stage a comeback for such an exquisite sweet as *peynirli baklava* (cheese baklava), which also survives in other parts of Turkey, such as the provinces of Isparta and Çorum.

The preeminent status enjoyed by baklava made it a yardstick by which other dishes were compared. The nineteenth-century cookery book writer and army officer Mahmud Nedim tells us that among the people of Rhodes meat pilaf was 'as esteemed as baklava', and that a meat and yogurt dish called *kalaços* was considered 'almost equal to baklava' in the eastern Turkish town of Çemişkezek.[38]

Most famous of the Ramazan traditions relating to baklava was the Baklava Procession, which had been instituted towards the end of the sixteenth century and took place annually on the fifteenth day of Ramazan. Hundreds of trays of baklava, one for every ten janissaries, were baked in the palace kitchens, tied in cloths to protect them from dust, and arrayed in the Second Court. The first tray was presented to the sultan, who was an honorary member of the First Janissary Company. Then two janissaries from each squad of ten would step forward by turn, pick up a tray and suspend it by the knot in the cloth from a pole they carried on their shoulders. When all the trays had been collected, the janissary companies, each led by their officers and standard bearer, would march out of the palace back to their barracks. The following day the empty copper trays and cloths were returned to the palace kitchens.[39] In later years, however, when the janissaries became infamous for the abuses and arrogance that led to their replacement by a new modernized army in 1826, they stopped returning the trays and cloths, claiming insolently that they had eaten those too.[40] Until the Janissary Corps was liquidated in 1826, one and a half months after the last Baklava Procession, this event remained a popular annual spectacle.

When the Museum of Ancient Costume was established in Istanbul in 1852, the around 140 models made for the museum in Austria included a pair of janissary soldiers carrying a tray of baklava in the Baklava Procession.[41] Sadly, none of these models, dressed in authentic Ottoman costume, has survived to the present day.

The Baklava Procession is the subject of the following verses recited by watchmen during Ramazan, as they drummed their way along the streets, waking people up for the pre-dawn meal of *sahur*:[42]

> As the sun and moon revolve
> May divine aid be your company
> The sultan gave baklava
> To his loyal janissaries.
>
> I watched the procession
> And see what I do
> I saw the ceremony
> And relate it to you.

Tonight is the sixteenth[43]
Ramazan is waning
Today to the janissaries
The sultan gave baklava.

I wanted to see the sight
The watchman said let's go
We reached the Palace Square
In time for the procession.

The guards raced about
The armourers jostled
Our sovereign gave permission
They snatched the baklava.

If it is true, as the historian Abdurrahman Şeref wrote in 1911, that baklava was distributed to around 10,000 janissaries, it would mean 1,000 trays in all.[44] Evidently unaware of the scale of the operation, the Reverend Robert Walsh, chaplain to the British embassy in the 1820s and 1830s, made the picturesque claim that the 'ladies of the Seraglio' prepared the baklava for the janissaries.[45] Although there is no evidence that those ladies were ever roped in to help, we do know that in 1573 a number of 'old women' were hired to roll out the prodigious quantities of *yufka* required for the Ramazan baklava at the palace.[46]

Wealthy Ottoman households suffered a similar staff shortage during Ramazan, when they distributed large quantities of baklava as gifts and kept open house for the *iftar* meal, at which the daylong fast was broken. In the nineteenth century we know that the need for additional kitchen staff was met by freelance pastrycooks, who used coffeehouses as their base, waiting for clients to hire their services for weddings and circumcision feasts, as well as Ramazan.[47]

Apart from its role on celebratory occasions, baklava was a feature of grand dinners given by the upper classes. Such a dinner, given by a woman in the town of Şuhut in western Turkey in the 1890s for her friends, is described by Lady Agnes Ramsay, who was guest of honour.[48] The third course was baklava with clotted cream: 'It was about eighteen inches in diameter and the colour of its crust was a gleaming golden brown. I will not attempt to describe the exquisite lightness of the flaky pastry or the delicate fragrance of the rich cream which filled it!' Lady Ramsay enthuses. However, not being aware that interspersing sweet dishes with savoury was a feature of Ottoman fine dining, she assumed that the 'huge cream tart' marked the end of the meal, and ate heartily. 'Alas!

Pride goeth before destruction and a haughty spirit before a fall! The dish that had contained the cream tart was removed only to give place to another just as large, piled with *dolmadhés*,' she laments. Obliged to taste course after relentless course, the meal that had started so enjoyably turned into a nightmare.

Not having foreknowledge of *nouvelle cuisine*, and forgetting that European meals had been arranged very differently before *à la russe* dining supplanted *à la française* in the 1830s, foreign guests at Ottoman dinners during the later nineteenth century were variously amused, appalled or outraged to be served sweet dishes in the middle instead of at the end of meals. By the same token, many Turkish people today find the idea almost shocking, so completely has this practice died out. Yet the succession of courses at these meals had its own rhythm of flavours, stimulating the palate with frequent contrasts between savoury, sour and sweet.

When Sir Harry Luke was invited to dinner by Huccetullah Mehmed Bahaeddin Veled, descendant of the mystic philosopher Mevlânâ Celâleddin Rûmî and head of the Mevlevi dervish order, at his country house near Konya in 1913, a meal very like the one that had caused Lady Ramsay such suffering was served. Luke, however, was a veteran traveller familiar with Ottoman customs, and so was able to enjoy the occasion and record the menu in detail:[49]

On the soft turf, under the shade of poplar trees, a table was spread, and for nearly two hours a dervish attendant brought and removed a bewildering number of viands, all contained in metal dishes from which one helped oneself directly with one's fork. The order of the courses was something as follows, meats, vegetables and sweet dishes being interspersed with delightful inconsequence:

- Grilled pieces of mutton (kebab).
- Meat patties (bürek).
- A sweet pastry with honey (baqlawa).
- Stuffed aubergines.
- Vegetable marrows stuffed with rice.
- Stuffed tomatoes.
- A sweet rice pudding with cream.
- Stewed okras.
- A sauté of mutton and vegetables.
- Pilav.
- Pears stewed in their skins.
- Melons.

In addition there were side dishes of cheese, salad and pimentos.

The higher echelons of society could afford baklava as regular fare rather than a rare treat. In the early seventeenth century Ottavio Bon, Venetian ambassador from 1604 to 1607, reported to a government evidently avid for the most mundane details of life at the Ottoman court that Sultan Ahmed I (r. 1603–17) 'closeth up his stomach with a *Bocklava* (A Tart), or some such thing' (i.e. he ended his meal with baklava). If correct, this suggests that at ordinary meals sweet pastries were reserved for the final course. Bon goes on to note the huge quantities of sugar expended in the making of sherbet and baklava in court circles:[50]

> As for sugar, there is spent an unspeakable deal of it in the making of *Sherbets* and *Boclavas*, which not only the Seraglio useth, but are also ordinary presents, from one Bashaw to another, and from one friend to another; insomuch that it is a thing to be admired, that so great a quantity should so suddenly be consumed.

Archive documents record that during 1648 and 1649 baklava was served almost weekly to the ministers attending the Imperial Council, which convened at the palace four days a week.[51] Baklava was also served at palace banquets, such as that held for the ambassador of Transylvania on 10 November 1650 and another to celebrate the Feast of Sacrifice on 4 December 1650. Baklava was the fifth course in the nineteen-course meal served to the ambassador, and the eighth course in the sixteen-course *bayram* banquet.[52] A curious feature of these banquet menus is that *mantı*, normally a dish of meat-stuffed noodles in yogurt sauce,[53] is here listed as a sweet dish. This illustrates the experimentation that characterized courtly Ottoman cuisine, and serves as a warning against jumping to conclusions about familiar dishes in a historical context.

Although baklava is always baked in ovens today, in past centuries few households had their own oven and such dishes were more often cooked over a gentle charcoal fire, either turning them upside down halfway through the cooking process or placing a metal sheet over the circular pan and spreading hot embers on top. Right up to the second half of the nineteenth century, Turkish cookery books still describe these methods.[54] Baklava could also be cooked in a *tandır* (tandoor oven), as the seventeenth-century Ottoman traveller, Evliyâ Çelebi, noted when visiting Belgrade. Again in the seventeenth century, we come across a reference to 'hot fried baklava' in Seyyid Hasan's diary,[55] but how the baklava was fried we have no idea.

Baklava is thought to have been the original inspiration for the Austrian strudel, itself introduced from Hungary.[56] Although baklava is not usually made today with pastry that is stretched rather than rolled, a relative of baklava, the *katmer* of Gaziantep in southeastern Turkey, is made by a similar method, as are some types of *börek*, its savoury counterpart.

RECIPES

AADI BAKLAWÄ (Türâbî Efendi, 1864)[57]

Make sufficient paste as No. 86 [Put a pound and a half of flour on a slab, make a hole in the centre, in which put a teaspoonful of salt and four eggs; mix all together, then add sufficient water, and form a softish flexible paste; then dip your hands into melted fresh butter, and work it for a few minutes longer] then divide it into fifty pieces the size of walnuts, sprinkle a little wheat starch under and over, and roll them out with a rolling-pin as thin as tissue-paper, quite round, and the size of the baking-tin you intend to lay them in; then butter the tin,* in which lay five of the pieces of paste one over the other, sprinkle a little fresh butter over the top one, and lay five more pieces over; then sprinkle either pounded almonds, pistachios, or filberts, all over, and lay five more pieces of paste over, butter again, and five more pieces of paste; then either of the above ingredients, and five more pieces of paste over, butter again, and so forth, until you have laid all the pieces of paste; then cut it up in diamonds, pour about half a pound or a little more of scalded fresh butter all over, and bake it a nice colour in a hot oven. While it is baking, put a pound of nice honey or loaf-sugar into a saucepan, with two pints of water, and set it to boil until it becomes a syrup; when the paste is nicely browned, pour it gently all over, and let it remain for five minutes or so; then dish up in pyramid, sprinkle some powdered sugar over, and serve hot or cold.

* In Turkey the baking-tins are made of copper from two to three inches deep. They are circular, and from one to two feet in diameter.

MELON BAKLAVA   (Anonymous, eighteenth century)[58]

Place a little butter and five to ten thinly rolled-out *yufka* in a suitable baking tray. Take spoonfuls of a very sweet melon and place these over the *yufka* until they are covered. Then place one more *yufka* over, sprinkle melted butter on top, and bake in the oven as usual. After it is baked, sprinkle plenty of sugar over for the best flavour.

BAKLAVA WITH ARTIFICIAL CLOTTED CREAM   (Mehmed Kâmil, 1844)[59]

The recipe describes three different fillings that can be used as substitutes for clotted cream, made with white beans (haricot beans), rice and cheese respectively.

Prepare the *yufka* as usual. If you have no *kaymak* (clotted cream), boil sufficient white beans in water until tender, strain, then mash them well. Pass through a hair sieve or colander. Then add a little milk and boil the purée until thickened. Whip a couple of egg whites well and stir into the mixture. Alternatively, cook rice well with milk, and when softened add well-whipped egg white. Or take unsalted *lor* cheese, or *çayır* cheese, soaked to remove the salt, and mix well with some sugar. All these fillings may be used, and they resemble clotted cream.

24 Kadayıf

> *Tel kadayıf* with plenty of sugar
> Gives joy to lovers of pleasure.
>
> Watchman's rhyme[1]

YASSI KADAYIF

KADAYIF IS THE PUDDING MOST frequently mentioned in the *Thousand and One Nights*.[2] This small yeast griddle cake with a rubbery texture is virtually identical to the English crumpet, and is probably its forefather. They were usually stuffed with nuts and soaked in syrup flavoured with rose water, as vividly described by Mas'ûdî in his world geography, *Muruj al-Dhahab wa-Ma'adin al-Jawahir* ('Meadows of Gold and Mines of Precious Stones'), completed in 947:[3]

> When in my friends the pang of hunger grows,
> I have *qatâ'if*, like soft folios;
> As flow of lambent honey brimming white
> So amid the other dainties it is bright,
> And, having drunk of almond-essence deep
> With oil it glitters, wherein it doth seep.
> Rose-water floats thereon, like flooding sea,
> Bubble on bubble swimming fragrantly;
> As foliated book, laid fold on fold
> Afflicted hearts rejoice when they behold:
> But when divided, like the spoils of war,
> All have their hearts' desire, and sated are.

Fortunately we know how this *kadayıf* that so inspired Mas'ûdî was made, because his contemporary, al-Warrâq, gives a recipe. A batter prepared from fine white flour, yeast, salt and borax is left to rise, then poured by the ladleful onto a marble slab or iron griddle heated over a fire.⁴ None of the later Arab cookery writers bothers to explain how *kadayıf* was made, presumably because it was always shop-bought, as is the case in Turkey and the rest of the Middle East today. The pancakes were then stuffed with a mixture of nuts – walnuts or almonds – sugar and rose water, and either rolled up or folded into half moons, and finally soaked in almond oil and syrup (optionally they could be fried before soaking in syrup).⁵ A thirteenth-century Arabic recipe uses a stuffing of pounded pistachios or almonds, sugar, musk and rose water.⁶

Kadayıf was usually cooked on one side only, which was the most delicious variety, according to the anonymous author of an eighteenth-century Turkish cookery manual.⁷ These pancakes are still made in Turkey, where they are known as *yassı kadayıf* ('flat *kadayıf*') in Istanbul, and in the southeastern provinces as *taş kadayıf* ('stone *kadayıf*') or *taş ekmeği* ('stone bread') in reference to the traditional practice of cooking them on a stone slab. In other parts of Turkey they are known as *cızlama* or *akıtma*. The method of preparing them has changed little since the tenth century. In Diyarbakır the *taş ekmeği* sold on street stalls is cooked on one side only, stuffed with walnuts and sugar, folded in half, then fried and tossed into syrup, just as described by al-Warrâq a thousand years ago. The home-made variety is cooked on both sides and eaten sprinkled with *pekmez*, sugar or jam.⁸

Stuffed *kadayıf* features in one late Ottoman cookery book under the name *yassı kadayıf dolması* ('stuffed flat *kadayıf*'), and is filled with pine nuts.⁹

The fifteenth-century Ottoman court physician Şirvânî gives a recipe for *kadayıf* pancakes, but only as an afterthought, introduced with the words 'And another variety is . . .', because for the Ottomans the term *kadayıf* referred primarily to the pastry strands known as *tel kadayıf* in Turkish and *kunâfa* in Arabic. The original *kadayıf* had been so overshadowed that Şirvânî had only the vaguest idea of how they were made, instructing his readers to make a dough with white flour, form it into flat circles, and lay these in a pan to cook. When describing Istanbul's *kadayıf* makers in the seventeenth century Evliyâ Çelebi mentions only *tel kadayıf*. Yet we know that *yassı kadayıf* continued to be made, since eighteenth- and nineteenth-century Ottoman cookery writers give recipes, although they do not describe the method, assuming – like earlier Arab writers – that they would be shop-bought.

In 1900 Mahmud Nedim tells us, 'This *yassı kadayıf* is made only in Istanbul and some other coastal provinces.' In fact, however, *yassı kadayıf* was made in plenty of other places under different names. In Edirne the home-made variety known as *akıtma* was a local speciality. When Sultan Ahmed III passed through the city during the Morean campaign of 1715, he was invited to the country house of Mirza, steward of the water engineers, to taste the 'renowned and legendary' *akıtma* made by his ninety-year-old mother.[10] Her recipe was as follows:

Akıtma

First take one *kıyye* of white flour, and add ash water made by mixing one *kıyye* of pure water with half a *kıyye* of woodash, leaving it to stand and then passing it through fine muslin.[11] Mix the flour and water to a batter with the consistency of *lalenk*.[12] Add 50 *dirhem*s of yeast and beat well until it acquires an almost glutinous texture. Then cover well and allow to rise for about three or four hours. Heat an earthenware griddle and pour the mixture onto it by the ladleful. When browned underneath turn over to cook on the other side. Remove with a spatula and place in a large dish. Then cook another. Melt some butter in a small pan and with a clean wing feather brush the melted butter over each pancake, cover again and set the dish on a tripod over a few embers until all the pancakes are ready. Leave to cool. Some people eat them plain, while others sprinkle each layer with a medium quantity of ground almonds, walnuts or hazelnuts. Alternatively, if each pancake is sprinkled with sugar after cooking they are delicious. They are even delightful without sweetening, because the sour flavour imparted by the yeast is most pleasant.

Finally, here is an early nineteenth-century recipe for *yassı kadayıf* prepared with clotted cream:[13]

Yağsız Kadayıf[14]

Arrange one layer of *yassı kadayıf* in a pan and pour over a couple of cups of milk, some sugar and some *kaymak* (clotted cream). Continue with another layer and if the milk is insufficient one or more cups may be added. Then place over the heat and simmer for a little while. Remove before the *kaymak* melts. Allow to cool slightly, then sprinkle with granulated sugar and eat.

TEL KADAYIF

While *kadayıf* in the medieval Arab world always meant *yassı kadayıf*, for the Ottoman Turks the term came to refer almost invariably to the fine pastry strands known as *tel kadayıf* (Arabic *kunâfa*). When Şirvânî translated al-Baghdâdî's thirteenth-century cookery book towards the middle of the fifteenth century, he added a recipe for *tel kadayıf* as the main *kadayıf* recipe, demoting al-Baghdâdî's *qatâyif* to 'another version'. This is the earliest recipe we have for *tel kadayıf*:[15]

Kadayıf

One kind is prepared with a batter of white flour and water, beaten until well combined. Let it stand. Then place a tinned pan over a gentle fire and using a large ladle punctured with holes, let the batter flow onto the pan to form long threads. When they are cooked remove from the pan and pour another batch. In this way the desired quantity of strands are prepared. Take the required quantity of these strands, lay them in a pan, and over them sprinkle almonds and ground sugar flavoured with musk. Roll it up and pour over sufficient sesame oil and syrup and rose water and ground pistachios. Then it is ready to eat.

During a guild procession in 1640, Istanbul's *kadayıf* makers marched through the streets with model shops decorated with strings of *tel kadayıf* dyed in many colours:[16] 'And the *kadayıf* makers made shops upon packhorses and decorated these little shops with strings of *kadayıf* in many colours and distributed *kadayıf* to the crowd.'

Although the Arabic term *kunâfa* today refers to *tel kadayıf*, in the thirteenth century the word meant a type of very thin flatbread.[17] This enables us to date the transformation of *kadayıf* and *kunâfa* into *tel kadayıf* roughly to some point between the thirteenth and fifteenth centuries.

A version of *kunâfa* made by shredding flatbread in the thirteenth-century *Kitâb al-Wusla ila al-Habîb* evidently represents an intermediate stage in this development.[18] However, it is a long leap from sliced flatbread to pouring threads of batter onto a griddle. Producing thin threads of batter is not easy without a special utensil. However, just such a utensil – a coconut shell with a hole in the bottom – appears in a recipe for *mushabbak* in the fourteenth-century Arabic cookery book *Kitâb Wasf al-At'ima al-Mu'tâda* in Topkapı Palace Library:[19]

Mushabbak ('Latticework')

Take some of this aforementioned batter and pour it into a coconut with a hole pierced in the base. Cover the hole with your finger as you fill it. Put sesame oil in the cauldron, and when it boils remove your finger from the hole and move [the coconut] in circles. So rings of latticework are created. Take them up and throw them in syrup and it comes out excellently.

33. Antique copper *tel kadayıf*
pot (Courtesy of Gökçen Adar;
photograph: Mustafa Dorsay).

Whether the first *tel kadayıf* was
made with a pierced coconut shell
we shall never know, but someone
used something of the kind to pour
threads of *kadayıf* batter onto a hot
griddle instead of into hot oil, and
thus *tel kadayıf* was born. The fact
that both are made of liquid batters
(minus yeast in the case of *tel kadayıf*)
cooked on a griddle explains why in
Turkish *tel kadayıf* and *yassı kadayıf*
share the name *kadayıf* despite
looking so different. On the other
hand, the Arabic name *kunâfa* must
hark back to the shredded flatbread
version.

In the fifteenth century a pierced
ladle was being used for making *tel
kadayıf*, and in time this evolved into a special copper pot with ten to fifteen
narrow brass pipes inserted in a row in the base. Known as *kadayıf kıfı* these pots
are still made in Gaziantep and Diyarbakır. Holding one palm across the pipes
to prevent the batter flowing out, the *kadayıfçı* (*kadayıf* maker) fills the vessel
and then swirls it over a circular and slightly domed copper griddle more than
a metre in diameter, to form dense parallel spirals that instantly set on the hot
surface.

The German confectioner Friedrich Unger watched *tel kadayıf* being made
in the 1830s and wrote the most detailed historical account we have, including
a description of the special stove into which the griddle fitted:[20]

> **Kataif**
> A very popular dish with a most delicious flavour. The halwadschi
> [*helvacı*, confectioner] prepares it in large quantities and sells the cakes
> both unmade and made.[21] The implements needed for the preparation of this
> *Kataif* consist of a tinned pan in which the batter is mixed, a fine sieve through

which it is passed so that there should be no lumps in it, a copper beaker, its inner side tinned, with 12–14 small brass pipes for pouring out the *Kataif*, and finally a big copper plate, onto which the *Kataif* is poured and cooked on a stove with hand-high edges, into which the *Kataif* cooking plate fits exactly.

The mixture for *Kataif*, which consists just of water and flour, is a thin liquid batter that is strained so that the narrow pipes do not get blocked. When the batter has been prepared in this way, place the round copper plate four feet in diameter on the aforementioned cooker, put sufficient charcoal under the plate to ensure that it is evenly heated, and try to maintain this even heat. After having oiled or buttered this cooking plate and then wiped it, pour the mixture with the help of the aforementioned beaker in circles onto the plate until it is full, leave for a few seconds, and the noodles are ready. Now remove them, and place them in portions on paper, grease the tray again and repeat this operation until your mixture has been used up.

These vermicelli-like noodles are subsequently prepared in the following way: For one *occa* of noodles, take 1 *occa* of honey, 125 drams of fat or butter. Grease a tinned copper tray, which must have an edge two fingers in height, with fat that must be warmed, spread the noodles in it and sprinkle over the 125 drams [of fat], press it a bit and place it in the oven, where it is baked at medium heat for half an hour until it is a golden colour. Meanwhile place the honey with some water on the fire, skim it and pour it over as soon as the noodles come out of the oven, leave to get cold and prick out in pieces. This is the famous *kataif*.

Charles White provides some additional details in his account published in 1846:[22]

The second and more common kind [of *kadayıf*] is somewhat like fine Neapolitan maccaroni. The paste, made fluid with rose-water, is placed in a small receiver, perforated at the bottom like the spout of a watering-pot. This implement is waved to and fro over a large circular copper-plate, moderately heated upon a stove; the mixture, passing through the holes in long filaments, soon dries, and is taken off ready for sale in bunches or strings, and sold by the *oka*.

If White is correct about adding rose water to the batter, this may have been a refinement enjoyed by the upper classes, since the usual variety consisted only of flour and water.

When he wrote his *Turkish Cookery Book* published in London in 1864, Türâbî Efendi was obliged to instruct his English readers how to make *tel kadayıf* from scratch, since they could not find it ready-made. They had to begin by manufacturing their own *kadayıf* pot, so it seems unlikely that anyone took up the challenge:[23]

Aadi Tel Kadayıf

Procure a tin pint pot, the shape of a tumbler, insert in the bottom eight or ten fine tubes; then put some flour in a basin, which mix with water to form a smooth batter; put a portion of the batter in the pot, let it run through the tubes, by passing the pot up and down on a very hot crumpet-stove, which is done in a few minutes in long threads like vermicelli; take them up, and spread them on a tray, and continue in this way till you have made about three pounds; then lay the vermicelli even in a buttered baking-tin, pour three-quarters of a pound of scalded fresh butter over, and bake it a nice brown on both sides in the oven, or on a charcoal fire; then put a pound of white sugar in a stewpan, with two pints of water, and set it to boil until it becomes a syrup; skim, and keep it hot. When the vermicelli is done, pour the syrup all over. If you wish it to be crisp, leave it uncovered; if soft, cover it the moment you have poured the syrup over, and let it remain for fifteen minutes or so; then cut it in four crossways, or any other shape you fancy, dish up. If any syrup is left in the baking tin, pour it over, and serve hot or cold.

In more recent times labour-saving devices for making *tel kadayıf* were developed. One of these is a swivel base enabling the copper griddles to be spun around. Another is a large vessel with twenty or so pipes underneath. This is hung from a horizontal arm that is then swung slowly across the spinning griddle. This system is used in many parts of Turkey today as well as other parts of the Middle East and North Africa.[24] Şevket Kılıç, a *kadayıfçı* in Gaziantep, describes a mechanized system he saw when visiting in Syria that consists of a heated revolving cylinder, but says he prefers the traditional manual method, since this produces curved strands, which are superior for making *kadayıf* pastries.

Leaving technical concerns aside, why did *tel kadayıf* win such overwhelming popularity at the expense of *yassı kadayıf*? This must be attributed to the unusual texture and the versatility of the pastry strands. *Tel kadayıf* could be prepared in all kinds of shapes: rolls, twists, buns and simple layers. It was made in private homes, by *medrese* students in their college rooms at weekends,[25] and of course at the palace for the sultan and his family,[26] not only by the royal confectioners but also by the sultan's private attendants (*enderun ağa*), as related by Charles White:[27]

That called *seraiee kataifi* ['palace *kadayıf*'] is most fashionable. Indeed, many officers of the Sultan's household pride themselves upon making this dish. In the palaces of Tcheraghan and Beshiktash the chamberlains, equerries, and superior black aghas have a kitchen fitted out with marble, and provided with stoves and utensils, where they beguile the tedium of 'waiting' by making these pancakes.[28] To produce a *seraiee kataif* worthy of being tasted by the Sultan, is regarded by them as a great honour.

One of the famous palace varieties involved baking the *tel kadayıf* with plenty of melted butter, straining off the excess butter and then rinsing the strands in hot water before adding the syrup. Another was *beyaz kadayıf* ('white *kadayıf*'), which was cooked on a stove instead of baked, and then steeped in a syrup made with sugar candy or *peynir şekeri*.[29]

In Damascus a version known as *katife* was prepared by frying the *tel kadayıf* in a pan with a little clarified butter, then adding honey or sugar, and heaping it onto a dish.[30]

A young Ottoman infantry officer and cookbook author, Mahmud Nedim, gives a simple *tel kadayıf* recipe for fellow officers who lack culinary skills, concluding with a warning against ready-made *kadayıf*:[31]

Tel Kadayıf

When you buy *kadayıf* from the *kadayıfçı* loosen the bundles on a sheet before laying them evenly into the baking tin and pour half-spoonfuls of melted clarified butter at intervals over the top. Place in the oven. Remove from the oven when coloured and leave to cool. Then pour boiling syrup over and cover to let it soften. After half an hour it will be ready to eat. This is what they call 'bachelor-style *kadayıf*'. It is undoubtedly better than the *kadayıf* cooked by the *kadayıf* makers with a thousand wiles and tricks, because they lay unbroken *kadayıf* strands like gilding over the top and fill the rest with the broken crumbs, which makes them a good profit.

Selling short-weight was another of the *kadayıfçı*'s tricks:[32]

Kataifjee are not always honest or fortunate in their attempts to sell light weight. It is related that the grand vizir, İzet Mehemet Pacha,[33] walking one day through the streets in disguise, stopped before one of the *kataif* shops, and, after watching the owner as he served different customers, thought that he detected short weight. He consequently demanded half an *oka*, which he received and paid for; then, calling to his attendants, he bade them draw forth the scales and weights carried by them for the purpose of discovering short measure. Upon weighing the *kataif* purchased by the grand vizir, it was proved that several drachms were wanting. Thereupon, İzet Mehemet ordered the dealer to produce his own weights, which turned out to be false. The punishment was summary, and not inappropriate. Half a dozen sturdy *kavass* seized the purveyor, who, in spite of shouts and protestations, was lifted and seated upon his own copper-plate, and there subjected during some minutes to the process of being converted into *kataif.*

Among the variations on basic *tel kadayıf* was *kadayıf micmeri*, an eighteenth-century innovation that has now been forgotten, but deserves to be revived.[34] When made by master chefs for banquets it was decorated with gold leaf. The method was to cook the *tel kadayıf* with a little clarified butter over a low heat, add ground almonds, pistachios and sugar, then form into cakes the shape of little Turkish coffee cups. These would keep for fifteen to twenty days, and boxes of them were sometimes sent as gifts to friends. According to a later recipe, the *micmer* could be shaped by pressing into the hollows of a fritter pan.[35]

Kadayıf twisted into ropes and then arranged in spirals was known as *çörek kadayıf* or *burma kadayıf*, and is first described in 1844.[36] The following recipe by Türâbî Efendi is dated 1864:[37]

Churèk Kadayıf

Prepare as much vermicelli as is required, as No. 149 [see Türâbî's *Aadi Tel Kadayıf* recipe on p. 197]; then twist it like a rope, twice the thickness of your thumb, and make it into cakes the size of a Bath bun; lay them in a buttered baking-tin, pour in about half a pound of scalded fresh butter, and bake it on both sides a nice brown. When done, pour some hot syrup all over, as above, and let it remain for ten minutes or so, dish up, and serve hot or cold.

Another variety was *kaymaklı kadayıf*, which had a layer of *kaymak* (clotted cream) in the centre; and another was *kadayıf* formed into twisted ropes filled with cinnamon, allspice, coconut and ground almonds.[38]

EKMEK KADAYIFI

Ekmek kadayıfı ('bread *kadayıf*') was originally just an alternative name for *yassı kadayıf*, but in the nineteenth century it came to denote a kind of bread pudding known as *saray etmeği* ('palace bread'), made from the crusts of the fine white loaves prepared for the sultan in the palace bakery. Gradually the bread was replaced by *Şam kehki* ('Damascus rusks'), and then by pairs of large circular rusks specially made for this popular pudding. Below is an eighteenth-century version of *saray etmeği* with clotted cream that marks the first stage in the evolution of what was to become one of Turkey's most delicious puddings:[39]

Kaymaklı Saray Etmeği

Take some of the fine white bread that the officers of the royal household call 'fodula' and which is baked in the royal bakery at the palace for his Majesty . . . The flour for this bread is specially ground in a watermill at Beykoz, and several varieties of wheat are mixed in equal quantities before being ground. When carefully kneaded the dough made from this flour makes bread that rises excellently and is filled with airholes like a sponge. So take one loaf of that bread and divide it in half. Remove the crumb from both sections so that only the crusts remain and fry each separately as if frying *kadayıf*, in plenty of butter. Then rinse with some hot water and after draining place one of the crusts in a baking tin with raised edges[40] and pour clarified sugar syrup over. When the syrup has been absorbed spread sufficient pure *kaymak* on top. Then prepare the other crust in another baking tin, and when it has absorbed the syrup lay it on top of the first. Add another ladleful of syrup and place the tin over the heat for a while. It may be eaten either hot or cold.

The fame of *saray etmeği* soon spread beyond the palace walls, and 'certain accomplished and discriminating gentlemen' adapted the recipe to produce a lighter version known as *fodula kadayıfı* that dispensed with frying in butter.[41] The first recipe for the *ekmek kadayıfı* as we know it today was published in 1844, using the 'famous ready-made *ekmek kadayıfı* rusks' or alternatively 'Damascus rusks'.[42] These were first soaked in boiling water to soften them, and then cooked in syrup, and served with *kaymak*. Türâbî Efendi's English version of this recipe, which is given below, calls for muffins (the original griddle-baked variety), since the special rusks were not available in England:[43]

Ekmek Kadayıfı

Put a pound of white sugar in a clean saucepan, with two pints of water, set it to boil until it becomes a syrup; then cut open four or five muffins, and put them in the syrup for two or three minutes, take them out carefully with a slice, lay half of them in a baking-tin, sprinkle some pounded pistachios or almonds over, then spread a layer of clotted cream a quarter of an inch thick, again pistachios or almonds, and cover them with the other half of the muffins; then pour three-quarters of a pint of the syrup over, and put it in the oven, or on a moderate charcoal fire, until the syrup is nearly absorbed; dish up, and serve hot or cold.

In the Ottoman period *kadayıf* puddings of all kinds were generally eaten hot rather than cold as they are today. Among the versions in the section headed 'Hot Sweet Pastries' in Mehmed Kâmil's book is a bread pudding with sour cherries (*vişne ekmeği*, 'sour cherry bread'), for which two recipes are given. One of these is made with thinly sliced bread fried in butter and eaten hot, while the other made with toasted bread is served cold.[44]

Vişne Ekmeği

Prepare the desired quantity of clarified sugar syrup and toss in sour cherries. Cook until the cherries shrivel and remove from the heat. Toast slices of fine white bread on a grill or using tongs, then arrange them in a pan. Add the cherries and syrup and some water and boil until the bread softens. Heap onto a dish and sprinkle with granulated sugar. Eat when cold. This is a very light dish. Dried apricots or plums can be substituted for the sour cherries, in which case these should be soaked in hot water for a few hours to soften them before cooking in syrup.

Alexis Soyer, renowned French master chef at the London Reform Club, tasted *ekmek kadayıfı* at a banquet given by Selim Pasha in 1856, and in a letter to *The Times* on 8 September 1856 mentioned the pudding among the many Turkish dishes 'which are indeed worthy of the table of the greatest epicure'.[45] Soyer intended to include Turkish recipes in a book to be called *The Culinary Wonder of All Nations*, but sadly died before it could be written, and all his papers were seized and destroyed by one of his creditors.[46]

25 Aşure

Aşure aşı hayli aşırı aştır.
(*Aşure* is an extremely excessive dish.)
                   Tongue-twister (sixteenth century)[1]

*A*ŞURE IS A PUDDING MADE of wheat grains cooked with a variety of pulses and dried fruits. Probably this multiplicity of ingredients is what the above tongue-twister meant when describing *aşure* as 'excessive'. It is descended from the grain porridges that were among the most ancient cooked foods, eaten before people discovered how to grind grain into flour. Making, eating and above all distributing *aşure* to others has sacred significance deriving from ancient rituals relating to fertility of the soil, abundance and rebirth. Variations on this dish made with whole wheat grains are to be found in many parts of the world from England to China, and are almost always associated with religious festivals, funerals or the new year. The *aşure* of Turkey and other parts of the Islamic world was eaten on the tenth day of Muharrem, the flummery, frumenty or fluffin of England was eaten at Christmas and Lent, the Greek and Romanian *koliva* at Christmas, Lent and funerals, the Armenian *anuş abur* at New Year and Christmas, the Russian *kutya* at Christmas and funerals, and the *ba bao zou* of China at New Year.[2] Mesopotamia was probably the original homeland of all these boiled wheat grain dishes, since it was here that wild wheat was first cultivated.

Wheat has always been the most esteemed of all grains grown in the Old World, due both to its high yield and the high gluten content of later varieties that made it suitable for pastry and bread making. In the 1960s American archaeologist Jack R. Harlan travelled to eastern Turkey to investigate how Neolithic man first harvested wild wheat in this region around the tenth millennium BC, and thereby throw light on the advent of arable farming, which began around a thousand years later. Harlan made himself a flint sickle and began to cut down wild wheat growing on Karacadağ mountain in the province of Diyarbakır. In one hour he was able to gather 2.45 kilograms of seed material, containing nearly 1 kilogram of clean grain. This proved that a Neolithic family only needed to work for three weeks to harvest more grain than they could eat in a year. Moreover, wild einkorn wheat contains 22.83 per cent protein, nearly double that of modern wheat varieties.[3]

Today the most widespread wild wheat species growing in Turkey is the wild einkorn *Triticum boeticum* var. *thaoudar*, which was domesticated in this region, while wild emmer *Triticum dicoccoides* is thought to have been domesticated in the upper Jordan watershed.[4]

Raw cereal grains cannot be digested by human beings, so cooking them is essential. How could people who did not yet possess clay pots, never mind copper cooking pans, have done this? It is thought that they may have cooked the wheat grains in skins, baskets sealed with clay or vessels hollowed from stone, using water heated with stones or clay balls previously heated in a fire.[5] The resulting porridge was probably the oldest grain food prepared by human beings. This is reflected in an Islamic legend that Adam and Eve's first food after being expelled from the Garden of Eden was wheat porridge:[6]

When Eve and Adam met at Arafat [a hill near Mecca] on the day of Ashura, the twelfth day of the month of Muharrem, they became hungry. They wandered aimlessly down the valley. Immediately God sent Gabriel with a plate of wheat ears and on the site of this mosque [Mosque of the Kitchen of the Lord Adam] he instructed Adam and Eve how to cook the wheat ears in a pot and they ate them. Once they had assuaged their hunger they gave thanks to God. In accordance with the word of the 'Possessor of Gifts' [God], they called the Lord Adam, Adam, because he appeared on the face of the earth and after the fall he again descended to the face of the earth and grazed on herbs until he met with Eve, and instructed by the Lord Gabriel they first ate soup. And still in the language of men when one man invites another to his house, he says, 'Let us eat food-of-the-father soup' . . . So now know you that the first most ancient food is soup, and all else was invented in modern times by the doctors of the law. And the first place on the face of the earth where a fire was lit and food cooked was this kitchen of the Lord Adam on Arafat.

According to the same legend the forbidden 'fruit' that resulted in Adam's expulsion from the Garden of Eden was wheat.[7] 'The Lord God commanded Adam not to eat of the wheat tree, but since human beings are forgetful he forgot this command and was sent down to earth.'

This story could be interpreted as an allegory of the transition from hunter-gathering to farming, when cereals began to replace the ancient diet of game meat and wild roots, fruits and herbs as the main source of sustenance. This was not just a revolution in diet but a revolution in lifestyle and world view. According to this legend the angel Gabriel taught Adam and Eve the skills they needed to survive on their new staple: cooking wheat porridge and grinding flour.[8]

Dependence on cereals for sustenance engendered beliefs about the sacred nature of wheat and bread, and the need for divine intervention to ensure next year's crop. Rituals similar to those associated with Tammuz, the Babylonian god of wheat and fertility,[9] spread hand in hand with farming throughout the Old World, from Scotland to China. The tenth-century Arab writer Abû Said Wahb bin Ibrahim witnessed a ceremony relating to Tâ-uz (Tammuz) in Harran, where the local people still held to the ancient pagan faith, and he lists boiled wheat among the foods eaten on this occasion:[10]

> Tammuz (July). In the middle of this month is the festival of el-Bûgât, that is, of the weeping women, and this is the Tâ-uz festival, which is celebrated in honour of the god Tâ-uz. The women bewail him, because his lord slew him so cruelly, ground his bones in a mill, and then scattered them to the wind. The women (during this festival) eat nothing which has been ground in a mill, but limit their diet to steeped wheat, sweet vetches, dates, raisins, and the like.

James George Frazer explains that the destruction of the corn at harvest time by scything, threshing and grinding was seen by the ancient farmers as an act of killing the god of the corn, who had to be propitiated by eating unmilled wheat grains and displays of grief and contrition. In Scotland the same idea that milling was an act of cruelty towards the ancient corn god lingered into the eighteenth century, as shown by these lines from 'John Barleycorn', a poem by Robert Burns:[11]

> But a miller us'd him worst of all,
> For he crush'd him between two stones.

Such beliefs and customs relating to wheat were found even in places where wheat cultivation was difficult or impossible. Rye, millet, oats and other cereals never quite matched the spiritual significance of wheat, and where small quantities of wheat could be obtained this was saved for festivals. In eighteenth-century Cumberland, even wealthy families were able to eat wheat only at Christmas.[12] Of the three Old World cereals – wheat, barley and rye – that contain gluten and so can be used for making yeast-risen bread, wheat is by far superior. Only wheat dough can be rolled out thinly, as pointed out in a Turkish proverb: 'Millet flour is no good for baklava, nor fig wood for rolling pins.' The versatility of wheat, whether in bread, pastry or pasta, certainly enhanced its culinary status, but its sacred persona as embodied in dishes such as *aşure* is far more ancient than any of these foods.

These ancient beliefs live on in traditional wheat berry dishes like *aşure*, frumenty, *koliva* and *anuş abur*, eaten at festivals symbolizing renewal and rebirth such as Christmas, New Year and Easter. This is also why unmilled grain dishes are associated with funerals in many cultures. With the addition of dried fruits, saffron and almond milk, the English frumenty acquired an increasingly Near Eastern flavour during the Middle Ages, as contact with the Levant and the Middle East increased.[13] At the other end of the world, the Chinese version known as *ba bao zou* is made with various grains, pulses and raisins.[14]

Koliva, the boiled wheat dish of eastern European countries, is made by Orthodox Christians for funerals and the Day of All Souls. Dr Covel, chaplain

34. Chinese *ba bao zou*, a version of *aşure* made of rice, beans, starch and sugar. It is served at New Year decorated with dried fruits (Photograph: Mustafa Dorsay).

at the British embassy in Istanbul under Sir John Finch, described *koliva* at the Greek Orthodox feast of the Assumption on 15 August 1671:[15]

> All being done, there is brought to the Church door a charger of boyl'd wheat, cover'd over with crosses made of blancht almonds and raisins; everyone that will takes one of it, but is obliged to say a Pater Noster and Ave for the souls of the dead there buried.

In the 1760s Richard Chandler described *koliva* decorated with almonds, gold leaf, raisins and pomegranate seeds at a Greek funeral in Athens:[16]

> Two [men] followed, carrying on their heads each a great dish of parboiled wheat; the surface, blanched almonds disposed in the figure of a dove, with gilding and a border of raisins and pomegranate-kernels. These, on our arrival at the church, were deposited over the body.

In the late nineteenth century Lucy Garnett gives this description of *koliva* at a ceremony held in Salonika:[17]

> The ceremony began with the bringing in the *Kolyva*, or Funeral Dish, of boiled wheat, decorated on the top with designs in coloured sugar, almonds and raisins, and other dried fruits, of crosses, coffins, leaves and flowers, monograms and inscriptions.

A Turkish writer relates how Muslim and Christian neighbours exchanged gifts of food on their respective festivals, those sent by Orthodox Christians at Easter including *koliva* that had been blessed in the church:[18]

> The gentry, merchants and tradesmen, whether Muslims or Christians, sent all their acquaintances a large tray of baklava at Ramazan and sweets and buns on the *kandil* festivals. Meanwhile at Easter Christians sent their friends and neighbours eggs dyed red, Easter cakes and oranges. Three days before Easter wheat cooked at home and decorated with almonds, sugar and spice was blessed in the churches and sent to their Muslim friends and neighbours.

Puddings similar to the Turkish *aşure* are made in Bulgaria and Bosnia, where they are known as *hašure* and *ashoure* respectively.[19] Sephardic Jews in the Balkans prepare a similar boiled wheat dish on the eve of the Jewish Arbor Day, Tu B'Shvat, signifying a wish for abundant crops during the coming year.[20] Known as *kofyas*, this is also made to celebrate a child's first tooth, which is a custom that is found in Turkey and many parts of the Middle East. In Syria cooked green wheat and barley grains in syrup were decorated with nuts and silver balls and offered to visitors when a baby cut its first tooth.[21] The Turkish equivalent is boiled wheat known as *diş buğdayı* ('tooth wheat'), which can be either sweet or savoury, and used to be distributed to relatives, friends and the poor. At a time when infant mortality was high, *diş buğdayı* was a way for the mother to express her joy that her child had survived the first dangerous year of its life. The late eighteenth-century Turkish historian Ahmed Câvid describes a version made with caramelized sugar which was a favourite snack among opium addicts.[22]

In the Islamic world *âşûra* is the name of the tenth day of Muharrem, the first month of the lunar year. Fasting on that day is an ancient custom that pre-dates Islam, and was widespread among the peoples of western Asia and the Middle East, including Arabs and Jews. Sunni Muslims abandoned this fast when Ramazan became the traditional fasting period, but Shiite and Alevî Muslims maintained the practice as a way of mourning the death of Hüseyin at Kerbela on the tenth of Muharrem, and combined it with the ancient ritual of preparing wheat berry porridge, symbolizing death and rebirth. The Umayyads, on the other hand, celebrated the day that Hüseyin was killed because of his refusal to pay allegiance to the Caliph Yezîd of the Umayyad dynasty.[23] Sunni Muslims continued to prepare *aşure*, associating it with various legends, such as Adam's penitence, Abraham's escape from the fire, the meeting between Jacob and his son Joseph, and the grounding of Noah's Ark on Mount Jûdî.[24]

In Turkey the Noah's Ark version is the most popular story about the invention of *aşure*. When the flood waters began to recede and the ark was grounded on the summit of Mount Jûdî, one last meal was prepared using up the remains of all the ark's food stores, hence the bewildering diversity of ingredients, including grains, pulses and dried fruits. Although boiled wheat is not mentioned in any versions of the Noah story,[25] nor in any other sacred texts of the monotheistic faiths, it nonetheless became associated with many religious events and festivals, and its ancient links with fertility, death and rebirth were never completely erased. In Ottoman Turkey cooking *aşure* during Muharrem was thought to bring good fortune and prosperity to the household. If the master of the house found a broad bean in his first spoonful of *aşure* he would wipe it clean and carry it around in his purse for the rest of the year for good luck. When the year was over the bean's power was deemed exhausted, and it was buried.[26]

Aşure played a particularly important role in the Bektaşî Sufi order. At the main lodge of the order in the village of Hacıbektaş a gigantic black cauldron used to cook *aşure* is held sacred.[27] Here the task of making *aşure* begins on the night of the ninth of Muharrem, and each family brings their contribution of wheat, chickpeas, beans, raisins, dried figs and nuts. The following account of cooking *aşure* in a Bektaşî dervish *tekke* was published in 1925:[28]

> When all the ingredients for the *âşûre* have been procured and cooked separately then the wheat is placed in a huge cauldron and the Aşçı Baba [cook] takes up a large ladle and declares 'By your leave, o İmâm.' Then he plunges the ladle into the cauldron, upon which all the dervishes present shout out 'Ya Hüseyin.' Whoever wishes to take up the ladle and stir declares, 'By your leave, o İmâm,' while the other dervishes shout 'Ya Hüseyin.' So they continue until the *âşûre* is cooked. Then the cook says to the Dede Efendi [head dervish], 'Let us occupy ourselves with the souls of the martyrs, the pottage is ready,' and the Dede Efendi replies 'By the will of God.' He stands next to the cauldron and all the dervishes stand in a row with their hands on their breasts. One who has a beautiful voice sings the Şeyh Safî Elegy or the Fuzûlî Elegy. When this is over the Dede Efendi chants a *gülbenk* prayer. Then the Aşçı Baba passes the ladle to the Dede Efendi and lifts the lid off the cauldron. The Dede Efendi says 'By your leave, o İmâm,' to which all the dervishes respond 'Ya Hüseyin', then the Dede Efendi stirs the pottage three times. All the dervishes salute the Dede Efendi by turns, then withdraw and salute one another. The Dede Efendi commands the Aşçı Baba, 'Divide out the pottage between the dervishes for the souls of the martyrs,' and declaring 'By your leave' he withdraws to his cell. Then the tables are set and everyone comes and eats. What is left is divided into small jugs and one is given to each of the dervishes.

In 1553 Hans Dernschwam watched a procession of Bektaşî dervishes in Istanbul during the month of Muharrem, which that year fell in November of the Julian calendar:[29]

> One of them takes the lead, singing, while the others follow behind, walking all through the city for some days in November. They talk of someone called Isaac or Isaia, and explain that it is in his memory that they do so, and also that the harvest may be fruitful. They [make] a kind of sacred soup that they call *aschray*.

Aşure was prepared during the month of Sefer as well as Muharrem by the Kâdirî dervishes,[30] and distributed at the Berat Kandili festival and in the evenings during the month of Ramazan at Eyüpsultan Imaret.[31] In parts of Turkey *aşure* is also a feature of the spring festival of Hıdrellez, held on 6 May.[32]

Aşure made in Muharrem by Sunni families also preserved its association with the dead, according to the following account dating from the late Ottoman period:[33]

> When the *âşûre* is ready the master of the house and other members of the family go down to the kitchen and sit around the cauldron while the Yâ Sîn and Al Mulk *sûra*s are recited in the name of all deceased members of the household. Then the tray used to cover the cauldron is removed and everyone lets the steam into their eyes, which is supposed to bring good luck. The first dishful of *âşûre* is not sent to neighbours but kept for eating in the house to bring prosperity. The rest is poured into Meissen jugs of different colours, and fine bowls with lids and saucers, and sprinkled with pistachio nuts, pine nuts, currants, and a few pomegranate kernels if in season. Then the lids are replaced and two bowls each placed on decorative trays, which are tightly wrapped in white cloths and sent to less intimate friends and acquaintances. The servant who delivers the *âşûre* is given a tip and the empty bowls are returned. The rest of the *âşûre* is poured into large dishes and sent to close friends and neighbours. It is considered rude to hand the dishes back without washing them, and they are carefully washed before returning.

People of a charitable disposition would distribute *aşure* not only to friends and neighbours, but to the poor of the neighbourhood, to students, and anyone who came to the door.[34] The Bulgarian writer Zani Ginchev wrote in 1887 that the dervishes of a Turkish *tekke* in Samovodine invited Christians into the convent only on the Day of *Aşure*:[35]

> In this convent, no Christians were allowed except on the Day of the Aşure – the Turkish All-Souls' Day, which the dervishes held on the 9th of March. On this day, the villagers from Samovodine were called in for the Aşure, because the convent had land in Samovodine, inherited with the *tekke* from the time when it was a Bulgarian Church, and this land was still worked by the villagers.

Mrs Mary Adelaide Walker, who lived with wealthy Ottoman families while painting portraits of women during her thirty years in Istanbul from 1856 onwards, recalled how *aşure* was distributed to the poor:[36]

> The 'aschourah', a sweet porridge which makes its appearance upon most festive occasions, deserves a few words of explanation, as this preparation has a legendary origin. *Aschourah* is composed of Indian wheat, barley,

wheat, dried raisins, nuts, almonds, walnuts, pistachio nuts, and even dry Windsor and haricot beans, boiled and sweetened, ten ingredients in all; a remembrance, says the legend, of Noah's residence in the Ark, 'into which the water must have penetrated at length, and produced an unexpected soup amongst the remnants of his dry stores.' *Aschourah* is made in great quantities in all respectable houses during the first ten days of the month Mouharem (the first month of the year) to be sent about to friends and to be liberally distributed to the poor; at this period, any persons presenting themselves at the door of a konak receive without question a bowl of *aschourah*.

Some philanthropists even established pious foundations for distributing *aşure*. Evliyâ Çelebi relates that Çelebi Abdurrahman Pasha set up a foundation of this kind when he was serving as governor of Egypt:[37]

> He arranged that ten cauldrons of *aşure* should be cooked and distributed to the poor in the name of İmâm Hüseyin each year in the month of Muharrem in the holy cities of Mecca and Medina, and endowed six thousand *para*s from his own property for the purchase of two *batman* of aloeswood and one *kantar* of beeswax and one *kantar* of twice-refined sugar and three *kantar*s of olive oil for the lamps for a ceremony in the name of İmâm Hüseyin on the twelfth night of the month of Âşûra.

Although *aşure* is sold throughout the year in some pudding shops in Turkey today, it is not usual to prepare it at home except during Muharrem. At the Ottoman palace, however, *aşure* was also eaten on ordinary days, as we see from documents recording meals served to dignitaries who served on the Divân (Council of State) and palace banquets.[38] *Aşure* also featured on the menus of two banquets given to the Transylvanian ambassador on 10 and 24 November 1649. Each banquet consisted of five puddings and eighteen and nineteen savoury dishes respectively: one pudding being served between every two or three savoury courses. Meals served to members of the Divân consisted of six courses, of which one or two were sweet. For example, the menu on 21 July 1648 was as follows: semolina helva, stuffed marrow, chicken soup, *aşure*, *fincan böreği* (pastries filled with cheese or minced meat), and roast pigeon. *Aşure* made with milk is recorded by the Sufî and gourmet Seyyid Hasan (1620–88).[39]

A famous variety of *aşure* made at the palace found its way into Ottoman cookery books. Known as *saray aşuresi* (palace *aşure*) or *süzme aşure* (strained *aşure*),[40] it was made with boiled wheat that had been strained to remove the fibre, leaving a smooth jelly. The following recipe dates from the eighteenth century:[41]

> If you wish to prepare palace *âşûre* then take only the strained liquid and add sugar and currants. When nearly cooked dissolve sufficient musk in a few cups of rose water, add this and some pistachio nuts, and pour into dishes. Decorate with more pistachios and that is your palace *âşûre*. Eat immediately.

When the German confectioner Friedrich Unger visited Istanbul in 1835 he was invited to several grand dinners at which palace-style *aşure* was one of the dishes. Unger gives the following brief description:[42]

Susme Aşure

Out of grain you prepare a decoction, and after having separated off the indissoluble parts, add raisins, sugar, almonds, pistachios and cinnamon, and boil it a while longer. This dish is eaten with wooden spoons.

Türâbî Efendi's recipe is one of the most detailed:[43]

Sèrây Ashûrassi

Put in a stewpan as much skinned wheat as is required,[44] with plenty of water, set it on the fire, and boil until the grains begin to crack; then take out with a wooden spoon what pulp there is on the top, and put it in a basin, add some more water, and continue so until you have extracted all the goodness from the grains; then strain the remaining grains through a sieve, and put all the pulp you have collected into a saucepan, add two or three ounces of washed currants, and a quarter or half a pound of loaf sugar, previously made into syrup as directed in the preceding receipts; put it on a charcoal fire and begin stirring it. When boiling, add a little musk mixed with two or three tablespoonfuls of rose-water, and stir it one or two minutes longer; then take it off and pour it into a dish, arrange on the top tastefully some skinned almonds and pistachios, and serve when cold.

One year in the 1980s my husband's Uncle Cevat, a merchant navy captain who was an excellent and enthusiastic cook, decided to cook palace-style *aşure* for Muharrem. The task of straining the boiled wheat was laborious, and whether the result really made up for so much hard work and extra washing up was questionable. But the fact that Uncle Cevat had not only heard of *saray aşuresi* but also knew how to make it (he would never have dreamed of consulting a cookery book) shows how the fame of this dish lived on in Istanbul long after the Ottoman period.

Ordinary *aşure* had been made at the palace at least since the sixteenth century, when palace documents record the ingredients as husked wheat grains, sugar, rice, almonds, dried broad beans, dried black-eye beans, dates, currants and roasted hazelnuts.[45] Seventeenth-century documents also list walnuts, dried *razakı* grapes, apples and eggs. Walnuts, apples and eggs do not appear in any recorded recipes for *aşure*, historical or modern, and may represent innovative versions of the pudding created by palace cooks.

Food for the sultan was not only prepared in the main kitchens, but also in the Kuşhane kitchen close to the harem, where the sultan's private attendants concocted specialities of their own devising. As well as the strained *aşure* discussed above, these officials also prepared *aşure* made with milk and pearl barley instead of wheat.[46]

Ayşe Fahriye's recipe for pearl barley *aşure* is a plain dish consisting only of boiled pearl barley, milk and sugar, poured into dishes and topped with almonds.[47] Whether the version made in the sultan's private kitchen was so simple we shall never know, but comparison of the few recipes recounted to Zarif Orgun by former attendants of the privy household with cookery books of the period suggests that although the basic recipes might be known outside the palace walls, the finer details were not. Of the eighteen different ingredients used in the *aşure* made in 1870 for distribution by Pertevniyal Sultan, the mother of Sultan Abdülaziz, five (dates, rice flour, clarified butter, black-eye beans and starch) do not feature in contemporary recipes:[48]

Wheat 400 *okka*s, white sugar 552 *okka*s, musk in the pod 23 *miskal*s, the finest razakı raisins 25 *okka*s, pine nuts 25 *okka*s [5 *okka*s of these are specified as being 'local' pine nuts], sultana raisins 22 *okka*s, Chios broad beans 20 *okka*s, Egyptian dates 25 *okka*s, black-eye beans 40 *okka*s, chickpeas 30 *okka*s, roasted hazelnuts 15 *okka*s, almonds 15 *okka*s, the finest rose water 50 *okka*s, beans 25 *okka*s, Konya currants 20 *okka*s, clarified butter 12 *okka*s, rice flour 20 *okka*s, starch 20 *okka*s.

This adds up to an astounding 1,316 *okka*s, equivalent to 1,684 kilograms or nearly 2 tons of dry ingredients, and when cooked would have doubled in quantity. In view of the lavish use of musk and other expensive ingredients it seems likely that Pertevniyal Sultan distributed this *aşure* to family members, friends, favoured retainers and state dignitaries rather than the poor.

Ayşe Osmanoğlu (1887–1960), the daughter of Sultan Abdülhamid II, described the custom of cooking and distributing *aşure* at the palace and to the poor in her memoirs:[49]

> *Âşûre* was cooked on the tenth day of Muharrem. This *âşûre* was brought in jugs to the different apartments and all the members of the royal family. Cauldrons were set up in the courtyard of Hamidiye Mosque and *âşûre* was distributed to the poor ... *Âşûre* was also sent to the sûfî *tekke*s, and these sent jugs of their own *âşûre* in return. Valuable jugs of *âşûre* wrapped in muslin were sent by the *pasha*s and eminent families. These were emptied, filled with *âşûre* made at the palace and returned, as was the custom.

Lady Dufferin, wife of the British ambassador, was offered *aşure* when she visited Nazlı Sultan, wife of the khedive of Egypt, at her house in Istanbul on 21 November 1882 (10 Muharrem 1300):[50]

> ... then we were given a peculiar dish which is eaten on this day, the tenth of the New Year. A silver table was brought in, and then an enormous silver tray, round which five of us sat. The stuff was in very large glass bowls, and we had one each, though one would have been enough for us all. Princess Nazli declared that it was a Biblical dish, and that Noah made it out of all the stores that remained in his ark at the end of the Deluge! It was rather good, and Shem, Ham and Japhet must have enjoyed it immensely. It was like thick barley gruel full of pistachio nuts, and walnuts, and almonds. After this, we wiped our fingers on napkins heavy with gold embroidery, and sipped something out of a golden cup, and took a stately departure.

Two days later Nazlı Sultan sent *aşure* in silver dishes to Lady Dufferin:

> This morning an A.D.C. from the Vice-Reine was announced, and he appeared, followed by a Hamal (porter), bearing on his head a tray covered over with a velvet cloth embroidered with gold and pearls; under it were three silver dishes with the barley gruel I have already described in them, and small gold coins spread over each. This was a little attention from the Khedive's wife. The cover and the dishes we returned, and I gave two 'lots' of the food and coins to the servants.

Since the word *aşure* derives from the Arabic *aşr*, meaning ten, and refers to the tenth day of Muharrem, some people followed a custom of preparing *aşure* with ten ingredients, as described by Mary Adelaide Walker.[51] In her list of ingredients she includes maize ('Indian wheat'), which is not mentioned in any Ottoman-period recipes, although it does feature in regional versions, as the example below illustrates.

In some of Turkey's eastern provinces a savoury version of *aşure* used to be made that included meat and onions as well as dried fruits, and a recipe for *aşure* of this kind from the Göle district of Ardahan is given below:[52]

Aşure with Meat

Soak beans, chickpeas, dried maize and wheat overnight. Cook the maize and wheat together until tender. Cook the chickpeas and beans separately, and when tender add to the wheat. Boil small pieces of mutton or beef on the bone until tender. Add one diced potato, dried mulberries, raisins, figs, apricots, prunes, apples and some dried cornelian cherries and any other similar ingredients you wish and cook all the ingredients together in one pan. When cooked remove from the heat. Fry sliced onion in butter and stir into the pan together with salt.

26 *Sütlü Tatlılar*

Milk Puddings

Muhallebi and *sütlaş* for me
The Maiden's Tower for you.

Watchman's rhyme[1]

A RICE PUDDING CALLED *UWA* IS mentioned in the eleventh century by Mahmud of Kashgar: 'Cook rice and place in cold water, then drain and add sugar. This is eaten as a cold dish.'[2] The version with milk called *sütlaç* today and *sütlü aş* ('milk food', elided to *sütlaş*) or *sütlü pirinç* (rice with milk) in historical sources is first encountered in fifteenth-century medical books[3] and the poems of Kaygusuz Abdal:[4]

> Forty thousand cauldrons of *pâlûze*, fifty thousand of *muhallebi*
> A thousand of *sütlü pirinç* in porcelain dishes.

In the mid-seventeenth century there were fifteen shops specializing in rice pudding in Istanbul.[5] Their first legendary patron was Şuayb Nebi, who cooked millet with milk, but he had been superseded by Enes bin Malik, who prepared rice cooked in milk for the Prophet Muhammed.

Turkish rice pudding entered Italian cuisine in the early sixteenth century by the name *riso turchesco*, and was served at the wedding of Ercole d'Este in 1529 as a filling for marzipan pastries.[6] Cristoforo Messisbugo makes frequent reference to *riso turchesco* made of rice, milk and sugar in his book on banquets published in 1549.[7] In 1570 Bartolomeo Scappi, chef to Pope Pius V, records it as 'Riso turcheso con latte, servito con zuccaro, canella sopra' ('Turkish rice with milk, served with sugar and sprinkled with cinnamon').[8]

Back in Turkey, too, *sütlaç* was a dish fit for the highest tables in the land. 'The Rice gellyed, a perfect fool in a platter' is how Covel described rice pudding served at a palace banquet given for the British ambassador Lord John Finch following his audience with Sultan Mehmed IV at Edirne Palace on 27 July 1675.[9] Another dish related to rice pudding was *pilav peltesi*, prepared by pouring a sauce made from starch, sugar and rose water on top of cooked rice.[10]

Muhallebi, a milk pudding thickened with ground rice, has a long history, apparently going back to Sassanid-period Persia (224–651). According to hearsay, the dish was introduced into the Arab cuisine in the late seventh century by a Persian cook who presented a dish of *muhallebi* to al-Muhallab bin Abî Sufra (d. 702), an Arab general in the service of the Umayyad caliphate. Al-Muhallab liked it so much that he named it *al-muhallabiyya* after himself.[11] The earliest recipes for *muhallebi* date from the tenth century, and describe three different versions: milk thickened with ground rice, milk with rice grains and chicken, and thirdly an egg custard without rice.[12] In two thirteenth-century Arab cookery books, that by al-Baghdâdî,[13] and another written in Spain, there are recipes for *muhallebi* made with mutton instead of chicken and flavoured with various spices.

Palace kitchen records suggest that *muhallebi* was always made with shredded chicken for the Ottoman sultan Mehmed II (1451–81), but a meatless version was also made, as shown by a recipe dated c. 1530.[14] The latter was flavoured with rose water, an ingredient that does not appear in the medieval Arabic *muhallabiyya* recipes, poured over the finished pudding, along with a little butter and powdered sugar.

Muhallebi made with shredded chicken also found its way into European cuisines, where very similar dishes, usually with the addition of ground almonds or almond milk, appear from the fourteenth century onwards by the names *blanc-manger* in French, *bianco mangiare* in Italian and *manjar blanco* in Spanish, all meaning 'white food'.[15] If the recipe books are anything to go by, this pudding, made of chicken, almonds, sugar, and a thickener such as rice flour or bread crumbs, was still going strong in the seventeenth century in England, France and Italy:[16]

To Make Blamanger in the Italian Fashion

Boil a Capon in water and salt very tender, or all to mash, then beat Almonds, and strain them with your Capon-Broth, rice flour, sugar, and rose-water; boil it like pap, and serve it in this form; sometimes in place of Broth use Cream.

As time went on, Europeans gradually dispensed with the minced chicken and rice, replacing them with breadcrumbs, calf's foot, hartshorn or veal jelly, which in the early eighteenth century were superseded by isinglass.[17] The isinglass was itself replaced by arrowroot in the first half of the nineteenth century, and cornstarch became the usual thickener in the second half of the nineteenth century, creating the blancmange we know today.[18] Despite spreading so far and wide across the Middle East and Europe, and remaining popular for so many centuries, *muhallebi* with shredded chicken has been forgotten everywhere except Turkey, where it is still made today by the name *tavukgöğüsü* ('chicken breast') because only the breast meat is used. This pudding does not retain any noticeable chicken flavour, and is only distinguishable from ordinary *muhallebi* by its texture. An enthusiastic description of this pudding is given in 1833 by the American naval physician Commodore de Kay, who tasted it at a grand repast of thirty or more courses given by the Ottoman naval commander of the port:[19]

> They were all new to us, and many of them exceedingly savoury, – one in particular seemed worthy of a *brêvet d'importation* into our hemisphere. It appears in the shape of an immense custard, and owes its peculiar excellent flavour to the presence of the breasts of very young chickens, which are by some means so intimately blended and incorporated with the custard as to be scarcely distinguishable. It is certainly an exquisite dish, and worthy of being classed with that French sauce which is said to be so palatable, that a person might be tempted with it to eat his own grandfather.

Mahmud Nedim, author of a cookery book for his fellow officers in the late nineteenth century, tells us that *tavukgöğüsü* was decorated with mottos in cinnamon and eaten sprinkled with rose water or orange-flower water. The *tavukgöğüsü* sold in Istanbul's pudding shops was sometimes adulterated by the substitution of minced tripe for chicken, but apparently even people who hated tripe were none the wiser.[20]

Arguably the most delicious of all Turkish milk puddings is *kazandibi* ('cauldron bottom'), a kind of *tavukgöğüsü* cooked until it forms a caramelized layer on the bottom of the pan. It is cut into squares, which are rolled up with the caramelized surface on top. The earliest description of this is by Mahmud Nedim, in his recipe for *muhallebi* made with chicken breast.[21] Making this variety demands a high degree of skill, and it is hardly ever made at home.

Hans Dernschwam, who visited Istanbul in 1553, describes a version without chicken but flavoured with musk:[22] 'Another one, which also is considered a delicious dish, is thus: one boils rice, milk and flour together, adds butter, sugar, rose water and musk; this dish is called *muhelleble*.' Muhallebi was served at the palace on feast days and featured on banquet menus for ambassadors,[23] but whether this was the meatless version flavoured with musk described by Dernschwam or the chicken breast variety is not specified.

Both *tavukgöğüsü* and plain *muhallebi* were decorated with words such as 'Maşallah' (May God protect), 'Padişahım çok yaşa' (Long live the Sultan), or the *tuğra* (royal monogram), applied using carved wooden moulds dipped in cinnamon.[24]

One of the foreign travellers who enjoyed *muhallebi* was the chaplain Robert Walsh:[25]

The itinerant confectioner . . . carries about upon his head a large wooden tray, and under his arm a stand with three legs. When required, he sets his stand, and lays his tray upon it covered with good things. The first is a composition of ground rice boiled to the consistence of a jelly, light and transparent, called *mahalabie*; from this he cuts off a slice with a brass shovel, lays it on a plate,

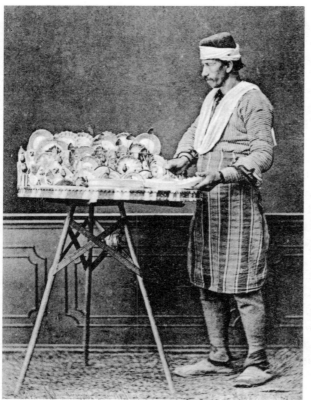

of which he has a pile on his tray, and, dividing it into square morsels, he drops on it attar of roses, or some other perfume, from a perforated silver vessel, and it forms a very cooling and delightful food.

35. A *muhallebi* seller as described by Mary Adelaide Walker in 1886: 'There is nothing prettier and more tempting than the mohalibé trays, when the white jelly is covered with a clean, wet cloth and surrounded with gaily-coloured and gilded saucers, while a richer display of ornamental porcelain rises in tiers at the back' (Courtesy of Mert Sandalcı).

A recipe for Turkish *muhallebi*, described as 'Ramazan cakes' – presumably because milk puddings were a feature of the pre-dawn Ramazan meal of *sahur* – found its way into a late nineteenth-century English cookery book:[26]

Ramazan Cakes

(a Turkish recipe) – Take half a pound of rice-flour, and dilute it with two glasses of milk; pass the preparation through a sieve into a stewpan. Boil over a moderate fire, stirring all the time. Add sugar to taste, let it reduce for seven or eight minutes, then add a few drops of extract of roses or of jessamine, turn it out on a round baking-sheet, previously moistened with cold water. Let the preparation be nearly an inch in thickness, and smooth its surface. When it is cold, sprinkle it with fine sugar, and divide it into small cakes, lozenge-shaped, round or oblong, according to taste.

36. Silver *muhallebi* spoons. Mary Adelaide Walker describes these 'slim metal arrow-shaped spoons' in her memoirs of her life in Istanbul in the nineteenth century (Courtesy of Sadberk Hanım Museum).

In the late nineteenth century Lady Dufferin, wife of the British ambassador, describes eating *muhallebi* with *kaymak* and sugar at a shop near the Grand Bazaar in Istanbul:[27] 'We also had rather a nice Turkish dish – squares of a sort of blanc-mange with Devonshire cream and sugar.'

Mary Adelaide Walker also recalled eating *muhallebi* topped with a piece of *kaymak* and eaten with special spoons:[28]

> They [Two Turkish girls] are, however, distracted during the negotiations by the rival charms of the mohalibé which an Albanian is dispensing at a neighbouring house-door. Mohalibé is a sort of cold jelly composed of ground rice and milk; it is served in saucers, powdered with sugar and sprinkled with rose-water: in the proper season a lump of clotted cream, called caimak, is added. There is nothing prettier and more tempting than the mohalibé trays, when the white jelly is covered with a clean, wet cloth and surrounded with gaily-coloured and gilded saucers, while a richer display of ornamental porcelain rises in tiers at the back. Then there are the slim metal arrow-shaped spoons, and the Oriental-looking flask of rose-water with its slender neck. The costume of the mohalibédji completes the picture: he wears the broad Albanian fez with a ponderous dark blue tassel, and a large striped cloth is bound round him like an apron.

Another variation is *su muhallebisi* ('water muhallebi') made with water instead of milk. The pudding itself is unsweetened but is served sprinkled with powdered sugar and rose water. In the past honey or *pekmez* sometimes replaced the powdered sugar, and lumps of *kaymak* were often placed on top when serving, which suggests that the *muhallebi* described by Lady Dufferin and Mary Walker was probably this version.[29] Although *su muhallebisi* originated as a cheap alternative sold in the streets, parks and public baths, and in 1844 was dismissively described by Mehmed Kâmil as the 'commonplace variety sold in shops',[30] this almost transparent white pudding gradually won acceptance among discriminating diners for its lightness and delicate flavour, and in the second half of the nineteenth century recipes begin to appear in Turkish cookery books.[31]

A late arrival on Turkey's milk pudding scene is *keşkül-i fukara*, meaning 'poor man's *keşkül*', which was introduced from Arab cuisine in the late nineteenth century.[32] *Keşkül* is a begging bowl in which dervishes collected foodstuffs given as alms – a 'tutti-frutti' as one observer put it – and this presumably inspired the pudding's name.[33] There is some heavy irony here, because the huge quantity of nuts makes this a rich pudding for rich people, certainly not anything a poor man could ever have hoped to taste.

Keşkül-i fukara makes its first appearance in print in 1882, with a recipe calling for ground pine nuts, pistachios and almonds.[34] Another version is made with ground pine nuts, almonds, coconut and coconut milk, and when cold is decorated with thin slices of coconut, chopped pistachios and other ground nuts, currants and sour pomegranate kernels (see recipe below). The same writer tells us that a cheap version of this pudding was made with a small amount of almonds and thickened with starch, which is the variety served in Turkish pudding shops today.

*Muhallebici*s or pudding shops are a venerable culinary institution in Turkey. Yet in the 1980s they began to close down one by one, until they were on the verge of extinction. Then, inspired partly by chains such as McDonald's, which had contributed to their decline, the old-fashioned pudding shops staged a triumphant renaissance. They too opened multiple branches with modern décor. It is astonishing that while thousands of *döner* restaurants were opening in Europe, no one thought to open a pudding shop, especially as the

'Pudding Shop' in Istanbul's Sultanahmet Square had become an international byword among hippies on the eastern trail in the 1960s and 1970s. While traditional *muhallebici*s were humble establishments serving a limited menu of chicken soup and chicken pilaf to go with their diverse array of milk puddings, the new-look pudding shops have expanded their menus to include meat

37. Shop selling *kaymak* (clotted cream) in the Kapalı Çarşı (Grand Bazaar) in Istanbul. This was eaten as a dessert sprinkled with honey, *pekmez* or sugar (Engraving after drawing by W.H. Bartlett, in *The Beauties of the Bosphorus*, London, undated [c. 1836], facing p. 34).

dishes and sweet pastries as well as milk puddings. Even in this new brash guise it is a pleasure to see them back.

RECIPES

SÜTLAÇ   (Mehmed Reşad, 1921)[35]
RICE PUDDING

Pick over a ladleful of pudding rice for stones and wash well, then boil in a moderate quantity of water. Add an *okka* of cold milk and set on the heat. Stir constantly until it comes to the boil. When the rice is well cooked add 75 *dirhem*s of sugar, and when this has dissolved and blended into the milk, ladle the pudding into bowls.

   Some housewives place copper milk bowls over hot embers and empty the *sütlaç* into these, then leave it to simmer for half an hour so that a thick creamy layer forms on top. Or they divide the *sütlaç* into bowls and after leaving it to cool slightly place it in the oven to brown on top. *Muhallebi* makers add rice flour, which gives it a thicker consistency.

SÜTLÜ MUHALLEBI   (Mahmud Nedim, 1900)[36]
BLANCMANGE WITH MILK

Place milk in a pan and set it on the heat. When it is warm add sufficient sugar and pour one or two ladlefuls into a bowl. Blend the rice flour, which has been ground and passed through a fine sieve, into the milk in the bowl to make a thick pap, then stir slowly into the pan of milk. When it begins to boil and is the consistency of fresh yogurt, remove the flaming charcoal so that only some embers remain, and leave to simmer for about a quarter of an hour (if a rose geranium leaf or a little orange-flower water is added while it simmers it will taste even better). To test whether it is cooked plunge a charcoal ember to which no ashes adhere into the pan (if the ember is extinguished it is not yet cooked, but if not it is). When you decide it is cooked then remove the pan from the heat and pour out the pudding into shallow dishes that have been wiped throroughly dry. When cold dip specially made moulds carved with words like 'maşallah', the Ottoman royal *tuğra*, or 'long live the sultan' into cinnamon and press them gently onto the surface. This is both decorative and a charming touch. Now they are ready to eat. Sometimes sugar is not added, but instead pounded sugar is sprinkled on top before eating, together with a little rose water or orange-flower water. This is pleasant too.

SU MUHALLEBISI   (Ayşe Fahriye, 1882–3)[37]
BLANCMANGE WITH WATER

This is prepared like ordinary *muhallebi*, but substituting plain water for milk and adding a little corn starch and a lump of alum the size of a hazelnut. When cooked it must be poured into plates in a thin layer [about 2 cm]. When serving pour over a little milk, top with some lumps of *kaymak*, and sprinkle with plenty of sugar, and rose water if desired.

If desired, the finest thick *pekmez* may be drizzled over the *su muhallebisi*. This is even more delicious if mixed half and half with sugar and brought to the boil, strained, then allowed to cool before using.

TAVUKGÖĞÜSÜ   (Mahmud Nedim, 1900)[38]
BLANCMANGE WITH CHICKEN BREAST

Begin to prepare *muhallebi* with milk and sugar, and after adding the rice flour blended with milk, take chicken breast that has been cooked without salt and soaked in water for five or ten hours and tease it into fibres. Rinse these again then sprinkle them into the pan and stir. Continue to cook as usual. When ready remove from the heat and pound with a wooden pestle, as one pounds *keşkek* and *herise*, until the chicken breast blends with the *muhallebi* and disappears. After this pour into shallow dishes and again decorate with cinnamon moulds, as you do for *muhallebi*, and serve sprinkled with a little rose or orange-flower water. It is delicious.

Most of the *muhallebici*s make their *tavukgöğüsü* from the fibres of beef tripe. No one can tell the difference. Even those who loathe tripe will eat *tavukgöğüsü* made from it with such a keen appetite that it must be seen to be believed. By preparing foods of this kind oneself or having someone else make them, one is preserved from deceptions of this kind.

If *muhallebi* or *tavukgöğüsü* are removed from the cooking pan using metal spatulas so that the scorched layer at the bottom of the pan is also taken up, and then the slices placed neatly on dishes with the browned sides upwards, they call it *kazgan dibi* ['bottom of the cauldron']. When cooking *muhallebi* with milk some people deliberately add a little soot, since *muhallebi* with a smoky flavour is supposedly famous.

KEŞKÜL-I FUKARA   (Mehmed Reşad, 1921–2)[39]
MILK PUDDING WITH GROUND NUTS

This is one of the delicious and celebrated puddings of Arabia. To prepare it take half an *okka* of sweet almonds and half an *okka* of pine nuts and pound them to a paste in a mortar. Tie this paste up in a piece of muslin and place in three *okkas* of milk. Also add the milk of one or two large coconuts. Bring to the boil and stir occasionally until the milk is reduced to two thirds by volume. Then squeeze the ground nuts and strain the liquid into the pan. Add the sugar, and when it is dissolved pour the pudding into small china bowls. Allow to cool.

Decorate the surface with coconut sliced very thinly in the shape of watermelon slices, chopped pistachios, almonds, roasted hazelnuts, pine nuts, a few currants and sour pomegranate kernels, and serve. A cheap version of this celebrated pudding is made by using a small amount of almonds and thickening with starch.

27 Zerde

You can't make *zerde* with just rice and no honey.
Turkish proverb[1]

ZERDE IS A RICE PUDDING coloured with saffron whose name derives from the Persian *zerd*, meaning golden. Legend has it that the first Umayyad caliph Muawiyah invented *zerde* as a dish of mourning for the death of Hamza, and presented it to the Prophet Muhammed. According to the seventeenth-century Turkish writer Evliyâ Çelebi, the Iranians refused to eat *zerde* because they regarded Muawiyah as a pretender who unjustly deprived Ali's descendants of the caliphate.[2] In fact, *shole zard* (*zerde*) is eaten in Iran in Muharrem to commemorate the Battle of Kerbela, at which Ali's younger son Hüseyin was killed.[3] In Ottoman Turkey, however, *zerde* was a dish for celebratory occasions, and enjoyed by enough people to merit a company of *zerde* makers.[4]

Zerde is mentioned several times in the *Thousand and One Nights*,[5] and in the thirteenth century by Mevlânâ:[6] 'O saffron, nourish thyself with water and enter into the zerde!' Surprisingly there are no recipes for this celebrated pudding in any of the medieval Arabic cookery books nor in any Ottoman Turkish cookbooks until 1900. Probably the method was considered too well known and too simple to require instructions. However, other documentary sources fill the gap. The earliest is a list of ingredients used by the Ottoman palace cooks when preparing *zerde* in 1539 for banquets celebrating the circumcision of Süleyman the Magnificent's sons Bâyezid and Cihângîr:[7] 6.4 kilograms of rice,[8] 10 kilograms of honey, 38 grams of saffron and 640 grams of butter. Another type was made with milk, using 1.6 kilograms of rice, 1.9 kilograms of sugar, 7.7 litres of milk and 640 grams of butter.[9] During this thirteen-day celebration *zerde* was served to rich and poor alike, from viziers to the city's poor, who were feasted at nine *imaret*s around the city.[10]

The expense of feasts and celebrations lasting several weeks was exorbitant, and from the eighteenth century onwards royal circumcisions and weddings began to be celebrated on a much more modest scale. Sultan Abdülhamid I (r. 1774–89) refused to hold public celebrations on the birth of his second son, declaring that 'such masquerades are unwarranted'. Instead he ordered that alms be distributed to dervish lodges, kaftans to school teachers, and schoolchildren treated to pilaf with *zerde* and pocket money.[11]

Süleyman the Magnificent used to provide a feast of *yahni* (mutton stew), pilaf and *zerde* at victory fêtes. *Zerde* served at celebrations of the conquest of Rhodes in 1522 was garnished with almonds.[12] Almonds are also mentioned by Hans Dernschwam in his description of *zerde* he ate during his visit to Turkey in 1553–5:[13] 'A czorba [soup] out of rice is a wonderful food, they make it yellow with saffron and sweeten it with sugar . . . [it is] served in a large full dish. On top of that is sprinkled almonds toasted in fat.'

Zerde's key ingredient is saffron. Dyeing clothing and foodstuffs yellow for sacred festivals is an ancient Near Eastern tradition that spread far and wide, to China and Europe.[14] Yellow was an auspicious colour symbolizing both the sun and gold, and it is *zerde*'s colour that the poet Latîfî stresses when he speaks of the '*zerrîn zerde*' ('golden *zerde*') served at the Fâtih Imaret in Istanbul in 1515.[15]

Zerde was closely associated with *imaret*s, public kitchens attached to mosques that provided meals twice daily for employees of the mosque complex, students, travellers and the poor. At most of these institutions *zerde* was a fixture on the Friday evening menu, as well as at *bayram*[16] and Ramazan meals.[17] Patients at some leprosy hospitals were served *zerde* on Monday and Thursday evenings.[18]

Zerde was one of the puddings made for Sultan Mehmed II in the fifteenth century,[19] and both ordinary *zerde* and the variation made with milk appeared regularly on palace dining tables in the sixteenth and seventeenth centuries.[20] Evliyâ Çelebi, the seventeenth-century courtier and traveller, tells us that Melek Ahmed Pasha served *zerde* flavoured with cloves and sweetened with honey at a banquet for Mehmed Giray Khan, ruler of the Crimea,[21] and that *zerde* made in Belgrade with almonds, cinnamon and cloves had a flavour 'unequalled in any other land'.[22]

Although *zerde* was served on so many different occasions, it was above all wedding feasts that were incomplete without *zerde*.[23] The English portraitist Mary Walker, who lived in Istanbul for nearly thirty years after the Crimean War (1853–6), accompanied many of her patronesses to weddings. She noted in her memoirs that *zerde* served with pilaf was 'an indispensable delicacy at every marriage feast' and tells us that it was 'ornamented with cinnamon, saffron, and pomegranate-seeds'.[24]

At wedding or circumcision banquets *zerde* was sometimes served in separate porcelain dishes together with pilaf, or poured on top of the pilaf like a sauce, when it was known as *pilav-zerde*.[25] This is how it was served at banquets given for the janissaries. Miniature paintings of such a banquet given in 1720 show dishes full of pilaf, topped with *zerde* (see Plate 14).

Ali Rıza Bey, director of Istanbul's wholesale fish market from 1883 to 1909, recounts in his memoirs how a foreign guest, Monsieur Obano, enjoyed *zerde* at the traditional annual banquet of fish and seafood given in the market at the beginning of March:[26]

> Bowls of *zerde* placed on the table amongst seasonal fruits attracted the attention of Monsieur Obano, who inquired of me as to its name and ingredients, then put a little on his plate to taste. He enjoyed the flavour so much that he helped himself to more and moreover recommended it to his foreign companions, and the bowls were passed from hand to hand. Indeed at his request his own cook was taught how to cook *zerde* with my assistance.
>
> Until twenty or twenty-five years ago never mind foreigners, most of our local Christian community had not heard of *zerde*. But now, seeing *zerde* in most of the restaurants of Galata and Istanbul, I am tempted to attribute this celebrity to that banquet.

A Bulgarian dictionary published in 1897 confirms that *zerde* was not being made by Christians in the Ottoman Empire. The definition emphasizes *zerde*'s Turkish-Islamic identity:[27] 'A boiled dish, which the Turks served to the poor at the mosques.'

The first recipe for *zerde* is recorded by Mahmud Nedim in 1900.[28] It is a simple version with none of the spices mentioned in earlier sources:

Zerde

Add a little washed and cleaned rice to water, together with sugar and simmer until it begins to thicken slightly. Toss in half or one *dirhem* of saffron and remove the pan from the heat. (Do not continue boiling after adding the saffron, as it would lose its fragrance.) Leave aside for quarter of an hour, then stir once and pour into bowls. Decorate with crumbled red *şerbetlik şeker*.[29]

There is no mention of the toasted almonds sprinkled on sixteenth-century *zerde*, nor do they appear in subsequent Ottoman recipes, which garnish with cinnamon, pine nuts, currants or pomegranate kernels. The following recipe dates from 1921:[30]

Zerde
This is one of the famous Turkish wedding puddings.

Method: Place 1 *dirhem* of saffron in a bowl with a ladleful of rose water, cover and leave for eight to ten hours. Take half an *okka* of *rizon* rice,[31] wash well and cook with four times the quantity of water until it starts disintegrating. Add some arrowroot diluted with a little water and cook, stirring constantly, until the aroma of rice and arrowroot has disappeared. Then add plenty of sugar. When this has dissolved, add the rose water and saffron, stir, and remove the pan from the heat. Cover and do not remove the lid until it has cooled. Then pour into small bowls, decorate with pine nuts, currants and crushed red *şerbet şekeri*, and serve.

Cooks attached great importance to the best type of rice for *zerde* but differed as to the variety they preferred. Hacıbeyzâde Ahmed Muhtar makes a strong case for his own preference, Ankara red rice, which 'makes excellent *zerde*. It keeps its shape and never confounds the cook.'[32]

The use of arrowroot in *zerde* is an interesting development. This form of starch produced from the roots of a plant native to South America and the West Indies seems to have become popular because of the transparency of puddings cooked with it. Arrowroot is mentioned among medicinal ingredients purchased for the Ottoman palace dispensary as early as the sixteenth century,[33] which is surprising since even the British, who of all European nations became most devoted to arrowroot, have no written record of it prior to 1696.[34]

Saffron was an expensive ingredient, and unscrupulous cooks used to substitute yellowberries[35] or turmeric, and pocket the difference.[36] The dried petals of bastard saffron (*Carthamus tinctorius*) is used in the cuisine of Gaziantep in southeastern Turkey today to colour *zerde* flavoured with rose water, orange-flower water or rose geranium, sprinkled with cinnamon and eaten in combination with unsweetened rice pudding.[37]

An unusual type of *zerde* was made with melons 'as fragrant as musk and ambergris' and flavoured with cinnamon and cloves.[38] According to Evliyâ Çelebi, even *zerde* made with Athenian honey was not as wonderful as the melon *zerde* of Diyarbakır; and the melons used for *zerde* in Beypazarı were so delicious and fragrant that they 'split the brain in two'.

When Evliyâ Çelebi visited Holland in 1663, he was given several ripe papayas (*Carica papaya*), which the Flemish had brought from the New World and were growing in gardens outside the city of Amsterdam.[39] Since the sweet yellow flesh resembled that of a melon, Evliyâ prepared *zerde* with some of his papayas, and all who tasted it declared that it was 'a flavour to be found only in heaven.'

In Istanbul the custom of serving *zerde* with pilaf at weddings was on the brink of oblivion in the last decade of the Ottoman Empire. Hacıbeyzâde Ahmed Muhtar, writing in 1916, noted sadly how traditional foodways were dying out:[40]

> Our national dishes have so far been abandoned that for ten or fifteen years now even the famous *düğün eti*,[41] so indispensable a part of such gatherings, is no longer served at weddings in our city. In the last five or six years some weddings do not even feature *zerde*, and if this trend continues, in 25 or 30 years there may be no one left who knows how to prepare these dishes, and the day might come when no one even remembers their name.

In fact his pessimism was unjustified. *Zerde* might have become a rarity at weddings and circumcisions in Istanbul, but the custom is very much alive in Konya and other provincial cities.[42]

RECIPES

ZERDE   (1539)

This recipe is based on the ingredients used to make zerde *in 1539 for the circumcision feast for Bâyezid and Cihângîr, the sons of Süleyman the Magnificent.*

   125 g rice
   5 cups water
   150 g honey
   1 g saffron
   10 g unsalted butter
   50 g almonds (blanched and coarsely chopped)

Place the rice with 5 cups of water in a covered pan and simmer over a very low heat for an hour and a quarter, stirring frequently to prevent the rice grains congealing into lumps. Add the honey and simmer for a further 5 minutes. Remove from the heat. Add the butter and saffron and stir gently for 5 minutes until the butter is absorbed. Stir occasionally until the *zerde* is lukewarm. Pour into small bowls. Allow to cool. Place the coarsely chopped almonds in a pan with a heavy base and stir continuously with a wooden spoon over a moderate heat until the almonds colour (about 10 minutes) and sprinkle over the *zerde*.

ZERDE WITH MILK   (1539)

This recipe is based on ingredients used to make zerde *with milk at the same feast in 1539.*

    125 g rice
    120 g sugar
    450 ml milk
    800 ml water
    40 g butter
    1 g saffron
    50 g almonds (blanched and coarsely chopped)

Prepare in the same way as the previous recipe.

MELON ZERDE   (Mid-seventeenth century)

This recipe is based on details about this pudding given by Evliyâ Çelebi in the mid-seventeenth century.

    1 medium-sized fragrant yellow-fleshed melon
    ½ cup rice
    ¼ tsp cinnamon
    ¼ tsp ground cloves
    ½ cup sugar
    1 tbsp lemon juice

Cut the melon flesh into chunks and blend in a food processor. Add water to make the quantity up to 5 cups. Place in a pan with the rice and simmer covered over a very low heat, stirring frequently, until the rice grains are very tender and the mixture thickens (about 1 hour 15 minutes). Stir in the ground cinnamon and cloves, sugar and lemon juice.

28 Dondurma   *Ice Cream*

This winter Istanbul is as cold as Erzurum
What need to spread cold comfort to all men
Fill the snowhouse this year Fâtima
So all can enjoy snow in the heat of summer.
                     Nailî of Monastir (1611–66)[1]

My ice cream with clotted cream
If you don't believe me taste it
Little ladies and gentlemen
To taste you must first pay for it.
         Turkish music-hall song, early twentieth century[2]

TURKISH NEWSPAPERS AND TV CHANNELS regularly feature the famous *dövme dondurma* ('beaten ice cream') of Turkey's southeastern province of Kahramanmaraş in stunts such as ice cream used as skipping ropes and 300 kilograms of ice cream stretched into a 30-metre-high pinnacle by the rising hydraulic platform of a fire engine. After the show is over this remarkable ice cream, which even in the scorching August sun takes nearly an hour to melt, is cut with cleavers and distributed to the spectators. When Prince Ali of Jordan visited Kahramanmaraş in September 1998 he was entertained by spectacles of this type and then invited to cut a block of ice cream with a cleaver. Finding this impossible, the prince was asked to try using his ceremonial sword but politely declined.[3]

Kahramanmaraş ice cream owes its stick-jaw consistency partly to the beating process and partly to the use of salep as a thickening and flavouring agent.[4] Just adding a little water to ground salep reveals the difference between salep and other thickeners such as starch or flour: the salep immediately takes on the consistency of drying concrete. This is due to its high glucomannan content.[5] The history of ice cream made with salep was never documented and rests on speculation and legend. The following story is told about its invention: one winter a pot of salep cooked with milk froze solid in the night and when the salep seller tasted it he found that it had a delicious flavour, and realized that this would be a popular new product to sell in the summer months.[6] All he had to do was to get hold of some ice in the winter, which, as we shall see, presented no difficulties in the Ottoman period.

Snow and ice were stored in vast quantities every winter, both by *karcıs* (snow collectors) in villages and towns, and in Istanbul by the state, which mustered all its resources for the task. Turkey is a mountainous country and most cities are close to high snowy peaks from which snow and blocks of ice from frozen lakes were carted and ferried to insulated ice houses and snow pits. Palace kitchen records for the fifteenth century record the huge amounts of ice and snow consumed. Even on summer hunting expeditions, ice was always available to cool the sultan's water and sherbets. When Sultan Mehmed II spent three weeks hunting around Lake Terkos in the summer of 1471, blocks of ice wrapped in felt were carried by porters from Istanbul, a distance of 50 kilometres as the crow flies.[7]

During the reign of his son Bâyezid II (1481–1512), considerable sums of money were spent on ice at the palace, and by the seventeenth century the quantity had multiplied to the point where ice and snow represented a major outlay.[8] According to the French traveller Michel Baudier, who visited Istanbul during the reign of Murad IV (r. 1623–40), annual expenditure on ice at the Ottoman palace was 20,000 *akçes*, equivalent to 8,000 pounds sterling.[9] In the middle of the seventeenth century the palace was using 780 camel-loads of snow each year.[10] Snow from the mountains of Uludağ and Katırlı near Bursa southwest of Istanbul, as well as ice cut from mountain lakes, was carried in felt bags by mule to the port of Mudanya on the southern shore of the Marmara Sea, and from there ferried by boat to Istanbul, where it was stored in seventy ice houses and snowpits around the city.[11]

The Reverend Robert Walsh describes the mule trains carrying ice down from these mountains in the early nineteenth century:[12]

The snow of this mountain [Uludağ] constitutes a considerable part of the treasures of the Turkish empire, as it does of its comforts and its luxuries. It is the exclusive property of the sultan, who farms it out to tenants, who vend it as more valuable than any produce of the soil. They are bound to supply the seraglio with a certain quantity, and the rest is disposed of to the population of Constantinople. It is sent down from the mountains cut into cuneiform wedges, and packed in felt, and caravans of mules are continually descending with such loads. It is brought to a promontory near Moudania, called from thence Booz Bournou, or 'the Cape of Ice,' whence it is embarked for the capital, and in such abundance, that the poorest *hummal* cools his sherbet with it during the hottest season of the year.

Snow collection was not just laborious but sometimes dangerous. In 1768 Albanian bandits captured a group of snow collectors on Mount Katırlı and demanded 5,000 *kuruş* in ransom from the *karcıbaşı* (superintendant of snow collectors). The local judge was instructed to rescue the snow collectors and arrest the bandits, but whether this operation to free the hostages was a success is not known.[13]

As well as snow and ice brought from nearby mountains, when there were sufficiently heavy snowfalls in Istanbul many thousands of soldiers, galley slaves and gardeners[14] were sent out with spades, picks, hoes and sleds. The snow was piled into heaps resembling 'bath-house domes' then rolled like gigantic snowballs into the snow pits and stamped down. When this task was over at the end of the winter season, the *karcıbaşı* gave a series of banquets to the grand vizier, the janissary commander, the *bostancıbaşı* (superintendant of the gardeners), the high admiral and the janissary soldiers. In guild processions the *karcıbaşı* and his men dressed in turbans and tall caps fashioned from snow and carrying lances and snow axes carved from ice marched through the streets, throwing snowballs at the crowd.[15]

Wealthy citizens in the provinces stored their own snow in pits, and commonly distributed some of the compacted snow, which by the summer had turned to ice, to people in the neighbourhood. This custom continued into the early years of the twentieth century. In Yatağan in southwestern Turkey the news that someone was distributing ice would spread like wildfire, and people would grab bowls, trays or any other containers that were to hand, and rush to collect their share of the ice as it was sawn into lumps.[16] Anyone too far from home to fetch a container wrapped the ice in their handkerchief. This is mentioned in a seventeenth-century poem by the folk poet Karacaoğlan, who declares, 'Send me snow wrapped in a handkerchief.'[17]

Philanthropists established charitable foundations for the provision of ice and snow to cool the water of public fountains in the hot summer months. The eighteenth-century French consul-general Claude Charles de Peyssonnel wrote:[18] 'Many have even carried their Benevolence so far as to assign sums of money for furnishing snow, during the summer, that [for] those who drink at these fountains may render the water more cool and refreshing.' One of the earliest such philanthropists was Hatice Sultan, the elder daughter of Mehmed

IV, who in 1663 made an endowment for snow to cool drinking water distributed at the *sebil* of Yeni Mosque in Istanbul. When Ramazan fell in the summer months, the same endowment provided free drinks of chilled honey sherbet to the congregation as they left the mosque after the evening *terâvih* prayers.[19]

European travellers were astonished at the abundance of snow and ice available in Ottoman Turkey during the summer. The French botanist Pierre Belon, who travelled in Turkey in 1546–51, gives a long account of the ice houses that he saw and proposes that the practice be introduced in France:[20]

> When it has snowed and frozen hard, when the Bora wind, also called the *Bise*, which blows between Greece and the North, and which is the coldest wind known, is in full force, the Turks gather the snow, filling certain houses constructed like vaults or else like a hillock of earth . . . and expressly made for the purpose, in the least southerly situation, such as in a low-lying place, behind some high wall, or in the shelter of a hill: the snow must be built up as though to make a wall of masonry, putting ice here and there. This wall will stand two years without melting. This manner is commonly followed throughout the country of Turkey . . . the same could be done in France: for we have seen it in several regions where the climate is hotter than in France, and it lasts all the summer.

The German physician and botanist Dr Leonhart Rauwolff, who spent the years 1573–6 travelling in Syria and southeastern Turkey, described the chilled sherbets sold in the bazaars of Aleppo during the summer months:[21] 'All these liquors are sold in their great batzars, where they have baskets full of ice and snow all the summer long, whereof they put so much into the drink that it maketh their teeth chatter and quake again.'

Although foreigners enjoyed these chilled drinks, they were also convinced that they were bad for the health. John Burbury, who accompanied the British ambassador Lord Henry Howard on his embassy to Istanbul in 1660, blamed 'eating much Fruit, and drinking Wine cooled excessively in Snow, which the Turks had procured' for the 'dire diseases' some of their companions suffered on the journey.[22] One early nineteenth-century traveller in southeastern Turkey, James Silk Buckingham, suggested that consuming much ice and raw lettuce might be causes of smallpox.[23] Turkish physicians, on the other hand, wrote of the benefits of cold water,[24] and Buckingham himself was equivocal, claiming at one point that ice was a 'cheap and healthy refreshment':[25]

> During all the summer, there is also an abundant supply of solid ice, brought down from the summits of Mount Taurus, in a journey of a day and night.

About an English pound of this is sold at present for a para or a farthing, and is a cheap and healthy refreshment, accessible to the poorest of the people. Iced milks, and sherbets of honey, cinnamon water, and perfumes, are also made for the rich, and furnish a great luxury during the heat of the day.

In Istanbul, too, even the poorest porter was able to afford a refreshing cup of iced water or sherbet, cooled by pouring the liquid over a block of ice attached to an iron prong or through a lump of snow attached to the spout of the vessel.[26] The latter method is described by Robert Walsh:[27]

In all convivial picnics on the grass, the *sougee*, or 'water-vender,' is in the greatest request. He is everywhere seen moving about, with his clear glass cup in one hand, and his jar with a long spout in the other, and the cry constantly heard is *sou, sook-sou*, 'water, cold water.' When called, he attaches a mass of snow to the spout, and the water comes limpid and refrigerated through the pores of it.

Storing ice and snow for the summer began in Mesopotamia thousands of years ago,[28] and was practised in China from an early date.[29] In Greece and Rome stored snow was a luxury reserved by the rich for cooling their wine. Pliny the Younger complained to a friend who missed a dinner to which he had been invited: 'I had prepared, you must know, a lettuce apiece, three snails, two eggs and a barley cake, with some sweet wine and snow; the snow I shall most certainly charge to your account, as a rarity that will not keep.'[30] In sixteenth-century Europe storing snow was so rare that when King Francis I of France travelled to Nice to negotiate a truce with the Holy Roman Emperor Charles V in June 1538, his doctor noted with amazement that the wine was chilled with ice brought down from the nearby mountains.[31]

The ancient Greeks cooled their wine by placing it in a *psycter*, a double-walled amphora with an inner compartment for the wine and an outer compartment surrounding the other for snow-chilled water.[32] During the Ottoman period similar vessels known as *karlık* ('snow vessels') with a special compartment for snow were used for cooling water and sherbet. The following Turkish riddle describes a *karlık*:[33]

What is that tent so singular
Inside is never summer but always winter?

The Turkic peoples of Central Asia had long been familiar with the gathering and storage of snow and ice. Mahmud of Kashgar's eleventh-century dictionary refers to ice houses called *buzluk* where ice was stored for use in the summer, and ice hooks called *ırgağ* used to drag ice into the ice house.[34] Snow played an important role in trade along the Asian Silk Road, as a way of refrigerating fresh foods on journeys lasting weeks and sometimes months. In the T'ang period (618–907) watermelons were exported from Khwarezm in Central Asia to China, a distance of over 4,000 kilometres, by packing them in snow-filled lead chests, and fresh mare's nipple grapes grown in Turfan in Turkistan must have been similarly packed in order to survive the gruelling 2,000 kilometre journey across scorching deserts to China.[35]

In the nineteenth century even Istanbul's many ice houses and snowpits with their vast snow and ice storage capacity were sometimes unable to keep up with demand. In 1844 a ball at the palace of the internuncio (the papal ambassador) had to be postponed because frozen snow for the ices and champagne could not be procured in sufficient quantities.[36] Gathering and storing enough snow and ice for Istanbul in the traditional way was probably becoming both difficult and expensive, because in 1856 Turkey imported shiploads of ice from the United States.[37] Norway had begun exporting ice cut from its frozen lakes in the first half of the nineteenth century, and Britain received its first shipment from Norway in 1822 and from America in 1844.[38]

Before returning to the subject of ice cream, there is one curious feature of ice that should not be passed over: the snow worms described by Evliyâ Çelebi.[39] In 1648 Evliyâ observed these worms on Syria's Jebel-i Hayy'u's-selc, the 'Mountain of Hard Snow', and tells us that the snow gatherers presented them as gifts to physicians. Although this phenomenon had been described by many geographers and travellers since antiquity, it was dismissed by scientists as a myth until late nineteenth-century research proved that a species of dark brown or black worm (*Mesenchytraeus solifugus*) does indeed live in glaciers and permanent snow.[40]

On the other hand, the myth that Marco Polo introduced ice cream to Italy from China has been exploded.[41] The Chinese, Greeks and Romans had certainly cooled drinks with snow and ice since very early times,[42] and according to *Larousse Gastronomique* Alexander the Great and the Emperor Nero had mixed snow with fruit purée,[43] but as Elizabeth David points out, it is a long leap from chilling drinks and foods with snow to the invention of true ice cream and sorbets.[44] The *yeh der bihişt* ('ice of paradise') mentioned by the fifteenth-century Persian poet Bushaq that at first sight could be taken to be an early reference to ice cream, is in fact nothing but a ground rice pudding whose name rests on 'the conceit that in Heaven, ice is sweet, has a toothsome texture and tastes of rose water'.[45]

A sorbet-like Turkish dessert called *kar helvası* (snow helva, and also known variously as *karma, karsanbaş* or *karlamaç*) is made by mixing *pekmez*, honey or fruit syrup with snow.[46] The snow used for this is not freshly fallen soft snow but long-lying compacted snow with a crunchy texture.[47] But real water ices and ice cream cannot be made either by mixing with snow or chilling with ice; salt or saltpetre must be added to reduce the temperature below freezing point.

The early history of ice cream, as distinguished from chilled sherbet or snow helva, is not easy to trace, not least because the name *sorbetto* that the Italians gave to Turkish *şerbet* when these fruit drinks became popular in the sixteenth century later acquired the meaning of fruit-flavoured water ices. Not until the first European recipes for ice cream were published in the late seventeenth century can *sorbetto* be assumed to mean water ices or ice cream.

China has often been credited with the invention, despite the doubt shed on this myth by scholars such as Edward Schafer.[48] Toussaint-Samat attributes the invention of the snow and saltpetre method for making water ices to the Chinese, as does *Larousse Gastronomique*, which has stuck to the Marco Polo legend through many editions. A more viable claim is made for the Moghuls, who in the sixteenth century are known to have cooled their water in summer by placing it in a solution of saltpetre.[49] Nonetheless, there is no evidence that they used the technique to make anything like ice cream, so we are once again in the realm of ice cream mythology.[50] However, the use of saltpetre as a cooling agent was a key link in the chain of events that that led to European experimentation with cooling techniques from the sixteenth century onwards. A nineteenth-century Turkish writer says that making ice by adding saltpetre to water was well known in Egypt, so it may be that this country played some part in the discovery of ices.[51]

In Europe experiments with refrigeration techniques began in Italy in the first half of the sixteenth century, when an Italian physician named Zimara wrote about the cooling properties of saltpetre.[52] For the next century this method was used to chill drinks and fruit, but not apparently to make ices, because in the 1660s the English physicist and chemist Robert Boyle wrote that although very little was known in England about cooling with a mixture of sea salt and snow, the method was widely used in Italy and other countries 'for the cooling of drinks and fruit, which is achieved by putting them into appropriate vessels which are then buried in the mixture'.[53] But although the invention of ices had evidently not yet reached Boyle's ears, it was at this time that the earliest indisputable references begin to appear in Italy, followed by France.[54]

The evidence points to ices having been introduced from Italy to Turkey, since the first mention of them in Istanbul dates from the late seventeenth century, when they were among the 130 dishes served at a banquet given in honour of the bailo of Venice in 1682.[55]

The modern Turkish term *dondurma* (from the verb *dondurmak*, 'to freeze')[56] for ices is first recorded in the late eighteenth century, when Ahmed Câvid says that they were being made from various fruits in Istanbul. However, the German confectioner Friedrich Unger wrote disparagingly of the ices served at dinners to which he was invited during his stay in Istanbul in 1835:[57]

In a few Turkish houses I also found a kind of ice (usually from dried fruit) prepared at home, although most imperfectly, so that I assume it has only recently been introduced to the Turks, that is into Constantinople. It is not worth our while to discuss the preparation of this ice, if it deserves that name.

The first Turkish recipe for ice cream was not published until 1882, although an earlier recipe book dated 1844 describes how to make ice in an ice cream pail:[58]

How to Freeze Ice When You Have Snow but no Ice

Place plenty of whittled snow into a container and mix it with several handfuls of salt, then fill a container made of lead and tin like an ice cream cylinder with water and bury it up to the rim in this snow mixture. Cover and place in a pit, and cover it against the air. After a few hours it will have frozen. They say it will even freeze in a celadon dish.

Although ice cream and ice cream pails were almost certainly introduced to Turkey from Italy, ice cream made with salep presents an anomaly that does not fit neatly into the story. This ice cream has to be beaten with a boxwood implement known as a *mablak*, like that traditionally used by Turkish confectioners for stirring helva.[59] To facilitate the beating process, the freezing cylinders used in Turkey had rounded rather than flat bottoms.[60] In the ice cream recipe below, dated 1882, Ayşe Fahriye describes how the mixture is beaten until it acquires a viscous consistency, and concludes by saying that the more it is beaten the more delicious it will be:[61]

Kaymaklı Dondurma

Pour one litre of milk into a pan and while stirring constantly add one and a half grams of ground salep. Continue stirring until the milk comes to the boil. When it is sufficiently well cooked, add 60 grams of sugar, bring to the boil again, then place in an ice cream mould made of lead or tin and set this into an ice cream pail. Sprinkle coarse salt around it and fill with snow, pressing it down firmly. Cover and turn the handle until the mixture inside the mould forms a frozen layer a finger in width. Scrape this away from the surface with a special spatula and push it down, then cover and turn the handle again. Repeat until the whole has become thick, then with an ice cream *mablak* begin to beat the ice cream until it acquires a viscous consistency. Place portions onto plates and eat.

As the snow melts, it is necessary to use the tap at the bottom of the pail to drain off the water, and then add more snow, which needs to be pressed down, and sprinkle on more salt. The more you scrape the sides of the mould as described and beat with the *mablak*, the more delicious the ice cream will be.

The very different technique and different shape of the moulds suggests two divergent traditions. In seventeenth-century Italy ice cream was made of cream, sugar, and flavourings such as lemon peel and cinnamon,[62] without any thickening agent. Not until the mid-eighteenth century did egg yolks appear in the mixture.[63] Even though the four egg yolks in Ayşe Fahriye's other recipe for ice cream suggest European influence, she still insists on the salep and the beating.[64] Fruit ices, on the other hand, are not beaten, with the exception of water ice made with melon, described in the following recipe published in 1926:[65]

Melon Ice

Take a very fragrant, juicy and soft melon, remove the rind and seeds, then mash it well, add sufficient sugar, and fill the tin [of the ice cream pail]. Stir, beat and turn as it freezes, as described in the recipe for *kaymaklı dondurma*.

While fruit ices vary very little from east to west, those made with milk differ considerably in terms of their ingredients as well as method: the condensed milk of Indian *kulfi*, the cream of European ice cream and the salep of Turkish *kaymaklı dondurma*.

In Istanbul ice cream making was largely the preserve of coffeehouse proprietors and street sellers.[66]

Neither confectioners nor pastrycooks sell ices. This is a distinct branch of trade, learned from Italians settled at Galata and Pera. There is, nevertheless, no lack of manufactured ice (*dondoormak*), or of *kar* (frozen snow), for cooling water and sherbets . . . Manufactured ices are sold in many shops at Galata and Pera. During summer evenings, the walk, crowding the small burying-ground, from the well-appointed hotel of Madame Giuseppini to the Hellenic minister's residence, is crowded with idlers of all nations, save perhaps those whom foreigners would naturally expect to meet – the Turks. Loungers seat themselves at tables placed in the road, and, defying dust and disagreeable emanations arising from the contiguous cemetery, smoke, drink punch, and eat 'gellati', furnished by the adjoining Greek coffee-houses. This is the principal solace of those who are detained during summer within the scorching and dusty precincts . . . Ambulatory ice-venders (*dondoormajee*) frequent public places of *kief*, such as the two Sweet Waters, and Armenian burying-grounds of Pera and Balykly. Their merchandize is contained in leaden pails immersed in snow, and placed within wooden buckets. Here and there, *dondoormajee* carry their ices in wooden celarets, gaily painted, and slung upon the backs of Mytelene ponies, neatly harnessed. In the centre is a tray and tripod stand, with the necessary cups and spoons.

Itinerant vendors carried their ice cream in a freezing pail wrapped in a white cloth, while the dishes, saucers and spoons, together with trays and water for washing the cups and spoons, were arranged on special brass stands – the chinaware on top and the washing facilities below. The pail and stand were hung from either end of a wooden yoke accross the vendor's shoulders.

Lady Alicia Blackwood, the wife of a churchman who came to Istanbul to work with Florence Nightingale during the Crimean War of 1853–6, relates how the vendors learned to cry out in English, 'Vera good ice, Johnny', for the benefit of the English

38. An itinerant ice cream vendor in Istanbul in the late nineteenth century. In his left hand he carries an ice cream bucket wrapped in cloths, and in his right a tin container with dishes for serving the ice cream stacked on top and water for rinsing them inside (Courtesy of Mert Sandalcı).

soldiers in Üsküdar,[67] instead of the usual Turkish cry of 'Ten paras for one plate, if you don't believe me try it.' Ices were so welcome in the unaccustomed heat that the vendors were besieged by more English customers than they could cope with.

Sometimes ice cream was adulterated by replacing the milk with boiled rice, as recorded by Mahmud Nedim, who tells us that the ice cream sold near Yeni Mosque at three piasters the kilogram was made of boiled rice.[68] Today, when most ice cream consists largely of stabilizers, emulsifiers, vegetable fats, artificial flavourings and colourings,[69] boiled rice seems desirable by comparison.

Notes

Introduction

1 Yusuf Has Hacib, *Kutadgu Bilig*, tr. Reşid Rahmeti Arat (Ankara, 1985), pp. 3614–15.

2 Evliyâ Çelebi, *Evliyâ Çelebi Seyahatnâmesi*, 10 vols, eds Seyit Ali Kahraman, Yücel Dağlı, Robert Dankoff et al. (Istanbul, 1996–2007), vol. 9, p. 180.

3 *Apicius: The Roman Cookery Book*, tr. Barbara Flower and Elisabeth Rosenbaum (London, 1958), p. 171.

4 *Apicius*, p. 171; Perry, Charles and Maxine Rodinson, *Medieval Arab Cookery* (Totnes, 2001), pp. 452–3; Woods, Sir Henry Felix, *Spunyarn from the Strands of a Sailor's Life*, 2 vols (London, 1924), p. 69.

5 Evliyâ Çelebi (1996–2007), vol. 1, p. 253; White, Charles, *Three Years in Constantinople or, Domestic Manners of The Turks in 1844*, 3 vols (London, 1845–6), vol. 2, p. 8.

6 See Chapters 13, 14, 15.

7 See Rodinson, Maxime, 'Ma'mûniyya East and West', *Petits Propos Culinaires*, 33 (November 1989).

8 See Ch. 15.

9 Ünver, Süheyl, *Tarihte 50 Türk Yemeği* (Istanbul, 1948), p. 14.

10 The size of a walnut or small egg. Sufficient for one very thin sheet of pastry about 30–40 cm in diameter.

11 Ünver, *Tarihte 50 Türk Yemeği*, pp. 6, 20; Sefercioğlu, M. Nejat (ed.), *Türk Yemekleri (XVIII. Yüzyıla Ait Yazma Bir Yemek Risalesi)* (Ankara, 1985), pp. 31–2. The sultan in question is probably Murad IV (r. 1623–40).

12 Ali Rıza (Balıkhane Nazırı), *Bir Zamanlar İstanbul*, ed. Niyazi Ahmet Banoğlu (Istanbul, n.d.), p. 131.

13 Hafız Hızır İlyas Ağa, *Tarih-i Enderun – Letaif-i Enderun*, ed. Cahit Kayra (Istanbul, 1987), pp. 164, 166.

14 Ali Rıza, *Bir Zamanlar İstanbul*, pp. 134–7.

15 Gökyay, Orhan Şaik, 'Sohbetnâme', *Tarih ve Toplum*, 3/14 (February 1985), pp. 56–64.

16 Ahmed Câvid, *Tercüme-i Kenzü'l-İştihâ*, eds Seyit Ali Kahraman and Priscilla Mary Işın (Istanbul, 2006), pp. 149–50.

17 Mahmud Nedim bin Tosun, *Aşçıbaşı*, ed. Priscilla Mary Işın (Istanbul, 1998), pp. 13–14.

18 See Ch. 16.
19 See Ch. 17.
20 Tannahill, Reay, *Food in History* (New York, 1973), p. 296.
21 Moltke, Helmuth von, *Türkiye Mektupları*, tr. Hayrullah Örs (Istanbul, 1969), p. 55.
22 Lear, Edward, *Journals of a Landscape Painter in Greece and Albania* (London, 1988), pp. 80–1.
23 Kut, Turgut, 'İstanbul'da Kâdirihâne Âsitânesinde 1906 Yılı Ramazan İftarları', *Dördüncü Milletlerarası Yemek Kongresi* (Konya, 1993), p. 192.
24 Koz, M. Sabri, 'Konya'da Bir Cevelan', *Güney'de Kültür*, 48 (February 1993), p. 27.
25 Dickie, John, *Delizia! The Epic History of the Italians and their Food* (New York, 2008), p. 95. My thanks to Michael Krondl for pointing out this source.
26 David, Elizabeth, *Harvest of the Cold Months: The Social History of Ice and Ices* (London, 1996), p. 10.
27 Luard, Elisabeth, *European Peasant Cookery* (London, 1988), pp. 392–3, 563–4; Müller, Georgina Adelaide, *Letters from Constantinople* (London, 1897), p. 183.
28 See Ch. 11.
29 David, *Harvest of the Cold Months*, p. 156.
30 See Ch. 28.
31 See Ch. 16.
32 Wechsberg, Joseph, *The Cooking of Vienna's Empire* (New York, 1968), p. 14.
33 Wechsberg, *The Cooking of Vienna's Empire*, p. 24.
34 Wechsberg, *The Cooking of Vienna's Empire*, pp. 105, 176.
35 See Ch. 13.
36 See Ch. 21.
37 Scappi, Bartolomeo, *The Opera of Bartolomeo Scappi* (1570): *The Art and Craft of a Master Cook*, tr. and ed. Terence Scully (Toronto, 2009), pp. 499, 532, 650.
38 Evliyâ Çelebi, *Evliyâ Çelebi Seyahatnâmesi*, eds Robert Dankoff, Seyit Ali Kahraman and Yücel Dağlı, vol. 1, 2nd edn (Istanbul, 2006), pp. 213, 289.
39 Nutku, Özdemir, *IV. Mehmet'in Edirne Şenliği 1675*, 2nd edn (Ankara, 1987), p. 73.
40 See Ch. 5 for further details.
41 White, *Three Years in Constantinople*, vol. 3, p. 244.
42 Türâbî Efendi, *Turkish Cookery Book, A Collection of Receipts Dedicated to those Royal and Distinguished Personages, the Guests of his Highness the Late Viceroy of Egypt, on the Occasion of the Banquet given at Woolwich, on Board his Highness's Yacht the Faiz-Jehad, the 16th July 1862. Compiled by Türabi Efendi from the Best Turkish Authorities* (London, n.d. [1864]), p. 62.
43 Arabacıyan, Mihran, *Miftâhü't-Tabbâhîin* (Istanbul, 1876), p. 213. My thanks to Garo Kürkman for providing a photocopy of this book.
44 Dufferin, Lady, *My Russian and Turkish Journals* (London, 1916), p. 302.
45 Mahmud Nedim, *Aşçıbaşı*, p. 108.
46 Mehmed Reşad, *Fenn-i Tabâhat*, 4 vols (Istanbul, AH 1340/1921–2), vol. 4, p. 13.
47 Ali Rıza, *Eski Zamanlarda İstanbul Hayatı*, ed. Ali Şükrü Çoruk (Istanbul, 2001), p. 325; Ali Rıza, *Bir Zamanlar İstanbul*, p. 176.

48 Ayşe Fahriye, *Ev Kadını* (Istanbul, AH 1300/1882–3), p. 230; Mehmed Reşad, *Fenn-i Tabâhat*, vol. 4, p. 13.
49 *Türk Kadının Tatlı Kitabı*, ed. Esat İren (Ankara, 1939).
50 *Türk Kadının Tatlı Kitabı*, 2nd edn, ed. Ekrem Muhittin Yeğen (Ankara, 1966).
51 See Ch. 23 for a recipe using cheese as a baklava filling. *Lokma* are doughnuts, and varieties with cheese appear in eighteenth-century recipes. Well-known regional flour confections made with fresh cheese include *peynirli helva*, some kinds of *hoşmerim*, *künefe* (*tel kadayıf* filled with cheese and eaten hot), and *Kemal Paşa tatlısı* (a kind of small cake soaked in syrup).
52 See Ch. 6.
53 Mevlânâ Celâleddin Rûmî, *Mesnevî*, 6 vols, tr. Veled İzbudak (Istanbul, 1990), vol. 3, p. 93, couplet 1156.

1 *Şeker* – Sugar

1 Mevlânâ Celâleddin Rûmî, *Divân-ı Kebîr*, 4 vols, tr. Abdülbâki Gölpınarlı (Istanbul, 1957), vol. 1, p. 18.
2 Weymarn, Niklas von, 'Process Development for Mannitol Production by Lactic Acid Bacteria', doctoral dissertation (Helsinki University, 2002), pp. 9, 13.
3 www.massmaple.org/history.php.
4 *Chambers Encyclopaedia*, 10 vols (London, 1874–80), vol. 9, p. 188.
5 Orman Kanunu no. 6831, 1956, section 3, article 14.
6 Burnaby, Frederick, *On Horseback through Asia Minor* (Gloucester, 1985), pp. 154–5.
7 Geerdes, Thomas, *Ana Besin Maddelerinden Şeker ve Tarihi*, tr. Cihad Gökdağ (Ankara, 1966), pp. 130ff; www.turkseker.gov.tr/sekerfabrikalari.aspx.
8 Üçer, Müjgân, *Sivas Halk Mutfağı* (Sivas, 1992), p. 40.
9 Kaşgarlı Mahmud, *Divanü Lûgat-it-Türk Tercümesi*, 4 vols, tr. Besim Atalay (Ankara, 1985–6), pp. 440, 459. A similar but unclarified product made in Roman times was known as *defrutum*, see Humphrey, John William, John Peter Oleson and Andrew Neil Sherwood, *Greek and Roman Technology: A Sourcebook* (London, 1998), pp. 165–6.
10 Schafer, Edward H., 'T'ang', in K.C. Chang (ed.), *Food in Chinese Culture* (New Haven, CT, 1977), p. 147.
11 İbn Battuta, *The Travels of Ibn Battuta*, tr. H.A.R. Gibb, (London, 1962), p. 64.
12 McNair, James Birtley, *Sugar and Sugar-Making* (Chicago, 1927), p. 188.
13 Davidson, Alan, *The Oxford Companion to Food* (Oxford, 1999), p. 765.
14 Schafer: 'T'ang', pp. 18, 152–3; Geerdes, *Ana Besin Maddelerinden Şeker*, p. 10.
15 Humphrey, *Greek and Roman Technology*, p. 165; *Chambers Encyclopaedia*, vol. 9, p. 188.
16 *Natural History* 12.32, in Humphrey, *Greek and Roman Technology*, p. 165.
17 Achaya, K.T., *Indian Food: A Historical Companion* (Delhi, 2005), p. 113.
18 Schafer, Edward H., *The Golden Peaches of Samarkand, A Study of T'ang Exotics* (Los Angeles and Berkeley, 1985), p. 153.

19 Beal, Samuel (tr.), *Si-Yu-Ki, Buddhist Records of the Western World*, 2 vols (London, 1881), vol. 1, pp. 90, 98.

20 Geerdes, *Ana Besin Maddelerinden Şeker*, p. 10.

21 Perry, Charles and Maxine Rodinson, *Medieval Arab Cookery* (Totnes, 2001), p. 464.

22 For example, 'Sugar is in Samarkand but he found it in Bukhara and it was that road he took', in Mevlânâ Celâleddin Rûmî, *Mesnevî*, 6 vols, tr. Veled İzbudak (Istanbul, 1990), vol. 3, couplet 3863. Poets particularly enjoyed rhyming Samarkand with *kand* (refined sugar).

23 Mevlânâ Celâleddin Rûmî, *Divân-ı Kebîr*, vol. 1, p. 327, couplet 3007.

24 Mustafa Ali of Gallipoli, *Cami'u'l-buhur der Mecalis-i Sur*, ed. Ali Öztekin (Ankara, 1996), p. 106.

25 Schafer, *The Golden Peaches of Samarkand*, p. 153; Yule, Henry and A.C. Burnell, *Hobson-Jobson, The Anglo-Indian Dictionary* (Ware, 1996), p. 863; Achaya, *Indian Food*, p. 113.

26 Yule, Henry (tr. and ed.), *The Book of Ser Marco Polo, the Venetian*, 2 vols (London, 1871), vol. 2, pp. 180, 183n (8).

27 Roe, Thomas, 'The Journal of Sir Thomas Roe, Ambassador from his Majesty King James the First', in Awnsham Churchill (ed.), *A Collection of Voyages and Travels* (London, 1752), p. 634.

28 Yule and Burnell, *Hobson-Jobson*, p. 863; for the derivation of the word *kand* I am indebted to Charles Perry, personal communication.

29 Yule and Burnell, *Hobson-Jobson*, p. 864.

30 Schafer, *The Golden Peaches of Samarkand*, p. 153.

31 Ali Rıza (Balıkhane Nazırı), *Bir Zamanlar İstanbul*, ed. Niyazi Ahmet Banoğlu (Istanbul, n.d.), p. 106.

32 *Türkiye Diyanet İşleri İslâm Ansiklopedisi*, 40 vols (Istanbul, 1989–2012), vol. 38, p. 487.

33 Achaya, *Indian Food*, p. 150; Rasonyi, Laszlo, *Tarihte Türklük* (Ankara, 1988), p. 97.

34 See Ch. 3.

35 Yusuf Has Hacib, *Kutadgu Bilig*, tr. Reşid Rahmeti Arat (Ankara, 1985), p. 263.

36 Mahmud al-Kāshgari, *Compendium of the Turkic Dialects (Dīwān Luγāt at-Turk)* 3 vols, ed. and tr. Robert Dankoff in collaboration with James Kelly (Cambridge, MA, 1984), vol. 1, pp. 124, 161.

37 Pegolotti, *La Pratica di Mercatura*, 1343, quoted in Yule and Burnell, *Hobson-Jobson*, p. 864.

38 Information supplied by Dr Bernard E. Nickl of the Leiter-Zucker Museum in Berlin in 2002.

39 Anonymous, 'An Account of the Method of Preparing and Refining Sugar', *Gentleman's and London Magazine* (Dublin, 1788), p. 407.

40 Geerdes, *Ana Besin Maddelerinden Şeker*, p. 12.

41 Yule and Burnell, *Hobson-Jobson*, p. 156.

42 Yule and Burnell, *Hobson-Jobson*, p. 864.

43 Ahmed Câvid, *Tercüme-i Kenzü'l-İştihâ*, eds Seyit Ali Kahraman and Priscilla Mary

Işın (Istanbul, 2006), pp. 130–1; *İslam Ansiklopedisi*, 13 vols (Eskişehir, 2001), vol. 11, 'Şeker'.

44 Mehmed Reşad, *Fenn-i Tabâhat*, 4 vols (Istanbul, AH 1340/1921–2), vol. 1, p. 43; Yule and Burnell, *Hobson-Jobson*, p. 864; Mason, Laura, *Sugar-Plums and Sherbet* (Totnes, 1998), pp. 39–40.

45 Redhouse, Sir James W., *A Turkish and English Lexicon* (Constantinople, 1890), p. 1877, 'Mısır'.

46 In Egypt in the seventeenth century a kind of basket woven from date palm branches used to package sugar is mentioned by the Turkish traveller Evliyâ Çelebi, who describes it as 'sugar cage' (*şeker kafesi*), see Evliyâ Çelebi, *Evliyâ Çelebi Seyahatnâmesi*, 10 vols, eds Seyit Ali Kahraman, Yücel Dağlı, Robert Dankoff et al. (Istanbul, 1996–2007), vol. 10, pp. 195–242. Old Cairo (Babul) was known in Europe as Babylonia. For example, the fifteenth-century Spanish traveller Pero Tafur writes, 'That day we went to see the city of Babylonia. It is divided into three sections. The first they call Greater Babylonia, the second Cairo, and the third Mistra', *Travels and Adventures 1435–1439*, ed. Malcolm Letts (London, 2004), p. 79. Pegolotti, Francesco Balducci, *La Pratica Della Mercatura*, ed. Allan Evans (Cambridge, MA, 1936), p. 434.

47 Rauwolff, Leonhart, 'Dr. Leonhart Rauwolff's Itinerary into the Eastern Countries, as Syria, Palestine, or the Holy Land, Armenia, Mesopotamia, Assyria, Chaldea Etc.', tr. Nicholas Staphorst, in John Ray (ed.), *A Collection of Curious Travels and Voyages* (London, 1693), pp. 48–9.

48 Yule and Burnell, *Hobson-Jobson*, p. 864.

49 Ayşe Fahriye, *Ev Kadını* (Istanbul, AH 1300/1882–3), p. 136.

50 Mahmud Nedim bin Tosun, *Aşçıbaşı*, ed. Priscilla Mary Işın (Istanbul, 1998), p. 113.

51 Bayramoğlu, Fuat, 'Türk Mutfağı ve Yazılı Kaynaklar', *Birinci Milletlerarasi Yemek Kongresi, Türkiye, 25–30 Eylül 1986* (Ankara, 1988), p. 38.

52 Ünver, Süheyl, *Tarihte 50 Türk Yemeği* (Istanbul, 1948), p. 15.

53 Karay, Refik Halid, *Üç Nesil Üç Hayat* (Istanbul, 1943), p. 131.

54 Dernschwam, Hans, *Istanbul ve Anadolu'ya Seyahat Günlüğü*, tr. Yaşar Önen (Ankara, 1987), pp. 70, 146.

55 Kütükoğlu, Mübahat S., *Osmanlılarda Narh Müessesi ve 1640 Tarihli Narh Defteri* (Istanbul, 1983), pp. 91, 98.

56 Evliyâ Çelebi, *Evliyâ Çelebi Seyahatnâmesi*, 10 vols, eds Seyit Ali Kahraman, Yücel Dağlı, Robert Dankoff et al. (Istanbul, 1996–2007), vol. 2, pp. 190–1.

57 Burnaby, Frederick, *On Horseback through Asia Minor* (Gloucester, 1985), p. 83; Moltke, Helmuth von, *Türkiye Mektupları*, tr. Hayrullah Örs (Istanbul, 1969), p. 150.

58 Geerdes, *Ana Besin Maddelerinden Şeker*, pp. 12–13.

59 Mason, Laura, *Sugar-Plums and Sherbet*, p. 31.

60 Geerdes, *Ana Besin Maddelerinden Şeker*, p. 10.

61 Geerdes, *Ana Besin Maddelerinden Şeker*, p. 11.

62 MacBane, Gavan, *From Cane to Kitchen: An Investigation into Medieval Processed Sugar*, 2006 (www.florilegium.org/files/FOOD-SWEETS/Cypriot-Sugr-art.html).

63 Brocquière, Bertrandon de la, 'The Travels of Bertrandon de la Brocquière 1432, 1433', in Thomas Wright (ed.), *Early Travels in Palestine* (London, n.d.), p. 323. The other gifts were fabrics, a peregrine falcon and two crossbows.
64 One *kantar* was equivalent to 56.452 kg.
65 Barkan, Lütfi Ömer, 'Istanbul Saraylarına ait Muhasebe Defterleri,' *Belgeler*, 12/13 (1979), p. 240.
66 MacBane, *From Cane to Kitchen*.
67 MacBane, *From Cane to Kitchen*, quotation from *Canon Pietro Casola's Pilgrimage to Jerusalem in the Year 1494*, tr. Newett, Margaret (Manchester, 1907).
68 Pîrî Reis, *Kitâb-ı Bahriye*, 4 vols, ed. Ertuğrul Zekâi Ökte (Istanbul, 1988), vol. 3, p. 1257; Galloway, J.H., 'The Mediterranean Sugar Industry', *Geographical Review*, 67/2 (April 1977), p. 180.
69 Lunde, Paul, 'Muslims and Muslim Technology in the New World', *Saudi Aramco World* (May–June 1992), pp. 38–41.
70 Tannahill, Reay, *Food in History* (London, 1988), pp. 218–19.
71 Wheler, George, *A Journey into Greece by George Wheler Esq. in Company of D'Spon of Lyons* (London, 1682), p. 353.
72 Tott, Baron François de, *Memoirs of the Turks and Tatars*, 2 vols (London and Dublin, 1785), vol. 2, part 4, p. 68.
73 Barkan, 'Istanbul Saraylarına ait Muhasebe Defterleri', p. 132; Ali Rıza (Balıkhane Nazırı), *Eski Zamanlarda İstanbul Hayatı*, ed. Ali Şükrü Çoruk (Istanbul, 2001), p. 315.
74 Olivier, G.A., *Travels in the Ottoman Empire, Egypt, and Persia Undertaken by Order of the Government of France, during the First Six Years of the Republic*, 2 vols (London, 1801), vol. 1, p. 238.
75 Bilgin, Arif, 'Seçkin Mekanda Seçkin Damaklar: Osmanlı Sarayında Beslenme Alışkınlıkları (15.–17. Yüzyıl)', in M. Sabri Koz (ed.), *Yemek Kitabı: Tarih – Halkbilimi – Edebiyat* (Istanbul, 2002), p. 56.
76 Lane-Poole, Stanley, *Turkey* (London, 1892), p. 293.
77 From the translation of Bon's account by Robert Withers, an official at the British embassy between 1611 and 1620, as published by John Greaves, who discovered the manuscript at the British embassy in Istanbul in 1638 and published it in 1650 (this excerpt is taken from the later edition of 1737). Greaves was unaware that Withers' translation had already been published by Samuel Purchas in 1625 (see Purchas, Samuel, *Hakluytus Posthumus or Purchas his Pilgrims*, 20 vols (Glasgow, 1905–7), vol. 9, p. 377). The two versions are slightly differently worded, and in the 1625 text, the 'Boclavas' (baklavas) are described as 'Tarts'. See Penzer, N.M., *The Harem* (London, 1965), pp. 34–7 for further discussion of Withers' text.
78 Evliyâ Çelebi (1996–2007), vol. 1, pp. 239–40.
79 Eton, William, *A Survey of the Turkish Empire* (London, 1799), p. 506.
80 Webster, James, *Travels Through the Crimea, Turkey and Egypt, 1825–28*, 2 vols (London, 1830), vol. 2, p. 181.
81 De Kay, James Ellsworth, *Sketches of Turkey in 1831 and 1832* (New York, 1833), p. 495; Ubicini, Jean Henri Abdolonyme, *Letters on Turkey: An Account of the Religious, Political, Social and Commercial Condition of the Ottoman Empire,*

2 vols, tr. Lady Easthope, facsimile of 1856 edn (New York, 1973), vol. 1, p. 356; Musahipzâde Celâl, *Eski Istanbul Yaşayışı* (Istanbul, 1946), p. 47.
82 Geerdes, *Ana Besin Maddelerinden Şeker*, pp. 17–21.
83 Evliyâ Çelebi (1996–2007), vol. 1, pp. 239–40.
84 *Meydan Larousse*, 12 vols (Istanbul, 1969–73), 'Şeker', vol. 11, p. 750.

2 *Nöbet Şekeri* – Sugar Candy

1 My thanks to M. Sabri Koz for providing this quotation.
2 Confectioner Nurtekin Erol, personal communication in 2003.
3 *Meydan Larousse*, 12 vols (Istanbul, 1969–1973), vol. 9, p. 422; Nostredame, Michel de (Nostradamus), *The Elixirs of Nostradamus*, ed. Knut Boeser (Rhode Island and London, 1996), p. 140.
4 McCrindle, J.W., *Ancient India as Described by Megasthenes and Arrian* (Calcutta, Bombay and London, 1877), p. 56.
5 Levey, Martin, Miroslav Krek and Husni Haddad, 'Some Notes on the Chemical Technology in an Eleventh Century Arabic Work on Bookbinding', *Isis*, 47/3 (September 1956), p. 241.
6 Yule, Henry and A.C. Burnell, *Hobson-Jobson: The Anglo-Indian Dictionary* (Ware, 1996), p. 864.
7 Nostredame, Michel de (Nostradamus), *Excellent et moult utile opuscule à tous nécessaire qui désirent avoir connoissance de plusieurs exquises receptes, divisé en deux parties. La première traicte de diverses façons de fardemens et senteurs pour illustrer et embelir la face. La seconde nous montre la façon et manière de faire confitures de plusieurs sortes* (Lyon, 1555), part 2, pp. 195–9 ('Pour faire le succre candi'). The English translation of this recipe is that by Peter Lemeseurier from the 1557 edition, see www.propheties.it/nostradamus/1555opuscole/opuscole.html). Boeser's translation of this recipe contains inaccuracies (see Nostredame, *The Elixirs of Nostradamus*, pp. 140–3).
8 *Encyclopaedia of Islam*, 2nd edn, 12 vols, eds P.J. Bearman, T. Bianquis, C.E. Bosworth, E. van Donzel, W.P. Heinrichs et al. (Leiden, 1960–2005), 'Sukkar'.
9 The date of the earliest reference in the *Oxford English Dictionary* under 'Sugar candy', see *Oxford English Dictionary*, CD-Rom version 3.01 (Oxford, 2002).
10 Martin, Benjamin, *The General Magazine of Arts and Sciences*, 1 (1755), p. 43.
11 Lecomte, Pretextat, *Les Arts et métiers de la Turquie de l'Orient* (Paris, 1902), p. 360.
12 İbn-i Şerif, *Yâdigâr, 15. Yüzyıl Türkçe Tıp Kitabı*, 2 vols, eds Ayten Altıntaş, Yahya Okutan, Doğan Koçer and Mecit Yıldız (Istanbul, 2003 and 2004), vol. 2, p. 440.
13 Evliyâ Çelebi (1996–2007), vol. 2, pp. 190–1.
14 Sefercioğlu, M. Nejat (ed.), *Türk Yemekleri (XVIII. Yüzyıla Ait Yazma Bir Yemek Risalesi)* (Ankara, 1985), p. 17.
15 Kütükoğlu, Mübahat S., *Osmanlılarda Narh Müessesi ve 1640 Tarihli Narh Defteri* (Istanbul, 1983), p. 96.
16 Evliyâ Çelebi (1996–2007), vol. 1, p. 241.
17 Personal communication by confectioner İsmail Erdoğan in 2006.

3 *Peynir Şekeri* – Pulled Sugar

1 Çelebioğlu, Âmil (ed.), *Ramazannâme* (Istanbul, n.d.), p. 253. This collection of rhymes recited by watchmen in Ramazan dates from the late eighteenth or early nineteenth century.

2 Mason, Laura, *Sugar-Plums and Sherbet* (Totnes, 1998), p. 88.

3 McNeill, Marion, *The Scots Kitchen* (London and Glasgow, 1929), p. 229.

4 Mason: *Sugar-Plums and Sherbet*, p. 83.

5 Nostredame, Michel de (Nostradamus), *Excellent et moult utile opuscule à tous nécessaire qui désirent avoir connoissance de plusieurs exquises receptes, divisé en deux parties. La première traicte de diverses façons de fardemens et senteurs pour illustrer et embelir la face. La seconde nous montre la façon et manière de faire confitures de plusieurs sortes* (Lyon, 1555), p. 205 (the English translation is by Peter Lemeseurier from the 1557 edition (www.propheties.it/nostradamus/1555opuscole/opuscole. html); Nostredame, Michel de (Nostradamus), *The Elixirs of Nostradamus*, ed. Knut Boeser (Rhode Island and London, 1996), p. 150.

6 Nasrallah, Nawal, *Annals of the Caliph's Kitchens, Ibn Sayyâr al-Warrâq's Tenth-Century Baġhdadi Cookbook* (Leiden and Boston, 2007), p. 596.

7 Nasrallah, *Annals of the Caliph's Kitchens*, p. 389.

8 Mason, *Sugar-Plums and Sherbet*, p. 83; Nostredame (1555), p. 205.

9 İbn-i Şerif, *Yâdigâr, 15. Yüzyıl Türkçe Tıp Kitabı*, 2 vols, eds Ayten Altıntaş, Yahya Okutan, Doğan Koçer and Mecit Yıldız (Istanbul, 2003 and 2004), p. 290.

10 Celâlüddin Hızır (Hacı Paşa), *Müntahab-ı Şifâ*, ed. Zafer Önler (Ankara, 1990), p. 181.

11 Ahmed Câvid, *Tercüme-i Kenzü'l-İştihâ*, eds Seyit Ali Kahraman and Priscilla Mary Işın (Istanbul, 2006), p. 97.

12 For a picture showing pulled sugar being worked in the hands in Turkey today, see Fig. 25.

13 Evliyâ Çelebi, *Evliyâ Çelebi Seyahatnâmesi*, 10 vols, eds Seyit Ali Kahraman, Yücel Dağlı, Robert Dankoff et al. (Istanbul, 1996–2007), vol. 1, p. 253.

14 Ahmed Câvid, *Tercüme-i Kenzü'l-İştihâ*, p. 116.

15 Unger, Friedrich, *A King's Confectioner in the Orient*, ed. Priscilla Mary Işın, tr. Merete Çakmak and Renate Ömeroğulları (London, 2003), p. 96.

16 Unger, *A King's Confectioner in the Orient*, p. 99.

17 Redhouse, Sir James W., *A Turkish and English Lexicon* (Constantinople, 1890), p. 455.

18 Hadiye Fahriye, *Tatlıcıbaşı* (Istanbul, AH 1342/1926), pp. 131–2.

19 *Larousse Gastronomique* (London, 1988), p. 105.

20 Tezcan, Semih, *Bir Ziyafet Defteri* (Istanbul, 1998), p. 7.

21 Musahipzâde Celâl, *Eski Istanbul Yaşayışı* (Istanbul, 1946), p. 13.

22 Ali Rıza (Balıkhane Nazırı), *Eski Zamanlarda İstanbul Hayatı*, ed. Ali Şükrü Çoruk (Istanbul, 2001), p. 39.

23 Davey, Richard, *The Sultan and his Subjects*, 2nd edn (London, 1907), pp. 424–5.

24 Morton, H.V., *Middle East* (London, 1941), p. 239.

25 Felek, Burhan, *Geçmiş Zaman Olur ki* (Istanbul, 1985), p. 79.

26 Weatherly, Henry, *A Treatise on the Art of Boiling Sugar* (Philadelphia, 1865), p. 66. Weatherley was English, although his book was published in the United States of America (see p. 9).

27 Şirvânî, Muhammed bin Mahmud, *15. Yüzyıl Osmanlı Mutfağı*, eds Mustafa Argunşah and Müjgân Çakır (Istanbul, 2005), pp. 110, 215; Perry, Charles (tr.), Muhammad b. al-Hasan b. Muhammed b. al-Karîm, *A Baghdad Cookery Book, the Book of Dishes (Kitâb al-Tabîkh)* (Totnes, 2005), p. 98. Arberry's translation reprinted in Perry, Charles and Maxine Rodinson, *Medieval Arab Cookery* (Totnes, 2001), pp. 83–5 contains a misunderstanding regarding the iron nail used for pulling the sugar which is corrected in Perry's new translation.

4 *Kudret Helvası* – Manna

1 Exodus 16:3–31; Quran, 2:57; Mevlânâ Celâleddin Rûmî, *Dîvân-ı Kebîr*, 4 vols, tr. Abdülbâki Gölpınarlı (Istanbul, 1957), vol. 2, p. 365.

2 Numbers 11:5–6.

3 Bodenheimer, F.S., *Insects as Human Food* (The Hague, 1951), p. 219; yunus. hacettepe.edu.tr/~ayguns/Cam_bali.htm.

4 Bodenheimer, *Insects as Human Food*, pp. 218–21.

5 Bodenheimer, *Insects as Human Food*, p. 221.

6 Sturtevant, E. Lewis, *Sturtevant's Edible Plants of the World*, ed. U.P. Hedrick (Albany, 1919), p. 375.

7 www.karahalli.com/haberoku.asp?haberID=43.

8 Personal communication, Kayseri, 25 May 2006.

9 yunus.hacettepe.edu.tr/~ayguns/Cam_bali.htm.

10 Evliyâ Çelebi, *Evliyâ Çelebi Seyahatnâmesi*, 10 vols, eds Seyit Ali Kahraman, Yücel Dağlı, Robert Dankoff et al. (Istanbul, 1996–2007), vol. 9, p. 70.

11 Petr Stary has identified the manna-producing aphids as *Thelaxes suberis* and *Lachnus* sp., see Stary, Petr, 'Aphids and their Parasites Associated with Oaks in Iraq', *Proceedings of the Entomological Society of Washington*, 71/4 (September 1969), p. 297.

12 Baytop, Turhan, *Türkçe Bitki Adları Sözlüğü* (Ankara, 1994), p. 117.

13 Bodenheimer, *Insects as Human Food*, p. 222.

14 Bodenheimer, *Insects as Human Food*, p. 223.

15 Evliyâ Çelebi (1996–2007): vol. 4, pp. 15, 37–8.

16 Hanbury, Daniel, *Science Papers, Chiefly Pharmacological and Botanical* (London, 1876), p. 272.

17 Burder, Samuel, *Oriental literature Applied to the Illustration of the Sacred Scriptures*, 2 vols (London, 1822), vol. 1, p. 152.

18 Bodenheimer, *Insects as Human Food*, pp. 222, 224; Stary, 'Aphids and their Parasites', p. 294.

19 Documentary film *Gezo* by Celal Vecel, 2006.

20 Bodenheimer, *Insects as Human Food*, p. 223.

21 Bodenheimer, *Insects as Human Food*, p. 222; Stary, 'Aphids and their Parasites', p. 294.

22 Pancirollus, Guido, *The History of Many Memorable Things Lost, which Were in Use Among the Ancients: and an Account of Many Excellent Things Found, Now in Use among the Moderns, both Natural and Artificial* (London, 1715), pp. 302–3.
23 Rauwolff, Leonhart, 'Dr. Leonhart Rauwolff's Itinerary into the Eastern Countries, as Syria, Palestine, or the Holy Land, Armenia, Mesopotamia, Assyria, Chaldea Etc.', tr. Nicholas Staphorst, in John Ray (ed.), *A Collection of Curious Travels and Voyages* (London, 1693), pp. 205–6.
24 Bodenheimer: *Insects as Human Food*, p. 224.
25 Millingen, Julius R. Van, *Turkey* (London, 1920), p. 27.
26 Fluckiger, F.A., 'Notiz über die Eichenmanna von Kurdistan', *Archiv der Pharmacie*, 200 (1872), p. 159.
27 Hanbury, Daniel, *Science Papers, Chiefly Pharmacological and Botanical* (London, 1876), pp. 287–8.
28 www.iranica.com/articles/gaz-.
29 Schafer, Edward H., *The Golden Peaches of Samarkand, A Study of T'ang Exotics* (Los Angeles and Berkeley, 1985), pp. 141, 187; Schafer, Edward H., 'T'ang', in K.C. Chang (ed.), *Food in Chinese Culture* (New Haven, CT, 1977), p. 108; Donkin, R.A., *Manna: An Historical Geography* (The Hague, 1980), p. 20; Mevlânâ Celâleddin Rûmî refers to 'manna that descends on the camel thorn' in *Dîvân-ı Kebîr*, 4 vols, tr. Abdülbâki Gölpınarlı (Istanbul, 1957), vol. 2, p. 408.
30 *Chambers Encyclopaedia*, 10 vols (London, 1874–80), vol. 9, p. 187; *Oxford English Dictionary*, CD-Rom version 3.01 (Oxford, 2002), 'Trehalose'.
31 Hanbury, *Science Papers*, p. 367.
32 Bodenheimer, *Insects as Human Food*, p. 221; *Brockhaus' Konverssationslexikon* (Leipzig, Berlin and Vienna 1894–6) (www.retrobibliothek.de/retrobib/seite.html?id=131092); Brehm, Alfred Edmund, *De ryggradslösa djurens lif* (Stockholm, 1882–8) (http://runeberg.org/brehm/ryggrad/0165.html), p. 155.
33 Grieve, M., *A Modern Herbal* (1931), 'Ash, Manna' (www.botanical.com/botanical/mgmh/mgmh.html).

5 Confectioners and Confectionery Shops

1 Halıcı, Feyzi, 'Mevlana'nın Eserlerinde Yemek ve Mutfak İmajı', *Birinci Milletlerarasi Yemek Kongresi 25–30 Eylül 1986* (Ankara, 1988), p. 116.
2 Ibn Battuta, *The Travels of Ibn Battuta*, tr. H.A.R. Gibb (London, 1962), p. 431. The Moroccan traveller Ibn Battuta listened to this account of Mevlânâ's meeting with Shems of Tabriz when he visited Konya in 1333, less than a century after the event had occurred.
3 Mevlânâ Celâleddin, *Mesnevî*, 6 vols, tr. Veled İzbudak (Istanbul, 1990), vol. 6, p. 103.
4 Skuse, E., *The Confectioners' Handbook*, 3rd edn (London, n.d. [1881]), pp. 2–4.
5 Skuse, E., *Skuse's Complete Confectioner*, 12th edn (London, 1928), p. 27–9.
6 Unger, Friedrich, *A King's Confectioner in the Orient*, ed. Priscilla Mary Işın, tr. Merete Çakmak and Renate Ömeroğulları (London, 2003), pp. 40–1.

7   White, Charles, *Three Years in Constantinople or, Domestic Manners of The Turks in 1844*, 3 vols (London, 1845–6), vol. 2, p. 7.

8   Unger, *A King's Confectioner*, p. 37; Felek, Burhan, *Geçmiş Zaman Olur ki* (Istanbul, 1985), p. 78.

9   Unger, *A King's Confectioner*, p. 37.

10 Published as a lithograph in *Stamboul, Recollections of Eastern Life* (Paris, 1858). Preziosi lived in Istanbul from 1851 until his death in 1882.

11 Evliyâ Çelebi, *Evliyâ Çelebi Seyahatnâmesi*, eds Robert Dankoff, Seyit Ali Kahraman and Yücel Dağlı, 10 vols, 2nd edn (Istanbul, 2006), vol. 1, p. 289.

12 White, *Three Years in Constantinople*, vol. 2, p. 8.

13 Gautier, Théophile, *Constantinople*, tr. F.C. de Sumichrast (New York, 1901), p. 65.

14 Soyer, Alexis, *A Culinary Campaign* (Lewes, East Sussex, 1995), p. 189.

15 Slade, Sir Adolphus, *Records of Travels in Turkey, Greece etc and of a Cruise in the Black Sea with the Capitan Pasha in the Years 1829, 1830 and 1831* (London, 1833), p. 407.

16 Auldjo, John, *Journal of a Visit to Constantinople* (London, 1835), p. 109.

17 White, *Three Years in Constantinople*, vol. 2, p. 7.

18 Abdülaziz Bey, *Osmanlı Âdet, Merasim ve Tabirleri*, eds Kâzım Arısan and Duygu Arısan Günay, 2 vols (Istanbul, 1995), vol. 1, p. 151.

19 Pardoe, Julia, *The City of the Sultan and Domestic Manners of the Turks in 1836*, 3 vols (London, 1838), vol. 1, p. 27.

20 Pardoe, *City of the Sultan*, vol. 2, p. 211.

21 Nerval, Gerard de, *Voyage en Orient*, 6th edn (Paris, 1862), pp. 351–2.

22 Saz, Leyla, *Harem'in İçyüzü* (Istanbul, 1974), p. 158.

23 Evliyâ Çelebi (2006), vol. 1, p. 289.

24 Dağlı, Hikmet Turhan, 'İstanbul'da Şekercilik', *Halk Bilgisi Haberleri* (May 1936), p. 112.

25 Evliyâ Çelebi (2006), vol. 1, pp. 276, 289; Dağlı, 'İstanbul'da Şekercilik', p. 112.

26 Dağlı, 'İstanbul'da Şekercilik', p. 112.

27 Dağlı, 'İstanbul'da Şekercilik', p. 112.

28 Tan, Nail, 'Türkiye'de Şekerciliğin Gelişmesinde Hacıbekir Müessesesinin Rolü', *Geleneksel Türk Tatlıları Bildirileri Sempozyumu* (Ankara, 1984), pp. 21–2.

29 Dağlı, 'İstanbul'da Şekercilik', p. 112; according to Nail Tan, however, Hacı Bekir's son was called Mehmed Muhiddin, see Tan, 'Türkiye'de Şekerciliğin Gelişmesinde Hacıbekir Müessesesinin Rolü', p. 23.

30 Ali Muhiddin's tombstone in Edirnekapı Cemetery is carved with a picture of a confectioner's mortar, see Tan, 'Türkiye'de Şekerciliğin Gelişmesinde Hacıbekir Müessesesinin Rolü', p. 22.

31 Felek, *Geçmiş Zaman Olur ki*, p. 79.

32 Tan, 'Türkiye'de Şekerciliğin Gelişmesinde Hacıbekir Müessesesinin Rolü', pp. 33–7.

33 Neave, Dorina Lockhart, *Twenty-six Years on the Bosphorus* (London, 1933), pp. 161–2.

34 Felek, *Geçmiş Zaman Olur ki*, pp. 78–9; Koçu, Reşat Ekrem, *İstanbul Ansiklopedisi*, 10 vols (Istanbul, 1958–73), vol. 7, pp. 3481–2; Uşaklıgil, Halid Ziya, *Kırk Yıl* (Istanbul, 1969), p. 39.

35 Evliyâ Çelebi, *Evliyâ Çelebi Seyahatnâmesi*, 10 vols, eds Seyit Ali Kahraman, Yücel Dağlı, Robert Dankoff et al. (Istanbul, 1996–2007), vol. 9, pp. 82–3; vol. 3, p. 20; Uşaklıgil, *Kırk Yıl*, p. 39.
36 Uşaklıgil, *Kırk Yıl*, p. 9.

6 Sugar Sculpture

1 Mustafa Ali of Gallipoli, *Cami'u'l-buhur der Mecalis-i Sur*, ed. Ali Öztekin (Ankara, 1996), p. 105.
2 Çelebioğlu, Âmil (ed.), *Ramazannâme* (Istanbul, n.d.), p. 270.
3 And, Metin, *Osmanlı Şenliklerinde Türk Sanatları* (Ankara, 1982), pp. 93–151.
4 Nutku, Özdemir, *IV. Mehmet'in Edirne Şenliği 1675*, 2nd edn (Ankara, 1987), pp. 56, 73; Hâfız Mehmed Efendi, *1720 Şehzadelerin Sünnet Düğünü*, ed. Seyit Ali Kahraman (Istanbul 2008), pp. 166–8.
5 Many miniature illustrations of *nahıl*s are found in Ottoman manuscripts, such as that reproduced in And, *Osmanlı Şenliklerinde Türk Sanatları*, pl. 47.
6 Nutku, *IV. Mehmet'in Edirne Şenliği 1675*, p. 67.
7 Evliyâ Çelebi, *Evliyâ Çelebi Seyahatnâmesi*, 10 vols, eds Seyit Ali Kahraman, Yücel Dağlı, Robert Dankoff et al. (Istanbul, 1996–2007), vol. 4, p. 203.
8 Mustafa Ali, *Cami'u'l-buhur der Mecalis-i Sur*, pp. 105–6.
9 Mustafa Ali, *Cami'u'l-buhur der Mecalis-i Sur*, p. 219.
10 And, *Osmanlı Şenliklerinde Türk Sanatları*, p. 218.
11 And, *Osmanlı Şenliklerinde Türk Sanatları*, pp. 93–4.
12 Lâtifî, *Evsâf-ı Istanbul*, ed. Nermin Suner (Pekin) (Istanbul, 1977), p. 54.
13 And, *Osmanlı Şenliklerinde Türk Sanatları*, p. 242.
14 Amicis, Edmondo de, *Constantinople*, 2 vols, tr. Maria Hornor Lansdale, (Philadelphia, 1896), vol. 1, p. 214.
15 Gerlach, Stephan, *Türkiye Günlüğü 1573–1576*, 2 vols (Istanbul, 2007), vol. 1, p. 99.
16 Gerlach, *Türkiye Günlüğü 1573–1576*, vol. 1, p. 319.
17 Tursun Bey, *Târîh-i Ebü'l-Feth*, ed. Mertol Tulum (Istanbul, 1977), p. 89.
18 Busbecq, Ogier Ghiselin de, *The Turkish Letters of Ogier Ghiselin de Busbecq Imperial Ambassador at Constantinople 1554–1562*, tr. Edward Seymour Forster (Oxford, 1927), pp. 8, 25.
19 Nutku, *IV. Mehmet'in Edirne Şenliği 1675*, p. 58.
20 Nutku, *IV. Mehmet'in Edirne Şenliği 1675*, p. 56.
21 Nutku, *IV. Mehmet'in Edirne Şenliği 1675*, p. 64.
22 And, *Osmanlı Şenliklerinde Türk Sanatları*, p. 222.
23 Covel, John, 'Dr. Covel's Diary (1670–1679)', in J. Theodore Bent (ed.), *Early Voyages and Travels in the Levant* (London, 1893), pp. 228–9.
24 Coke, Thomas, 'A True Narrative of the Great Solemnity of the Circumcision of Mustapha, Prince of Turky, Eldest Son of Mahomet, Present Emperor of the Turks: Together with an Account of the Marriage of his Daughter to his Great Favourite Mussaip, at Adrianople, as it Was Sent in a Letter to a Person of Honour: by Mr Coke, Secretary of the Turky Company, Being in Company with his Excellency the

Lord Ambassador Sir John Finch', in *Harleian Miscellany*, vol. 5 (London, 1676), p. 366.

25 Koçu, Reşat Ekrem, *Tarihimizde Garip Vakalar* (Istanbul, 1952), pp. 75, 83; And, *Osmanlı Şenliklerinde Türk Sanatları*, p. 120; Hâfız Mehmed Efendi, *Şehzadelerin Sünnet Düğünü*, ed. Seyit Ali Kahraman (Istanbul, 2008), p. 160; Vehbî, *Surnâme: Sultan Ahmet'in Düğün Kitabı*, ed. Mertol Tulum (Istanbul 2007), pp. 403, 684.

26 And, *Osmanlı Şenliklerinde Türk Sanatları*, pp. 223–4.

27 Schafer, Edward H., 'T'ang', in K.C. Chang (ed.) *Food in Chinese Culture* (New Haven, CT, 1977), p. 153.

28 Perry, Charles (tr.), *An Anonymous Andalusian Cookbook of the Thirteenth Century* (n.d.), at http://daviddfriedman.com/Medieval/Cookbooks/Andalusian/andalusian_contents.htm.

29 The translator, Charles Perry, gives the following explanatory footnote: 'The "eyebrow" and the "eye" may be technical terms for parts of a mould. The gilding referred to is also ambiguous in the Arabic; both gold leaf and egg-yolk endoring were practised in the Islamic world.'

30 Hieatt, Constance B. and Sharon Butler, *Curye on Inglysch* (London, 1985), p. 153.

31 Mason, Laura, *Sugar-Plums and Sherbet* (Totnes, 1998), p. 141.

32 Kubilay, Ayşe Yetişkin, 'Nahıllar', *Skylife* (January 2002).

33 Day, Ivan, 'The Art of Confectionery', www.historicfood.com/The%20Art%20of%20Confectionery.pdf.

34 Nutku, *IV. Mehmet'in Edirne Şenliği 1675*, p. 73.

35 Galata was a former Genoese colony established in Byzantine times, and during the Ottoman period was a cosmopolitan quarter of Istanbul on the north bank of the Golden Horn.

36 Evliyâ Çelebi, *Evliyâ Çelebi Seyahatnâmesi*, eds Robert Dankoff, Seyit Ali Kahraman and Yücel Dağlı, vol. 1, 2nd edn (Istanbul, 2006), p. 289.

37 Perry, *An Anonymous Andalusian Cookbook*.

38 Unger, Friedrich, *A King's Confectioner in the Orient*, ed. Priscilla Mary Işın, tr. Merete Çakmak and Renate Ömeroğulları (London, 2003), pp. 101–2.

39 Tarancı, Cahit Sıtkı, *Otuz Beş Yaş*, ed. Asım Bezirci (Istanbul, 2003), p. 164. The Affan Dede mentioned in the poem kept a toyshop in the district of Üsküdar, Istanbul in the early twentieth century.

40 Plat, Hugh, *Delightes for Ladies* (London, 1609), reproduced in *A Collection of Medieval and Renaissance Cookbooks*, vol. 1, 4th edn, eds Duke Cariadoc of the Bow and Duchessa Diana Alena (1987), recipe 44.

41 Weatherly, Henry, *A Treatise on the Art of Boiling Sugar* (Philadelphia, 1865), p. 56. Although Weatherley's treatise was published in the United States, he was an English confectioner writing in England.

42 Skuse, E., *The Confectioners' Handbook*, 3rd edn (London, n.d. [1881]), p. 82.

43 Abdülaziz Bey, *Osmanlı Âdet, Merasim ve Tabirleri*, eds Kâzım Arısan and Duygu Arısan Günay, 2 vols (Istanbul, 1995), vol. 1, pp. 151, 268; personal communication by Nalan Aydın.

7 *Akide* – Drops

1   Mercan Çarşısı (Coral Bazaar) is the name of a busy shopping area in Istanbul.
2   Tietze, Andreas, *Tarihi ve Etimolojik Türkiye Türkçesi Lugatı* (Istanbul and Vienna, 2002), pp. 110, 126–7.
3   Celâlüddin Hızır (Hacı Paşa), *Müntahab-ı Şifâ*, ed. Zafer Önler, (Ankara, 1990), p. 203; Şirvânî, Muhammed bin Mahmud, *15. Yüzyıl Osmanlı Mutfağı*, eds Mustafa Argunşah and Müjgân Çakır (Istanbul, 2005), pp. 234–6.
4   'Osmanlı Toplum Yaşayışıyla İlgili Belgeler-Bilgiler: Esnaf Suç ve Cezaları', *Tarih ve Toplum*, 10 (October 1984), p. 31.
5   The form *ağda* is used in the Bursa Commercial Code of 1502, see Akgündüz, Ahmet, *Osmanlı Kanunnameleri ve Hukukî Tahlilleri*, vol. 2 (Istanbul, 1990), p. 200.
6   Evliyâ Çelebi, *Evliyâ Çelebi Seyahatnâmesi*, eds Robert Dankoff, Seyit Ali Kahraman and Yücel Dağlı, vol. 1, 2nd edn (Istanbul, 2006), p. 287.
7   Sertoğlu, Midhat, *Osmanlı Tarih Lûgatı* (Istanbul, 1986), pp. 13–14.
8   Sertoğlu, *Osmanlı Tarih Lûgatı*, pp. 13–14.
9   Koçu, Reşat Ekrem, *İstanbul Ansiklopedisi*, 10 vols (Istanbul, 1958–73), vol. 2, pp. 521–2, 'Akîde Şekeri'.
10 Tietze, *Tarihi ve Etimolojik Türkiye Türkçesi Lugatı*, p. 127 (the quotation is from Mustafa Ali's *Kavâ'idü'l-mecâlis*).
11 Ahmed Refik, *Onuncu Asr-ı Hicrîde Istanbul Hayatı (1495–1591)* (Istanbul, 1988), p. 122; Koçu, *İstanbul Ansiklopedisi*, vol. 2, p. 522, 'Akîde Şekeri'.
12 Nutku, Özdemir, *IV. Mehmet'in Edirne Şenliği 1675*, 2nd edn (Ankara, 1987), p. 73.
13 Koçu, Reşat Ekrem, *Tarihimizde Garip Vakalar* (Istanbul, 1952), p. 81.
14 Osmanoğlu, Ayşe, *Babam Sultan Abdülhamid* (Istanbul, 1984), pp. 65–6.
15 Evliyâ Çelebi (2006), vol. 1, p. 289.
16 Evliyâ Çelebi (2006), vol. 1, pp. 276, 289.
17 Evliyâ Çelebi (2006), vol. 1, 289.
18 Tezcan, Semih, *Bir Ziyafet Defteri* (Istanbul, 1998), p. 9.
19 Evliyâ Çelebi (2006), vol. 1, p. 253.
20 Kütükoğlu, Mübahat S., *Osmanlılarda Narh Müessesi ve 1640 Tarihli Narh Defteri* (Istanbul, 1983), p. 101.
21 Çelebioğlu, Âmil (ed.), *Ramazannâme* (Istanbul, n.d.), p. 194.
22 Abdülaziz Bey, *Osmanlı Âdet, Merasim ve Tabirleri*, eds Kâzım Arısan and Duygu Arısan Günay, 2 vols (Istanbul, 1995), vol. 1, p. 151.
23 Ahmed Câvid, *Tercüme-i Kenzü'l-İştihâ*, eds Seyit Ali Kahraman and Priscilla Mary Işın (Istanbul, 2006), p. 86.
24 Nutku, *IV. Mehmet'in Edirne Şenliği*, p. 73.
25 Perry, Charles and Maxine Rodinson, *Medieval Arab Cookery* (Totnes, 2001), pp. 425, 454, 471.
26 Mevlânâ Celâleddin, *Dîvân-ı Kebîr*, 4 vols, tr. Abdülbâki Gölpınarlı (Istanbul, 1957), vol. 1, p. 83, couplet 771.
27 Koçu, *İstanbul Ansiklopedisi*, vol. 2, p. 522; Unger, Friedrich, *A King's Confectioner*

in the Orient, ed. Priscilla Mary Işın, tr. Merete Çakmak and Renate Ömeroğulları (London, 2003), p. 100.

28 Unger, *A King's Confectioner in the Orient*, p. 100.
29 Unger, *A King's Confectioner in the Orient*, p. 100.
30 Writers including Abdülaziz Bey, Burhan Felek, Reşat Ekrem Koçu and Hadiye Fahriye mention these varieties of *akide*. Koçu and Hadiye Fahriye both agree that cinnamon and clove were the most common.
31 Ahmed Câvid, *Tercüme-i Kenzü'l-İştihâ*, p. 115.
32 Hadiye Fahriye, *Tatlıcıbaşı* (Istanbul, AH 1342/1926), p. 129.
33 Hadiye Fahriye, *Tatlıcıbaşı*, p. 129.
34 Koçu, *Istanbul Ansiklopedisi*, vol. 2, p. 522.
35 *Melceü't-Tabbâhîn (Aşçıların Sığınağı)*, ed. Cüneyt Kut (Istanbul, 1997), pp. 69, 71.
36 Şirvânî, Muhammed bin Mahmud, *15. Yüzyıl Osmanlı Mutfağı*, eds Mustafa Argunşah and Müjgân Çakır (Istanbul, 2005), pp. 127–8.
37 A type of helva in fine threads (see Ch. 17 *Keten Helva*) that was stored in airtight boxes.
38 Unger, *A King's Confectioner in the Orient*, p. 100.
39 Hadiye Fahriye, *Tatlıcıbaşı*, p. 128.
40 Arabacıyan, Mihran, *Miftâhü't-Tabbâhîn* (Istanbul, 1876), p. 192. This cookery book is written in Turkish using Armenian script.

8 *Ağız Miski* – Musk Lozenges

1 Dr Yücel Dağlı's archive.
2 Kütükoğlu, Mübahat S., *Osmanlılarda Narh Müessesi ve 1640 Tarihli Narh Defteri* (Istanbul, 1983), p. 101.
3 Koçu, Reşat Ekrem, *Tarihimizde Garip Vakalar* (Istanbul, 1952), p. 81.
4 Unpublished cookery manual, f. 25v. For the transcription of an almost identical recipe dating from the mid-nineteenth century see Halıcı, Feyzi (ed.), *Ali Eşref Dede'nin Yemek Risalesi* (Ankara, 1992), p. 23.
5 Baytop, Turhan, *Türkiye'de Bitkilerle Tedavi*, 2nd. edn (Istanbul, 1999), pp. 272–4.
6 Weatherly, Henry, *A Treatise on the Art of Boiling Sugar* (Philadelphia, 1865), p. 102.
7 Demirhan, Ayşegül, *Mısır Çarşısı Drogları* (Istanbul, 1974), p. 103.
8 Skuse, E., *Skuse's Complete Confectioner*, 12th edn (London, 1928), pp. 380–1.
9 Shakespeare, William, *The Works of William Shakespeare*, (London, n.d. [c. 1893]), p. 68. My thanks to Charles Perry for pointing out this reference.
10 May, Robert, *The Accomplisht Cook* (Totnes, 2000), pp. 275–6.
11 Pardoe, Julia, *The Beauties of the Bosphorus* (London, n.d. [c. 1840]), p. 34.
12 Kut, Günay (ed.), *Et-Terkibât Fî Tabhi'l-Hülviyyât (Tatli Pişirme Tarifleri)* (Ankara, 1986), p. 26.
13 Unger, Friedrich, *A King's Confectioner in the Orient*, ed. Priscilla Mary Işın, tr. Merete Çakmak and Renate Ömeroğulları (London, 2003), p. 102.

9 *Misk* – Musk

1 Yusuf Has Hacib, *Kutadgu Bilig*, tr. Reşid Rahmeti Arat (Ankara, 1985), p. 17.
2 Mahmud al-Kāshgari, *Compendium of the Turkic Dialects (Dīwān Luyāt at-Turk)* 3 vols, ed. and tr. Robert Dankoff in collaboration with James Kelly (Cambridge, MA, 1984), vol. 2, p. 465.
3 Mustafa Ali of Gallipoli, *Cami'u'l-buhur der Mecalis-i Sur*, ed. Ali Öztekin (Ankara, 1996), p. 128.
4 For discussions of the term Tatar used in this sense see 'Tatar' in *İslam Ansiklopedisi*, 13 vols (Eskişehir, 2001), vol. 2, pp. 50–1; and Mehmet Maksudoğlu, 'Tatarlar Kimdir?', *Kalgay Dergisi*, 22 (October–December 2001) at www.kalgaydergisi.org/index.php?sayfa=dergiicerik&sayi=22&kod=490.
5 Aryal, Achyut, 'A Report on Status and Distribution of Himalayan Musk Deer Moschus Chrysogaster in Annapurna Conservation Area of Manang District, Nepal', 2005, p. 13, report to ITNC, UK see www.itnc.org/FinalReportonMuskdeerManang.pdf.
6 Yule, Henry (tr. and ed.), *The Book of Ser Marco Polo, the Venetian*, 2 vols (London, 1871), vol. 2, pp. 28–9.
7 Yule, *The Book of Ser Marco Polo*, vol. 2, p. 242.
8 Macartney, Clement, 'The Deer with a Fatal Scent', *Unasylva*, 35 (1983), report written for the World Wildlife Fund, excerpts at www.fao.org/docrep/q1093e/q1093e03.htm.
9 Baoliang, Zhang, 'Musk-deer: Their Capture, Domestication and Care According to Chinese Experience and Methods', *Unasylva*, 35/139 (1983), pp. 16–8 (www.fao.org/docrep/q1093e/q1093e02.htm).
10 Seyyid Mehmed İzzet, *Çay Risâlesi* (Istanbul, AH 1295/1878), pp. 80–1.
11 Roe, Thomas, 'The Journal of Sir Thomas Roe, Ambassador from his Majesty King James the First', in Awnsham Churchill (ed.), *A Collection of Voyages and Travels* (London, 1752), p. 634.
12 Ahmed Refik, *Onbirinci Asr-ı Hicrî'de Istanbul Hayatı (1592–1688)* (Istanbul, 1988), p. 37.
13 Unpublished cookery manual, f. 26r.
14 Tom Stobart's *Cooks Encyclopaedia*, quoted in Davidson, Alan, *The Oxford Companion to Food* (Oxford, 1999), p. 523.
15 Aryal, 'A Report on Status and Distribution of Himalayan Musk Deer Moschus Chrysogaster', p. 50.
16 Sandwich, Earl of, *A Voyage Performed by the Late Earl of Sandwich Round the Mediterranean in the Years 1738 and 1739* (London, 1799), p. 175.
17 Tott, Baron François de, *Memoirs of the Turks and Tatars*, 2 vols (London and Dublin, 1785), vol. 1, p. 35.
18 Kâşgarlı Mahmud, *Divanü Lûgat-it-Türk*, vol. 3, pp. 48–9.

10 *Badem Şekeri* – Sugared Almonds

1 Çelebioğlu, Âmil (ed.), *Ramazannâme* (Istanbul, n.d.), p. 194.

2 Mevlânâ Celâleddin Rûmî, *Mesnevî*, 6 vols, tr. Veled İzbudak (Istanbul, 1990), vol. 1, p. 120, couplet 1494.

3 Evliyâ Çelebi, *Evliyâ Çelebi Seyahatnâmesi*, eds Robert Dankoff, Seyit Ali Kahraman and Yücel Dağlı, vol. 1, 2nd edn. (Istanbul, 2006), p. 289.

4 Ahmed Câvid, *Tercüme-i Kenzü'l-İştihâ*, eds Seyit Ali Kahraman and Priscilla Mary Işın (Istanbul, 2006), p. 81.

5 Unger, Friedrich, *A King's Confectioner in the Orient*, ed. Priscilla Mary Işın, tr. Merete Çakmak and Renate Ömeroğulları (London, 2003), p. 101.

6 Panwork or panning is the process whereby seeds and nuts were coated in sugar by swinging pans suspended by chains from the ceiling.

7 Tursun Bey, *Târîh-i Ebü'l-Feth*, ed. Mertol Tulum (Istanbul, 1977), p. 89.

8 Evliyâ Çelebi, *Evliyâ Çelebi Seyahatnâmesi*, 10 vols, eds Seyit Ali Kahraman, Yücel Dağlı, Robert Dankoff et al. (Istanbul, 1996–2007), vol. 1, p. 253.

9 Ahmed Câvid, *Tercüme-i Kenzü'l-İştihâ*, p. 81; Mütercim Âsım, *Burhân-ı Katı* (Ankara, 2000), p. 34.

10 Şirvânî, Muhammed bin Mahmud, *15. Yüzyıl Osmanlı Mutfağı*, eds Mustafa Argunşah and Müjgân Çakır (Istanbul, 2005), p. 228.

11 Evliyâ Çelebi (1996–2007), vol. 1, p. 253; Mütercim Âsım, *Burhân-ı Katı*, p. 34.

12 Clavijo, Ruy Gonzalez de, *Embassy to Tamerlane 1403–1406* (London, 1928), p. 243.

13 Tott, Baron François de, *Memoirs of the Turks and Tatars*, 2 vols (London and Dublin, 1785), vol. 1, p. 36.

14 Witteveen, Joop, 'Rose Sugar and Other Mediaeval Sweets', *Petits Propos Culinaires*, 20 (July 1985), pp. 24–5.

15 Reşat Ekrem Koçu, *Tarihimizde Garip Vakalar* (Istanbul, 1952), p. 83; Hafız Mehmed, *1720 Şehzadelerin Sünnet Düğünü*, ed. Seyit Ali Kahraman (Istanbul 2008), p. 32.

16 Coke, Thomas, 'A True Narrative of the Great Solemnity of the Circumcision of Mustapha, Prince of Turky, Eldest Son of Mahomet, Present Emperor of the Turks: Together with an Account of the Marriage of his Daughter to his Great Favourite Mussaip, at Adrianople, as it Was Sent in a Letter to a Person of Honour: By Mr Coke, Secretary of the Turky Company, Being in Company with his Excellency the Lord Ambassador Sir John Finch', in *Harleian Miscellany*, vol. 5 (London, 1676), p. 366.

17 Ali Rıza (Balıkhane Nazırı), *Bir Zamanlar İstanbul*, ed. Niyazi Ahmet Banoğlu (Istanbul, n.d.), p. 108.

18 Saz, Leylâ, *Harem'in İçyüzü* (Istanbul, 1974), p. 256.

19 Garnett, Lucy, *The Women of Turkey and their Folklore*, 2 vols (London, 1893), vol. 1, p. 85.

20 Neave, Dorina Lockhart, *Twenty-six Years on the Bosphorus* (London, 1933), p. 128.

21 Day, Ivan, 'Bridecup and Cake', in Laura Mason (ed.), *Food and the Rites of Passage* (Totnes, 2002), p. 36; Hensel Sebastian, *The Mendelssohn Family (1729–1847) from Letters and Journals* (New York, 1882), pp. 86–7.

22 Redhouse, Sir James W., *A Turkish and English Lexicon* (Constantinople, 1890), 'Saçı', p. 1152.
23 Kalafat, Yaşar, *Balkanlardan Uluğ Türkistan'a Türk Halk İnançları II* (Ankara, 2005), pp. 51, 66; Çetin, Cengiz, 'Türk Düğün Gelenekleri ve Kutsal Evlilik Ritüeli', *Ankara Üniversitesi Dil ve Tarih-Coğrafya Fakültesi Dergisi*, 48/2 (2008), p. 119.
24 Kurtoğlu, Orhan, 'Klasik Türk Şiirinde Saçı Geleneği', *Milli Folklor*, 81 (2009), p. 90.
25 Tott, *Memoirs of the Turks and Tatars*, vol. 1, part 2, p. 213.
26 Mason, Laura, *Sugar-Plums and Sherbet* (Totnes, 1998), p. 121.
27 Şirvânî, Muhammed bin Mahmud, *15. Yüzyıl Osmanlı Mutfağı*, eds Mustafa Argunşah and Müjgân Çakır (Istanbul, 2005), p. 228.
28 The fourteenth-century recipe in *Curye on Inglysche* specifies a *fourneys* (furnace) as a heat source, but instead of swinging the pan on chains, instructs that the confectioner stir the comfits with the flat of his hand, while turning the pan over the heat with the other.
29 Gautier, Théophile, *Constantinople*, tr. F.C. de Sumichrast (New York, 1901), p. 65.
30 Gülhan, Abdülkerim, 'Divan Şiirinde Meyveler ve Meyvelerden Hareketle Yapılan Teşbih ve Mecazlar', *Turkish Studies: International Periodical for the Languages, Literature and History of Turkish or Turkic*, 3/5 (2008), pp. 353–75.

11 *Şerbetlik Şeker* – Sherbet Sugar

1 Lines from a poem celebrating the birth of the Prophet Muhammed. They describe how Muhammed's mother Emine becomes thirsty during labour and is given cold sherbet. See Onay, Ahmet Talât, *Eski Türk Edebiyatında Mazmunlar ve İzahı*, ed. Cemal Kurnaz (Ankara, 2000), p. 425.
2 See Ch. 13.
3 Unger, Friedrich, *A King's Confectioner in the Orient*, ed. Priscilla Mary Işın, tr. Merete Çakmak and Renate Ömeroğulları (London, 2003), pp. 79–80; Abdülaziz Bey, *Osmanlı Âdet, Merasim ve Tabirleri*, eds Kâzım Arısan and Duygu Arısan Günay, 2 vols (Istanbul, 1995), vol. 1, p. 151; Pakalın, Mehmet Zeki, *Osmanlı Tarih Deyimleri ve Terimleri Sözlüğü*, 3 vols (Istanbul, 1983), vol. 3, p. 339.
4 Unger, *A King's Confectioner*, pp. 81, 155.
5 Unger, *A King's Confectioner*, pp. 80–1.
6 Abdülaziz, *Osmanlı Âdet, Merasim ve Tabirleri*, vol. 1, p. 151.
7 Unger, *A King's Confectioner*, p. 81.
8 Sarı, Nil et al. (eds), *Klasik Dönem İlaç Hazırlama Yöntemleri ve Terkipleri* (Istanbul, 2003), pp. 61–2.
9 Celâlüddin Hızır (Hacı Paşa), *Müntahab-ı Şifâ*, ed. Zafer Önler (Ankara, 1990), p. 195.
10 *Oxford English Dictionary*, CD-Rom version 3.01 (Oxford, 2002), 'Conserve'.
11 Tezcan, Semih, *Bir Ziyafet Defteri* (Istanbul, 1998), p. 7.
12 Abdülaziz, *Osmanlı Âdet, Merasim ve Tabirleri*, vol. 1, p. 111.
13 Abdülaziz, *Osmanlı Âdet, Merasim ve Tabirleri*, vol. 1, p. 151; the red colouring was

mainly provided by cochineal, but alternatively by a decoction of rose petals or carmine, see Unger, *A King's Confectioner*, pp. 65, 74.

14 Ali Rıza (Balıkhane Nazırı), *Bir Zamanlar İstanbul*, ed. Niyazi Ahmet Banoğlu (Istanbul, n.d.), p. 106.

15 Abdurrahman Şeref, 'Topkapı Saray-ı Hümâyûn', *Tarih-i Osmanî Encümeni Mecmuası* (Istanbul, AH 1328–9/1910–11), pp. 336–7.

16 Hançerlioğlu, Orhan, *İslâm İnançları Sözlüğü*, 3rd edn (Istanbul, 2000), pp. 334–5. Two couplets from the poem are quoted at the beginning of this chapter.

17 David, Elizabeth, *Harvest of the Cold Months: The Social History of Ice and Ices* (London, 1996), p. 49.

18 David, *Harvest of the Cold Months*, p. 10.

19 Bacon, Francis, *The Works of Francis Bacon*, 2 vols, ed. James Spedding (Cambridge, 1857), vol. 2, p. 565.

20 Blount, Sir Henry, *A Voyage into the Levant* (London, 1636), p. 105.

21 Walker, John, *A Selection of Curious Articles from the Gentleman's Magazine*, vol. 1, 2nd edn (London, 1811), p. 381.

22 Houghton, John, *Husbandry and Trade Improv'd: Being a Collection of Many Valuable Materials Relating to Corn, Cattle, Coals, Hops, Wool, etc.* (London, 1728), vol. 4, p. 187.

23 Bruslons, Jacques Savary des, *Dictionnaire Universel de Commerce*, 3 vols (Paris, 1742), vol. 3, p. 797. Elizabeth David writes that sorbec is mentioned in the 1723 edition of this work (see David, *Harvest of the Cold Months*, p. 131).

24 *Encyclopaedia Britannica*, vol. 17 (Edinburgh, 1797), p. 358.

25 Jarrin, G.A., *The Italian Confectioner*, 3rd edn (London, 1827), pp. 91–3.

26 *Assiettes montées* ('raised dishes') were dessert dishes such as jellies, so named because in the medieval period they were served on a platform in the middle of the table, see Lacroix, Paul, *Manners, Customs, and Dress During the Middle Ages, and During the Renaissance Period* (Paris, 1874), 'Sweet Dishes, Desserts'.

27 Mayhew, Henry, *London Labour and the London Poor*, 3 vols (London, 1861), vol. 1, p. 198.

28 Weatherly, Henry, *A Treatise on the Art of Boiling Sugar* (Philadelphia, 1865), p. 75.

29 Unger, *A King's Confectioner*, p. 79.

30 See Ch. 13.

12 *Macun* – Soft Toffee

1 Onay, Ahmet Talât, *Eski Türk Edebiyatında Mazmunlar ve İzahı*, ed. Cemal Kurnaz (Ankara, 2000), p. 352.

2 Koçu, Reşat Ekrem, *İstanbul Ansiklopedisi*, 10 vols (Istanbul 1958–1973), vol. 3, pp. 1405–6, 'Macuncular'.

3 Prof. Dr Nihat Falay, personal communication, Bitlis, June 2009.

4 Ömür Tufan, keeper of the kitchens at Topkapı Palace, personal communication, 30 April 2011.

5 Ömür Tufan, personal communication, 2006.

6 Koçu, *İstanbul Ansiklopedisi*, vol. 3, pp. 1405–6.
7 Walker, Mary Adelaide, *Eastern Life and Scenery with Excursions in Asia Minor, Mytilene, Crete, and Roumania*, 2 vols (London, 1886), vol. 1, p. 85.
8 İlter Uzel and Kenan Süveren in their introduction to Şerefeddin Sabuncuoğlu (Amasyalı), *Mücerrebnâme (İlk Türkçe Deneysel Tıp Eseri – 1468)*, eds İlter Uzel and Kenan Süveren (Ankara, 1999), pp. 16–17.
9 Sarı, Nil et al. (eds), *Klasik Dönem İlaç Hazırlama Yöntemleri ve Terkipleri* (Istanbul, 2003), p. 63.
10 Pakalın, Mehmet Zeki, *Osmanlı Tarih Deyimleri ve Terimleri Sözlüğü*, 3 vols (Istanbul, 1983), vol. 2, pp. 636–8, 'Nevruz'.
11 Maksetof, Kabil, 'Ebû Reyhan Beyrûnî ve Nevruz Hakkında', tr. Kudaybergen Elubaev, in Sadık Tural and Elmas Kılıç (eds), *Nevruz ve Renkler* (Ankara, 1996).
12 Vámbéry, Armin, *Scenes from the East* (Budapest, 1974), p. 1954; for an account of Vámbéry's life and travels in the 1860s see *Tarih ve Toplum*, 2 (February 1984), pp. 145–6.
13 Mustafa Ali of Gallipoli, *Ziyâfet Sofraları (Mevâidü'n-nefâis fî kavâidi'l mecâlis)*, 2 vols, ed. Orhan Şaik Gökyay (Istanbul, 1978), vol. 1, p. 149.
14 Musahipzâde Celâl, *Eski Istanbul Yaşayışı* (Istanbul, 1946), p. 99.
15 Pakalın, *Osmanlı Tarih Deyimleri*, vol. 2, pp. 636–8, 'Nevruz'.
16 Onay, *Eski Türk Edebiyatında*, p. 352. Seyyid Vehbî died in 1736.
17 Osmanoğlu, Ayşe, *Babam Sultan Abdülhamid* (Istanbul, 1984), p. 106.
18 Pakalın, *Osmanlı Tarih Deyimleri*, vol. 1, p. 797, 'Helvahâne Ocağı'; Baylav, Naşid, *Eczacılık Tarihi* (Istanbul, 1968), p. 179.
19 Baylav, *Eczacılık Tarihi*, pp. 173–6; Nalbandoğlu, A., 'Nevruz ve Nevruziyye', *Tarih Hazinesi*, ed. İbrahim Hakkı Konyalı, 8 (15 November 1950), p. 368. The latter source contains a photograph of a *Nevruz macunu* jar still with its greeting card that was originally in the Topkapı Palace collections, but was later given to the museum at Istanbul University Department of Pharmacy.
20 Nalbandoğlu, 'Nevruz ve Nevruziyye', p. 368.
21 Osmanoğlu, *Babam Sultan Abdülhamid*, p. 106.
22 Baylav, *Eczacılık Tarihi*, pp. 172, 179.
23 Evliyâ Çelebi, *Evliyâ Çelebi Seyahatnâmesi*, eds Robert Dankoff, Seyit Ali Kahraman and Yücel Dağlı, vol. 1, 2nd edn (Istanbul, 2006), p. 213.
24 Onay, *Eski Türk Edebiyatında*, p. 352.
25 Gökyay, Orhan Şaik, 'Sohbetnâme', *Tarih ve Toplum*, 3/14 (February 1985), p. 132.

13 Çevirme – Fondant

1 Culpeper, Nicholas, *Culpeper's Complete Herbal* (Ware, 1995), p. 450.
2 In Greece the mastic-flavoured variety is for some reason described as vanilla-flavoured: *vanilla ipovrichio* (Βανίλια Υποβρύχιο).
3 Celâl Paşa, *Şurup İmalâtı* (Istanbul, AH 1309/1891), p. 17; Mehmed Reşad, *Fenn-i Tabâhat*, 4 vols (Istanbul, AH 1340/1921–2), vol. 4, p. 32.
4 Charlemont, James Caulfield (fourth Viscount Charlemont), *The Travels of Lord*

Charlemont in Greece and Turkey, eds W.B. Stanford and E.J. Finopoulos (London, 1984), pp. 166–7.

5 Tott, Baron François de, *Memoirs of the Turks and Tatars*, 2 vols (London and Dublin, 1785), vol. 1, part 1, p. 96; Pardoe, Julia, *The City of the Sultan and Domestic Manners of the Turks in 1836*, 3 vols (London, 1838), vol. 1, p. 158.

6 Celâlüddin Hızır (Hacı Paşa), *Müntahab-ı Şifâ*, ed. Zafer Önler (Ankara, 1990), f. 172v.

7 Şirvânî, Muhammed bin Mahmud, *15. Yüzyıl Osmanlı Mutfağı*, eds Mustafa Argunşah and Müjgân Çakır (Istanbul, 2005), pp. 112, 217.

8 Culpeper, *Culpeper's Complete Herbal*, pp. 450–3.

9 Mehmed Kâmil, *Melceü't-Tabbâhîn*, 8th edn (Istanbul, AH 1290/1873), pp. 132–3; Celâl Paşa, *Şurup İmalâtı*, p. 18.

10 Unger, Friedrich, *A King's Confectioner in the Orient*, ed. Priscilla Mary Işın, tr. Merete Çakmak and Renate Ömeroğulları (London, 2003), p. 72.

11 Selim İleri, personal communication, 30 April 2011.

12 Felek, Burhan, *Geçmiş Zaman Olur ki* (Istanbul, 1985), p. 115.

13 İleri, Selim, *Oburcuk Mutfakta* (Istanbul, 2010), p. 378.

14 The term *tatlı* (sweet) was used for either *çevirme* or fruit preserves in a thick syrup eaten with a spoon, the equivalent of the Greek 'spoon sweet'.

15 Unger, *A King's Confectioner*, p. 73.

16 Celâl Paşa, *Şurup İmalâtı*, p. 18.

17 Mehmed Reşad, *Fenn-i Tabâhat*, vol. 4, p. 32.

18 Poullet, le Sieur, *Nouvelles Relations Du Levant* (Paris, 1668), p. 109.

19 Unger, *A King's Confectioner*, pp. 72–8.

20 White, Charles, *Three Years in Constantinople or, Domestic Manners of The Turks in 1844*, 3 vols (London, 1846), vol. 3, p. 7.

21 Mehmed Kâmil (1873), pp. 132–3; Arabacıyan, Mihran, *Miftâhü't-Tabbâhîin*, (Istanbul, 1876), pp. 252, 257; Ayşe Fahriye, *Ev Kadını* (Istanbul, AH 1300/1882–3), pp. 262, 286; Mehmed Reşad, *Fenn-i Tabâhat*, vol. 4, p. 32; Ahmed Şevket, *Aşçı Mektebi*, (Istanbul, AH 1341/1925), p. 85.

22 Abdülaziz Bey, *Osmanlı Âdet, Merasim ve Tabirleri*, eds Kâzım Arısan and Duygu Arısan Günay, 2 vols (Istanbul, 1995), vol. 1, pp. 110–11. Here the term *tatlı* is used for *çevirme*.

23 Unger, *A King's Confectioner*, p. 72.

24 Gouffé, Jules, *The Book of Preserves (Le Livre de conserves)*, tr. Alphonse Gouffé (London, 1871), p. 257. The French edition of this book is *Recettes pour préparer et conserver les viandes et les poissons salés et fumés, les terrines, les galantines, les légumes, les fruits, les confitures, les liqueurs de famille, les sirops, les petits fours, etc.* (Paris, 1869).

25 Gouffé, Jules, *Le Livre de patisserie* (Paris, 1873), p. 85.

26 Under 'Fondant' in *Oxford English Dictionary*, CD-Rom (Oxford, 2002).

27 Skuse, E., *The Confectioners' Handbook*, 3rd edn (London, n.d. [1881]), pp. 51–2.

28 Skuse, E., *Skuse's Complete Confectioner*, 12th edn (London, 1928), p. 242.

29 Unger, *A King's Confectioner*, p. 50.

30 Skuse, *Confectioners' Handbook*, p. 52.

31 Skuse, *Confectioners' Handbook*, p. 53, 'Pink and White Mice'.

32 Unger, *A King's Confectioner*, p. 73.

33 Skuse, *Confectioners' Handbook*, p. 52.

34 Celâl Paşa, *Şurup İmalâtı*, pp. 17–18.

35 Mehmed Reşad, *Fenn-i Tabâhat*, vol. 4, p. 32.

36 Hadiye Fahriye, *Tatlıcıbaşı* (Istanbul, AH 1342/1926), p. 184.

14 *Reçel* – Preserves

1 Mevlânâ Celâleddin Rûmî, *Dîvân-ı Kebîr*, 4 vols, tr. Abdülbâki Gölpınarlı (Istanbul, 1957), p. 95.

 2 Columella, Lucius Junius Moderatus, *Of Husbandry* (London, 1745), p. 550; *Apicius: The Roman Cookery Book*, tr. Barbara Flower and Elisabeth Rosenbaum (London, 1958), p. 53; Toussaint-Samat, Maguelonne, *History of Food*, tr. Anthea Bell (Massachusetts, 2000), p. 265.

 3 Davidson, Alan, *The Oxford Companion to Food* (Oxford, 1999), p. 645; Hehn, Victor, *Cultivated Plants and Domestic Animals in their Migration from Asia to Europe*, ed. James Steven Stallybrass (London, 1891), p. 186.

 4 Ünver, Süheyl, *Fatih Devri Yemekleri* (Istanbul, 1952), p. 50.

 5 Mevlânâ, *Dîvân-ı Kebîr*, vol. 1, p. 13.

 6 Celâlüddin Hızır (Hacı Paşa), *Müntahab-ı Şifâ*, ed. Zafer Önler (Ankara, 1990), pp. 77, 84, 117, 202–3. Green walnuts were used for preserves, as specified by later sources. Gourd at this time, before the introduction of *Cucurbita* gourds such as the pumpkin from the New World, would have been one of the Old World *Lagenaria* family of gourds, which includes the bottle gourd.

 7 *Phyllanthus emblica*, the fruit of a tropical tree native to India. See Redhouse, Sir James W., *A Turkish and English Lexicon* (Constantinople, 1890); Ahmed Câvid, *Tercüme-i Kenzü'l-İştihâ*, eds Seyit Ali Kahraman and Priscilla Mary Işın (Istanbul, 2006), p. 82; Bilgin, Arif, 'Seçkin Mekanda Seçkin Damaklar: Osmanlı Sarayında Beslenme Alışkınlıkları (15.–17. Yüzyıl)', in M. Sabri Koz (ed.), *Yemek Kitabı: Tarih – Halkbilimi – Edebiyat* (Istanbul, 2002), p. 63.

 8 Barkan, Lütfi Ömer, 'İstanbul Saraylarına ait Muhasebe Defterleri', *Belgeler*, 12/13 (1979), p. 225; Şirvânî, Muhammed bin Mahmud, *15. Yüzyıl Osmanlı Mutfağı*, eds Mustafa Argunşah and Müjgân Çakır (Istanbul, 2005), p. 246; Ünver: *Fatih Devri Yemekleri*, p. 83.

 9 Ali Rıza (Balıkhane Nazırı), *Bir Zamanlar İstanbul*, ed. Niyazi Ahmet Banoğlu (Istanbul, n.d.), p. 62.

10 Outlying districts of Istanbul.

11 Perry, Charles and Maxine Rodinson, *Medieval Arab Cookery* (Totnes, 2001), p. 402; Ahmed Câvid, *Tercüme-i Kenzü'l-İştihâ*, pp. 38, 117; Mütercim Âsım, *Burhân-ı Katı* (Ankara, 2000), p. 629.

12 Şükûn, Ziya, *Farsça-Türkçe Lûgat, Gencinei Güftar Ferhengi Ziya* (Istanbul, 1996), vol. 2, p. 1043n.

13 Derived from the Portuguese *marmelada*, a name for quince jelly made with honey, which is regarded as the prototype of all jams.

14 Şirvânî, *15. Yüzyıl Osmanlı Mutfağı*, p. 246. The majority of Şirvânî's recipes are translations of al-Bağdadî's thirteenth-century Arabic cookery book, but this is one of the seventy-seven original recipes that he added.

15 See explanation near the end of this chapter.

16 Ünver, *Fatih Devri Yemekleri*, p. 16; Hammer-Purgstall, Joseph von, *Devlet-i Osmaniye Tarihi*, 10 vols (Istanbul, AH 1329/1917), vol. 3, p. 35.

17 Celâl Paşa, *Şurup İmalâtı* (Istanbul, AH 1309/1891), pp. 19–20.

18 White, Charles, *Three Years in Constantinople or, Domestic Manners of The Turks in 1844*, 3 vols (London, 1846), vol. 2, p. 7.

19 Pardoe, Julia, *The City of the Sultan and Domestic Manners of the Turks in 1836*, 3 vols (London, 1838), vol. 2, p. 111. Also see Uluçay, M. Çağatay, *Padişahların Kadınları ve Kızları* (Ankara, 1985), p. 131; and Moltke, Helmuth von, *Türkiye Mektupları*, tr. Hayrullah Örs (Istanbul, 1969), p. 53.

20 Witteveen, Joop, 'Rose Sugar and Other Mediaeval Sweets', *Petits Propos Culinaires*, 20 (July 1985), p. 23.

21 Mehmed Kâmil, *Melceü't-Tabbâhîn (Aşçıların Sığınağı)*, ed. Cüneyt Kut (Istanbul, 1997), p. 80.

22 Musahipzâde Celâl, *Eski Istanbul Yaşayışı* (Istanbul, 1946), p. 115.

23 Abdülaziz Bey, *Osmanlı Âdet, Merasim ve Tabirleri*, eds Kâzım Arısan and Duygu Arısan Günay, 2 vols (Istanbul, 1995), vol. 1, p. 265.

24 Celâl Paşa, *Şurup İmalâtı*.

25 Mason, Laura, *Sugar-Plums and Sherbet* (Totnes, 1998), p. 51.

26 Nostredame, Michel de (Nostradamus), *The Elixirs of Nostradamus*, ed. Knut Boeser (Rhode Island and London, 1996), pp. xix, 87–146. Nostradamus's book consists of two tracts, the first devoted to cosmetics and the second to jams and other sweetmeats.

27 Şirvânî, *15. Yüzyıl Osmanlı Mutfağı*, p. 246.

28 Schumacher-Voelker, Uta, 'German Cookery Books, 1485–1800', *Petits Propos Culinaires*, 6 (October 1980), pp. 39–40.

29 A species of citrus described as orange coloured and resembling a cross between a bitter orange and a lemon. It remains unidentified. See Tezcan, Semih, *Bir Ziyafet Defteri* (Istanbul, 1998), pp. 32–3; Bilgin, 'Seçkin Mekanda', p. 62; Mütercim Âsım, *Burhân-ı Katı*, p. 62, 'Bekrâyî'.

30 Tezcan suggests that this may be the sweet lemon, *Citrus limetta*. See Tezcan, *Bir Ziyafet Defteri*, p. 33.

31 A type of small green pear, perhaps the wild pear (*ahlat*). See Günay Kut 'Meyve Bahçesi', *Journal of Turkish Studies: Festschrift in Honor of Eleazar Birnbaum*, 29 (2005), pp. 210, 212.

32 Tezcan, *Bir Ziyafet Defteri*, p. 7.

33 Rolamb, Nicholas, 'A Relation of a Journey to Constantinople', in Awnsham Churchill (ed.), *A Collection of Voyages and Travels* (London, 1752), vol. 4, p. 682.

34 The term *tatlı* (sweet) also referred to *çevirme*, a type of fondant (see Ch. 13), but today it is used for puddings in general.

35 Unger, Friedrich, *A King's Confectioner in the Orient*, ed. Priscilla Mary Işın, tr.

Merete Çakmak and Renate Ömeroğulları (London, 2003), p. 54; Ayşe Fahriye, *Ev Kadını* (Istanbul, AH 1300/1882–3), p. 431.

36 Hadiye Fahriye, *Tatlıcıbaşı* (Istanbul, AH 1342/1926) pp. 144–5.
37 Mehmed Reşad, *Fenn-i Tabâhat*, 4 vols (Istanbul, AH 1340/1921–2), vol. 4, p. 32.
38 Mehmed Kâmil (1997), pp. 79–80.
39 Pardoe, *City of the Sultan*, vol. 1, p. 117.
40 Tott, Baron François de, *Memoirs of the Turks and Tatars*, 2 vols (London and Dublin, 1785), vol. 1, p. 96.
41 Mehmed Kâmil (1997), p. 82.
42 İleri, Selim, *Oburcuk Mutfakta* (Istanbul, 2010), p. 378.
43 Pardoe, *City of the Sultan*, vol. 1, p. 158.
44 Personal communications by members of the Gurmeyizbiz group in February 2006, and Vecihe Zaman Arseven in Antalya in October 2007.
45 Blunt, Lady Fanny Janet, *The People of Turkey, Twenty Years Residence among Bulgarians, Greeks, Albanians, Turks and Armenians*, 2 vols, ed. Stanley Lane Poole (London, 1878), vol. 2, p. 46.
46 Maundrell, Henry, 'A Journey from Aleppo to Jerusalem at Easter A.D. 1697', in Thomas Wright (ed.), *Early Travels in Palestine* (London, 1848), p. 407.
47 Hill, Aaron, *The Present State of the Turkish Empire* (London, n.d. [1740]) (first published in 1709 as *A History of the Ottoman Empire*), pp. 220–1.
48 Burnaby, Frederick, *On Horseback Through Asia Minor* (Gloucester, 1985), p. 38.
49 Schneider, E.C.A., *Letters from Broosa, Asia Minor* (Chambersburg, PA, 1846), p. 83.
50 Tott, *Memoirs of the Turks*, vol. 1, part 2, p. 36.
51 Çelebioğlu, Âmil (ed.), *Ramazannâme* (Istanbul, n.d.), pp. 223–4.
52 Ahmed Câvid, *Tercüme-i Kenzü'l-İştihâ*, p. 94.
53 Moltke, *Türkiye Mektupları*, p. 105.
54 Fontmagne, Baronne Durand de, *Un Séjour à l'Ambassade de France à Constantinople sous le Second Empire* (Paris, 1902), p. 146.
55 Coke, Thomas, 'A True Narrative of the Great Solemnity of the Circumcision of Mustapha, Prince of Turky, Eldest Son of Mahomet, Present Emperor of the Turks: Together with an Account of the Marriage of his Daughter to his Great Favourite Mussaip, at Adrianople, as it Was Sent in a Letter to a Person of Honour: by Mr Coke, Secretary of the Turky Company, Being in Company with his Excellency the Lord Ambassador Sir John Finch', in *Harleian Miscellany*, vol. 5 (London, 1676), p. 366.
56 Bilgin, 'Seçkin Mekanda', p. 64; İbn-i Şerif, *Yâdigâr, 15. Yüzyıl Türkçe Tıp Kitabı*, 2 vols, eds Ayten Altıntaş, Yahya Okutan, Doğan Koçer and Mecit Yıldız (Istanbul, 2003 and 2004), p. 264; Evliyâ Çelebi, *Evliyâ Çelebi Seyahatnâmesi*, 10 vols, eds Seyit Ali Kahraman, Yücel Dağlı, Robert Dankoff et al. (Istanbul, 1996–2007), vol. 9, p. 60; vol. 10, p. 267.
57 Bilgin, 'Seçkin Mekanda', pp. 62–4; Saz, Leylâ, *Harem'in İçyüzü* (Istanbul, 1974), p. 159; Ahmed Câvid, *Tercüme-i Kenzü'l-İştihâ*, pp. 83, 106; Olivier, G.A., *Travels in the Ottoman Empire, Egypt, and Persia Undertaken by Order of the Government of France, during the First Six Years of the Republic*, 2 vols (London, 1801), vol. 1, p. 236; vol. 2, p. 93; Evliyâ Çelebi (1996–2007), vol. 2, p. 98.

58 Musahipzade Celâl, *Eski Istanbul Yaşayışı*, p. 156.
59 Evliyâ Çelebi (1996–2007), vol. 5, pp. 14, 87; vol. 8, p. 45; Ahmed Câvid, *Tercüme-i Kenzü'l-İştihâ*, pp. 106 'Cebe', 82 'Âmüle', 83 'Edrek'. Some archive documents record these as coming from Egypt (Bilgin, 'Seçkin Mekanda', p. 64), presumably because this was the main trading centre for goods in transit from India and the Far East. Similarly Bursa is given as the source of *chebulic myrobalan* preserves in 1489–90 (see Barkan, 'Istanbul Saraylarına', p. 89), yet since this tropical fruit did not grow in Bursa the preserve must have been brought from India by merchants on the trade route via Bursa to Istanbul.
60 Evliyâ Çelebi (1996–2007), vol. 4, p. 159.
61 Terzioğlu, Arslan, *Helvahane Defteri ve Topkapı Sarayında Eczacılık* (Istanbul, 1992), pp. 57–8, 61, 63, 64, 66.
62 Neave, Dorina Lockhart, *Twenty-six Years on the Bosphorus* (London, 1933), p. 103.
63 Terzioğlu, *Helvahane Defteri*, pp. 62, 70–1.
64 Karay, Refik Halid, *Üç Nesil Üç Hayat* (Istanbul, 1943), p. 132.
65 Rauwolff, Leonhart, 'Dr. Leonhart Rauwolff's Itinerary into the Eastern Countries, as Syria, Palestine, or the Holy Land, Armenia, Mesopotamia, Assyria, Chaldea Etc.', tr. Nicholas Staphorst, in John Ray (ed.), *A Collection of Curious Travels and Voyages* (London, 1693), p. 98.
66 Ayşe Fahriye, *Ev Kadını*, pp. 276, 278.
67 Personal communication by Gezgen Tugay (b. 1925) about the jams her mother used to make.
68 Hadiye Fahriye, *Tatlıcıbaşı*, p. 156, 173.
69 Lecomte, Pretextat, *Les Arts et métiers de la Turquie de l'Orient* (Paris, 1902), pp. 351–3.
70 Alus, Sermet Muhtar, *Istanbul Yazıları*, eds Erol Sadi Erdinç and Faruk Ilıkan (Istanbul, 1994), p. 137.
71 Mehmed Reşad, *Fenn-i Tabâhat*, vol. 4, p. 31.
72 Sage apples are a gall produced by the sage species *Salvia pomifera* and *Salvia fructicosa* after being pierced by the gall wasp *Aulacidea levantina*. According to Kirby, William and William Spence, *Introduction to Entomology* (Philadelphia, 1846), p. 211 these galls 'are esteemed in the Levant for their aromatic and acid flavour, especially when prepared with sugar, and form a considerable article of commerce from Scio to Constantinople, where they are regularly exposed in the market'. Friedrich Unger saw confectioners preparing sage apple preserve in Istanbul in 1835. The vernacular Greek name for these is *faskomilia*.
73 Terzioğlu, *Helvahane Defteri*, p. 61.
74 Unger, *A King's Confectioner*, p. 60.
75 Mehmed Kâmil (1997), p. 82.
76 İbn-i Şerif, *Yâdigâr*, vol. 2, p. 248, 'Koruk Perverdesi'.
77 Terzioğlu, *Helvahane Defteri*, pp. 61, 63, 29r.
78 Cerrahoğlu, Abdurrahman, *Sofra Nimetleri* (Istanbul, 1996), p. 405; Kolak, Cevat, *Tatlılar – Pastalar Yemekler* (Istanbul, n.d.), pp. 24–5.
79 Use a long steel or wooden spoon to stir the quicklime into the water and keep

your face away from the pan as you stir it in. Avoid using an aluminium container. Quicklime (calcium oxide) is unslaked lime; when diluted with water, as here, it becomes slaked lime (calcium hydroxide), a substance widely used in the food industry. It is commonly used in preparing pickles, hence its alternative English name, pickling lime.

80 Terzioğlu, *Helvahane Defteri*, pp. 61, 29r.
81 Kolak, *Tatlılar – Pastalar Yemekler*, p. 24.

15 Helva: Home-made Varieties

1 Mevlânâ Celâleddin, *Dîvân-ı Kebîr*, 4 vols, tr. Abdülbâki Gölpınarlı (Istanbul, 1957), vol. 1, p. 33, couplet 264.
2 Galland, Antoine, *İstanbul'a Ait Günlük Anılar (1672–3)*, tr. Nahid Sırrı Örik (Ankara, 1987), pp. 110–11; Galland, Antoine, *Journal d'Antoine Galland pendant son séjour à Constantinople (1672–1673)*, vol. 1, ed. Charles Schefer (Paris, 1881), pp. 118–19.
3 Terzioğlu, Arslan, *Helvahane Defteri ve Topkapı Sarayında Eczacılık* (Istanbul, 1992), pp. 58, 23r. For the possible reading of *sad* I am grateful to Seyit Ali Kahraman.
4 Barkan, Lütfi Ömer, 'Istanbul Saraylarına ait Muhasebe Defterleri', *Belgeler*, 12/13 (1979), p. 224.
5 Barkan, 'Istanbul Saraylarına', p. 112.
6 Meninski, Francisci a Mesgnien, *Lexicon Arabico Persico, Turcicum*, 4 vols (Vienna, 1780), vol. 3, p. 501; for the recipe as made in the province of Burdur see Cerrahoğlu, Abdurrahman, *Sofra Nimetleri* (Istanbul, 1996), pp. 376–7.
7 İvgin, Hayrettin, 'Bazı Halk Şiirlerimizde Yemeklerimiz', *Türk Mutfağı Sempozyumu Bildirileri* (Ankara, 1982), pp. 236–7.
8 Mehmed Tevfik, *İstanbul'da Bir Sene*, ed. Nuri Akbayar (Istanbul, 1991), p. 84.
9 Evliyâ Çelebi, *Evliyâ Çelebi Seyahatnâmesi*, 10 vols, eds Seyit Ali Kahraman, Yücel Dağlı, Robert Dankoff *et al.* (Istanbul, 1996–2007), vol. 9, p. 121.
10 Mahmud Nedim bin Tosun, *Aşçıbaşı*, ed. Priscilla Mary Işın (Istanbul, 1998), p. 130; Işın, Priscilla Mary, 'A Nineteenth Century Ottoman Gentleman's Cookbook', *Petits Propos Culinaires*, 61 (May 1999), pp. 33, 36–7.
11 Mehmed Tevfik, *İstanbul'da Bir Sene*, p. 84.
12 Bayramoğlu, Fuat, 'Türk Mutfağı ve Yazılı Kaynaklar', *Birinci Milletlerarasi Yemek Kongresi, Türkiye, 25–30 Eylül 1986* (Ankara, 1988), p. 41.
13 Halıcı, Feyzi (ed.), *Ali Eşref Dede'nin Yemek Risalesi* (Ankara, 1992). This recipe dates from 1836.
14 *Revani* is a kind of sponge cake made with eggs and semolina and soaked in syrup.
15 Tezcan, Semih, *Bir Ziyafet Defteri* (Istanbul, 1998), p. 29.
16 Sefercioğlu, M. Nejat (ed.), *Türk Yemekleri (XVIII. Yüzyıla Ait Yazma Bir Yemek Risalesi)* (Ankara, 1985), p. 25; Mehmed Kâmil, *Melceü't-Tabbâhîn (Aşçıların Sığınağı)*, ed. Cüneyt Kut (Istanbul, 1997), p. 53; Halıcı: *Ali Eşref Dede*, pp. 22–3.
17 Kut, Günay, 'Türklerde Yeme-İçme Geleneği ve Kaynakları', in *Eskimeyen Tatlar* (Istanbul, 1996), p. 63.

18 Halıcı, *Ali Eşref Dede*, pp. 22–3; Sefercioğlu, *Türk Yemekleri*, p. 25. Modern cookery books give recipes for a very different confection by this name, a kind of deep-fried pastry soaked in syrup.
19 Şirvânî, Muhammed bin Mahmud, *15. Yüzyıl Osmanlı Mutfağı*, eds Mustafa Argunşah and Müjgân Çakır (Istanbul, 2005), pp. 233, 237.
20 Barkan, 'Istanbul Saraylarına', pp. 192, 202, 207. For translations of several Arabic recipes see Rodinson, Maxime, 'Ma'munıyya East and West', *Petits Propos Culinaires*, 33 (November 1989), p. 17.
21 Tezcan, *Bir Ziyafet Defteri*, p. 25.
22 Rodinson, 'Ma'munıyya', p. 16; Meninski, *Lexicon*, vol. 4, p. 270. Rodinson's article includes translations of several Arabic recipes dating from the thirteenth century and one dating from the fifteenth century.
23 See Ch. 26.
24 The earliest European recipe for the dish is in *Liber de Coquina*, dated 1300. See Rodinson, 'Ma'munıyya', p. 19.
25 Şirvânî, *15. Yüzyıl Osmanlı Mutfağı*, p. 233.
26 Meninski, *Lexicon*, vol. 4, p. 270.
27 Redhouse, Sir James W., *A Turkish and English Lexicon* (Constantinople, 1890), p. 1661.
28 Barkan, 'Istanbul Saraylarına', pp. 226 (year 1471), 117 (year 1573–4), 142 (year 1573–4).
29 Ünver, Süheyl, *Tarihte 50 Türk Yemeği* (Istanbul, 1948), p. 18; Sefercioğlu, *Türk Yemekleri*, p. 26.
30 Ünver, *Tarihte 50 Türk Yemeği*, p. 17; Kut, Günay (ed.), *Et-Terkibât Fî Tabhi'l-Hülviyyât (Tatlı Pişirme Tarifleri)* (Ankara, 1986), p. 17; Halıcı, *Ali Eşref Dede*, pp. 24–5; Mehmed Kâmil (1997), p. 54.
31 Unger, Friedrich, *A King's Confectioner in the Orient*, ed. Priscilla Mary Işın, tr. Merete Çakmak and Renate Ömeroğulları (London, 2003), p. 94.
32 Perry, Charles and Maxine Rodinson, *Medieval Arab Cookery*, (Totnes, 2001), pp. 84, 142, 417, 492.
33 Mehmed Kâmil (1997), p. 55; Türâbî Efendi, *Turkish Cookery Book, A Collection of Receipts Dedicated to those Royal and Distinguished Personages, the Guests of his Highness the Late Viceroy of Egypt, on the Occasion of the Banquet Given at Woolwich, on Board his Highness's Yacht the Faiz-Jehad, the 16th July 1862. Compiled by Türabi Efendi from the Best Turkish Authorities* (London, n.d. [1864]), p. 58; Ünver, *Tarihte 50 Türk Yemeği*, p. 18.
34 Ünver, *Tarihte 50 Türk Yemeği*, p. 18. The author tells us only that he was the grandson of Şeyhülislâm Paşmakzâde.
35 Türâbî Efendi, *Turkish Cookery Book*, p. 58.
36 Güzel, Abdurrahman, 'Türk Kültürü'nde Mevlid ve Yoğ Gelenekleri Etrafında Teşekkül Eden Folklorik Unsurlar', *Üçüncü Milletlerarası Yemek Kongresi, 7–12 Eylül 1990* (Ankara, n.d.), p. 91.
37 Yücel Dağlı, personal communication, citing glossary in Can, Şefik, *Mevlânâ, Hayatı, Şahsiyeti, Fikirleri* (Istanbul, 1995); Göncüoğlu, Süleyman Faruk, 'İstanbul'un Fethi Sonrası Kurulan İlk Semt: Saraçhane', *Atatürk Üniversitesi Güzel*

Sanatlar Enstitüsü Dergisi, 2009 (online journal, dergi.atauni.edu.tr/index.php/GSED/article/viewFile/2192/2191), p. 41.

38 Ahmed Câvid, *Tercüme-i Kenzü'l-İştihâ*, eds Seyit Ali Kahraman and Priscilla Mary Işın (Istanbul, 2006), p. 7.
39 Abdülaziz Bey, *Osmanlı Âdet, Merasim ve Tabirleri*, eds Kâzım Arısan and Duygu Arısan Günay, 2 vols (Istanbul, 1995), vol. 1, p. 262.
40 Ali Rıza (Balıkhane Nazırı), *Bir Zamanlar İstanbul*, ed. Niyazi Ahmet Banoğlu (Istanbul, n.d.), p. 200.
41 Şirvânî, *15. Yüzyıl Osmanlı Mutfağı*, p. 231.
42 Sefercioğlu, *Türk Yemekleri*, p. 26.
43 Kut, *Et-Terkibât*, p. 18.

16 Helva: Commercial Varieties

1 A term used in the seventeenth century by Evliyâ Çelebi, *Evliyâ Çelebi Seyahatnâmesi*, 10 vols, eds Seyit Ali Kahraman, Yücel Dağlı, Robert Dankoff et al. (Istanbul, 1996–2007), vol. 1, p. 253; vol. 2, p. 23.
2 Lecomte, Pretextat, *Les Arts et métiers de la Turquie de l'Orient* (Paris, 1902), pp. 357–9.
3 Baytop, Turhan, *Türkiye'de Bitkilerle Tedavi*, 2nd. edn (Istanbul, 1999), pp. 190–1; Baytop, Turhan, *Türkçe Bitki Adları Sözlüğü* (Ankara, 1994), pp. 77–8.
4 Fellows, Charles, *An Account of Discoveries in Lycia* (London, 1841), p. 230.
5 Saberi, Helen J., with Anissa Helou and Esteban Pombo-Villar, 'A Spicy Mystery', *Petits Propos Culinaires*, 47 (August 1994), p. 10. Pharmacologist Turhan Baytop gives the main source of helva root as the *Gypsophila* species of *G. arrostii, G. bicolor, G. eriocalyx, G. perfoliata* and *G. venusta*, and some other plants whose roots are used as substitutes (*Acantholimon, Ankyropetalum, Astragalus, Echinophora* and *Scorzonera* spp.), but *Saponaria officinalis* is not among them. See Baytop, *Türkçe Bitki Adları*, pp. 77–8. Its pharmaceutical name is *Radix Saponariae albae*, whereas soapwort root is *Radix Saponariae rubrae*.
6 Unger, Friedrich, *A King's Confectioner in the Orient*, ed. Priscilla Mary Işın, tr. Merete Çakmak and Renate Ömeroğulları (London, 2003), p. 95.
7 *Pekmez*, grape molasses.
8 Unger, *A King's Confectioner*, pp. 90, 92.
9 White, Charles, *Three Years in Constantinople or, Domestic Manners of The Turks in 1844*, 3 vols (London, 1845–6), vol. 2, p. 2.
10 M. Sabri Koz, personal communication.
11 Olivier, G.A., *Travels in the Ottoman Empire, Egypt, and Persia Undertaken by Order of the Government of France, During the First Six Years of the Republic*, 2 vols (London, 1801), vol. 2, p. 44.
12 White, *Three Years in Constantinople*, vol. 2, p. 2; Davis, Edwin John, *Anatolica, or the Journal of a Visit to Some of the Ancient Ruined Cities of Caria, Phrygia, Lycia, and Pisidia* (London, 1874), p. 143.
13 Lecomte, *Les Arts et métiers*, p. 357.
14 *Kebabçı*, meaning a kebab cook.

15 MacFarlane, Charles, *Constantinople in 1828* (London, 1829), p. 201.

16 İbn-i Şerif, *Yâdigâr, 15. Yüzyıl Türkçe Tıp Kitabı*, 2 vols, eds Ayten Altıntaş, Yahya Okutan, Doğan Koçer and Mecit Yıldız (Istanbul, 2003 and 2004), vol. 2, p. 311.

17 Nasrallah, Nawal, *Annals of the Caliph's Kitchens, Ibn Sayyâr al-Warrâq's Tenth-Century Bağhdadi Cookbook* (Leiden and Boston, 2007), p. 428.

18 Perry, Charles and Maxine Rodinson, *Medieval Arab Cookery*, (Totnes, 2001), pp. 425, 471–2.

19 Perry and Rodinson, *Medieval Arab Cookery*, pp. 471–2.

20 Bilgin, 'Seçkin Mekanda Seçkin Damaklar', p. 62.

21 Kütükoğlu, Mübahat S., *Osmanlılarda Narh Müessesi ve 1640 Tarihli Narh Defteri* (Istanbul, 1983), p. 92.

22 Tezcan, Semih, *Bir Ziyafet Defteri* (Istanbul, 1998), p. 7.

23 Dernschwam, Hans, *Tabebuch Einer Reise Nach Konstantinopel und Kleinasien (1553–1555)*, ed. Franz Babinger (Munich and Leipzig, 1923), pp. 172–3.

24 Wechsberg, Joseph, *The Cooking of Vienna's Empire* (New York, 1968), p. 14; Tasnadi, Edit, 'Macar Mutfağında Türk Yemekleri', *Dördüncü Milletlerarası Yemek Kongresi* (Konya, 1993), p. 274.

25 *Larousse Gastronomique* (London, 1988), p. 867.

26 Lecomte, *Les Arts et métiers*, p. 353.

27 Unger, *A King's Confectioner*, p. 44.

28 Lecomte, *Les Arts et métiers*, p. 357.

29 Ahmed Câvid, *Tercüme-i Kenzü'l-İştihâ*, eds Seyit Ali Kahraman and Priscilla Mary Işın, (Istanbul, 2006), p. 134; Mütercim Âsım, *Burhân-ı Katı* (Ankara, 2000), p. 405.

30 Davidson, Alan, *The Oxford Companion to Food*, 2nd edn (Oxford, 2006), p. 835; Mercer, Dr Henry C., 'Wafer Irons', *A Collection of Papers Read Before the Bucks County Historical Society*, vol. 5 (Pennsylvania, 1926), p. 248. According to Mercer, the source of this information is an entry by Augustus Joseph Schulte in the *Catholic Encyclopedia* of 1908, but I have been unable to check this or discover any more information about the wafer iron.

31 Murat Kargılı and Stephanie Ateş, personal communications, 2007.

32 From an unpublished manuscript c. 1800, f. 25v. Ünver, Süheyl, *Tarihte 50 Türk Yemeği* (Istanbul, 1948), pp. 16–17. Here Ünver gives the same recipe with slight variations transcribed from an eighteenth-century manuscript. Both recipes are derived from a common eighteenth-century source.

33 Ünver, *Tarihte 50 Türk Yemeği*, pp. 16–17; Unger, *A King's Confectioner*, p. 93.

34 Baytop, *Türkçe Bitki Adları*, p. 78; *çalma pekmez* in Aysel Özen's unpublished book about the cuisine of İncesu; Hadiye Fahriye, *Tatlıcıbaşı* (Istanbul, AH 1342/1926), p. 166 also mentions adding helva root to *pekmez*.

35 Mehmed Reşad, *Fenn-i Tabâhat*, 4 vols (Istanbul, AH 1340/1921–2), vol. 1, p. 44.

36 Kut, Günay (ed.), *Et-Terkibât Fî Tabhi'l-Hülviyyât (Tatli Pişirme Tarifleri)* (Ankara, 1986), p. 27.

37 *Kurs* is an incense tablet made principally of aloes, musk, ambergris and tragacanth gum.

38 Childs, W., *Across Asia Minor on Foot* (New York and London, 1917), p. 70; Fisher, John, 'Gentleman Spies in Asia', *Asian Affairs*, 41/2 (2010), p. 208.
39 Ahmed Câvid, *Tercüme-i Kenzü'l-İştihâ*, p. 99.
40 Rauwolff, Leonhart, 'Dr. Leonhart Rauwolff's Itinerary into the Eastern Countries, as Syria, Palestine, or the Holy Land, Armenia, Mesopotamia, Assyria, Chaldea Etc.', tr. Nicholas Staphorst, in John Ray (ed.) *A Collection of Curious Travels and Voyages* (London, 1693), p. 94.
41 Çıkla, Fatma, *Çukurova Yemekleri* (Istanbul, 1998), p. 238; Tokuz, Gonca, *Gaziantep ve Kilis Mutfak Kültürü* (Gaziantep, 2002), pp. 296, 324; *Antakya Mutfağı* (Antakya, 1990), p. 100.
42 For examples of early Arabic *nâtif* recipes see Nasrallah, *Annals of the Caliph's Kitchens*, pp. 428–31; Perry and Rodinson, *Medieval Arab Cookery*, pp. 471, 454; Saberi, 'A Spicy Mystery', May 1995, pp. 18–21.
43 Saberi: 'A Spicy Mystery', August 1994, p.10.
44 Charles Perry, personal communication. Also see, Saberi, 'A Spicy Mystery', November 1994, pp. 14–15.

17 *Keten Helva (Pişmâniye)*

1   This song was performed by the famous female music-hall singer Şamram (1870–1955); see Koçu, Reşat Ekrem, *Istanbul Ansiklopedisi*, 10 vols (Istanbul, 1958–73), vol. 3, p. 1388.
2   Erevnidis, Pavlos, 'Yunanistan'da (veya Türkiye'de) Mutfak ve Yakovos Dizikirikis'in Dil Milliyetçiliği', *Yemek ve Kültür*, 3 (2005), pp. 38–52, p. 44.
3   The Chinese version of *keten helva* is made of rice flour.
4   Hadiye Fahriye, *Tatlıcıbaşı* (Istanbul, AH 1342/1926), pp. 44–5.
5   Kâmil Küpçü of Adapazarı (b. 1928), personal communication, 11 November 2008.
6   Mahmud Nedim bin Tosun, *Aşçıbaşı*, ed. Priscilla Mary Işın (Istanbul, 1998), pp. 163–4. In Konya forty-five folds are usual (Halıcı, Nevin, *Akdeniz Bölgesi Yemekleri* (Konya, 1983), p 139), in Burdur forty folds (Cerrahoğlu, Abdurrahman, *Sofra Nimetleri* (Istanbul, 1996), pp. 384–5), in Sivas fifteen to twenty folds (Üçer, Müjgân, *Sivas Halk Mutfağı* (Sivas, 1992), p. 71). In the village of Şıhlar it is folded at least thirty times.
7   Ahmed Şevket, *Aşçı Mektebi*, (Istanbul, AH 1341/1925), p. 164.
8   Hadiye Fahriye, *Tatlıcıbaşı*, p. 47.
9   Güzelbey, Cemil Cahit, 'Gaziantep'e Özgü Yemekler', *Türk Mutfağı Sempozyumu Bildirileri* (Ankara, 1982), p. 102.
10 Şirvânî, Muhammed bin Mahmud, *15. Yüzyıl Osmanlı Mutfağı*, eds Mustafa Argunşah and Müjgân Çakır (Istanbul, 2005), p. 179.
11 Tezcan, Semih, *Bir Ziyafet Defteri* (Istanbul, 1998), p. 7.
12 Prochazka-Eisl, Gisela, *Das Surnâme-i Hümâyûn* (Istanbul, 1995), p. 148.
13 Lecomte, Pretextat, *Les Arts et métiers de la Turquie de l'Orient* (Paris, 1902), pp. 359–60.
14 *Cheveux de vieille.* This is Lecomte's French translation of the Greek term *molia tis grias.*

15 *Meydan Larousse*, 12 vols (Istanbul, 1969–73), vol. 5, p 764, 'Helva'.
16 Cerrahoğlu, *Sofra Nimetleri*, p. 384.
17 Musahipzâde Celâl, *Eski Istanbul Yaşayışı* (Istanbul, 1946), pp. 90–1.
18 Selmân al-Farisî, the first Persian to convert to Islam, one of the most foremost disciples of Muhammed, and the founder of Sufism, see Hançerlioğlu, Orhan, *İslâm İnançları Sözlüğü*, 3rd edn (Istanbul, 2000), p. 525.
19 Nasrattınoğlu, İrfan Ünver, 'Afyonkarahisar Mutfağı', *Türk Mutfağı Sempozyumu Bildirileri* (Ankara, 1982), pp. 230–1.
20 Hadiye Fahriye, *Tatlıcıbaşı*, p. 47.

18 *Helva Sohbeti* – Helva Parties

1 Onay, Ahmet Talât, *Eski Türk Edebiyatında Mazmunlar ve İzahı*, ed. Cemal Kurnaz (Ankara, 2000), p. 243.
2 Kaşgarlı Mahmud, *Divanü Lûgat-it-Türk Tercümesi*, 4 vols, tr. Besim Atalay (Ankara, 1985–6), vol. 1, p. 455.
3 Kut, Günay, 'Türklerde Yeme-İçme Geleneği ve Kaynakları', in *Eskimeyen Tatlar* (Istanbul, 1996), p. 53; Hançerlioğlu, Orhan, *İslâm İnançları Sözlüğü*, 3rd edn (Istanbul, 2000), p. 109.
4 Ibn Battuta, *The Travels of Ibn Battuta*, tr. H.A.R. Gibb (London, 1962), pp. 426–7.
5 Musahipzâde Celâl, *Eski Istanbul Yaşayışı* (Istanbul, 1946), p. 99.
6 Soysal, Sahrap, *Bir Yemek Masalı* (Istanbul, 2003), p. 187; Kut, 'Türklerde Yeme-İçme Geleneği', p. 53; Ünver, Süheyl, 'Selçuklular, Beylikler ve Osmanlılarda Yemek Usûlleri ve Vakitleri', *Türk Mutfağı Sempozyumu Bildirileri* (Ankara, 1982), p. 3.
7 Hacıbeyzâde Ahmed Muhtâr, *Aşevi – Aşçılık, Beyne'l-milel Sofracılık* (Istanbul, AH 1332/1916–17), pp. 14–15; Kut, Turgut, *Açıklamalı Yemek Kitapları Bibliyografyası (Eski Harfli Yazma ve Basma Eserler)* (Ankara, 1985), pp. 16–17.
8 The only one of these games I could identify was *esir alma*, which in English is known as prisoner's base.
9 Evliyâ Çelebi, *Evliyâ Çelebi Seyahatnâmesi*, 10 vols, eds Seyit Ali Kahraman, Yücel Dağlı, Robert Dankoff et al. (Istanbul, 1996–2007), vol. 7, p. 235.
10 Akarca, Döndü, 'Şitâiyyelerde Sosyal Yaşantı', *Çukurova Üniversitesi Sosyal Bilimler Enstitüsü Dergisi*, 14/1 (2005), p. 7.
11 Mustafa Ali of Gallipoli, *Ziyâfet Sofraları (Mevâidü'n-nefâis fî kavâidi'l mecâlis)*, 2 vols, ed. Orhan Şaik Gökyay (Istanbul, 1978), p. 129.
12 Mehmed Tevfik, *İstanbul'da Bir Sene*, ed. Nuri Akbayar (Istanbul, 1991), pp. 46–63; Kut, Günay (ed.), *Et-Terkibât Fî Tabhi'l-Hülviyyât (Tatli Pişirme Tarifleri)* (Ankara, 1986), pp. xii–xiii; Kazancıgil, Ratip, *Edirne Helva Sohbetleri ve Kış Gecesi Eğlenceleri* (Edirne, 1993), pp. 32ff; Tokuz, Gonca, *20. Yüzyılda Gaziantep'te Eğlence Hayatı* (Gaziantep, 2004), p. 52.
13 Onay, *Eski Türk Edebiyatında*, p. 467.
14 Onay, *Eski Türk Edebiyatında*, p. 467; Mehmet Tevfik, *İstanbul'da Bir Sene*, p. 50.
15 Kazancıgil, *Edirne Helva Sohbetleri*, p. 32.
16 Kazancıgil, *Edirne Helva Sohbetleri*, pp. 23–33.
17 Kazancıgil, *Edirne Helva Sohbetleri*, p. 32.

18 *Keşkek* is a porridge-like dish of mutton and wheat berries.
19 Develi, Hayati (ed.), *Risâle-i Garîbe* (Istanbul, 2001), p. 39.
20 Mehmed Tevfik, *İstanbul'da Bir Sene*, pp. 47–8; Musahipzâde Celâl, *Eski Istanbul Yaşayışı*, p. 90; Ali Rıza (Balıkhane Nazırı), *Bir Zamanlar İstanbul*, ed. Niyazi Ahmet Banoğlu (Istanbul, n.d.), p. 286.
21 Musahipzâde Celâl, *Eski Istanbul Yaşayışı*, p. 90.
22 Üçer, Müjgân, *Sivas Halk Mutfağı* (Sivas, 1992), p. 72; Atilla Özbek, personal communication, 2006.
23 Musahipzade Celâl, *Eski Istanbul Yaşayışı*, p. 90; Mehmed Tevfik, *İstanbul'da Bir Sene*, pp. 62–3.
24 Mehmed Tevfik, *İstanbul'da Bir Sene*, p. 47.
25 Onay, *Eski Türk Edebiyatında*, p. 243.
26 Doğanay, Mehmet, 'Bir Mekân Unsuru Olarak İstanbul'un Ahmed Midhat Efendinin Romanlarına Tesiri', *Dumlupınara Üniversitesi Sosyal Bilimler Dergisi*, 15 (August 2006), p. 102.
27 *Çağrı*, 36/394 (September 1992), p. 14.
28 A reference to tiny dried okra threaded on strings.
29 İlhami was the pen name of Sultan Selim III.
30 Musahipzâde Celâl, *Eski Istanbul Yaşayışı*, pp. 90–1.
31 Davidson, Alan, *The Oxford Companion to Food*, 1st edn (Oxford, 1999), p. 797; Bradley, Mary Emily, *Douglass Farm: A Juvenile Story of Life in Virginia* (New York, 1858), p. 138.
32 Akarca, 'Şitâiyyelerde Sosyal Yaşantı', p. 5.
33 Evliyâ Çelebi (1996–2007), vol. 7, p. 252.
34 Evliyâ Çelebi (1996–2007), vol. 7, pp. 115–16.
35 Ali Rıza (Balıkhane Nazırı), *Bir Zamanlar İstanbul*, ed. Niyazi Ahmet Banoğlu (Istanbul, n.d.), p. 183.

19 *Sucuk* and *Köfte*

1 Schafer, Edward H., *The Golden Peaches of Samarkand, A Study of T'ang Exotics* (Los Angeles and Berkeley, 1985), pp. 119, 142.
2 Kaşgarlı Mahmud, *Divanü Lûgat-it-Türk Tercümesi*, 4 vols, tr. Besim Atalay (Ankara, 1985–6), vol. 1, p. 440.
3 Brocquière, Bertrandon de la, 'The Travels of Bertrandon de la Brocquière 1432, 1433', in Thomas Wright (ed.), *Early Travels in Palestine* (London, n.d.), pp. 328–9.
4 Evliyâ Çelebi, *Evliyâ Çelebi Seyahatnâmesi*, 10 vols, eds Seyit Ali Kahraman, Yücel Dağlı, Robert Dankoff et al. (Istanbul, 1996–2007), vol. 1, p. 286.
5 Evliyâ Çelebi (1996–2007), vol. 9, p. 180.
6 Today Edincik in the northwestern province of Balıkesir.
7 Evliyâ Çelebi (1996–2007), vol. 4, p. 17; vol. 5, pp. 152, 164.
8 Walsh, Robert, *Constantinople and the Seven Churches of Asia Minor*, 2 vols (London, n.d. [c. 1840]), vol. 1, pp. 33–4.
9 Strange, Guy le, *Palestine Under the Moslems, a Description of Syria and the Holy*

Land from A.D. 650 to 1500, Translated from the Works of the Mediaeval Arab Geographers (London, 1890), p. 298; Steingass, Francis Joseph, *A Comprehensive Persian–English Dictionary, Including the Arabic Words and Phrases to be Met with in Persian Literature* (London, 1892), http://dsal.uchicago.edu/dictionaries/ steingass, p. 368.

10 Kut, Günay (ed.), *Et-Terkibât Fî Tabhi'l-Hülviyyât (Tatlı Pişirme Tarifleri)* (Ankara, 1986), pp. ix, 27. In other parts of Turkey *pelte* is a starch-thickened pudding, for details see Ch. 20.

11 Özen, Aysel, 'Tarihin İzleri ile İncesu Yemek Kültürü', unpublished manuscript (İncesu, 2006).

12 Ünver, Süheyl, 'Yemek Hakkında Defter', unpublished transcription of a nineteenth-century manuscript cookery book, Süleymaniye Library, Dr A. Süheyl Ünver Bağışı no. 652 (Istanbul, 1964), ff. 13–14.

13 Clarke, Edward Daniel, *Travels in Various Countries of Europe, Asia and Africa* (New York, 1970), p. 529.

14 Walsh, Robert, *Narrative of a Journey from Constantinople to England* (London, 1828), p. 111.

15 Pardoe, Julia, *The City of the Sultan and Domestic Manners of the Turks in 1836*, 3 vols (London, 1838), vol. 2, p. 211.

16 Smyth, Warrington W.M.A., *A Year with the Turks or Sketches of Travel in the European and Asiatic Dominions of the Sultan* (New York, 1854), p. 200.

17 Musahipzâde Celâl, *Eski Istanbul Yaşayışı* (Istanbul, 1946), p. 156.

18 Kut, Günay, *Et-Terkibât*, p. 26.

19 Unger, Friedrich, *A King's Confectioner in the Orient*, ed. Priscilla Mary Işın, tr. Merete Çakmak and Renate Ömeroğulları (London, 2003), p. 108.

20 Ünver, 'Yemek Hakkında Defter', ff. 13–14.

21 Ayşe Fahriye, *Ev Kadını* (Istanbul, AH 1300/1882–3), p. 356.

22 The grape juice is clarified by adding lumps of marl, a calcareous clay, to precipitate the solid particles which would impart a bitter flavour to the *pekmez*.

20 Pelte

1 Özkan, Ömer, *Divan Şiirinin Penceresinden Ösmanlı Toplum Hayatı (XIV–XV. Yüzyıl)* (Istanbul, 2007), p. 632.

2 Perry, Charles (tr.), *A Baghdad Cookery Book, the Book of Dishes (Kitâb al-Tabîkh)* (Totnes, 2005), p. 100 n1.

3 Mevlânâ Celâleddin Rûmî, 4 vols, *Dîvân-ı Kebîr*, tr. Abdülbâki Gölpınarlı (Istanbul, 1957), vol. 4, p. 124, couplet 1105.

4 Nasrallah, Nawal, *Annals of the Caliph's Kitchens, Ibn Sayyâr al-Warrâq's Tenth-Century Bağhdadi Cookbook* (Leiden and Boston, 2007), pp. 382–7. The recipes for *faludhaj* in this source include variations with almonds, olive oil or butter instead of sesame oil, egg yolks or rice instead of starch, and melon juice instead of honey and oil.

5 Perry, Charles and Maxine Rodinson, *Medieval Arab Cookery* (Totnes, 2001), p. 85; and Perry, *A Baghdad Cookery Book*, p. 100. See Perry and Rodinson, *Medieval*

Arab Cookery, pp. 419–20 for two similar recipes, one with saffron and one with camphor; the second is shaped into rolls or geometric shapes.

6 Şirvânî, Muhammed bin Mahmud, *15. Yüzyıl Osmanlı Mutfağı*, eds Mustafa Argunşah and Müjgân Çakır (Istanbul, 2005), pp. 218–19.

7 İvgin, Hayrettin, 'Bazı Halk Şiirlerimizde Yemeklerimiz', *Türk Mutfağı Sempozyumu Bildirileri* (Ankara, 1982), p. 78; Gökyay, Orhan Şaik, 'Kaygusuz Abdal'ın Sımâtiyeleri', *Türk Folkloru Dergisi*, 13 (August 1980), pp. 3–5; 14 (September 1980), pp. 3–6, 14, p. 3.

8 Mevlânâ, *Dîvân-ı Kebîr*, vol. 2, p. 1887.

9 Şirvânî, *15. Yüzyıl Osmanlı Mutfağı*, p. 231. Şirvânî's book consists of a Turkish translation of Baghdadî's thirteenth-century Arabic cookery book, with the addition of over seventy additional recipes that include the two *pelte* recipes discussed here.

10 Akgündüz, Ahmet, *Osmanlı Kanunnameleri ve Hukukî Tahlilleri*, vol. 2 (Istanbul, 1990), p. 198.

11 Bilgin, Arif, 'Seçkin Mekanda Seçkin Damaklar: Osmanlı Sarayında Beslenme Alışkınlıkları (15.–17. Yüzyıl)', in M. Sabri Koz (ed.), *Yemek Kitabı: Tarih – Halkbilimi – Edebiyat* (Istanbul, 2002), p. 60.

12 Reindel-Kiel, Hedda, 'Cennet Taamları', *Soframız Nur Hanemiz Mamur*, eds Suraiya Faroqhi and Christoph K. Neumann (Istanbul, 2006), pp. 79–87.

13 Sefercioğlu, M. Nejat (ed.), *Türk Yemekleri (XVIII. Yüzyıla Ait Yazma Bir Yemek Risalesi)* (Ankara, 1985), pp. 31–2; Ünver, Süheyl, *Tarihte 50 Türk Yemeği* (Istanbul, 1948), pp. 6, 20; *Türkiye Diyanet Vakfı İslam Ansiklopedisi*, 40 vols (Istanbul, 1989–2010), vol. 4, pp. 40–2.

14 Sefercioğlu, *Türk Yemekleri*, pp. 31–2; Ünver, *Tarihte 50 Türk Yemeği*, pp. 6, 20.

15 Strong wheat suitable for making *peksimet* (ship's biscuit, rusk).

16 Sefercioğlu, *Türk Yemekleri*, p. 31.

17 Sefercioğlu, *Türk Yemekleri*, p. 26.

18 Pakalın, Mehmet Zeki, *Osmanlı Tarih Deyimleri ve Terimleri Sözlüğü*, 3 vols (Istanbul, 1983), vol. 3, p. 244, 'Sofalılar Pâlûdecisi'.

19 Kütükoğlu, Mübahat S., *Osmanlılarda Narh Müessesi ve 1640 Tarihli Narh Defteri* (Istanbul, 1983), p. 311. This seventeenth-century register of retail prices includes Kütahya ware *pelte* dishes, 2.5 *parmak*s (approximately 7.5 cm) in diameter costing 5 *akçe*s.

20 Evliyâ Çelebi, *Evliyâ Çelebi Seyahatnâmesi*, 10 vols, eds Seyit Ali Kahraman, Yücel Dağlı, Robert Dankoff et al. (Istanbul, 1996–2007), vol. 1, p. 149.

21 Halıcı, Nevin, 'Antalya'da Yemek ile İlgili Töreler ve Antalya Yemekleri', *Geleneksel Türk Yemekleri ve Beslenme (Geleneksel Türk Mutfağı Sempozyumu Bildirileri, 10–11 Eylül 1982)* (Konya, 1982), p. 169.

22 Evliyâ Çelebi (1996–2007), vol. 1, p. 299.

23 Sumac is the tiny sour red berries of *Rhus coriaria*, a small tree native to the Mediterranean.

24 Ahmed Câvid, *Tercüme-i Kenzü'l-İştihâ*, eds Seyit Ali Kahraman and Priscilla Mary Işın (Istanbul, 2006), pp. 83, 90, 120.

25 Mehmed Kâmil, *Melceü't-Tabbâhîn*, pp. 91, 60.

26 Hadiye Fahriye, *Tatlıcıbaşı* (Istanbul, AH 1342/1926), pp. 80, 81.

27 Ayşe Fahriye, *Ev Kadını* (Istanbul, AH 1300/1882-3), pp. 234-5.

28 Nasrallah, *Annals of the Caliph's Kitchens*, p. 387.

29 Türâbî Efendi, *Turkish Cookery Book, A Collection of Receipts Dedicated to Those Royal and Distinguished Personages, the Guests of his Highness the Late Viceroy of Egypt, on the Occasion of the Banquet given at Woolwich, on Board his Highness's Yacht the Faiz-Jehad, the 16th July 1862. Compiled by Türabi Efendi from the Best Turkish Authorities* (London, n.d. [1864]), p. 64.

30 Evliyâ Çelebi (1996-2007), vol. 1, p. 286.

31 White, Charles, *Three Years in Constantinople or, Domestic Manners of The Turks in 1844*, 3 vols (London, 1845-6), vol. 2, p. 6.

32 Ünver, *Tarihte 50 Türk Yemeği*, p. 46; Halıcı, Feyzi (ed.), *Ali Eşref Dede'nin Yemek Risalesi* (Ankara, 1992), p. 34.

33 Nasrallah, *Annals of the Caliph's Kitchens*, pp. 274-5; Perry: *Baghdad Cookery Book*, p. 33; Perry and Rodinson, *Medieval Arab Cookery*, p. 495.

34 Ünver, Süheyl, *Fatih Devri Yemekleri* (Istanbul, 1952), p. 28; also see Ergin, Nina, Christoph K. Neumann and Amy Singer (eds), *Feeding People, Feeding Power: Imarets in the Ottoman Empire* (Istanbul, 2007), pp. 205-6.

35 Tezcan, Semih, *Bir Ziyafet Defteri* (Istanbul, 1998), pp. 9, 13, 15, 17.

36 Apricots from wild or ungrafted trees grown from seed.

37 Barkan, Lütfi Ömer, 'Istanbul Saraylarına ait Muhasebe Defterleri', *Belgeler*, 12/13 (1979), p. 24.

38 Ünver, *Fatih Devri Yemekleri*, p. 28.

39 Celâlüddin Hızır (Hacı Paşa), *Müntahab-ı Şifâ*, ed. Zafer Önler, (Ankara, 1990), p. 39.

40 Şirvânî, *15. Yüzyıl Osmanlı Mutfağı*, p. 239.

41 Ünver, *Fatih Devri Yemekleri*, p. 28. Physician and food historian Prof. Süheyl Ünver (1898-1986) gives the ingredients and quantities used in late Ottoman *imaret*s as recounted to him by the scholar İsmail Saip Sencer, who died in 1940.

42 Perhaps due to the sloppy texture or mixture of many ingredients. Today this metaphorical use has been taken a step further to form the verb *zırvalamak*, to talk nonsense.

43 Şirvânî, *15. Yüzyıl Osmanlı Mutfağı*, p. 231.

44 Ayşe Fahriye, *Ev Kadını*, pp. 234-5.

45 'Kıyye-i aşarî'. The metric system of weights and measures was officially adopted in Turkey in 1869.

21 *Lokum* – Turkish Delight

1 Nahya, Zümrüt, 'Geleneksel Türk Kültüründe Tatlı', *Geleneksel Türk Tatlıları Sempozyumu Bildirileri 17-18 Aralık 1983* (Ankara, 1984), p. 94.

2 Vámbéry, Armin, *Scenes from the East* (Budapest, 1974), pp. 98-9.

3 De Kay, James Ellsworth, *Sketches of Turkey in 1831 and 1832* (New York, 1833), p. 126.

4 White, Charles, *Three Years in Constantinople or, Domestic Manners of The Turks in 1844*, 3 vols (London, 1845–6), vol. 2, p. 8.

5 Kernels of apricots grown on grafted trees are sweet and taste somewhat like almonds.

6 Unger, Friedrich, *A King's Confectioner in the Orient*, ed. Priscilla Mary Işın, tr. Merete Çakmak and Renate Ömeroğulları (London, 2003), p. 97.

7 Baillie, E.C.C., *A Sail to Smyrna: Or, An Englishwoman's Journal including Impressions of Constantinople, a Visit to a Turkish Harem and a Railway Journey to Ephesus* (London, 1873), p. 76.

8 Lecomte, Pretextat, *Les Arts et métiers de la Turquie de l'Orient* (Paris, 1902), pp. 353–4.

9 See Ch. 13.

10 www.cadbury.co.uk/cadburyandchocolate/ourstory/Pages/OurstoryDetail. aspx?id=1914_turkish_delight&category=product&era=1901_1940&mode=det ail. Cadbury's has continued to produced Fry's Turkish Delight since taking over J.S. Fry & Sons in 1919.

11 Skuse, E., *Skuse's Complete Confectioner*, 12th edn (London, 1928), p. 177.

12 Unger, Friedrich, *Conditorei des Orients* (Athens and Nauplia, 1838), pp. 88–9.

13 Dernschwam, Hans, *Tabebuch Einer Reise Nach Konstantinopel und Kleinasien (1553–1555)*, ed. Franz Babinger (München and Leipzig, 1923), p. 124, 'Krafft Meel'.

14 Redhouse, Sir James W., *A Turkish and English Lexicon* (Constantinople, 1890), p. 2082: 'Starch from wheat used for food'. Redhouse's definition of the Arabic word *neşâ* stresses the same point: '*neşa*: starch of wheat, used as food.'

15 Redhouse, *A Turkish and English Lexicon*, p. 1362: '*fâlûzec*: jelly or blanc-mange of strained wheat or rice flour etc.'

16 Blunt, Lady Fanny Janet, *The People of Turkey, Twenty Years Residence among Bulgarians, Greeks, Albanians, Turks and Armenians*, 2 vols, ed. Stanley Lane Poole (London, 1878), vol. 1, pp. 206–7.

17 Beeton, Isabella, *Beeton's Book of Household Management*, facsimile edn (London, 1968), pp. 706–7; Acton, Eliza, *Modern Cookery for Private Families* (East Sussex, 1993), pp. 397–9; Skuse, E., *The Confectioners' Handbook*, 3rd edn (London, n.d. [1881]), p. 165. For blancmanges with chicken breast see May, Robert, *The Accomplisht Cook* (Totnes, 2000), p. 300. Beeton and Acton also give recipes for blancmange thickened with rice flour or arrowroot.

18 See Chs 21 and 22.

19 Reindel-Kiel, Hedda, 'Cennet Taamları', *Soframiz Nur Hanemiz Mamur*, eds Suraiya Faroqhi and Christoph K. Neumann (Istanbul, 2006), p. 96. The document in question specifies that the *kesme* was made with *pekmez*, precluding any possibility that this might be an early reference to *lokum*.

20 Pakalın, Mehmet Zeki, *Osmanlı Tarih Deyimleri ve Terimleri Sözlüğü*, 3 vols (Istanbul, 1983), vol. 3, p. 5.

21 Perry, Charles and Maxine Rodinson, *Medieval Arab Cookery* (Totnes, 2001), p. 219.

22 This form was in use in the eighteenth century for pastries such as *yumurtalı lokum* and *hacı lokumu*, see Sefercioğlu, M. Nejat (ed.), *Türk Yemekleri (XVIII. Yüzyıla Ait*

Yazma Bir Yemek Risalesi) (Ankara, 1985), p. 6 and Ünver, Süheyl, *Tarihte 50 Türk Yemeği* (Istanbul, 1948), p. 9. The term 'sugar lokum' used in a seventeenth-century source is therefore more likely to refer to a small sweet pastry than to anything like the sweetmeat of later centuries, see Evliyâ Çelebi, *Evliyâ Çelebi Seyahatnâmesi*, 10 vols, eds Seyit Ali Kahraman, Yücel Dağlı, Robert Dankoff et al. (Istanbul, 1996–2007), vol. 9, p. 444.

23 Üsküdar, a district of Istanbul on the Asian shore of the Bosphorus strait.

24 Soyer, Alexis, *A Culinary Campaign* (Lewes, East Sussex, 1995), p. 196.

25 Musahipzâde Celâl, *Eski Istanbul Yaşayışı* (Istanbul, 1946), p. 7; Mehmed Reşad, *Fenn-i Tabâhat*, 4 vols (Istanbul, AH 1340/1921–2), vol. 4, p. 35.

26 Lecomte, *Les Arts et métiers*, p. 353.

27 Vane, Frances Anne, Marchioness of Londonderry, *Narrative of a Visit to the Courts of Vienna, Constantinople, Athens and Naples* (London, 1840), p. 150.

28 Türâbî Efendi, *Turkish Cookery Book, A Collection of Receipts Dedicated to those Royal and Distinguished Personages, the Guests of his Highness the Late Viceroy of Egypt, on the Occasion of the Banquet given at Woolwich, on Board his Highness's Yacht the Faiz-Jehad, the 16th July 1862. Compiled by Türabi Efendi from the Best Turkish Authorities* (London, n.d. [1864]), p. v.

29 *Punch*, 12 January 1861, p. 12.

30 'The Latest Novelty for Dessert, Genuine Rahat Lakoum, A Delicious Turkish Sweetmeat Imported from Turkey by Krikorian Bros', pamphlet, 1878, British Library, Evan.7548.

31 Dickens, Charles, *Edwin Drood* (London, n.d. [1870]), pp. 22–3. This shop still existed in 1891, see Hughes, William R., *A Week's Tramp in Dickens-land* (London, 1891), p. 132.

32 Kesnin Bey, *The Evil of the East, or Truths about Turkey* (London, 1888), p. 135. Kesnin Bey is a pseudonym used by Eugène Chesnel.

33 Unpublished manuscript, private collection, ff. 26r–27v.

34 Mehmed Kâmil, *Melceü't-Tabbâhîn (Aşçıların Sığınağı)*, ed. Cüneyt Kut (Istanbul, 1997), p. 80.

35 Sefercioğlu, *Türk Yemekleri*, p. 26.

36 Unger, *A King's Confectioner*, pp. 97–8.

37 Ayşe Fahriye, *Ev Kadını* (Istanbul, AH 1300/1882–3), pp. 250–2.

38 'Double-cooked' *lokum* is cooked for a longer time to give a thicker consistency.

39 Hadiye Fahriye, *Tatlıcıbaşı* (Istanbul, AH 1342/1926), pp. 117–23.

40 Abdülaziz Bey, *Osmanlı Âdet, Merasim ve Tabirleri*, eds Kâzım Arısan and Duygu Arısan Günay, 2 vols (Istanbul, 1995), vol. 1, p. 327.

41 Nordegren, Thomas, *The A–Z Encyclopedia of Alcohol and Drug Abuse* (Florida, 2002), p. 549: 'Rahat lakoum: Turkish colloquial term for confection containing hashish'.

42 Şirvânî, Muhammed bin Mahmud, *15. Yüzyıl Osmanlı Mutfağı*, eds Mustafa Argunşah and Müjgân Çakır (Istanbul, 2005), p. 216; Perry and Rodinson, *Medieval Arab Cookery*, pp. 84, 417, 456; Perry, Charles (tr.), Muhammad b. al-Hasan b. Muhammed b. al-Karîm, *A Baghdad Cookery Book, the Book of Dishes (Kitâb al-Tabîkh)* (Totnes, 2005), p. 99.

43 Unger, *A King's Confectioner*, p. 94.

22 *Güllaç* – Starch Wafers

1 Özkan, Ömer, *Divan Şiirinin Penceresinden Osmanlı Toplum Hayatı (XIV–XV. Yüzyıl)* (Istanbul, 2007), p. 644.
2 Lâmi'î Çelebi, *Şem' ü Pervâne* (Istanbul, 1522), Süleymaniye Library, Esat Efendi 2744, f. 63v; Perry, Charles and Maxine Rodinson, *Medieval Arab Cookery* (Totnes, 2001), p. 222. Ibn Rûmî uses the term *lauzinaj*, the almond sweetmeat that in his time was wrapped in these wafers.
3 Dr Paul Buell translates it as 'flower pastry', see Buell, Paul D., 'Mongol Empire and Turkicization: The Evidence of Food and Foodways', in Reuven Amitai-Preiss and David O. Morgan (eds), *The Mongol Empire and its Legacy* (Leiden, Boston and Cologne, 1999), p. 220.
4 Mütercim Âsım, *Burhân-ı Katı* (Ankara, 2000), pp. 295, 296; Ahmed Câvid, *Tercüme-i Kenzü'l-İştihâ*, eds Seyit Ali Kahraman and Priscilla Mary Işın (Istanbul, 2006), pp. 55, 59, 142.
5 Nasrallah, Nawal, *Annals of the Caliph's Kitchens, Ibn Sayyâr al-Warrâq's Tenth-Century Baghdadi Cookbook* (Leiden and Boston, 2007), p. 125. *Lauz* means almonds, and here *lauzinaj* is the name for confections made of ground almonds or sometimes other nuts, usually wrapped in *güllaç* wafers. See other recipes for *lauzinaj* in *Kitâb Wasf al-At'ima al-Mu'tâda*, Perry and Rodinson, *Medieval Arab Cookery*, p. 419 and note 3, pp. 456–7, 'Another Variety'.
6 Perry and Rodinson, *Medieval Arab Cookery*, pp. 84–5, 456, 'As for the Moist'; Perry, Charles (tr.), Muhammad b. al-Hasan b. Muhammed b. al-Karîm, *A Baghdad Cookery Book, the Book of Dishes (Kitâb al-Tabîkh)* (Totnes, 2005), pp. 99–100.
7 Şirvânî, Muhammed bin Mahmud, *15. Yüzyıl Osmanlı Mutfağı*, eds Mustafa Argunşah and Müjgân Çakır (Istanbul, 2005), p. 237. The term 'kneading' is used in the earliest Turkish recipe for *güllaç*, and in the thirteenth-century Arabic recipe. In al-Warraq's tenth-century recipe, on the other hand, the term 'dissolve' is used, which more closely approaches the process of preparing a starch batter. The inappropriate term 'knead' may have also meant 'beating until well blended' or reflect the unfamiliarity of the authors with a technique that was not used in domestic kitchens but only by specialist *güllaç* makers.
8 Barkan, Lütfi Ömer, 'Istanbul Saraylarına ait Muhasebe Defterleri', *Belgeler*, 12/13 (1979), pp. 112, 131.
9 Evliyâ Çelebi, *Evliyâ Çelebi Seyahatnâmesi*, eds Robert Dankoff, Seyit Ali Kahraman and Yücel Dağlı, vol. 1, 2nd edn (Istanbul, 2006), p. 266.
10 See Şirvânî's fifteenth-century recipe, the sixteenth-century description by Hans Dernschwam and Türâbî Efendi's nineteenth-century recipe in this chapter. Türâbî Efendi specifies that the egg whites be whipped. Modern *güllaç* wafers often include no egg white, only maize starch and wheat flour.
11 Şirvânî, *15. Yüzyıl Osmanlı Mutfağı*, p. 233. For his other recipes see pp. 237 and 232.

12 Buell, 'Mongol Empire and Turkicization', p. 220. The Turkicization of Mongol foodways at this period is discussed at length by Buell in this article.

13 Tezcan, Semih, *Bir Ziyafet Defteri* (Istanbul, 1998), p. 7.

14 Dernschwam, Hans, *Tabebuch Einer Reise Nach Konstantinopel und Kleinasien (1553–1555)*, ed. Franz Babinger (Munich and Leipzig, 1923), p. 124. I am grateful to Merete Çakmak for her translation from the German. I also wish to thank Berrin Torolsan for drawing my attention to this description of *güllaç*.

15 Evliyâ Çelebi, *Evliyâ Çelebi Seyahatnâmesi*, 10 vols, eds Seyit Ali Kahraman, Yücel Dağlı, Robert Dankoff et al. (Istanbul, 1996–2007), vol. 5, p. 199. The thousand layers must be literary hyperbole.

16 Mehmed Kâmil, *Melceü't-Tabbâhîn (Aşçıların Sığınağı)*, ed. Cüneyt Kut (Istanbul, 1997), p. 59.

17 Türâbî Efendi, *Turkish Cookery Book, A Collection of Receipts Dedicated to those Royal and Distinguished Personages, the Guests of his Highness the Late Viceroy of Egypt, on the Occasion of the Banquet Given at Woolwich, on Board his Highness's Yacht the Faiz-Jehad, the 16th July 1862. Compiled by Türabi Efendi from the Best Turkish Authorities* (London, n.d. [1864]), p. 63.

18 Türâbî Efendi, *Turkish Cookery Book*, title page and Preface.

19 Torolsan, Berrin, 'Trade Secrets: Fine Fast Food', *Cornucopia*, 27 (2002), p. 108.

20 White, Charles, *Three Years in Constantinople or, Domestic Manners of The Turks in 1844*, 3 vols (London, 1845-6), vol. 3, p. 92.

21 Ünver, Süheyl, *Tarihte 50 Türk Yemeği* (Istanbul, 1948), p. 19. Paşmakçızâde Abdullah Efendi served as *şeyhülislam*, the highest Ottoman religious dignitary.

22 Mahmud Nedim bin Tosun, *Aşçıbaşı*, ed. Priscilla Mary Işın (Istanbul, 1998), p. 101.

23 Üçer, Müjgân, *Anamın Aşı Tandırın Başı – Sivas Mutfağı* (Istanbul, 2006), p. 601. This regional variation is made with walnuts.

24 Türâbî Efendi, *Turkish Cookery Book*, p. 63.

25 Çelebioğlu, Âmil (ed.), *Ramazannâme* (Istanbul, n.d.), p. 126, 'Fasl-ı Ramazan'.

26 Abdülaziz Bey, *Osmanlı Âdet, Merasim ve Tabirleri*, eds Kâzım Arısan and Duygu Arısan Günay, 2 vols (Istanbul, 1995), vol. 1, p. 251. Abdülaziz Bey was writing in 1910–12.

27 Saz, Leylâ, *Harem'in İçyüzü* (Istanbul, 1974), p. 124. Leylâ Saz (1850–1936) was a woman composer and poet, who as a child was companion to the Ottoman princess Münîre Sultan.

28 Mehmed Tevfik, *İstanbul'da Bir Sene*, ed. Nuri Akbayar (Istanbul, 1991), p. 142.

29 Tulgar, Ahmet, 'Güllaç bize sanatı ve sabrı öğretti', *Milliyet*, 26 October 2003.

23 Baklava

1 Çelebioğlu, Âmil (ed.), *Ramazannâme* (Istanbul, n.d.) p. 152.

2 Uğurlu, Nurer, *Bilmece Bildirmece* (Istanbul, 1984), p. 22.

3 Luke, Harry, *An Eastern Chequer Board* (London, 1934), p. 272.

4 Nesin, Aziz, *Böyle Gelmiş Böyle Gitmez 1: Yol*, 13th edn (Istanbul, 1998), p. 32.

5   Abdülaziz Bey, *Osmanlı Âdet, Merasim ve Tabirleri*, eds Kâzım Arısan and Duygu Arısan Günay, 2 vols (Istanbul, 1995), vol. 1, pp. 76, 273.
6   Gürpınar, Hüseyin Rahmi, *Eti Senin Kemiği Benim*, 2nd edn (Istanbul, 1973), pp. 19–20.
7   Barkan, Lütfi Ömer, 'Istanbul Saraylarına ait Muhasebe Defterleri', *Belgeler*, 12/13 (1979), p. 275.
8   Assistant Prof. Abdülkadir Dündar kindly provided me with a translation of the *imaret* foundation deed, dated 1495.
9   Gökyay, Orhan Şaik, 'Kaygusuz Abdal', ın Sımâtiyeleri', *Türk Folkloru Dergisi*, 14 (September 1980), p. 4.
10 This jesting claim has been around since the seventeenth century, see Evliyâ Çelebi, *Evliyâ Çelebi Seyahatnâmesi*, 10 vols, eds Seyit Ali Kahraman, Yücel Dağlı, Robert Dankoff et al. (Istanbul, 1996–2007), vol. 2, p. 53. For another later example see Yüksel, Murat, *Türk Edebiyatında Hamsi* (Trabzon, 1989), p. 45.
11 Barkan, 'Istanbul Saraylarına', pp. 275, 277.
12 Barkan, 'Istanbul Saraylarına', p. 354.
13 Bayramoğlu, Fuat, 'Türk Mutfağı ve Yazılı Kaynaklar', *Birinci Milletlerarasi Yemek Kongresi, Türkiye, 25–30 Eylül 1986* (Ankara, 1988), pp. 43–4.
14 Barkan, 'Istanbul Saraylarına', pp. 24, 147.
15 Perry, Charles, 'Early Turkish Influence on Arab and Iranian Cuisine', *Dördüncü Milletlerarası Yemek Kongresi, Türkiye 3–6 Eylül 1992* (Konya, 1993), pp. 242–3.
16 Mahmud al-Kāshgari, *Compendium of the Turkic Dialects (Dīwān Luγāt at-Turk)* 3 vols, ed. and tr. Robert Dankoff in collaboration with James Kelly (Cambridge, MA, 1984), vol. 2, p. 159.
17 Dr Paul Buell, in a letter dated 1993.
18 Perry, Charles, 'The Taste for Layered Bread among the Nomadic Turks and the Central Asian Origins of Baklava', in *Culinary Cultures of the Middle East*, ed. Sami Zubaida and Richard Tapper (London, 1994), p. 89: 'A pastry called *qatlama* is known among the Uzbeks, Kazakhs, Tatars, Bashkirs, Azarbayjanis and Turkmens, and the Uyghurs of Xinjiang Province, China.'
19 Mahmud Nedim bin Tosun, *Aşçıbaşı*, ed. Priscilla Mary Işın (Istanbul, 1998), p. 28.
20 Ahmed Câvid, *Tercüme-i Kenzü'l-İştihâ*, eds Seyit Ali Kahraman and Priscilla Mary Işın (Istanbul, 2006), pp. 149–50.
21 Brocquière, Bertrandon de la, 'The Travels of Bertrandon de la Brocquière 1432, 1433', in Thomas Wright (ed.), *Early Travels in Palestine* (London, n.d.), pp. 314–15.
22 Kaşgarlı Mahmud, *Divanü Lûgat-it-Türk Tercümesi*, 4 vols, tr. Besim Atalay (Ankara, 1985–6), vol. 2, p. 106.
23 Algar, Ayla Esen, 'Bushaq of Shiraz: Poet, Parasite and Gastronome', *Petits Propos Culinaires*, 31 (March 1989), p. 11.
24 Prochazka-Eisl, Gisela, *Das Surnâme-i Hümâyûn* (Istanbul, 1995), p. 85.
25 Evliyâ Çelebi (1996–2007), vol. 5, p. 199.
26 Bayramoğlu, Fuat, 'Türk Mutfağı ve Yazılı Kaynaklar', *Birinci Milletlerarasi Yemek Kongresi, Türkiye, 25–30 Eylül 1986* (Ankara, 1988), p. 43 (eight layers); Sefercioğlu, M. Nejat (ed.), *Türk Yemekleri (XVIII. Yüzyıla Ait Yazma Bir Yemek Risalesi)* (Ankara, 1985), p. 21 (forty layers); Mehmed Kâmil, *Melceü't-Tabbâhîn (Aşçıların*

Sığınağı), ed. Cüneyt Kut (Istanbul, 1997), p. 47 (thirty-five to sixty layers); Türâbî Efendi, *Turkish Cookery Book* (London, n.d. [1864]), p 47 (fifty layers).

27 Oğuz, Burhan, *Türkiye Halkının Kültür Kökenleri*, vol. 1, (Istanbul, 1976), p 711.

28 Bayramoğlu, 'Türk Mutfağı', p. 43–4.

29 Friedrich Unger, *A King's Confectioner in the Orient*, ed. Priscilla Mary Işın, tr. Merete Çakmak and Renate Ömeroğulları (London, 2003), p. 103.

30 Barkan, Lütfi Ömer, 'Fatih Cami ve İmareti Tesislerinin 1489–1490 Yıllarına ait Muhasebe Bilançoları', *İktisat Fakültesi Mecmuası*, 23/1–2 (October 1962, February 1963), pp. 394–5.

31 Ünver, Süheyl, *Fatih Devri Yemekleri* (Istanbul, 1952), p. 68.

32 Mahmud Nedim, *Aşçıbaşı*, pp. 164–5.

33 Evliyâ Çelebi (1996–2007), vol. 5, p. 228.

34 Arlı, Mine, 'Türk Mutfağına Genel Bir Bakış', *Türk Mutfağı Sempozyumu Bildirileri* (Ankara, 1982), p. 30.

35 Bell, James Stanislaus, *Journal of a Residence in Circassia during the Years 1837, 1838 and 1839*, 2 vols (London, 1840), vol. 1, p. 417.

36 See recipes at end of chapter for melon baklava and three fillings used as a substitute for clotted cream.

37 Türâbî Efendi, *Turkish Cookery Book, A Collection of Receipts Dedicated to those Royal and Distinguished Personages, the Guests of his Highness the Late Viceroy of Egypt, on the Occasion of the Banquet given at Woolwich, on Board his Highness's Yacht the Faiz-Jehad, the 16th July 1862. Compiled by Türabi Efendi from the Best Turkish Authorities* (London, n.d. [1864]), pp. iv, 47.

38 Mahmud Nedim, *Aşçıbaşı*, pp. 126, 170.

39 Ali Rıza (Balıkhane Nazırı), *Eski Zamanlarda İstanbul Hayatı*, ed. Ali Şükrü Çoruk (Istanbul, 2001), pp. 200–1; Koçu, Reşat Ekrem, *İstanbul Ansiklopedisi*, 10 vols (Istanbul, 1958–73), vol. 4, pp. 1939–40.

40 *Dünden Bugüne İstanbul Ansiklopedisi*, 8 vols (Istanbul, 1993), vol. 2, p. 5, 'Baklava Alayı'.

41 Gautier, Théophile, *Constantinople*, tr. F.C. de Sumichrast (New York, 1901), p. 261.

42 Çelebioğlu, *Ramazannâme*, pp. 150–2.

43 In the former system of Turkish time the new day began at sunset.

44 Abdurrahman Şeref, 'Topkapı Saray-ı Hümâyûn', *Tarih-i Osmanî Encümeni Mecmuası* (Istanbul, AH 1328–9/1910–11), p. 335.

45 Walsh, Robert, *A Residence at Constantinople*, 2 vols (London, 1836), vol. 1, p. 365.

46 Barkan, 'İstanbul Saraylarına', p. 133.

47 Alus, Sermet Muhtar, *İstanbul Yazıları*, eds Erol Sadi Erdinç and Faruk Ilıkan (Istanbul, 1994), p. 138.

48 Ramsay, Lady Agnes Dick, *Everyday Life in Turkey* (London, 1897), pp. 151–2.

49 Luke, *Eastern Chequer Board*, pp. 112–13.

50 Withers, Robert, 'A Description of the Grand Seignor's Seraglio', in Thomas Birch (ed.), *Miscellaneous Works of Mr John Greaves*, vol. 2 (London, 1737), p. 721. This account of the Ottoman palace by Ottavio (or Ottaviano) Bon dating from the period 1604–7 was translated into English by Robert Withers and published as his own work in 1625. In 1737 the translation was republished by John Greaves.

51 Reindel-Kiel, Hedda, 'Cennet Taamları', *Soframiz Nur Hanemiz Mamur*, eds Suraiya Faroqhi and Christoph K. Neumann (Istanbul, 2006), pp. 78–87.
52 Reindel-Kiel, 'Cennet Taamları', p. 95.
53 *Mantı* is a dish of ancient Central Asian origin introduced into China by the ninth century, consisting of stuffed noodles, usually filled with minced mutton, served with garlic yogurt. See Anderson, E.N., 'The Yin-Shan Cheng-Yao and the West: Central Asian Components in China's Foodways', paper, Sixth International Conference on the History of Science in China, Cambridge, England, 1990; Anderson, E.N., Paul D. Buell and Charles Perry, *A Soup for the Qan* (London, 2000), p. 313.
54 Bayramoğlu, 'Türk Mutfağı', pp. 43–4; Ahmed Câvid, *Tercüme-i Kenzü'l-İştihâ*, pp. 149–50.
55 Gökyay, Orhan Şaik, 'Sohbetnâme', *Tarih ve Toplum*, 3/14 (February 1985), p. 132.
56 *Larousse Gastronomique* (London, 1988), p. 1234: 'inspired by the Turkish baklava, the recipe was apparently created by a Hungarian'; Wechsberg, Joseph, *The Cooking of Vienna's Empire* (New York, 1968), p. 176: 'The *Apfelstrudel* is not of Viennese origin. It was the Hungarians who took their incredibly thin Strudel dough from the great Turkish delicacy *baklava* and then filled it with apples.'
57 Türâbî Efendi, *Turkish Cookery Book*, p. 47.
58 Sefercioğlu, M. Nejat (ed.), *Türk Yemekleri (XVIII. Yüzyıla Ait Yazma Bir Yemek Risalesi)* (Ankara, 1985), p. 31.
59 Mehmed Kâmil (1997), p. 47.

24 Kadayıf

1 Çelebioğlu, Âmil (ed.), *Ramazannâme* (Istanbul, n.d.), p. 49.
2 Perry, Charles and Maxine Rodinson, *Medieval Arab Cookery* (Totnes, 2001), p. 492.
3 Perry and Rodinson, *Medieval Arab Cookery*, pp. 34–5. This translation by A.J. Arberry sacrifices a good deal of the original meaning for the sake of making the English rhyme, as shown by this more literal translation by Nawal Nasrallah (*Annals of the Caliph's Kitchens, Ibn Sayyâr al-Warrâq's Tenth-Century Baghdadi Cookbook* (Leiden and Boston, 2007), p. 424): 'I have for friends when hunger strikes, qatâyif like piles of books stacked. / They resemble honeycombs – with holes and white – when closely seen. / Swimming in almond oil, disgorged after they had their fill of it. / With glistening bubbles, back and forth, rose water sways. / Rolled and aligned like purest of arrows, their sight the smitten-hearted rejoice. / More delicious than they are is seeing them plundered, for man's joy lies in what is most hankered.'
4 Nasrallah, *Annals of the Caliph's Kitchens*, p. 420.
5 Nasrallah, *Annals of the Caliph's Kitchens*, pp. 420–4.
6 Perry and Rodinson, *Medieval Arab Cookery*, p. 460 ('Qatâ'if Mahshuwwa', from a copy of *Kitâb al-Wusla ila al-Habîb*).
7 Sefercioğlu, M. Nejat (ed.), *Türk Yemekleri (XVIII. Yüzyıla Ait Yazma Bir Yemek Risalesi)* (Ankara, 1985), p. 8.

8 *Diyarbakır Mutfağı* (Istanbul, 2003), p. 71; *Antakya Mutfağı* (Antakya, 1990), p. 96, 'Cevizli Kadayıf'; Çıkla, Fatma, *Çukurova Yemekleri* (Istanbul, 1998), p. 243; *Malatya Mutfağından* (Malatya, n.d. [1990]), p. 41.

9 Mehmed Reşad, *Fenn-i Tabâhat*, 4 vols (Istanbul, AH 1340/1921–2), vol. 3, p. 38. Pine nuts used as a stuffing for sweet pastries is so unusual in Turkish cuisine that I am inclined to think this is a printing error, the correct rendering being pistachios; the Turkish names differ by a single letter (*çam fıstığı, şam fıstığı*).

10 Sefercioğlu, *Türk Yemekleri*, pp. 8–9; Ünver, Süheyl, *Tarihte 50 Türk Yemeği* (Istanbul, 1948), pp. 11–12.

11 Ash water (*küllü su*) was used as a raising agent in flour bakery until recent times in Turkey, but has now largely been replaced by baking powder.

12 A pouring batter as used to make *lalenk* or *lalanaga*, a kind of pancake made with beaten eggs and flour.

13 Mehmed Kâmil, *Melceü't-Tabbâhîn (Aşçıların Sığınağı)*, ed. Cüneyt Kut (Istanbul, 1997), p. 51. English crumpets may be used for this recipe.

14 'Fat-free *kadayıf*'.

15 Şirvânî, Muhammed bin Mahmud, *15. Yüzyıl Osmanlı Mutfağı*, eds Mustafa Argunşah and Müjgân Çakır (Istanbul, 2005), pp. 222–3.

16 Evliyâ Çelebi, *Evliyâ Çelebi Seyahatnâmesi*, 10 vols, eds Seyit Ali Kahraman, Yücel Dağlı, Robert Dankoff et al. (Istanbul, 1996–2007), vol. 1, p. 265.

17 Perry and Rodinson, *Medieval Arab Cookery*, pp. 453, 456.

18 Perry and Rodinson, *Medieval Arab Cookery*, p. 494.

19 Perry and Rodinson, *Medieval Arab Cookery,* p. 421. There are two copies of this manuscript in Topkapı Palace Library: TSKM 62 Tıp/1992 and TSKM 22/74 Tıp/2004.

20 Unger, Friedrich, *A King's Confectioner in the Orient*, ed. Priscilla Mary Işın, tr. Merete Çakmak and Renate Ömeroğulları (London, 2003), pp. 104–5.

21 By this Unger means that the *kadayıf* pancakes were sold plain or made up into a pudding.

22 White, Charles, *Three Years in Constantinople or, Domestic Manners of the Turks in 1844*, 3 vols (London, 1845–6), vol. 2, pp. 10–11.

23 Türâbî Efendi, *Turkish Cookery Book, A Collection of Receipts Dedicated to those Royal and Distinguished Personages, the Guests of his Highness the Late Viceroy of Egypt, on the Occasion of the Banquet Given at Woolwich, on Board his Highness's Yacht the Faiz-Jehad, the 16th July 1862. Compiled by Türabi Efendi from the Best Turkish Authorities* (London, n.d. [1864]), p. 51.

24 My thanks to Suphi Görgen for his account of *kadayıf* makers in Alexandria.

25 Sefercioğlu, *Türk Yemekleri*, p. 15; Musahipzâde Celâl, *Eski Istanbul Yaşayışı* (Istanbul, 1946), pp. 90, 99; Abdülaziz Bey, *Osmanlı Âdet, Merasim ve Tabirleri*, eds Kâzım Arısan and Duygu Arısan Günay, 2 vols (Istanbul, 1995), vol. 1, p. 77.

26 Bilgin, Arif, 'Seçkin Mekanda Seçkin Damaklar: Osmanlı Sarayında Beslenme Alışkınlıkları (15.–17. Yüzyıl)', in M. Sabri Koz (ed.), *Yemek Kitabı: Tarih – Halkbilimi – Edebiyat* (Istanbul, 2002), p. 60.

27 White, *Three Years in Constantinople*, vol. 2, p. 10. For a palace-style *kadayıf* recipe see Sefercioğlu: *Türk Yemekleri*, p. 16, 'Saray Katayıfı'.

28 White is confusing *tel kadayıf* with *yassı kadayıf*, in fact palace-style *kadayıf* was the former.
29 Sefercioğlu, *Türk Yemekleri*, pp. 16, 17.
30 Sefercioğlu, *Türk Yemekleri*, pp. 14–15. The anonymous eighteenth-century author surmises that *katife* is a corruption of the term Arabic *kunâfa*.
31 Mahmud Nedim bin Tosun, *Aşçıbaşı*, ed. Priscilla Mary Işın (Istanbul, 1998), p. 133.
32 White, *Three Years in Constantinople*, pp. 11–12.
33 İzzet Mehmed Paşa (1723–84) served twice as grand vizier, in 1774–5 and 1781–2, during the reigns of Mustafa III and Abdülhamid I.
34 Sefercioğlu, *Türk Yemekleri*, p. 18.
35 Halıcı, Feyzi (ed.), *Ali Eşref Dede'nin Yemek Risalesi* (Ankara, 1992), p. 16.
36 Mehmed Kâmil (1997), p. 49.
37 Türâbî Efendi, *Turkish Cookery Book*, p. 52.
38 Ayşe Fahriye, *Ev Kadını* (Istanbul, AH 1300/1882–3), p. 216; Mahmud Nedim, *Aşçıbaşı*, p. 136 has a similar recipe filled with ground walnuts, hazelnuts or almonds.
39 Ünver, *Tarihte 50 Türk Yemeği*, pp. 15–16.
40 *Fodula* loaves were in the form of circular cakes, and the baking tins used for *saray etmeği* were also circular.
41 Mehmed Kâmil (1997), p. 52, 'Fodula Kadayıfı'.
42 Mehmed Kâmil (1997), p. 52.
43 Türâbî Efendi, *Turkish Cookery Book*, p. 54. Because the muffins were fresh he misses out the process of soaking in water.
44 Mehmed Kâmil (1997), p. 55.
45 Soyer, Alexis, *A Culinary Campaign* (Lewes, East Sussex, 1995), p. 305. Soyer spelt *ekmek kadayıfı*, 'ekmekataive'.
46 Frank Clement Lorford, www.soyer.co.uk. Soyer died in August 1858.

25 *Aşure*

1 Mustafa Ali of Gallipoli, *Ziyâfet Sofraları* (*Mevâidü'n-nefâis fî kavâidi'l mecâlis*), 2 vols, ed. Orhan Şaik Gökyay (Istanbul, 1978), vol. 1, p. 160.
2 Tannahill, Reay, *Food in History*, 2nd edn (London, 1988), p. 96; White, Florence, *Food in England* (London, 1951), pp. 26, 348–9, 361; Davidson, Alan, *The Oxford Companion to Food*, 2nd edn (Oxford, 2006), p. 83; Aylin Öney Tan, 'Be Merry, Around a Wheat Berry! The Significance of Wheat in Anatolian Rituals and Celebrations', *Celebration: Proceedings of the Oxford Symposium on Food and Cookery, 2011* (Totnes, 2012), pp. 346–55; Kaneva-Johnson, Maria, *The Melting Pot, Balkan Food and Cookery* (Totnes, 1999), p. 208.
3 Harlan, Jack R., 'A Wild Wheat Harvest in Turkey', *Archaeology*, 20/3 (June 1967), pp. 197–8.
4 Harlan, 'Wild Wheat Harvest', pp. 197, 201.
5 Archaeologist and ethnobotanist Dr Füsun Ertuğ, personal communication, 2010.

6 Evliyâ Çelebi, *Evliyâ Çelebi Seyahatnâmesi*, 10 vols, eds Seyit Ali Kahraman, Yücel Dağlı, Robert Dankoff et al. (Istanbul, 1996–2007), vol. 9, p. 356.

7 Evliyâ Çelebi (1996–2007), vol. 1, p. 230.

8 Evliyâ Çelebi, *Evliyâ Çelebi Seyahatnâmesi*, eds Robert Dankoff, Seyit Ali Kahraman and Yücel Dağlı, vol. 1, 2nd edn (Istanbul, 2006), p. 264.

9 Frazer, James George, *The Golden Bough* (London, 1924), pp. 324ff.

10 Frazer, *Golden Bough*, p. 338. Abû Said Wahb bin Ibrahim's account is quoted by al-Nedîm in his *Fihrist el-'Ulûm* dated 987 (see Smith, William, *Dictionary of the Bible: Comprising its Antiquities, Biography, Geography and Natural History*, 4 vols (New York, 1870), vol. 4, p. 3175, 'Tammûz'). Harran is in the province of Urfa in southeastern Turkey.

11 Quoted by Frazer, *Golden Bough*, p. 338.

12 *Chambers Encyclopaedia*, 10 vols (London, 1874–80), vol. 4, p. 159, 'Wheat': 'So small was the quantity of wheat used in the county of Cumberland . . . that it was only a rich family that used a peck of wheat in the course of the year, and that was used at Christmas.' This quotation is from Eden, Frederick Morton, *The State of the Poor; or, A History of the Labouring Classes in England*, 3 vols (London, 1797), vol. 1, p. 562.

13 Appleby, Mrs, *Yorkshire Cookery* (Lancaster, 1971), p. 92; Tannahill, *Food in History* (2nd edn), p. 182; Davidson, Alan, *The Oxford Companion to Food*, 1st edn (Oxford, 1999), p. 323; Hartley, Dorothy, *Food in England* (London, 1996), pp. 534–5.

14 Wei-Jun, Zhov, 'Çin'in Geleneksel Yeni Yıl Arefesi Yemeği', *Üçüncü Milletlerarası Yemek Kongresi, 7–12 Eylül 1990* (Ankara, n.d.), pp. 16–20. I also wish to thank Aylin Öney Tan for further information about this Chinese grain food, as related to her by Coşkun Aral, and my friend Nâlan Aydın, who purchased a tin sold under the name 'mixed congee' produced in Taiwan in America for me to taste and photograph. Mixed congee contains no raisins, but only a mixture of pulses and grains, including rice and sometimes wheat berries, but is decorated with dried fruits when serving.

15 Covel, John, 'Dr. Covel's Diary (1670–1679)', in J. Theodore Bent (ed.), *Early Voyages and Travels in the Levant* (London, 1893), p. 145.

16 Chandler, Richard, *Travels in Asia Minor and Greece*, 3rd edn (London, 1817), vol. 1, pp. 153–4.

17 Garnett, Lucy, *The Women of Turkey and their Folklore*, 2 vols (London, 1893), vol. 1, p. 66. For a description of modern *koliva* see Kaneva-Johnson, *Melting Pot*, pp. 209–10.

18 Abdülaziz Bey, *Osmanlı Âdet, Merasim ve Tabirleri*, eds Kâzım Arısan and Duygu Arısan Günay, 2 vols (Istanbul, 1995), vol. 1, p. 273. Abdülaziz Bey was writing in 1910–12.

19 Kaneva-Johnson, *Melting Pot*, p. 211.

20 Sperling, Devorah S., 'Boiled Wheat', *Petits Propos Culinaires*, 9 (October 1981), p. 61.

21 Roden, Claudia, *The Book of Jewish Food* (London, 1997), p. 494.

22 Ahmed Câvid, *Tercüme-i Kenzü'l-İştihâ*, eds Seyit Ali Kahraman and Priscilla Mary Işın (Istanbul, 2006), p. 112, 'Dânek'.

23 *Türkiye Diyanet Vakfı İslam Ansiklopedisi*, 40 vols (Istanbul, 1989–2010), vol. 4, p. 26, 'Âşûra'.

24 Hançerlioğlu, Orhan, *İslâm İnançları Sözlüğü*, 3rd edn (Istanbul, 2000), p. 28; Sertoğlu, Midhat, *Osmanlı Tarih Lûgatı* (Istanbul, 1986), pp. 21–2. Mount Jûdî lies south of Lake Van, in eastern Turkey. Mount Ararat is located about 200 km to the northeast.

25 In the Sumerian flood story and the Bible animals are sacrificed and presumably eaten, while in the Quran no mention is made of either sacrifices or other food.

26 Abdülaziz Bey, *Osmanlı Âdet*, p. 246.

27 Algar, Ayla Esen, 'Bektaşilik'te Yemeğin Yeri', *İkinci Milletlerarası Yemek Kongresi 3–10 Eylül 1988* (Ankara, 1989), pp. 22–3.

28 Samancıgil, Kemal, *Bektaşilik Tarihi* (Istanbul, 1945), pp. 89–90.

29 Dernschwam, Hans, *Tabebuch Einer Reise Nach Konstantinopel und Kleinasien (1553–1555)*, ed. Franz Babinger (Munich and Leipzig, 1923), p. 120.

30 İşli, H. Necdet, 'Kâdirîhâne'de Aşûre', in M. Sabri Koz (ed.), *Yemek Kitabı: Tarih, Halkbilim, Edebiyatı* (Istanbul, 2002), pp. 719–32.

31 Ünver, Süheyl, *Fatih Devri Yemekleri* (Istanbul, 1952), p. 3.

32 Toygar, Kâmil, 'Türkiye'de Hıdrellez Çevresinde Oluşan Mutfak Kültürü', *Üçüncü Milletlerarası Yemek Kongresi, 7–12 Eylül 1990* (Ankara, n.d.), pp. 70–1.

33 Abdülaziz Bey, *Osmanlı Âdet*, p. 246.

34 Abdülaziz Bey, *Osmanlı Âdet*, p. 76.

35 Kaneva-Johnson, Maria, 'Boiled Wheat and Aşure', *Petits Propos Culinaires*, 5 (May 1980), p. 69.

36 Walker, Mary Adelaide, *Eastern Life and Scenery with Excursions in Asia Minor, Mytilene, Crete, and Roumania*, 2 vols (London, 1886), vol. 1, p. 260.

37 Evliyâ Çelebi (1996–2007), vol. 4, p. 17.

38 Reindel-Kiel, Hedda, 'Cennet Taamları', *Soframiz Nur Hanemiz Mamur*, eds Suraiya Faroqhi and Christoph K. Neumann (Istanbul, 2006), pp. 79–97.

39 Gökyay, Orhan Şaik, 'Sohbetnâme', *Tarih ve Toplum*, 3/14 (February 1985), p. 61.

40 Abdülaziz Bey, *Osmanlı Âdet*, p. 246.

41 Ünver, Süheyl, *Fatih Devri Yemekleri* (Istanbul, 1952), p. 4.

42 Unger, Friedrich, *A King's Confectioner in the Orient*, ed. Priscilla Mary Işın, tr. Merete Çakmak and Renate Ömeroğulları (London, 2003), p. 116.

43 Türâbî Efendi, *Turkish Cookery Book, A Collection of Receipts Dedicated to those Royal and Distinguished Personages, the Guests of his Highness the Late Viceroy of Egypt, on the Occasion of the Banquet Given at Woolwich, on Board his Highness's Yacht the Faiz-Jehad, the 16th July 1862. Compiled by Türabi Efendi from the Best Turkish Authorities* (London, n.d. [1864]), pp. 60–1.

44 Half a cup of wheat is sufficient to make around six servings.

45 Bilgin, Arif, *Osmanlı Saray Mutfağı* (Istanbul, 2004), p. 59.

46 Ali Rıza (Balıkhane Nazırı), *Eski Zamanlarda İstanbul Hayatı*, ed. Ali Şükrü Çoruk (Istanbul, 2001), p. 325; Ali Rıza (Balıkhane Nazırı), *Bir Zamanlar İstanbul*, ed.

Niyazi Ahmet Banoğlu (Istanbul, n.d.), p. 176. The Turkish term for pearl barley is *Frenk arpası* ('European barley').

47 Ayşe Fahriye, *Ev Kadını* (Istanbul, AH 1300/1882–3), p. 229.

48 Orgun, Zarif, 'Osmanlı Sarayında Yemek Yeme Adabı', *Türk Mutfağı Sempozyumu Bildirileri* (Ankara, 1982), p. 149.

49 Osmanoğlu, Ayşe, *Babam Sultan Abdülhamid* (Istanbul, 1984), pp. 105–6.

50 Dufferin and Ava, Harriet Georgina Blackwood, Dowager Marchioness of, *My Russian and Turkish Journals* (London, 1916), pp. 246–7.

51 Walker, *Eastern Life and Scenery*, vol. 1, p. 260.

52 My thanks to Hanım Özdağ of Göle for this family recipe.

26 *Sütlü Tatlılar* – Milk Puddings

1 Çelebioğlu, Âmil (ed.), *Ramazannâme* (Istanbul, n.d.), p. 241.

2 Kaşgarlı Mahmud, *Divanü Lûgat-it-Türk Tercümesi*, 4 vols, tr. Besim Atalay (Ankara, 1985–6), vol. 1, pp. 90–1.

3 Mehmed oğlu Eşref, *Hazâinü's-saadat*, pp. 32–1, quoted in *Tarama Sözlüğü*, 8 vols (Ankara, 1988), vol. 5, p. 3639, 'Sütlaç'; İbn-i Şerif, *Yâdigâr, 15. Yüzyıl Türkçe Tıp Kitabı*, 2 vols, eds Ayten Altıntaş, Yahya Okutan, Doğan Koçer and Mecit Yıldız (Istanbul, 2003 and 2004), vol. 2, pp. 306, 345; Koşay, Hâmit and Akile Ülkücan, *Anadolu Yemekleri ve Türk Mutfağı* (Ankara, 1961), p. 139.

4 Gökyay, Orhan Şaik, 'Kaygusuz Abdal'ın Sımâtiyeleri', *Türk Folkloru Dergisi*, 14 (1980), p. 5.

5 Evliyâ Çelebi, *Evliyâ Çelebi Seyahatnâmesi*, 10 vols, eds Seyit Ali Kahraman, Yücel Dağlı, Robert Dankoff et al. (Istanbul, 1996–2007), vol. 1, pp. 249–50.

6 Dickie, John, *Delizia! The Epic History of the Italians and Their Food* (New York, 2008), p. 95. At this banquet the guests were served 'fried marzipan pastries filled with Turkish-style rice', the Turkish-style rice being made with rice cooked in milk with sugar, butter and rose water. My thanks to Michael Krondl for telling me about this source.

7 Messisbugo, Cristoforo, *Banchetti, compositioni di vivande et apparecchio generale* (Ferrara, 1549), pp. 19, 48, 53, 71.

8 Scappi, Bartolomeo, *Opera di M. Bartolomeo Scappi, cuoco Secreto di Papa Pio V.* (Venice, 1570), Book 4, f. 241v.

9 Covel, John, 'Dr. Covel's Diary (1670–1679)', in J. Theodore Bent (ed.), *Early Voyages and Travels in the Levant* (London, 1893), p. 262.

10 Unger, Friedrich, *A King's Confectioner in the Orient*, ed. Priscilla Mary Işın, tr. Merete Çakmak and Renate Ömeroğulları (London, 2003), p. 108.

11 This story is recorded in a thirteenth-century Andalusian cookery book *Anwâ al-Saydala fi Alwân al-At'ima*. See 'Making Muhallabiyya' in the English translation of this manuscript by Charles Perry accessible at www.daviddfriedman.com/Medieval/Cookbooks/Andalusian/andalusian_contents.htm. For a discussion of the story see Nasrallah, Nawal, *Annals of the Caliph's Kitchens, Ibn Sayyâr al-Warrâq's Tenth-Century Bağhdadi Cookbook* (Leiden and Boston, 2007), p. 535.

12 Nasrallah, *Annals of the Caliph's Kitchens*, pp. 407–8.

13 Perry, Charles, (tr.), Muhammad b. al-Hasan b. Muhammed b. al-Karîm, *A Baghdad Cookery Book, the Book of Dishes (Kitâb al-Tabîkh)*, (Totnes, 2005), p. 50.

14 Barkan, Lütfi Ömer, 'Saray Mutfağının 894–895 (1489–1490) yılına ait Muhasebe Bilançosu', *İktisat Fakültesi Mecmuası*, 23/1–2 (October 1962, February 1963), pp. 189, 193, 199, 204, 206, 212; Şirvânî, Muhammed bin Mahmud, *15. Yüzyıl Osmanlı Mutfağı*, eds Mustafa Argunşah and Müjgân Çakır (Istanbul, 2005), p. 229.

15 Perry, Charles and Maxine Rodinson, *Medieval Arab Cookery* (Totnes, 2001), p. 263; Wilson, C. Anne, 'The French Connection: Part II', *Petits Propos Culinaires*, 4 (February 1980), p. 17. Anne Wilson says there is a recipe for blancmange with 'brayed almonds and pounded capon's flesh' in the thirteenth-century *Viandier*, and one similar to the Turkish version made with teased threads of cooked chicken and rice in the early fourteenth-century *Traité de cusine*. For a discussion of the possible connection between the Arabic *isfidhabâj*, which has the same literal meaning of 'white food', but refers to a type of meat stew using pale-coloured ingredients (comparable to the *beyaz yahni* or 'white stew' of Turkish cuisine) see Perry and Rodinson, *Medieval Arab Cookery*, pp. 263ff. There appears to be no connection apart from the name (for examples of *isfidhabâj* recipes see Nasrallah, *Annals of the Caliph's Kitchens*, pp. 282–4 and Perry and Rodinson, *Medieval Arab Cookery*, pp. 55, 341). *Muhallabiyya* recipes, on the other hand, are clearly the origin of most *blanc mange* recipes. As Charles Perry says, white dishes were valued in medieval Arab cuisine, and possibly the term 'white food' was current for *muhallabiya* in vernacular speech. In Turkish the equivalent term *ak aş* for *muhallebi* is recorded in two nineteenth-century dictionaries.

16 May, Robert, *The Accomplisht Cook* (Totnes, 2000), pp. 298–300 (facsimile of the 1685 edition of Robert May's book). For discussions of the origins of blancmange see Perry and Rodinson, *Medieval Arab Cookery*, pp. 263ff. and Davidson, Alan, *The Oxford Companion to Food*, 2nd edn (Oxford, 2006), pp. 82–3.

17 Williams, T., *The Accomplished Housekeeper and Universal Cook* (London, 1717), p. 192.

18 The earliest recipe I have been able to find for blancmange made with corn starch is in an American cookery book published in 1853, see Leslie, Eliza, *Directions for Cookery in its Various Branches*, 49th edn (Philadelphia, 1858), p. 500.

19 De Kay, James Ellsworth, *Sketches of Turkey in 1831 and 1832* (New York, 1833), p. 325.

20 Mahmud Nedim, *Aşçıbaşı*, p. 103.

21 Mahmud Nedim, *Aşçıbaşı*, p. 103.

22 Dernschwam, Hans, *Tabebuch Einer Reise Nach Konstantinopel und Kleinasien (1553–1555)*, ed. Franz Babinger (Munich and Leipzig, 1923), p. 124. I am grateful to Merete Çakmak for her English translations from this German source.

23 Reindel-Kiel, Hedda, 'Cennet Taamları', *Soframiz Nur Hanemiz Mamur*, eds Suraiya Faroqhi and Christoph K. Neumann (Istanbul, 2006), pp. 83, 85, 95.

24 Mahmud Nedim bin Tosun, *Aşçıbaşı*, ed. Priscilla Mary Işın (Istanbul, 1998), pp. 101–2.

25 Walsh, Robert, *Constantinople and the Seven Churches of Asia Minor*, 2 vols (London, n.d. [c. 1840]), vol. 1, pp. 33–4.

26 *Cassell's Dictionary of Cookery* (London, Paris and New York, n.d.), p. 705, 'Ramazan Cakes'.

27 Dufferin and Ava, Harriet Georgina Blackwood, Dowager Marchioness of, *My Russian and Turkish Journals* (London, 1916), p. 171.

28 Walker, Mary Adelaide, *Eastern Life and Scenery with Excursions in Asia Minor, Mytilene, Crete, and Roumania*, 2 vols (London, 1886), vol. 1, pp. 85–6.

29 Mehmed Kâmil, *Melceü't-Tabbâhîn (Aşçıların Sığınağı)*, ed. Cüneyt Kut (Istanbul, 1997), p. 57; Ayşe Fahriye, *Ev Kadını* (Istanbul, AH 1300/1882–3), p. 230 (recipe no. 465); Mehmed Reşad, *Fenn-i Tabâhat*, 4 vols (Istanbul, AH 1340/1921–2), vol. 4, p. 7.

30 Mehmed Kâmil, *Melceü't-Tabbâhîn*, p. 57.

31 Ayşe Fahriye, *Ev Kadını*, p. 230. This recipe is given at the end of the chapter.

32 Mehmed Reşad, *Fenn-i Tabâhat*, vol. 4, pp. 8–9.

33 Vámbéry, Armin, *Scenes from the East* (Budapest, 1974), p. 231.

34 Ayşe Fahriye, *Ev Kadını*, p. 240.

35 Mehmed Reşad, *Fenn-i Tabâhat*, vol. 4, pp. 5–6.

36 Mahmud Nedim, *Aşçıbaşı*, pp. 101–2.

37 Ayşe Fahriye, *Ev Kadını*, p. 230.

38 Mahmud Nedim, *Aşçıbaşı* p. 103.

39 Mehmed Reşad, *Fenn-i Tabâhat*, vol. 4, p. 8.

27 Zerde

1 Aksoy, Ömer Asım, *Atasözleri ve Deyimler Sözlüğü*, 3 vols (Ankara 1971), vol. 1, p. 340.

2 Evliyâ Çelebi, *Evliyâ Çelebi Seyahatnâmesi*, eds Robert Dankoff, Seyit Ali Kahraman and Yücel Dağlı, vol. 1, 2nd edn (Istanbul, 2006), pp. 284–5; Evliyâ Çelebi, *Evliyâ Çelebi Seyahatnâmesi*, 10 vols, eds Seyit Ali Kahraman, Yücel Dağlı, Robert Dankoff et al. (Istanbul, 1996–2007), vol. 4, p. 178.

3 Arndt, Alice, 'Saffron: The Festive Spice', *Üçüncü Milletlerarası Yemek Kongresi, 7–12 Eylül 1990*, (Ankara, n.d.), p. 36. In Iran thinly sliced almonds are added to *shole zard*, and the top is garnished with cinnamon and chopped pistachio nuts, see Zafari, Mahin, *Iranian Cooking for Foreigners* (Tahran, 1966) p. 61.

4 Evliyâ Çelebi (2006), pp. 284–5.

5 Burton, Richard F., *The Book of the Thousand Nights and a Night*, 11 vols (London, 1885), vol. 2, p. 313; vol. 7, p. 185. Burton translates *zerde* as 'a sauce yellowed with saffron' and 'yellow rice' respectively, giving explanations in footnotes.

6 Mevlânâ Celâleddin, *Mesnevî*, 6 vols, tr. Veled İzbudak (Istanbul, 1990), vol. 4, couplet 1085. Also see Cunbur, Müjgân, 'Mevlânâ'nın Mesnevi'sinde ve Divan-ı Kebir'inde Yemekler', *Türk Mutfağı Sempozyumu Bildirileri* (Ankara, 1982), p. 79.

7 Tezcan, Semih, *Bir Ziyafet Defteri* (Istanbul, 1998), p. 25.

8 In the original document quantities are given in *kiles* and *dirhems* (3.2 g). The *kile* was a grain measure. Different sources give widely differing values for the *kile*, since it varied from place to place and according to the type of grain being

measured. I have based my metric weights on the equivalent in *dirhem*s given in
the endowment deed for Sultan Mehmed II's hospice, which in connection with
making pilaf for hospice guests tells us that two *kile*s of rice was equivalent to
4,000 *dirhem*s, which makes 1 *kile* 6.4 kg, see Ünver, Süheyl, *Fatih Devri Yemekleri*
(Istanbul, 1952), pp. 7–8). Other values for the *kile* are far too large to be applicable
to the ingredients of *zerde* in this list.

9 Tezcan, *Bir Ziyafet Defteri*, p. 27.
10 Tezcan, *Bir Ziyafet Defteri*, p. 9.
11 Uzunçarşılı, İsmail Hakkı, *Osmanlı Devletinin Saray Teşkilâtı*, (Ankara, 1988),
   p. 109.
12 Lâmiî Çelebi, see Kut, Günay (ed.), *Et-Terkibât Fî Tabhi'l-Hülviyyât (Tatli Pişirme
   Tarifleri)* (Ankara, 1986), pp. x–xi.
13 Dernschwam, Hans, *Tabebuch Einer Reise Nach Konstantinopel und Kleinasien
   (1553–1555)*, ed. Franz Babinger (Munich and Leipzig, 1923), pp. 36, 123. English
   translations by Merete Çakmak.
14 Arndt, 'Saffron', pp. 34–7.
15 Kut, Günay, *Et-Terkibât*, p. 51; Lâtifî, *Evsâf-ı Istanbul*, ed. Nermin Suner (Pekin)
   (Istanbul, 1977), p. 36.
16 The two major Islamic festivals, *îd* in Arabic, are the four-day Kurban Bayramı or
   Feast of Sacrifice and the three-day Şeker Bayram or Feast of Sugar at the end of
   Ramazan.
17 Ünver, *Fatih Devri Yemekleri*, pp. 81–3.
18 Pakalın, *Osmanlı Tarih Deyimleri*, vol. 2, p. 546, 'Miskinhâne'.
19 Ahmed Refik, *Eski Istanbul* (Istanbul, 1931), p. 17.
20 Sarı, Nil, 'Osmanlı Sarayında Yemeklerin Mevsimlere Göre Düzenlenmesi ve
   Devrin Tababetiyle İlişkisi', *Türk Mutfağı Sempozyumu Bildirileri* (Ankara, 1982),
   p. 250; Reindel-Kiel, Hedda, 'Cennet Taamları', *Soframız Nur Hanemiz Mamur*, eds
   Suraiya Faroqhi and Christoph K. Neumann (Istanbul, 2006), pp. 79, 81.
21 Evliyâ Çelebi (1996–2007), vol. 5, p. 88.
22 Evliyâ Çelebi (1996–2007), vol. 5, p. 199.
23 Saz, Leylâ, *Harem'in İçyüzü* (Istanbul, 1974), p. 262.
24 Walker, Mary Adelaide, *Eastern Life and Scenery with Excursions in Asia Minor,
   Mytilene, Crete, and Roumania*, 2 vols (London, 1886), vol. 2, pp. 10–11.
25 In a nineteenth-century Turkish–English dictionary *pilav zerde* is defined as 'pilaw
   decorated with a sweet sauce of saffron', see Redhouse, Sir James W., *A Turkish and
   English Lexicon* (Constantinople, 1890), p. 451.
26 Ali Rıza (Balıkhane Nazırı), *Eski Zamanlarda İstanbul Hayatı*, ed. Ali Şükrü Çoruk
   (Istanbul, 2001), p. 282.
27 Johnson, Maria, 'Notes on Turkish Contributions to Balkan Flour Confectionery',
   Birinci Milletlerarasi Yemek Kongresi, 25–30 Eylül 1986 (Ankara, 1988), p. 158.
28 Mahmud Nedim bin Tosun, *Aşçıbaşı*, ed. Priscilla Mary Işın (Istanbul, 1998),
   p. 104.
29 For details of *şerbetlik şeker* see Ch. 11.
30 Mehmed Reşad, *Fenn-i Tabâhat*, 4 vols (Istanbul, AH 1340/1921–2), vol. 4, p. 10.
31 A type of rice imported at this period. It is mentioned in the gazette published by

the Ottoman Chamber of Trade in 1899 and 1900, along with Egyptian rice and Rangon rice.

32 Hacıbeyzâde Ahmed Muhtar, *Aşevi – Aşçılık, Beyne'l-milel Sofracılık* (Istanbul, AH 1332/1916–17), p. 160. Ankara red rice has small reddish grains and a delicious flavour. Sadly it is no longer grown except by a few local people for their own consumption.
33 Barkan, Lütfi Ömer, 'İstanbul Saraylarına ait Muhasebe Defterleri', *Belgeler*, 12/13 (1979), p. 78, entry for the year AH 962 (1554–5).
34 *Oxford English Dictionary*, CD-Rom version 3.01 (Oxford, 2002), 'Arrowroot'.
35 The berries of *Rhamnus infectorius*, used as a textile dye.
36 Ahmed Câvid, *Tercüme-i Kenzü'l-İştihâ*, eds Seyit Ali Kahraman and Priscilla Mary Işın (Istanbul, 2006), p. 84.
37 Tokuz, Gonca, *Gaziantep ve Kilis Mutfak Kültürü* (Gaziantep, 2002), p. 312.
38 Evliyâ Çelebi (1996–2007), vol. 2, pp. 242–3; vol. 4, pp. 39, 89.
39 Evliyâ Çelebi (1996–2007), vol. 6, pp. 223–4. Evliyâ Çelebi says that the name of this New World fruit is *hunza*. The papaya was carried rapidly throughout the Old World, and had reached India by the late sixteenth century (which explains why another name for the papaya in Turkish was *inebe-i hindiye*, 'Indian grape', a name also used for the mango), and China by the mid-seventeenth century.
40 Hacıbeyzâde, *Aşevi*, pp. 19–20.
41 'Wedding meat', slices of boiled mutton dipped in yogurt, fried and served in their own juice, sometimes with the addition of spices.
42 Halıcı, Nevin, 'Konya Düğün Yemeği', *Üçüncü Milletlerarası Yemek Kongresi, 7–12 Eylül 1990* (Ankara, n.d.), p. 198.

28 *Dondurma* – Ice Cream

1 Pakalın, Mehmet Zeki, *Osmanlı Tarih Deyimleri ve Terimleri Sözlüğü*, 3 vols (Istanbul, 1983), vol. 2, pp. 201–2, 'Karhane'.
2 Koçu, Reşat Ekrem, *İstanbul Ansiklopedisi*, 10 vols (Istanbul, 1958–1973), vol. 3, p. 1388, 'Ayak Esnafı'.
3 *Milliyet* newspaper, 14 September 1998, p. 17.
4 Salep is the ground tuber of several species of orchid in four genera (*Orchis, Ophrys, Dactylorhiza, Serapias*), used to make a hot winter drink (also called salep) as well as ice cream.
5 Tekinşen, O. Cenap and K. Kaan Tekinşen, *Dondurma: Temel Bilgiler, Teknoloji, Kalite Kontrolü* (Kahramanmaraş, 2008), p. 101.
6 Eric Hansen, 'The Search for Turkey's Mr Whippy', *Sunday Telegraph*, 'Travel' supplement, 1 April 2001, pp. 1–2 (the story was related by Mehmet Kambur, one of the foremost ice cream makers in Kahramanmaraş).
7 Barkan, Lütfi Ömer, 'İstanbul Saraylarına ait Muhasebe Defterleri', *Belgeler*, 12/13 (1979), p. 249.
8 Evliya Çelebi, *Evliyâ Çelebi Seyahatnâmesi*, 10 vols, eds Seyit Ali Kahraman, Yücel Dağlı, Robert Dankoff et al. (Istanbul, 1996–2007), vol. 1, p. 251.
9 Baudier, Michel, *The History of the Imperial Estate of the Grand Seigneurs: Their*

Habitations, Lives, Titles, Qualities, Exercises, Workes, Revenewes, Habit, Discent, Ceremonies, Magnificence, Judgments, Officers, Favourites, Religion, Power, Government and Tyranny (London, 1635), p. 141.

10 Pakalın, *Osmanlı Tarih Deyimleri*, vol. 2, p. 281, 'Kilâr-ı Âmire'.

11 Evliyâ Çelebi (1996–2007), vol. 1, p. 251.

12 Walsh, Robert, *Constantinople and the Seven Churches of Asia Minor*, 2 vols (London, n.d. [c. 1840]), vol. 1, p. 30.

13 Ahmed Refik. *Onikinci Asr-ı Hicrî'de Istanbul Hayatı (1689–1785)* (Istanbul, 1988), p. 219.

14 *Bostancı*. Although the Bostancı Corps were originally palace gardeners, they came to serve in many other capacities, such as guards and policing the Bosphorus.

15 Evliyâ Çelebi (1996–2007), vol. 1, p. 251.

16 'Türk Kültüründe Kar, Buz, Dondurma', *Uysal-Walker Archive of Turkish Oral Narrative*, Texas Technical University, http://aton.ttu.edu/Turk_kulturunde.asp.

17 'Türk Kültüründe Kar, Buz, Dondurma'.

18 Peyssonnel, Claude Charles de, 'Strictures and Remarks on the Preceding Memoirs', in Baron François de Tott, *Memoirs of the Turks and Tatars*, 2 vols (London and Dublin, 1785), vol. 2, Part 4, p. 203.

19 Konyalı, İbrahim Hakkı, 'Yeni Cami Kapılarında Halka Bal Şerbeti Dağıtılırdı', *Tarih Hazinesi*, 1 (15 November 1950), p. 23.

20 David, Elizabeth, *Harvest of the Cold Months: The Social History of Ice and Ices* (London, 1996), p. 41. Translation by Elizabeth David from the French of Pierre Belon, *Les Observations de plusieurs singularitez et choses memorables . . .* (Paris, 1553), pp. 417–19.

21 Rauwolff, Leonhart, 'Dr. Leonhart Rauwolff's Itinerary into the Eastern Countries, as Syria, Palestine, or the Holy Land, Armenia, Mesopotamia, Assyria, Chaldea Etc.', tr. Nicholas Staphorst, in John Ray (ed.) *A Collection of Curious Travels and Voyages* (London, 1693), p. 95.

22 Burbury, John, *A Relation of a Journey of the Right Honourable My Lord Henry Howard from London to Vienna and thence to Constantinople* (London, 1671), p. 137.

23 Buckingham, James Silk, *Travels in Mesopotamia. Including a Journey from Aleppo to Baghdad, by the Route of Beer, Orfah, Diarbekr, Mardin and Mousul*, 2 vols (London, 1827), vol. 1, p. 153.

24 The fifteenth-century Turkish physician Celâlüddin Hızır recommends drinking snow water to strengthen the stomach, see Celâlüddin Hızır (Hacı Paşa), *Müntahab-ı Şifâ*, ed. Zafer Önler, (Ankara, 1990), p. 89. Another early fifteenth-century physician, İbn-i Şerif, recommends water chilled with ice and snow for gynaecological complaints.

25 Buckingham, *Travels in Mesopotamia*, vol. 1, p. 149.

26 Walsh, Robert, *Constantinople and the Seven Churches of Asia Minor*, 2 vols (London, n.d. [c. 1840]), vol. 1, pp. 30, 33; White, Charles, *Three Years in Constantinople or, Domestic Manners of The Turks in 1844*, 3 vols (London, 1845–6), vol. 2, p. 14.

27 Walsh, *Constantinople and the Seven Churches*, vol. 1, p. 33.

28 *Economist*, 'Before Fridges: The Ice Trade', *Economist*, 21 December 1991–3 January 1992, pp. 71–2.
29 Schafer, Edward H., *The Golden Peaches of Samarkand, A Study of T'ang Exotics* (Low Angeles and Berkeley, 1985), p. 120.
30 *Economist*, 'Before Fridges', pp. 71–2.
31 Toussaint-Samat, Maguelonne, *History of Food*, tr. Anthea Bell (Massachusetts, 2000), pp. 749–50; Dumas, Alexandre, *Dumas on Food*, tr. Alan Davidson and Jane Davidson (London, 1979), p. 146.
32 Forbes, Robert James, *Studies in Ancient Technology*, vol. 2, (Leiden, 1964), p. 116. At a later date the double-compartmental amphora type *psycter* was replaced by a jar with a tall cylindrical foot which was placed inside a krater filled with snow or cold water.
33 Abdülaziz Bey, *Osmanlı Âdet, Merasim ve Tabirleri*, eds Kâzım Arısan and Duygu Arısan Günay, 2 vols (Istanbul, 1995), vol. 2, p. 460.
34 Kaşgarlı Mahmud, *Divanü Lûgat-it-Türk Tercümesi*, 4 vols, tr. Besim Atalay (Ankara, 1985–6), vol. 1, pp. 141, 467.
35 Schafer, *The Golden Peaches of Samarkand*, p. 119.
36 White, *Three Years in Constantinople*, vol. 2, p. 14.
37 'Türk Arşivlerinden', *Tarih Hazinesi*, 2 (1 December 1950), p. 100.
38 *Economist*, 'Before Fridges', pp. 71–2.
39 Evliyâ Çelebi (1996–2007), vol. 9, p. 281.
40 www.nichols.edu/departments/glacier/iceworm.htm.
41 Toussaint-Samat, *History of Food*, p. 749.
42 Schafer, *The Golden Peaches of Samarkand*, p. 168; David, *Harvest of the Cold Months*, pp. 227–8.
43 *Larousse Gastronomique* (London, 1988), pp. 662–3.
44 David, *Harvest of the Cold Months*, pp. 47, 168.
45 Ahmed Câvid, *Tercüme-i Kenzü'l-İştihâ*, eds Seyit Ali Kahraman and Priscilla Mary Işın (Istanbul, 2006), p. 152; Charles Perry, personal communication, 6 June 2006.
46 'Türk Kültüründe Kar, Buz, Dondurma'.
47 Hanım Özdağ of Göle, personal communication, 23 February 2006.
48 Schafer, *The Golden Peaches of Samarkand*, p. 168. The Chinese stored ice and chilled beverages in ice pools, but there is no evidence that they made ice cream or water ices.
49 Abu al-Fazl, *Ain-i Akbarî* (http://persian.packhum.org/persian/main), vol. 2, ch. 134.
50 Achaya, K.T., *Indian Food: A Historical Companion*, 4th edn (Delhi, 2005), p. 116. Although Achaya says the *Ain-i-Akbari* written in 1590 describes making ice cream, none of the recipes in the section on the imperial kitchen bears such an interpretation. Also see Tannahill, Reay, *Food in History* (New York, 1973), p. 314; Davidson, Alan, *The Oxford Companion to Food*, 1st edn (Oxford, 1999), p. 393.
51 Mehmed Kâmil, *Melceü't-Tabbâhîn*, 1st edn, (Istanbul, 1844), p. 123.
52 David, Elizabeth, 'The Harvest of Cold Months', *Petits Propos Culinaires*, 3 (November 1979), p. 15.

53 David, Elizabeth, 'Fromages Glacés and Iced Creams', *Petits Propos Culinaires*, 2 (August 1979), p. 28.

54 David, *Harvest of the Cold Months*, pp. 25ff.

55 Hubbard, G.E., *The Day of the Crescent: Glimpses of Old Turkey* (Cambridge, 1920), p. 57.

56 Even this term could be misleading, since *dondurma* was also used for savoury jelly dishes made with calves' feet.

57 Unger, Friedrich, *A King's Confectioner in the Orient*, ed. Priscilla Mary Işın, tr. Merete Çakmak and Renate Ömeroğulları (London, 2003), p. 87.

58 Mehmed Kâmil, *Melceü't-Tabbâhîn*, p. 119 (margin).

59 Ayşe Fahriye, *Ev Kadını* (Istanbul, AH 1300/1882–3), pp. 300–1; Hadiye Fahriye, *Tatlıcıbaşı* (Istanbul, AH 1342/1926), p. 187.

60 Mahmud Nedim bin Tosun, *Aşçıbaşı* (Istanbul AH 1317/1900), p. 230.

61 Ayşe Fahriye, *Ev Kadını*, pp. 300–1.

62 David, 'Fromages Glacés', p. 32; Davidson, *The Oxford Companion to Food*, p. 392.

63 David, 'Fromages Glacés', p. 32.

64 Ayşe Fahriye, *Ev Kadını*, p. 301.

65 Hadiye Fahriye, *Tatlıcıbaşı*, pp. 188–9.

66 White, *Three Years in Constantinople*, vol. 2, pp. 13–16.

67 Blackwood, Lady Alicia, *A Narrative of Personal Experiences and Impressions During a Residence on the Bosphorus throughout the Crimean War* (London, 1881), p. 199.

68 Mahmud Nedim, *Aşçıbaşı*, p. 159.

69 McGee, Harold, *On Food and Cooking: The Science and Lore of the Kitchen* (London, 1992), p. 26.

Bibliography

Abdülaziz Bey, *Osmanlı Âdet, Merasim ve Tabirleri*, eds Kâzım Arısan and Duygu Arısan Günay, 2 vols (Istanbul, 1995).

Abdurrahman Şeref, 'Topkapı Saray-ı Hümâyûn', *Tarih-i Osmanî Encümeni Mecmuası* (Istanbul, AH 1328–9/1910–11).

Abu al-Fazl, *Ain-i Akbarî*, http://persian.packhum.org/persian/main.

Achaya, K.T., *Indian Food: A Historical Companion*, 4th edn. (Delhi, 2005).

Acton, Eliza, *Modern Cookery for Private Families* (East Sussex, 1993).

Ahmed Câvid, *Tercüme-i Kenzü'l-İştihâ*, eds Seyit Ali Kahraman and Priscilla Mary Işın (Istanbul, 2006).

Ahmed Cevat Paşa, *Târîh-i Askerî-i Osmanî*, vol. 1 (Istanbul, AH 1297/1880).

Ahmed Refik, *Onuncu Asr-ı Hicrî'de Istanbul Hayatı (1495–1591)* (Istanbul, 1988).

—— *Onbirinci Asr-ı Hicrî'de Istanbul Hayatı (1592–1688)* (Istanbul, 1988).

—— *Onikinci Asr-ı Hicrî'de Istanbul Hayatı (1689–1785)* (Istanbul, 1988).

—— *Eski Istanbul* (Istanbul, 1931).

Ahmed Şevket, *Aşçı Mektebi* (Istanbul, AH 1341/1925).

Akarca, Döndü, 'Şitâiyyelerde Sosyal Yaşantı', *Çukurova Üniversitesi Sosyal Bilimler Enstitüsü Dergisi*, 14/1 (2005), pp. 1–13.

Akbayar, Nuri, *Osmanlı Yer Adları Sözlüğü* (Istanbul, 2001).

Akgündüz, Ahmet, *Osmanlı Kanunnameleri ve Hukukî Tahlilleri*, vol. 2 (Istanbul, 1990).

Aksoy, Ömer Asım, *Atasözleri ve Deyimler Sözlüğü*, 3 vols (Ankara, 1971).

Alarcón, Claudia, 'Tamales in Mesoamerica: Food for Gods and Mortals', *Petits Propos Culinaires*, 63 (December 1999), pp. 15–34.

Algar, Ayla Esen, 'Bektaşilik'te Yemeğin Yeri', *İkinci Milletlerarası Yemek Kongresi, 3–10 Eylül 1988* (Ankara, 1989), pp. 22–3.

—— 'Bushaq of Shiraz: Poet, Parasite and Gastronome', *Petits Propos Culinaires*, 31 (March 1989), pp. 9–20.

Ali Rıza (Balıkhane Nazırı), *Bir Zamanlar İstanbul*, ed. Niyazi Ahmet Banoğlu (Istanbul, n.d.).

—— *Eski Zamanlarda İstanbul Hayatı*, ed. Ali Şükrü Çoruk (Istanbul, 2001).

Altınay, Ahmed Refik, *Lâle Devri*, ed. Haydar Ali Diriöz (Ankara, 1973).

Alus, Sermet Muhtar, *Istanbul Yazıları*, eds Erol Sadi Erdinç and Faruk Ilıkan (Istanbul, 1994).

Amicis, Edmondo de, *Constantinople*, 2 vols, tr. Maria Hornor Lansdale (Philadelphia, 1896).

And, Metin, *Osmanlı Şenliklerinde Türk Sanatları* (Ankara, 1982).

Anderson, E.N., 'The Yin-Shan Cheng-Yao and the West: Central Asian Components in China's Foodways', paper, Sixth International Conference on the History of Science in China, Cambridge, England, 1990.

Anderson, E.N., Paul D. Buell and Charles Perry, *A Soup for the Qan* (London, 2000).

Andrew, Malcolm, *The Canterbury Tales: The General Prologue* (Oklahoma, 1993).

Anonymous, 'An Account of the Method of Preparing and Refining Sugar', *Gentleman's and London Magazine* (Dublin, 1788), pp. 406–8.

Anonymous, 'The Latest Novelty for Dessert, Genuine Rahat Lakoum, A Delicious Turkish Sweetmeat Imported from Turkey by Krikorian Bros', pamphlet, 1878, British Library, Evan.7548.

Antakya Mutfağı (Antakya, 1990).

Apicius: The Roman Cookery Book, tr. Barbara Flower and Elisabeth Rosenbaum (London, 1958).

Appleby, Mrs, *Yorkshire Cookery* (Lancaster, 1971).

Arabacıyan, Mihran, *Miftâhü't-Tabbâhîin* (Istanbul, 1876).

Arlı, Mine, 'Türk Mutfağına Genel Bir Bakış', *Türk Mutfağı Sempozyumu Bildirileri* (Ankara, 1982), pp. 19–34.

Arndt, Alice, 'Saffron: The Festive Spice', *Üçüncü Milletlerarası Yemek Kongresi, 7–12 Eylül 1990* (Ankara, n.d.), pp. 34–7.

Aryal, Achyut, 'A Report on Status and Distribution of Himalayan Musk Deer Moschus Chrysogaster in Annapurna Conservation Area of Manang District, Nepal', 2005, report to ITNC, UK, at www.itnc.org/FinalReportonMuskdeerManang.pdf.

Atasoy, Nurhan, *Hasbahçe: Osmanlı Kültüründe Bahçe ve Çiçek* (Istanbul, 2002).

Auldjo, John, *Journal of a Visit to Constantinople* (London, 1835).

Ayşe Fahriye, *Ev Kadını* (Istanbul, AH 1300/1882–3).

Bacon, Francis, *The Works of Francis Bacon*, 2 vols, ed. James Spedding (Cambridge, 1857).

Baillie, E.C.C., *A Sail to Smyrna: Or, An Englishwoman's Journal including Impressions of Constantinople, a Visit to a Turkish Harem and a Railway Journey to Ephesus* (London, 1873).

Baoliang, Zhang, 'Musk-deer, Their Capture, Domestication and Care According to Chinese Experience and Methods', *Unasylva*, 35/139 (1983), pp. 16–18, www.fao.org/docrep/q1093e/q1093e02.htm.

Barkan, Lütfi Ömer, 'Fatih Cami ve İmareti Tesislerinin 1489–1490 Yıllarına ait Muhasebe Bilançoları', *İktisat Fakültesi Mecmuası*, 23/1–2 (October 1962, February 1963) pp. 297–341.

—— 'Saray Mutfağının 894–895 (1489–1490) Yılına ait Muhasebe Bilançosu', *İktisat Fakültesi Mecmuası*, 23/1–2 (October 1962, February 1963), pp. 380–98.

—— 'İstanbul Saraylarına ait Muhasebe Defterleri', *Belgeler*, 12/13 (1979), pp. 1–380.

Baudier, Michel, *The History of the Imperial Estate of the Grand Seigneurs: Their Habitations, Lives, Titles, Qualities, Exercises, Workes, Revenewes, Habit, Discent,*

Ceremonies, Magnificence, Judgments, Officers, Favourites, Religion, Power, Government and Tyranny (London, 1635).

Baylav, Naşid, *Eczacılık Tarihi* (Istanbul, 1968).

Bayramoğlu, Fuat, 'Türk Mutfağı ve Yazılı Kaynaklar', *Birinci Milletlerarasi Yemek Kongresi, Türkiye, 25–30 Eylül 1986* (Ankara, 1988), pp. 38–49.

Baytop, Turhan, *Türkiye'nin Tıbbî ve Zehirli Bitkileri* (Istanbul, 1963).

—— *Türkçe Bitki Adları Sözlüğü* (Ankara, 1994).

—— *Türkiye'de Bitkilerle Tedavi*, 2nd edn (Istanbul, 1999).

Beal, Samuel (tr.), *Si-Yu- Ki, Buddhist Records of the Western World*, 2 vols (London, 1906).

Beeton, Isabella, *Beeton's Book of Household Management*, facsimile edn (London, 1968).

Bell, James Stanislaus, *Journal of a Residence in Circassia during the years 1837, 1838 and 1839*, 2 vols (London, 1840).

Bilgin, Arif, 'Seçkin Mekanda Seçkin Damaklar: Osmanlı Sarayında Beslenme Alışkınlıkları (15.–17. Yüzyıl)', in M. Sabri Koz (ed.), *Yemek Kitabı: Tarih – Halkbilimi – Edebiyat* (Istanbul, 2002), pp. 35–75.

—— *Osmanlı Saray Mutfağı* (Istanbul, 2004).

Blackwood, Lady Alicia, *A Narrative of Personal Experiences and Impressions During a Residence on the Bosphorus throughout the Crimean War* (London, 1881).

Blount, Sir Henry, *A Voyage into the Levant* (London, 1636).

Blunt, Lady Fanny Janet, *The People of Turkey, Twenty Years Residence among Bulgarians, Greeks, Albanians, Turks and Armenians*, 2 vols, ed. Stanley Lane Poole (London, 1878).

Bodenheimer, F.S., *Insects as Human Food* (The Hague, 1951).

Bradley, Mary Emily, *Douglass Farm: A Juvenile Story of Life in Virginia* (New York, 1858).

Brehm, Alfred Edmund, *De Ryggradslösa Djurens Lif* (Stockholm, 1882–8), http://runeberg.org/brehm/ryggrad/0165.html.

Brockhaus' Konverssationslexikon (Leipzig, Berlin and Vienna, 1894–6), www.retrobibliothek.de/retrobib/seite.html?id=131092.

Brocquière, Bertrandon de la, 'The Travels of Bertrandon de la Brocquière 1432, 1433', in Thomas Wright (ed.), *Early Travels in Palestine* (London, n.d.), pp. 283–382.

—— *The Travels of Bertrandon de la Brocquiere, Counsellor and First Esquire – Carver to Philippe le Bon, Duke of Burgundy, to Palestine, and his Return from Jerusalem Overland to France, During the Years 1432 and 1433*, tr. Thomas Johnes (Hafod Uchtryd, 1807).

Bruslons, Jacques Savary des, *Dictionnaire Universel de Commerce*, 3 vols (Paris, 1742).

Bruyn, Corneille le, *A Voyage to the Levant* (London, 1702).

Buckingham, James Silk, *Travels in Mesopotamia: Including a Journey from Aleppo to Baghdad, by the Route of Beer, Orfah, Diarbekr, Mardin and Mousul*, 2 vols (London, 1827).

Buell, Paul D., 'Mongol Empire and Turkicization: The Evidence of Food and Foodways', in Reuven Amitai-Preiss and David O. Morgan (eds), *The Mongol Empire and its Legacy* (Leiden, Boston and Cologne, 1999), pp. 200–23.

—— 'Steppe Foodways and History', *Asian Medicine*, 2/2 (2006), pp. 171–203.

Büngül, Nurettin Rüştü, *Eski Eserler Ansiklopedisi*, 2 vols (Istanbul, n.d.).

Burbury, John, *A Relation of a Journey of the Right Honourable My Lord Henry Howard from London to Vienna and thence to Constantinople* (London, 1671).

Burder, Samuel, *Oriental Literature Applied to the Illustration of the Sacred Scriptures*, 2 vols (London, 1822).

Burnaby, Frederick, *On Horseback through Asia Minor* (Gloucester, 1985).

Burton, Richard F., *The Book of the Thousand Nights and a Night*, 11 vols (London, 1885).

Busbecq, Ogier Ghiselin de, *The Turkish Letters of Ogier Ghiselin de Busbecq Imperial Ambassador at Constantinople 1554–1562*, tr. Edward Seymour Forster (Oxford, 1927).

Çağrı (Kültür Sanat Bilim Dergisi), 36/394 (September 1992).

Cassell's Dictionary of Cookery (London, Paris and New York, n.d. [nineteenth century]).

Celâl Paşa, *Şurup İmalâtı* (Istanbul, AH 1309/1891).

Celâlüddin Hızır (Hacı Paşa), *Müntahab-ı Şifâ*, ed. Zafer Önler (Ankara, 1990).

Çelebioğlu, Âmil (ed.), *Ramazannâme* (Istanbul, n.d.).

Cerrahoğlu, Abdurrahman, *Sofra Nimetleri* (Istanbul, 1996).

Çetin, Cengiz, 'Türk Düğün Gelenekleri ve Kutsal Evlilik Ritüeli', *Ankara Üniversitesi Dil ve Tarih-Coğrafya Fakültesi Dergisi*, 48/2 (2008), pp. 111–26.

Chambers Encyclopaedia, 10 vols (London, 1874–80).

Chandler, Richard, *Travels in Asia Minor and Greece*, 2 vols, 3rd edn (London, 1817).

Charlemont, James Caulfeild (fourth Viscount Charlemont), *The Travels of Lord Charlemont in Greece and Turkey*, eds W.B. Stanford and E.J. Finopoulos (London, 1984).

Childs, W., *Across Asia Minor on Foot* (New York and London, 1917).

Çığ, Muazzez İlmiye, *Kuran İncil ve Tevrat'ın Sumer'deki Kökeni* (Istanbul, 2006).

Çıkla, Fatma, *Çukurova Yemekleri* (Istanbul, 1998).

Clarke, Edward Daniel, *Travels in Various Countries of Europe, Asia and Africa* (New York, 1970).

Clavijo, Ruy Gonzalez de, *Embassy to Tamerlane 1403–1406* (London, 1928).

Coke, Thomas, 'A True Narrative of the Great Solemnity of the Circumcision of Mustapha, Prince of Turky, Eldest Son of Mahomet, Present Emperor of the Turks: Together with an Account of the Marriage of his Daughter to his Great Favourite Mussaip, at Adrianople, as it Was Sent in a Letter to a Person of Honour: by Mr Coke, Secretary of the Turky Company, Being in Company with his Excellency the Lord Ambassador Sir John Finch', in *Harleian Miscellany*, vol. 5 (London, 1676), pp. 365–6.

Columella, Lucius Junius Moderatus, *Of Husbandry* (London, 1745).

Covel, John, 'Dr. Covel's Diary (1670–1679)', in J. Theodore Bent (ed.), *Early Voyages and Travels in the Levant* (London, 1893), pp. 101–287.

Culpeper, Nicholas, *Culpeper's Complete Herbal* (Ware, 1995).

Cunbur, Müjgân, 'Mevlânâ'nın Mesnevi'sinde ve Divan-ı Kebir'inde Yemekler', *Türk Mutfağı Sempozyumu Bildirileri* (Ankara, 1982), pp. 69–85.

Dağlı, Hikmet Turhan, 'Istanbul'da Şekercilik', *Halk Bilgisi Haberleri* (May 1936), p. 112.

Davey, Richard, *The Sultan and his Subjects*, 2nd edn (London, 1907).

David, Elizabeth, *English Bread and Yeast Cookery* (London, 1978).

—— 'Hunt the Ice Cream', *Petits Propos Culinaires*, 1 (1979), pp. 8–13.

——'Fromages Glacés and Iced Creams', *Petits Propos Culinaires*, 2 (August 1979), pp. 23–35.

—— 'The Harvest of Cold Months', *Petits Propos Culinaires*, 3 (November 1979), pp. 9–16.

—— *Harvest of the Cold Months: The Social History of Ice and Ices* (London, 1996).

Davidson, Alan, *The Oxford Companion to Food*, 1st edn (Oxford, 1999).

—— *The Oxford Companion to Food*, 2nd edn (Oxford, 2006).

Davis, Edwin John, *Anatolica, or the Journal of a Visit to Some of the Ancient Ruined Cities of Caria, Phrygia, Lycia, and Pisidia* (London, 1874).

—— *Life in Asiatic Turkey. A Journal of Travel in Cilicia (Pedias and Trachoea), Isauria, and Parts of Lycaonia and Cappadocia* (London, 1879).

Day, Ivan, 'The Art of Confectionery', www.historicfood.com/The%20Art%20of%20 Confectionery.pdf.

—— 'Bridecup and Cake', in Laura Mason (ed.), *Food and the Rites of Passage* (Totnes, 2002).

De Kay, James Ellsworth, *Sketches of Turkey in 1831 and 1832* (New York, 1833).

Demirhan, Ayşegül, *Mısır Çarşısı Droglar ı* (Istanbul, 1974).

Dernschwam, Hans, *Tabebuch Einer Reise Nach Konstantinopel und Kleinasien (1553–1555)*, ed. Franz Babinger (Munich and Leipzig, 1923).

—— *Istanbul ve Anadolu'ya Seyahat Günlüğü*, tr. Yaşar Önen (Ankara, 1987).

Develi, Hayati (ed.), *Risâle-i Garîbe* (Istanbul, 2001).

Dickens, Charles, *Edwin Drood* (London, n.d. [1870]).

Dickie, John, *Delizia! The Epic History of the Italians and their Food* (New York, 2008).

Dispensatory of the United States of America, 1918, www.swsbm.com/Dispensatory/ USD-1918-complete.pdf.

Diyarbakır Mutfağı (Istanbul, 2003).

Doğanay, Mehmet, 'Bir Mekân Unsuru Olarak İstanbul'un Ahmed Midhat Efendinin Romanlarına Tesiri', *Dumlupınara Üniversitesi Sosyal Bilimler Dergisi*, 15 (August 2006), pp. 95–108.

Donkin, R.A., *Manna: An Historical Geography* (The Hague, 1980).

Dufferin and Ava, Harriet Georgina Blackwood, Dowager Marchioness of, *My Russian and Turkish Journals* (London, 1916).

Duhanî, Said Naum, *Beyoğlu'nun adı Pera iken*, tr. Nihal Önol (Istanbul, 1990).

Dumas, Alexandre, *Dumas on Food*, tr. Alan Davidson and Jane Davidson (London, 1979).

Dünden Bugüne İstanbul Ansiklopedisi, 8 vols (Istanbul, 1993).

Edebiyat Ansiklopedisi (Istanbul, 1991).

Economist, 'Before Fridges: The Ice Trade', 21 December 1991–3 January 1992, pp. 71–2.

Encyclopaedia Britannica, vol. 17 (Edinburgh, 1797).

Encyclopaedia of Islam, 2nd edn, 12 vols, eds P.J. Bearman, T. Bianquis, C.E. Bosworth, E. van Donzel, W.P. Heinrichs et al. (Leiden, 1960–2005).

Erevnidis, Pavlos, 'Yunanistan'da (veya Türkiye'de) Mutfak ve Yakovos Dizikirikis'in Dil Milliyetçiliği', *Yemek ve Kültür*, 3 (2005), pp. 38–52.

Ergin, Nina, Christoph K. Neumann and Amy Singer (eds), *Feeding People, Feeding Power: Imarets in the Ottoman Empire* (Istanbul, 2007).

Ergin, Osman, *Türk Dilinde Yanlış Anlamlı Kelimeler, Tabirler ve Yakıştırmalar Sözlüğü* (Istanbul, 1999).

Eton, William, *A Survey of the Turkish Empire* (London, 1799).

Evci, İsmail, *Kayseri ve Kayseri Sofrası* (Kayseri, n.d.).

Evliyâ Çelebi, *Evliyâ Çelebi Seyahatnâmesi*, 10 vols, eds Seyit Ali Kahraman, Yücel Dağlı, Robert Dankoff et al. (Istanbul, 1996–2007).

—— *Evliyâ Çelebi Seyahatnâmesi*, eds Robert Dankoff, Seyit Ali Kahraman and Yücel Dağlı, vol. 1, 2nd edn (Istanbul, 2006).

Felek, Burhan, *Geçmiş Zaman Olur ki* (Istanbul, 1985).

Fellows, Charles, *A Journal Written during an Excursion in Asia Minor* (London, 1838).

—— *An Account of Discoveries in Lycia* (London, 1841).

Felter, Harvey Wickes and John Uri Lloyd, *King's American Dispensatory*, 18th edn (1898), www.henriettesherbal.com/eclectic/kings.

Fisher, John, 'Gentleman Spies in Asia', *Asian Affairs*, 41/2 (2010), pp. 202–12.

Fluckiger, F.A., 'Notiz über die Eichenmanna von Kurdistan', *Archiv der Pharmacie*, 200 (1872), pp. 159–64.

Fontmagne, Baronne Durand de, *Un Séjour à l'Ambassade de France a Constantinople sous le Second Empire* (Paris, 1902).

—— *Kırım Harbi Sonrasında Istanbul*, tr. Gülçiçek Soytürk (Istanbul, 1977).

Forbes, Robert James, *Studies in Ancient Technology*, vol. 2 (Leiden, 1964).

Frazer, James George, *The Golden Bough* (London, 1924).

Galland, Antoine, *Journal d'Antoine Galland pendant son séjour à Constantinople (1672–1673)*, vol. 1, ed. Charles Schefer (Paris, 1881).

—— *Istanbul'a Ait Günlük Anılar (1672–3)*, tr. Nahid Sırrı Örik (Ankara, 1987).

Galloway, J.H., 'The Mediterranean Sugar Industry', *Geographical Review*, 67/2 (April 1977), pp. 177–94.

Garnett, Lucy, *The Women of Turkey and their Folklore*, 2 vols (London, 1893).

Gautier, Théophile, *Constantinople*, tr. F.C. de Sumichrast (New York, 1901).

Geerdes, Thomas, *Ana Besin Maddelerinden Şeker ve Tarihi*, tr. Cihad Gökdağ (Ankara, 1966).

Gerlach, Stephan, *Türkiye Günlüğü 1573-1576*, 2 vols (Istanbul, 2007).

Gökyay, Orhan Şaik, 'Kaygusuz Abdal'ın Sımâtiyeleri', *Türk Folkloru Dergisi*, 13 (August 1980), pp. 3–5; 14 (September 1980), pp. 3–6.

—— 'Sohbetnâme', *Tarih ve Toplum*, 3/14 (February 1985), pp. 56–64.

Göncüoğlu, Süleyman Faruk, 'İstanbul'un Fethi Sonrası Kurulan İlk Semt: Saraçhane', *Atatürk Üniversitesi Güzel Sanatlar Enstitüsü Dergisi*, 2009 (online journal, e-dergi. atauni.edu.tr/index.php/GSED/article/viewFile/2192/2191).

Gouffé, Jules, *Le Livre de patisserie* (Paris 1867).

—— *The Book of Preserves (Le Livre de conserves)*, tr. Alphonse Gouffé (London, 1871).

—— *Le Livre de patisserie* (Paris, 1873).

Grieve, M., *A Modern Herbal* (1931), www.botanical.com/botanical/mgmh/mgmh. html.

Gülhan, Abdülkerim, 'Divan Şiirinde Meyveler ve Meyvelerden Hareketle Yapılan Teşbih ve Mecazlar', *Turkish Studies: International Periodical for the Languages, Literature and History of Turkish or Turkic*, 3/5 (2008), pp. 353–75.

Gürpınar, Hüseyin Rahmi, *Eti Senin Kemiği Benim*, 2nd edn (Istanbul, 1973).

Güzel, Abdurrahman, 'Türk Kültürü'nde Mevlid ve Yoğ Gelenekleri Etrafında Teşekkül Eden Folklorik Unsurlar', *Üçüncü Milletlerarası Yemek Kongresi, 7–12 Eylül 1990* (Ankara, n.d.), pp. 80–93.

Güzelbey, Cemil Cahit, 'Gaziantep'e Özgü Yemekler', *Türk Mutfağı Sempozyumu Bildirileri* (Ankara, 1982), pp. 87–103.

Hacıbeyzâde Ahmed Muhtar, *Aşevi – Aşçılık, Beyne'l-milel Sofracılık* (Istanbul, AH 1332/1916–17).

Hadiye Fahriye, *Tatlıcıbaşı* (Istanbul, AH 1342/1926).

Hâfız Hızır İlyas Ağa, *Tarih-i Enderun – Letaif-i Enderun*, ed. Cahit Kayra (Istanbul, 1987).

Hâfız Mehmed Efendi, *1720, Şehzadelerin Sünnet Düğünü*, ed. Seyit Ali Kahraman (Istanbul, 2008).

Halıcı, Feyzi, 'Mevlana'nın Eserlerinde Yemek ve Mutfak İmajı', *Birinci Milletlerarasi Yemek Kongresi, 25–30 Eylül 1986* (Ankara, 1988), pp. 114–18.

—— (ed.), *Ali Eşref Dede'nin Yemek Risalesi* (Ankara, 1992).

Halıcı, Nevin, 'Konya Düğün Yemeği', *Üçüncü Milletlerarası Yemek Kongresi, 7–12 Eylül 1990* (Ankara, n.d.), pp. 196–8.

—— 'Antalya'da Yemek ile İlgili Töreler ve Antalya Yemekleri', *Geleneksel Türk Yemekleri ve Beslenme (Geleneksel Türk Mutfağı Sempozyumu Bildirileri, 10–11 Eylül 1982)* (Konya, 1982), pp. 165–87.

—— *Akdeniz Bölgesi Yemekleri* (Konya, 1983).

Hamamîzâde İhsan, *Hamsinâme* (Istanbul, 1928).

Hammer-Purgstall, Joseph von, *Devlet-i Osmaniye Tarihi*, 10 vols (Istanbul, AH 1329/1917).

Hanbury, Daniel, *Science Papers, Chiefly Pharmacological and Botanical* (London, 1876).

Hançerlioğlu, Orhan, *İslâm İnançları Sözlüğü*, 3rd edn (Istanbul, 2000).

Harlan, Jack R., 'A Wild Wheat Harvest in Turkey', *Archaeology*, 20/3 (June 1967), pp 197–201.

Hartley, Dorothy, *Food in England* (London, 1996).

Hehn, Victor, *Cultivated Plants and Domestic Animals in their Migration from Asia to Europe*, ed. James Steven Stallybrass (London, 1891).

Hensel Sebastian, *The Mendelssohn Family (1729–1847) from Letters and Journals* (New York, 1882).

Hieatt, Constance B. and Sharon Butler, *Curye on Inglysch* (London, 1985).

Hill, Aaron, *The Present State of the Turkish Empire* (London, n.d. [1740]) (first published in 1709 as *A History of the Ottoman Empire*).

Houghton, John, *Husbandry and Trade Improv'd: Being a Collection of Many Valuable Materials Relating to Corn, Cattle, Coals, Hops, Wool, etc.*, vol. 4 (London, 1728).

Hubbard, G.E., *The Day of the Crescent: Glimpses of Old Turkey* (Cambridge, 1920).

Hughes, William R., *A Week's Tramp in Dickens-land* (London, 1891).

Humphrey, John William, John Peter Oleson and Andrew Neil Sherwood, *Greek and Roman technology: A Sourcebook* (London, 1998).

Işın, Priscilla Mary, 'A Nineteenth Century Ottoman Gentleman's Cookbook', *Petits Propos Culinaires*, 61 (May 1999), pp. 30–7.

—— 'Kudret Helvası Göklerden Yağıyor mu?', IX. *Türk Tıp tarihi Kongresi Bildirileri*, eds Esin Kahya, Sevgi Şar, Adnan Ataç and Mümtaz Mazıcıoğlu (Ankara, 2006), pp. 261–71.

—— 'Şıhlar Köyü'nün Ballı Külük Helvası', *Ballı Yazılar*, ed. Nilhan Aras (Istanbul, 2010), pp. 307–13.

—— *Osmanlı Mutfak Sözlüğü* (Istanbul, 2010).

Ibn Battuta, *The Travels of Ibn Battuta*, tr. H.A.R. Gibb (London, 1962).

İbn-i Şerif, *Yâdigâr, 15. Yüzyıl Türkçe Tıp Kitabı*, 2 vols, eds Ayten Altıntaş, Yahya Okutan, Doğan Koçer and Mecit Yıldız (Istanbul, 2003 and 2004).

İleri, Selim, *Oburcuk Mutfakta* (Istanbul, 2010).

İslam Ansiklopedisi, 13 vols (Eskişehir, 2001).

İşli, H. Necdet, 'Kâdirîhâne'de Aşûre', in M. Sabri Koz (ed.), *Yemek Kitabı: Tarih, Halkbilim, Edebiyatı* (Istanbul, 2002).

İvgin, Hayrettin, 'Bazı Halk Şiirlerimizde Yemeklerimiz', *Türk Mutfağı Sempozyumu Bildirileri* (Ankara, 1982), pp. 235–43.

—— 'Geleneksel Bir Türk Tatlısı: Pelte', *Geleneksel Türk Tatlıları Bildirileri Sempozyumu* (Ankara, 1984), pp. 77–85.

Jarrin, G.A., *The Italian Confectioner*, 3rd edn (London, 1827).

Johnson, Maria, 'Notes on Turkish Contributions to Balkan Flour Confectionery', *Birinci Milletlerarası Yemek Kongresi, 25–30 Eylül 1986* (Ankara, 1988), pp. 153–62.

Kalafat, Yaşar, *Balkanlardan Uluğ Türkistan'a Türk Halk İnançları II* (Ankara, 2005).

Kalças, Evelyn Lyle, *Food from the Fields* (İzmir, 1984).

Kaneva-Johnson, Maria, 'Boiled Wheat and Aşure', *Petits Propos Culinaires*, 5 (May 1980), pp. 67–9.

—— *The Melting Pot, Balkan Food and Cookery* (Totnes, 1999).

Karagöz Matbahda (Istanbul, AH 1329/1913).

Karay, Refik Halid, *Üç Nesil Üç Hayat* (Istanbul, 1943).

Kaşgarlı Mahmud, *Divanü Lûgat-it-Türk Tercümesi*, 4 vols, tr. Besim Atalay (Ankara, 1985–6).

—— *Divânü Lugâti't-Türk*, eds Seçkin Erdi and Serap Tuğba Yurteser (Istanbul, 2005).

Kazancıgil, Ratip, *Edirne Helva Sohbetleri ve Kış Gecesi Eğlenceleri* (Edirne, 1993).

Kesnin Bey [Eugène Chesnel], *The Evil of the East, or Truths about Turkey* (London, 1888).

Kırby, William and William Spence, *Introduction to Entomology* (Philadelphia, 1846).

Koçu, Reşat Ekrem, *Tarihimizde Garip Vakalar* (Istanbul, 1952).

—— *İstanbul Ansiklopedisi*, 10 vols (Istanbul, 1958–73).

Kolak, Cevat, *Tatlılar – Pastalar Yemekler* (Istanbul, n.d.).

Konyalı, İbrahim Hakkı, 'Yeni Cami Kapılarında Halka Bal Şerbeti Dağıtılırdı', *Tarih Hazinesi*, 1 (15 November 1950), pp. 21–3, 48.

Koşay, Hâmit and Akile Ülkücan, *Anadolu Yemekleri ve Türk Mutfağı* (Ankara, 1961).

Koz, M. Sabri 'Konya'da Bir Cevelan', *Güney'de Kültür*, 48 (February 1993), pp. 23–8.

—— (ed.), *Yemek Kitabı: Tarih, Halkbilim, Edebiyatı* (Istanbul, 2002).

Kömürciyan, Eremya Çelebi, *Istanbul Tarihi*, ed. Kevork Pamukciyan (Istanbul, 1988).

Kubilay, Ayşe Yetişkin, 'Nahıllar', *Skylife* (January 2002).

Kur'ân-ı Kerîm ve Türkçe Anlamı (Ankara, 1984).

Kurtoğlu, Orhan, 'Klasik Türk Şiirinde Saçı Geleneği', *Milli Folklor* 81 (2009), pp. 89–99.

Kut, Günay (ed.), *Et-Terkibât Fî Tabhi'l-Hülviyyât (Tatlı Pişirme Tarifleri)* (Ankara, 1986).

—— 'Türklerde Yeme-İçme Geleneği ve Kaynakları', in *Eskimeyen Tatlar* (Istanbul, 1996), pp. 38–71.

—— 'Meyve Bahçesi', *Journal of Turkish Studies: Festschrift in Honor of Eleazar Birnbaum*, 29 (2005), pp. 201–56.

Kut, Turgut, *Açıklamalı Yemek Kitapları Bibliyografyası (Eski Harfli Yazma ve Basma Eserler)* (Ankara, 1985).

—— '18. Yüzyılın İkinci Yarısında Hazırlanmış Bir Yemek Lügatı', *Birinci Milletlerarası Yemek Kongresi (Türkiye, 25–30 Eylül 1986)* (Ankara, 1988), pp. 181–5.

—— 'İstanbul'da Kâdirihâne Âsitânesinde 1906 Yılı Ramazan İftarları', *Dördüncü Milletlerarası Yemek Kongresi, Türkiye 3–6 Eylül 1992* (Konya, 1993), pp. 183–99.

Kürkman, Garo, *Anadolu Ağırlık ve Ölçüleri* (Istanbul, 2003).

Kütükoğlu, Mübahat S., *Osmanlılarda Narh Müessesi ve 1640 Tarihli Narh Defteri* (Istanbul, 1983).

Lacroix, Paul, *Manners, Customs, and Dress During the Middle Ages, and During the Renaissance Period* (Paris, 1874), www.archive.org/stream/mannerscustomand10940gut/10940.txt.

Lâmi'î Çelebi, *Şem' ü Pervâne* (Istanbul, 1522), Süleymaniye Library, Esat Efendi 2744, ff. 62v–82r.

Lane-Poole, Stanley, *Turkey* (London, 1892).

Larousse Gastronomique (London, 1990).

Lâtifî, *Evsâf-ı Istanbul*, ed. Nermin Suner (Pekin) (Istanbul, 1977).

Lear, Edward, *Journals of a Landscape Painter in Greece and Albania* (London, 1988).

Lecomte, Pretextat, *Türkiye'de Sanatlar ve Zeneatlar*, ed. Ayda Düz (Istanbul, n.d.).

—— *Les Arts et métiers de la Turquie et de l'Orient* (Paris, 1902).

Leslie, Eliza, *Directions for Cookery in its Various Branches*, 49th edn (Philadelphia, 1858).

Levey, Martin, Miroslav Krek and Husni Haddad, 'Some Notes on the Chemical Technology in an Eleventh Century Arabic Work on Bookbinding', *Isis*, 47/3 (September 1956), pp. 239–43.

Luard, Elisabeth, *European Peasant Cookery* (London, 1988).

Luke, Harry, *An Eastern Chequer Board* (London, 1934).

Lunde, Paul, 'Muslims and Muslim Technology in the New World', *Saudi Aramco World* (May–June 1992), pp. 38–41.

Macartney, Clement, 'The Deer with a Fatal Scent', *Unasylva*, 35 (1983), report written for the World Wildlife Fund, excerpts at www.fao.org/docrep/q1093e/q1093e03.htm.

MacBane, Gavan, *From Cane to Kitchen: An Investigation into Medieval Processed Sugar*, 2006, www.florilegium.org/files/FOOD-SWEETS/Cypriot-Sugr-art.html.

McCrindle, J.W., *Ancient India as described by Megasthenes and Arrian* (Calcutta, Bombay and London, 1877).

MacFarlane, Charles, *Constantinople in 1828* (London, 1829).

McGee, Harold, *On Food and Cooking, The Science and Lore of the Kitchen* (London, 1992).

McNair, James Birtley, *Sugar and Sugar-Making* (Chicago, 1927).

McNeill, Marion, *The Scots Kitchen* (London and Glasgow, 1929).

Mahmud al-Kāshgari, *Compendium of the Turkic Dialects (Dīwān Luyāt at-Turk)* 3 vols, ed. and tr. Robert Dankoff in collaboration with James Kelly (Cambridge, MA, 1984).

Mahmud Nedim bin Tosun, *Aşçıbaşı* (Istanbul, AH 1317/1900).

—— *Aşçıbaşı*, ed. Priscilla Mary Işın (Istanbul, 1998).

Maksetof, Kabil, 'Ebû Reyhan Beyrûnî ve Nevruz Hakkında', tr. Kudaybergen Elubaev, in Sadık Tural and Elmas Kılıç (eds), *Nevruz ve Renkler* (Ankara, 1996), pp. 269–73.

Maksudoğlu, Mehmet, 'Tatarlar Kimdir?', *Kalgay Dergisi*, 22 (October–December 2001), www.kalgaydergisi.org/index.php?sayfa=dergiicerik&sayi=22&kod=490.

Malatya Mutfağından (Malatya, n.d. [1990]).

March, Lourdes, 'Rice in Spanish Mediterranean Cooking', *İkinci Milletlerarası Yemek Kongresi, 3–10 Eylül 1988* (Konya, 1989), pp. 248–52.

Martin, Benjamin, *The General Magazine of Arts and Sciences*, 1 (1755).

Mason, Laura, *Sugar-Plums and Sherbet* (Totnes, 1998).

Maundrell, Henry, 'A Journey from Aleppo to Jerusalem at Easter A.D. 1697', in Thomas Wright (ed.), *Early Travels in Palestine* (London, 1848), pp. 383–512.

May, Robert, *The Accomplisht Cook* (Totnes, 2000).

Mayhew, Henry, *London Labour and the London Poor*, 3 vols (London, 1861).

Mehmed Kâmil, *Melceü't-Tabbâhîn*, 1st edn (Istanbul, 1844).

—— *Melceü't-Tabbâhîn*, 8th edn (Istanbul, AH 1290/1873).

—— *Melceü't-Tabbâhîn (Aşçıların Sığınağı)*, ed. Cüneyt Kut (Istanbul, 1997).

Mehmed Reşad, *Fenn-i Tabâhat*, 4 vols (Istanbul, AH 1340/1921-2).

Mehmed Tevfik, *İstanbul'da Bir Sene*, ed. Nuri Akbayar (Istanbul, 1991).

Meninski, Francisci a Mesgnien, *Lexicon Arabico Persico, Turcicum*, 4 vols (Vienna, 1780).

Mercer, Dr Henry C., 'Wafer Irons', *A Collection of Papers Read Before the Bucks County Historical Society*, vol. 5 (Pennsylvania, 1926), pp. 246–50.

Messisbugo, Cristoforo, *Banchetti, compositioni di vivande et apparecchio generale* (Ferrara, 1549).

Mevlânâ Celâleddin Rûmî, *Mesnevî*, 6 vols, tr. Veled İzbudak (Istanbul, 1990).

—— *Dîvân-ı Kebîr*, 4 vols, tr. Abdülbâki Gölpınarlı (Istanbul, 1957).

Meydan Larousse, 12 vols (Istanbul, 1969–73).

Miller, Barnette, *Beyond the Sublime Porte: The Grand Seraglio of Stambul* (New Haven, CT, 1931).

Millingen, Julius R. Van, *Turkey* (London, 1920).

Moltke, Helmuth von, *Türkiye Mektupları*, tr. Hayrullah Örs (Istanbul, 1969).

Mont, Sieur de, *A New Voyage to the Levant, 1691* (London, 1696).

Morris, Desmond, *Christmas Watching* (London, 1992).

Morton, H.V., *Middle East* (London, 1941).

Müller, Georgina Adelaide, *Letters from Constantinople* (London, 1897).

Musahipzâde Celâl, *Eski Istanbul Yaşayışı* (Istanbul, 1946).

Mustafa Ali of Gallipoli, *Ziyâfet Sofraları (Mevâidü'n-nefâis fî kavâidi'l mecâlis)*, 2 vols, ed. Orhan Şaik Gökyay (Istanbul, 1978).

—— *Hâlâtü'l-Kahire Mine'l-Âdâti'z-Zâhire*, ed. Orhan Şaik Gökyay (Ankara, 1984).

—— *Cami'u'l-buhur der Mecalis-i Sur*, ed. Ali Öztekin (Ankara, 1996).

Mütercim Âsım, *Burhân-ı Katı* (Ankara, 2000).

Nahya, Zümrüt, 'Geleneksel Türk Kültüründe Tatlı', *Geleneksel Türk Tatlıları Sempozyumu Bildirileri 17–18 Aralık 1983* (Ankara, 1984), pp. 91–6.

Nalbandoğlu, A., 'Nevruz ve Nevruziyye', *Tarih Hazinesi*, ed. İbrahim Hakkı Konyalı, 8 (15 November 1950), pp. 367–8, 414.

Nasrallah, Nawal, *Annals of the Caliph's Kitchens, Ibn Sayyâr al-Warrâq's Tenth-Century Bağhdadi Cookbook* (Leiden and Boston, 2007).

Nasrattınoğlu, İrfan Ünver, 'Afyonkarahisar Mutfağı', *Türk Mutfağı Sempozyumu Bildirileri* (Ankara, 1982), pp. 215–34.

Neave, Dorina Lockhart, *Twenty-six Years on the Bosphorus* (London, 1933).

Nerval, Gerard de, *Voyage en Orient*, 6th edn (Paris, 1862).

—— *Doğu'ya Seyahat*, tr. Muharrem Taşçıoğlu (Ankara, 1984).

Nesin, Aziz, *Böyle Gelmiş Böyle Gitmez 1: Yol*, 13th edn (Istanbul, 1998).

Nordegren, Thomas, *The A–Z Encyclopedia of Alcohol and Drug Abuse* (Florida, 2002).

Nostredame, Michel de (Nostradamus), *Excellent et moult utile opuscule à tous nécessaire qui désirent avoir connoissance de plusieurs exquises receptes, divisé en deux parties. La première traicte de diverses façons de fardemens et senteurs pour illustrer et embelir la face. La seconde nous montre la façon et manière de faire confitures de plusieurs sortes* (Lyon, 1555). English translations of extracts from the 1557 edition by Peter Lemeseurier (2000) are taken from www.propheties.it/nostradamus/1555opuscole/opuscole.html.

—— *The Elixirs of Nostradamus*, ed. Knut Boeser (Rhode Island and London, 1996).

Nott, John, *The Cook's and Confectioner's Dictionary* (London, 1723).

Nutku, Özdemir, *IV. Mehmet'in Edirne Şenliği 1675*, 2nd edn (Ankara, 1987).

Oberling, Gerry and Grace Martin Smith, *The Food Culture of the Ottoman Palace* (Istanbul, 2001).

Ögel, Bahaeddin, 'Türklerde Tatlı Anlayışı ve Şeker', *Geleneksel Türk Tatlıları Sempozyumu Bildirileri 17–18 Aralık 1983* (Ankara, 1984), pp. 17–20.

Oğuz, Burhan, *Türkiye Halkının Kültür Kökenleri*, vol. 1 (Beslenme Teknikleri) (Istanbul, 1976).

Ohsson, Ignatius Mouradgea de, *Tableau Genéral de l'Empire Ottoman*, 7 vols (Paris, 1791).

Olivier, G.A., *Travels in the Ottoman Empire, Egypt, and Persia Undertaken by Order of the Government of France, During the First Six Years of the Republic*, 2 vols (London, 1801).

Onay, Ahmet Talât, *Eski Türk Edebiyatında Mazmunlar ve İzahı*, ed. Cemal Kurnaz (Ankara, 2000).

Önder, Ali Rıza, 'Ürgüp Düğünlerinde Nahıl', *Türk Folklor Araştırmaları*, 83 (June 1956), pp. 1315–16.

Önder, Mehmet, *Mevlana, Hayatı-Eserleri* (Istanbul, n.d.).

—— 'Konya'da Tarih Boyunca Helvacılık', *Türk Folkloru Araştırmaları*, 1/11 (1950), pp. 159–60.

Önler, Zafer, *Müntahab-ı Şifa II Sözlük* (Istanbul, 1999).

Orgun, Zarif, 'Osmanlı Sarayında Yemek Yeme Adabı', *Türk Mutfağı Sempozyumu Bildirileri* (Ankara, 1982), pp. 139–51.

Orman Kanunu no. 6831, 1956, section 3, article 14.

'Osmanlı Toplum Yaşayışıyla İlgili Belgeler-Bilgiler: Esnaf Suç ve Cezaları', *Tarih ve Toplum*, 10 (October 1984).

Osmanoğlu, Ayşe, *Babam Sultan Abdülhamid* (Istanbul, 1984).

Oxford English Dictionary, CD-Rom version 3.01 (Oxford, 2002).

Özdeniz, B., *Alaturka-Alafranga 500 Yemek ve Tatlı Reçeteleri* (Istanbul, 1975).

Özen, Aysel, 'Tarihin İzleri ile İncesu Yemek Kültürü', unpublished manuscript (İncesu, 2006).

Özkan, Ömer, *Divan Şiirinin Penceresinden Osmanlı Toplum Hayatı (XIV–XV. Yüzyıl)* (Istanbul, 2007).

Özsabuncuoğlu, Özden, *Dört Mevsim Gaziantep Yemekleri* (Gaziantep, 2003).

Öztuna, Yılmaz, *Resimlerle Türkiye Tarihi* (Istanbul, 1970).

Pakalın, Mehmet Zeki, *Osmanlı Tarih Deyimleri ve Terimleri Sözlüğü*, 3 vols (Istanbul, 1983).

Pancirollus, Guido, *The History of Many Memorable Things Lost, which Were in Use Among the Ancients: And an Account of Many Excellent Things Found, Now in Use Among the Moderns, Both Natural and Artificial* (London, 1715).

Pardoe, Julia, *The City of the Sultan and Domestic Manners of the Turks in 1836*, 3 vols (London, 1838).

—— *The Beauties of the Bosphorus* (London, n.d. [c. 1840]).

Pegolotti, Francesco Balducci, *La Pratica Della Mercatura*, ed. Allan Evans (Cambridge, MA, 1936).

Pegge, S. (ed.), *Forme of Cury* (1780), www.gutenberg.org/ebooks/8102.

Penzer, N.M., *The Harem* (London, 1965).

Perry, Charles (tr.), *An Anonymous Andalusian Cookbook of the Thirteenth Century* (n.d.), http://daviddfriedman.com/Medieval/Cookbooks/Andalusian/andalusian_contents.htm.

—— 'Early Turkish Influence on Arab and Iranian Cuisine', *Dördüncü Milletlerarası Yemek Kongresi, Türkiye 3–6 Eylül 1992* (Konya, 1993), pp. 241–4.

—— 'The Taste for Layered Bread among the Nomadic Turks and the Central Asian Origins of Baklava', in Sami Zubaida and Richard Tapper (eds), *Culinary Cultures of the Middle East* (London, 1994), pp. 87–91.

—— (ed.), *Medieval Arab Cookery* (Totnes, 2001).

—— (tr.), Muhammad b. al-Hasan b. Muhammed b. al-Karîm, *A Baghdad Cookery Book: The Book of Dishes (Kitâb al-Tabîkh)* (Totnes, 2005).

Peyssonnel, Claude Charles de, 'Strictures and Remarks on the Preceding Memoirs', in Baron François de Tott, *Memoirs of the Turks and Tatars*, vol. 2, part 4 (London and Dublin, 1785), pp. 161–287.

Pîrî Reis, *Kitâb-ı Bahriye*, 4 vols, ed. Ertuğrul Zekâi Ökte (Istanbul, 1988).

Plat, Hugh, *Delightes for Ladies* (London, 1609), reproduced in *A Collection of Medieval and Renaissance Cookbooks*, vol. 1, 4th edn, eds Duke Cariadoc of the Bow and Duchessa Diana Alena (n.p., 1987).

Poullet, le Sieur, *Nouvelles relations du Levant* (Paris, 1668).

Prochazka-Eisl, Gisela, *Das Surnâme-i Hümâyûn* (Istanbul, 1995).

Purchas, Samuel, *Hakluytus Posthumus or Purchas his Pilgrims*, 20 vols (Glasgow, 1905–7).

Ramsay, Lady Agnes Dick, *Everyday Life in Turkey* (London, 1897).

Rasonyi, Laszlo, *Tarihte Türklük* (Ankara, 1988).

Rauwolff, Leonhart, 'Dr. Leonhart Rauwolff's Itinerary into the Eastern Countries, as Syria, Palestine, or the Holy Land, Armenia, Mesopotamia, Assyria, Chaldea Etc.', tr. Nicholas Staphorst, in John Ray (ed.), *A Collection of Curious Travels and Voyages*, vol. 2 (London, 1693), pp. 1–338.

Redhouse, Sir James W., *A Turkish and English Lexicon* (Constantinople, 1890).

Reindel-Kiel, Hedda, 'Cennet Taamları', *Soframiz Nur Hanemiz Mamur*, eds Suraiya Faroqhi and Christoph K. Neumann (Istanbul, 2006), pp. 55–110.

Richardson, Tim, *Sweets, A History of Temptation* (London, 2002).

Roden, Claudia, 'Early Arab Cooking and Cookery Manuscripts', *Petits Propos Culinaires*, 6 (October 1980), pp. 16–27.

—— *The Book of Jewish Food* (London, 1997).

Rodinson, Maxime, 'Ma'munıyya East and West', *Petits Propos Culinaires*, 33 (November 1989), pp. 15–25. The article is reprinted in Charles Perry (ed.), *Medieval Arab Cookery* (Totnes, 2001), pp. 185–95.

Roe, Thomas, 'The Journal of Sir Thomas Roe, Ambassador from his Majesty King James the First', in Awnsham Churchill (ed.), *A Collection of Voyages and Travels* (London, 1752), pp. 617–67.

—— *The Embassy of Sir Thomas Roe to the Court of the Great Mogul 1615–1619*, 2 vols, ed. William Foster (London, 1899).

Rolamb, Nicholas, 'A Relation of a Journey to Constantinople', in Awnsham Churchill (ed.), *A Collection of Voyages and Travels*, vol. 4 (London, 1752), pp. 671–718.

Saberi, Helen J., with Anissa Helou and Esteban Pombo-Villar, 'A Spicy Mystery', *Petits Propos Culinaires*, 47 (August 1994), pp. 8–17; 48 (November 1994), pp. 10–15; 49 (May 1995), pp. 18–21.

Samancıgil, Kemal, *Bektaşilik Tarihi* (Istanbul, 1945).

Sandwich, Earl of, *A Voyage Performed by the Late Earl of Sandwich Round the Mediterranean in the Years 1738 and 1739* (London, 1799).

Sandys, George, *Sandys Travells, Containing an History of the Original and Present State of the Turkish Empire . . .*, 6th edn (London, 1670).

Sarı, Nil, 'Osmanlı Sarayında Yemeklerin Mevsimlere Göre Düzenlenmesi ve Devrin Tababetiyle İlişkisi', *Türk Mutfağı Sempozyumu Bildirileri* (Ankara, 1982), pp. 245–55.

Sarı, Nil et al. (eds), *Klasik Dönem İlaç Hazırlama Yöntemleri ve Terkipleri* (Istanbul, 2003) (transcription of *Gunyetü'l-Muhassılîn*, a Turkish translation from the Persian made in 1733 by Ahmed Sânî of Muhammed Mü'min et-Tenkabunî's *Tuhfetü'l-Mü'minîn*, dated 1699).

Saz, Leylâ, *Harem'in İçyüzü* (Istanbul, 1974).

Scappi, Bartolomeo, *Opera di M. Bartolomeo Scappi, cuoco Secreto di Papa Pio V.* (Venice, 1570).

—— *The Opera of Bartolomeo Scappi (1570): The Art and Craft of a Master Cook*, tr. and ed. Terence Scully (Toronto, 2009).

Schafer, Edward H., 'T'ang', in K.C. Chang (ed.), *Food in Chinese Culture* (New Haven, CT, 1977), pp. 85–140.

—— *The Golden Peaches of Samarkand, A Study of T'ang Exotics* (Los Angeles and Berkeley, 1985).

Schneider, E.C.A., *Letters from Broosa, Asia Minor* (Chambersburg, PA, 1846).

Schumacher-Voelker, Uta, 'German Cookery Books, 1485–1800', *Petits Propos Culinaires*, 6 (October 1980), pp. 34–46.

Sefercioğlu, M. Nejat (ed.), *Türk Yemekleri (XVIII. Yüzyıla Ait Yazma Bir Yemek Risalesi)* (Ankara, 1985).

Şemseddin Sâmî, *Kâmûs-ı Türkî* (Istanbul, 1989), facsimile of AH 1317 edn.

Şerefeddin Sabuncuoğlu (Amasyalı), *Mücerrebnâme (İlk Türkçe Deneysel Tıp Eseri – 1468)*, eds İlter Uzel and Kenan Süveren (Ankara, 1999).

Sertoğlu, Midhat, *Osmanlı Tarih Lûgatı* (Istanbul, 1986).

Seyyid Mehmed İzzet, *Çay Risâlesi* (Istanbul, AH 1295/1878).

Shakespeare, William, *The Works of William Shakespeare* (London, n.d. [c. 1893]).

Şirvânî, Muhammed bin Mahmud, *15. Yüzyıl Osmanlı Mutfağı*, eds Mustafa Argunşah and Müjgân Çakır (Istanbul, 2005).

Skuse, E., *The Confectioners' Handbook*, 3rd edn (London, n.d. [1881]).

—— *Skuse's Complete Confectioner*, 12th edn (London, 1928).

Slade, Sir Adolphus, *Records of Travels in Turkey, Greece etc and of a Cruise in the Black Sea with the Capitan Pasha in the Years 1829, 1830 and 1831* (London, 1833).

Smith, William, *Dictionary of the Bible: Comprising its Antiquities, Biography, Geography and Natural History*, 4 vols (New York, 1870).

Smyth, Warrington W.M.A., *A Year with the Turks or Sketches of Travel In the European and Asiatic Dominions of the Sultan* (New York, 1854).

Soyer, Alexis, *A Culinary Campaign* (Lewes, East Sussex, 1995).

Soysal, Sahrap, *Bir Yemek Masalı* (Istanbul, 2003).

Sperling, Devorah S., 'Boiled Wheat', *Petits Propos Culinaires*, 9 (October 1981), pp. 61–2.

Stary, Petr, 'Aphids and their Parasites Associated with Oaks in Iraq', *Proceedings of the Entomological Society of Washington*, 71/4 (September 1969), pp. 279–98.

Steingass, Francis Joseph, *A Comprehensive Persian–English Dictionary, Including the Arabic Words and Phrases to be Met with in Persian Literature* (London, 1892), http://dsal.uchicago.edu/dictionaries/steingass.

Strange, Guy le, *Palestine under the Moslems: A Description of Syria and the Holy*

Land from A.D. 650 to 1500, Translated from the Works of the Mediaeval Arab Geographers (London, 1890).

Sturtevant, E. Lewis, *Sturtevant's Edible Plants of the World*, ed. U.P. Hedrick (Albany, NY, 1919).

Şükûn, Ziya, *Farsça-Türkçe Lûgat, Gencinei Güftar Ferhengi Ziya* (Istanbul, 1996).

Tan, Aylin Öney 'Be Merry, Around a Wheat Berry! The Significance of Wheat in Anatolian Rituals and Celebrations', *Celebration: Proceedings of the Oxford Symposium on Food and Cookery, 2011* (Totnes, 2012), pp. 346–55.

Tan, Nail, 'Türkiye'de Şekerciliğin Gelişmesinde Hacıbekir Müessesesinin Rolü', *Geleneksel Türk Tatlıları Bildirileri Sempozyumu* (Ankara, 1984), pp. 21–44.

Tannahill, Reay, *Food in History* (New York, 1973).

—— *Food in History*, 2nd edn (London, 1988).

Tarama Sözlüğü, 8 vols (Ankara, 1988).

Tarancı, Cahit Sıtkı, *Otuz Beş Yaş*, ed. Asım Bezirci (Istanbul, 2003).

Tasnadi, Edit, 'Macar Mutfağında Türk Yemekleri', *Dördüncü Milletlerarası Yemek Kongresi, Türkiye 3–6 Eylül 1992* (Konya, 1992), pp. 272–5.

Tekinşen, O. Cenap and K. Kaan Tekinşen, *Dondurma: Temel Bilgiler, Teknoloji, Kalite Kontrolü* (Kahramanmaraş, 2008).

Terzioğlu, Arslan, *Helvahane Defteri ve Topkapı Sarayında Eczacılık* (Istanbul, 1992).

Tezcan, Semih, *Bir Ziyafet Defteri* (Istanbul, 1998).

Thevenot, Jean, *The Travels of Monsieur de Thevenot into the Levant 1655–56* (London, 1687).

Tietze, Andreas, *Tarihi ve Etimolojik Türkiye Türkçesi Lugatı* (Istanbul and Vienna, 2002).

Tokuz, Gonca, *Gaziantep ve Kilis Mutfak Kültürü* (Gaziantep, 2002).

—— *20. Yüzyılda Gaziantep'te Eğlence Hayatı* (Gaziantep, 2004).

Torolsan, Berrin, 'Trade Secrets: Fine Fast Food', *Cornucopia*, 27 (2002), pp. 106–10.

Tott, Baron François de, *Memoirs of the Turks and Tatars*, 2 vols (London and Dublin, 1785).

Toussaint-Samat, Maguelonne, *History of Food*, tr. Anthea Bell (Massachusetts, 2000).

Toygar, Kâmil, 'Türkiye'de Hıdrellez Çevresinde Oluşan Mutfak Kültürü', *Üçüncü Milletlerarası Yemek Kongresi, 7–12 Eylül 1990* (Ankara, n.d.), pp. 67–75.

Tulgar, Ahmet, 'Güllaç bize sanatı ve sabrı öğretti', *Milliyet*, 26 October 2003, www.milliyet.com.tr/2003/10/26/pazar/paz06.html.

Türâbî Efendi, *Turkish Cookery Book, A Collection of Receipts Dedicated to those Royal and Distinguished Personages, the Guests of his Highness the Late Viceroy of Egypt, on the Occasion of the Banquet Given at Woolwich, on Board his Highness's Yacht the Faiz-Jehad, the 16th July 1862. Compiled by Türabi Efendi from the Best Turkish Authorities* (London, n.d. [1864]).

'Türk Arşivlerinden', *Tarih Hazinesi*, 2 (1 December 1950), pp. 100–1.

Türkiye Diyanet Vakfı İslâm Ansiklopedisi, 40 vols (Istanbul, 1989–2012).

Türk Kadının Tatlı Kitabı, ed. Esat İren (Ankara, 1939).

Türk Kadının Tatlı Kitabı, 2nd edn, ed. Ekrem Muhittin Yeğen (Ankara, 1966).

'Türk Kültüründe Kar, Buz, Dondurma', Uysal-Walker Archive of Turkish Oral Narrative, Texas Technical University, http://aton.ttu.edu/Turk_kulturunde.asp.

Tursun Bey, *Târîh-i Ebü'l-Feth*, ed. Mertol Tulum (Istanbul, 1977).

Ubicini, Jean Henri Abdolonyme, *Letters on Turkey: An Account of the Religious, Political, Social and Commercial Condition of the Ottoman Empire*, 2 vols, tr. Lady Easthope, facsimile of 1856 edn (New York, 1973).

Üçer, Müjgân, 'Horoz Şekerleri', *Sivas Folkloru*, 11 (December 1973), pp. 8–9.

—— *Sivas Halk Mutfağı* (Sivas, 1992).

—— *Anamın Aşı Tandırın Başı – Sivas Mutfağı* (Istanbul, 2006).

Uluçay, M. Çağatay, *Padişahların Kadınları ve Kızları* (Ankara, 1985).

Unger, Friedrich, *Conditorei des Orients* (Athens and Nauplia, 1838).

—— *A King's Confectioner in the Orient*, ed. Priscilla Mary Işın, tr. Merete Çakmak and Renate Ömeroğulları (London, 2003).

Ünver, Süheyl, *Tarihte 50 Türk Yemeği* (Istanbul, 1948).

—— *Fatih Devri Yemekleri* (Istanbul, 1952).

—— 'Yemek Hakkında Defter', unpublished transcription of a nineteenth-century manuscript cookery book, Süleymaniye Library, Dr A. Süheyl Ünver Bağışı no. 652 (Istanbul, 1964).

—— 'Selçuklular, Beylikler ve Osmanlılarda Yemek Usûlleri ve Vakitleri', *Türk Mutfağı Sempozyumu Bildirileri* (Ankara, 1982), pp. 1–13.

Uşaklıgil, Halid Ziya, *Kırk Yıl* (Istanbul, 1969).

Uysal, Abdullah, *Zanaatkarlar Kanunu: Kanunname-i Ehl-i Hıref* (Ankara, 1982).

Uzunçarşılı, İsmail Hakkı, *Osmanlı Devletinin Saray Teşkilâtı* (Ankara, 1988).

Vámbéry, Armin, *Scenes from the East* (Budapest, 1974).

Vane, Frances Anne, Marchioness of Londonderry, *Narrative of a Visit to the Courts of Vienna, Constantinople, Athens and Naples* (London, 1840).

Vehbî, *Surnâme: Sultan Ahmet'in Düğün Kitabı*, ed. Mertol Tulum (Istanbul, 2007).

Walker, John, *A Selection of Curious Articles from the Gentleman's Magazine*, vol. 1, 2nd edn (London, 1811).

Walker, Mary Adelaide, *Eastern Life and Scenery with Excursions in Asia Minor, Mytilene, Crete, and Roumania*, 2 vols (London, 1886).

Walsh, Robert, *Narrative of a Journey from Constantinople to England* (London, 1828).

—— *A Residence at Constantinople*, 2 vols (London, 1836).

—— *Constantinople and the Seven Churches of Asia Minor*, 2 vols (London, n.d. [c. 1840]).

Weatherly, Henry, *A Treatise on the Art of Boiling Sugar* (Philadelphia, 1865).

Webster, James, *Travels Through the Crimea, Turkey and Egypt, 1825–28*, 2 vols (London, 1830).

Wechsberg, Joseph, *The Cooking of Vienna's Empire* (New York, 1968).

Wei-Jun, Zhov, 'Çin'in Geleneksel Yeni Yıl Arefesi Yemeği', *Üçüncü Milletlerarası Yemek Kongresi, 7–12 Eylül 1990* (Ankara, n.d.), pp. 16–20.

Weymarn, Niklas von, 'Process Development for Mannitol Production by Lactic Acid Bacteria', doctoral dissertation (Helsinki University, 2002).

Wheler, George, *A Journey into Greece by George Wheler Esq. in Company of D'Spon of Lyons* (London, 1682).

White, Charles, *Three Years in Constantinople or, Domestic Manners of The Turks in 1844*, 3 vols (London, 1845–6).

White, Florence, *Food in England* (London, 1951).

Williams, T., *The Accomplished Housekeeper and Universal Cook* (London, 1717).

Wilson, C. Anne, 'The French Connection: Part II', *Petits Propos Culinaires*, 4 (February 1980), pp. 8–20.

Withers, Robert, 'A Description of the Grand Seignor's Seraglio', in Thomas Birch (ed), *Miscellaneous Works of Mr John Greaves*, vol. 2 (London, 1737), pp. 541–800.

—— 'The Grand Signiors Serraglio: Written by Master Robert Withers', in Samuel Purchas (ed.), *Hakluytus Posthumus or Purchas his Pilgrims*, vol. 9 (Glasgow, 1905), pp. 322–406.

Witteveen, Joop, 'Rose Sugar and Other Mediaeval Sweets', *Petits Propos Culinaires*, 20 (July 1985), pp. 22–8.

Woods, Sir Henry Felix, *Spunyarn from the Strands of a Sailor's Life,* 2 vols (London, 1924).

Wright, Thomas (ed.), *Early Travels in Palestine* (London, 1848).

Yetkin, Haşim, *Dünden Bugüne Alanya Sofrası* (Alanya, n.d.).

Yıldır, Mehmet, *Modern Yemek Kitabı* (Istanbul, 1976).

Yüksel, Murat, *Türk Edebiyatında Hamsi* (Trabzon, 1989).

Yule, Henry (tr. and ed.), *The Book of Ser Marco Polo, the Venetian,* 2 vols (London, 1871).

—— and A.C. Burnell, *Hobson-Jobson, The Anglo-Indian Dictionary* (Ware, 1996).

Yusuf Has Hacib, *Kutadgu Bilig*, tr. Reşid Rahmeti Arat (Ankara, 1985).

Zafari, Mahin, *Iranian Cooking for Foreigners* (Tahran, 1966).

Zhukovsky, P., *Türkiye'nin Ziraî Bünyesi*, tr. Celâl Kıpçak, Haydar Nouruzhan and Sâbir Türkistanlı (Istanbul, 1951).

Websites

www.iranica.com.

www.karahalli.com/haberoku.asp?haberID=43.

www.massmaple.org/history.php.

yunus.hacettepe.edu.tr/~ayguns/Cam_bali.htm.

General Index